A2 PE for AQA

Nesta Wiggins-James

Rob James

Graham Thompson

Heinemann Educational Publishers
Halley Court, Jordan Hill, Oxford OX2 8EJ
Part of Harcourt Education

Heinemann is the registered trademark of
Harcourt Education Limited

First published 2006

11 10 09 08 07
10 9 8 7 6 5 4 3

British Library Cataloguing in Publication Data is available
from the British Library on request.

ISBN 978 0 435 49937 2

Typeset by TA Tek-Art, Croydon, Surrey

Illustrated by TA Tek-Art, Croydon, Surrey

Printed in the UK by Scotprint

Cover photo: © Alamy/Image State

Picture research by Jemma Street

Photo credits
Fig 1.02 Michael Steele/Getty Images; Fig 1.03 Ramzi Haidar/AFP/Getty Images; Fig 2.08 Stu Forster/Getty Images; Fig 2.10 Jeff Haynes/AFP/Getty Images; Fig 3.01 Pawel Kopczynski/Reuters/Corbis UK Ltd; Fig 3.04 Stefano Rellandini/Reuters/Corbis UK Ltd; Fig 4.01 Empics; Fig 4.04 Empics; Fig 5.01 Toshifumi Kitamura/AFP/Getty Images; Fig 5.02 Doug Pensinger/Getty Images; Fig 5.03 Mark Shearman/Action Plus; Fig 5.05 Empics; Fig 5.07 Alexander Zemlianichenko/Associated Press/Empics; Fig 6.01 Jason Reed/Reuters/Corbis UK Ltd; Fig 6.04 Empics; Fig 6.06 Eddie Keogh/Reuters/Corbis UK Ltd; Fig 6.07 Kazuhiro Nogi/AFP/Getty Images; Fig 6.18 Gary C. Caskey/Epa/Corbis UK Ltd; Fig 6.19 Stephane Reix/For Picture/Corbis UK Ltd; Fig 6.20 Adam Pretty/Getty Images; Fig 9.01 Eddie Keogh/Reuters/Corbis UK Ltd; Fig 9.02 Patrick Price/Reuters/Corbis UK Ltd; Fig 9.06 PA WIRE/Empics; Fig 10.01 Odd Andersen/AFP/Getty Images; Fig 15.01 Johannes Simon/AFP/Getty Images; Fig 15.02 Stephen Munday/Getty Images; Fig 15.03 Kin Cheung/Reuters/Corbis UK Ltd; Fig 15.04 Empics; Fig 16.01 Paul Seiser/Action Plus; Fig 16.02 Empics; Fig 17.06 Gregorio Borgia/Associated Press/Empics; Fig 17.07 Otto Greule Jr./Allsport/Getty Images; Fig 19.01 Bettmann/Corbis UK Ltd; Fig 19.02 Tim De Waele/Corbis UK Ltd; Fig 19.03 Clive Brunskill/Getty Images for Pepsi/Getty Images; Fig 19.04 Getty Images; Fig 19.05 Kevin Lamarque/Reuters/Corbis UK Ltd; Fig 20.02 Empics; Fig 20.03 Fox Photos/Hulton Archive/Getty Images; Fig 20.04 William Manning/Corbis UK Ltd; Fig 20.05 Mike King/Corbis UK Ltd; Fig 20.06 George Tiedemann/Newsport/Corbis UK Ltd; Fig 21.01 Empics

Acknowledgements
Every effort has been made to contact copyright holders of material reproduced in this book. Any omissions will be rectified in subsequent printings if notice is given to the publishers.

AQA examination questions are reproduced courtesy of the Assessment and Qualifications Alliance.

Contents

Introduction v

Unit 4: Physiological, biomechanical and psychological factors which optimise performance

Section 1: Physiological and biomechanical factors
Chapter 1: The physiology of skeletal muscle 1
Chapter 2: The sources and supply of energy in the body 12
Chapter 3: Factors that contribute to successful endurance performance 29
Chapter 4: Causes of fatigue and recovery from exercise 39
Chapter 5: Planning training regimes for elite performers 51
Chapter 6: Applying mechanics to sporting activity 67

Section 2: Psychological factors 86
Chapter 7: Personality 88
Chapter 8: Attitude 99
Chapter 9: Aggression 107
Chapter 10: Achievement motivation 114
Chapter 11: Arousal 119
Chapter 12: Social facilitation 126
Chapter 13: Attribution theory 131
Chapter 14: Self-efficacy 135
Chapter 15: Group dynamics 140
Chapter 16: Leadership 147
Chapter 17: Stress and stress management 153
Unit 4 questions 167

Unit 5: Factors affecting the nature and development of elite performance

Chapter 18: Talent identification and talent development 173
Chapter 19: Sport ethics, deviancy and the law 190
Chapter 20: The international perspective – World Games and the sport systems of the UK, the USA and France 219
Section B & PED5 – What can you expect? 251
Unit 5 questions 254

Unit 6: Coursework

Chapter 21: Practical coursework 259

Index 270

Introduction

This book has been specifically designed for students following the AQA A2 sport and physical education course. For maximal benefit this book should be used in conjunction with the student workbook written alongside this text, which provides a much greater range of tasks and past paper questions.

This text will support and reinforce the teaching that you receive in your centre and attempts to help you apply your understanding of theory to practical performance.

The content of the book is presented in a form that is identical to the AQA specification and is arranged under the same sections and sub-headings.

The book is divided into three sections – one for each module of your study:

- Module 4 (Unit PED4) – Physiological, Biomechanical and Psychological factors which optimise performance
- Module 5 (PED5) – Factors affecting the nature and development of elite performance
- Module 6 (PE6P or PE6C) – Analysis and critical evaluation of the factors which optimise performance.

Each section is divided into chapters which begin with a list of learning objectives. These are invaluable when it comes to preparing for your examination. Make sure that you can achieve each learning objective stated before you sit your examination.

Throughout each chapter you will find a series of tasks which are designed to help you understand and apply your knowledge in a way required by the final examination. Look out also in the margins for KEYWORDS – important definitions, HOT TIPS – helpful exam advice and APPLICATION – relevant application of theory. These have been specifically written to help improve your examination performance.

Some essential guidance, preparing you for your practical assessment and for the successful completion of your synoptic assignment and your project coursework (optional) is also contained in section 3. Do use this, if you follow the advice carefully you can't go wrong!

How you will be examined

There are three units you must complete in order to gain your A level in Sport and Physical Education. PED4 and PED5 are assessed by written examination whilst in PE6P/C your coursework is assessed by your teachers in the first instance and then subject to moderation by the examination board. The synoptic assignment will also be assessed externally.

Unit 4 (PED4) Physiological, Biomechanical and Psychological factors which optimise performance	**Unit 5 (PED5)** a) Factors affecting the nature and development of elite performance b) Synoptic assessment	**Unit 6 (PE6P or PE6C)** a) Analysis and critical evaluation of factors which optimise performance b) Synoptic assignment
$1\frac{1}{2}$ hours written examination 4 from 5 x 15 mark questions + 4 marks QWC 30% of A2 mark 15% of the total A level marks	$1\frac{1}{2}$ hours written examination a) 2 from 3 x 15 mark questions b) Synoptic assessment 3 from 4 x 12 mark questions + 4 marks QWC 35% of A2 mark $17\frac{1}{2}$% of total A level marks	a) Practical demonstration Or Written project (10%) b) Synoptic assignment ($7\frac{1}{2}$%) 35% of A2 mark $17\frac{1}{2}$% of total A level marks

Unit 4: Physiological, biomechanical and psychological factors which optimise performance

Section 1: Physiological and biomechanical factors

Chapter 1: The physiology of skeletal muscle

Learning outcomes

By the end of this chapter you should be able to:

- explain the basic structure of skeletal muscle
- distinguish between the different muscle fibre types in the body and explain how each can be of benefit to specific performers
- give a definition of a motor unit and explain its role in muscle contraction
- account for the variations in the strength of a muscle response by multiple unit summation and wave summation
- differentiate between synchronous and asynchronous contraction
- explain the function of muscle spindle apparatus and its role in the control of movement
- state the adaptive responses expected of the muscle following a period of resistance training.

Introduction

The coach and athlete must have a sound understanding of the muscular system in order to devise training programmes which lead to improved performance. In your study of AS Physical Education you will recall that you considered the role of the muscles in performing a range of movements from sporting activity. The purpose of this chapter, however, is to discuss both the structure and function of skeletal muscle, detailing how knowledge at this microscopic level can be applied in order to enhance the effectiveness of training.

The structure of skeletal muscle

Muscle belly

The whole muscle composed of many individual muscle fibres.

Epimysium, perimysium and endomysium

Connective tissue that surrounds the muscle belly, fasciculi and muscle fibres respectively.

Fasciculi

Bundles of muscle fibres that make up the muscle belly.

When viewed at a molecular level you will see that there are a number of different structures that make up a muscle. The **muscle belly** is wrapped in a thick connective tissue that allows for movement of the muscles and carries nerves and blood vessels, called the **epimysium**. Another connective tissue, the **perimysium**, surrounds bundles of muscle fibres named **fasciculi.** Finally, the **endomysium** surrounds each individual muscle fibre. Together, the epimysium, perimysium and endomysium extend to form tendons which attach the muscle to the bones of the body.

Upon closer inspection it can be seen that individual muscle fibres are made up of hundreds of smaller elements called myofibrils. These myofibrils contain the proteins responsible for muscle contraction, actin and myosin, together with the components necessary for energy production and the control of movement (namely mitochondria, glycogen and fat deposits, and muscle spindles).

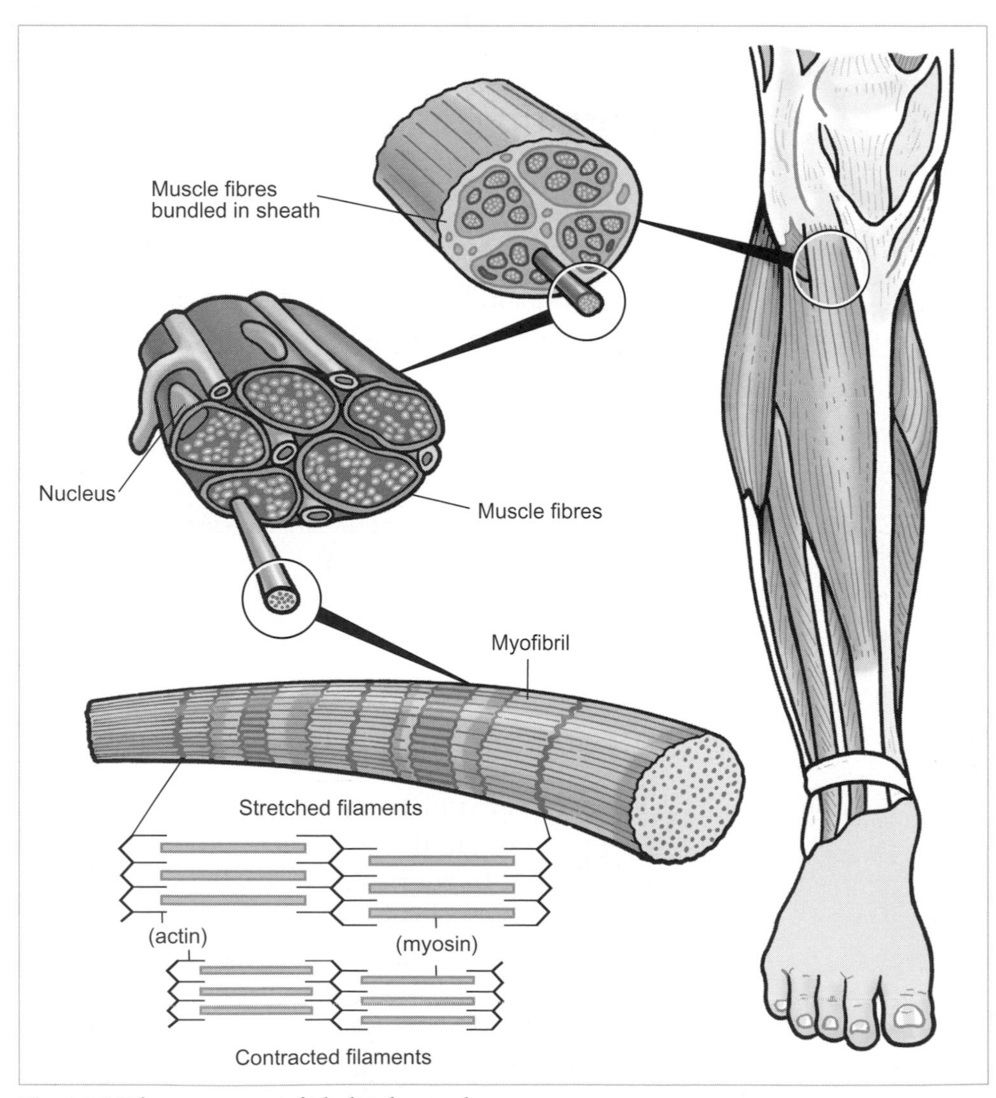

Fig 1.01 The structure of skeletal muscle

Types of muscle fibre

Slow twitch muscle fibre
A type of muscle fibre that uses oxygen to produce energy (high oxidative capacity). They are associated with endurance-based activities.

Fast twitch muscle fibre
A type of muscle fibre that has a high glycolytic capacity (anaerobic). They are associated with speed and power-based activities.

Skeletal muscle fibres are not all uniform; in fact they can differ in both structure and function. A single muscle such as the bicep brachii will be composed of two principal types of muscle fibres: **slow twitch (type 1)** and **fast twitch (type 2)**. Slow twitch fibres contract more slowly but are highly resistant to fatigue and are therefore favoured by endurance athletes, whilst fast twitch fibres can contract more rapidly, generating greater forces, but are more liable to fatigue. These fibres are more prevalent in sprinters and power athletes. Fast twitch fibres have been further classified into type 2a and type 2b. Type 2a fibres, also known as fast oxidative glycolytic (FOG) muscle fibres, are more resistant to fatigue than type 2b fibres, which have a greater anaerobic capacity and are termed fast twitch glycolytic (FTG) muscle fibres.

An average muscle will typically be composed of approximately 50 per cent slow twitch fibres, 25 per cent fast twitch (a) fibres with the remaining 25 per cent fast twitch (b) fibres.

Fig 1.02 An endurance athlete will possess a high number of slow twitch muscle fibres

Fig 1.03 A weightlifter will possess a high percentage of fast twitch glycolytic fibres (type 2b)

Table 1.01 summarises the main structural and functional characteristics of each of the three types of muscle fibres.

There are many differences in the distribution of fibres between different muscles of the same person and between different people. In humans, virtually all muscles are a mixture of all three fibre types.

Table 1.01 Structural and functional characteristics of slow and fast twitch muscle fibres

	Slow twitch (type 1)	**Fast oxidative glycolytic (FOG) (type 2a)**	**Fast twitch glycolytic (FTG) (type 2b)**
Functional characteristic			
Speed of contraction (ms)	Slow (110)	Fast (50)	Fast (50)
Force of contraction	Low	High	Highest
Resistance to fatigue	Very high	Moderate	Low
Aerobic capacity	Very high	Moderate	Low
Anaerobic capacity	Low	High	High
Structural characteristic			
Fibre size	Small	Large	Large
Mitochondrial density	High	Moderate	Low
Capillary density	High	Moderate	Low
Myoglobin content	High	Moderate	Low
PC store	Low	High	High
Glycogen store	Low	High	High
Triglyceride store	High	Moderate	Low
Motor neuron size	Small	Large	Large
Activity suited	Marathon	1500m	Shot put

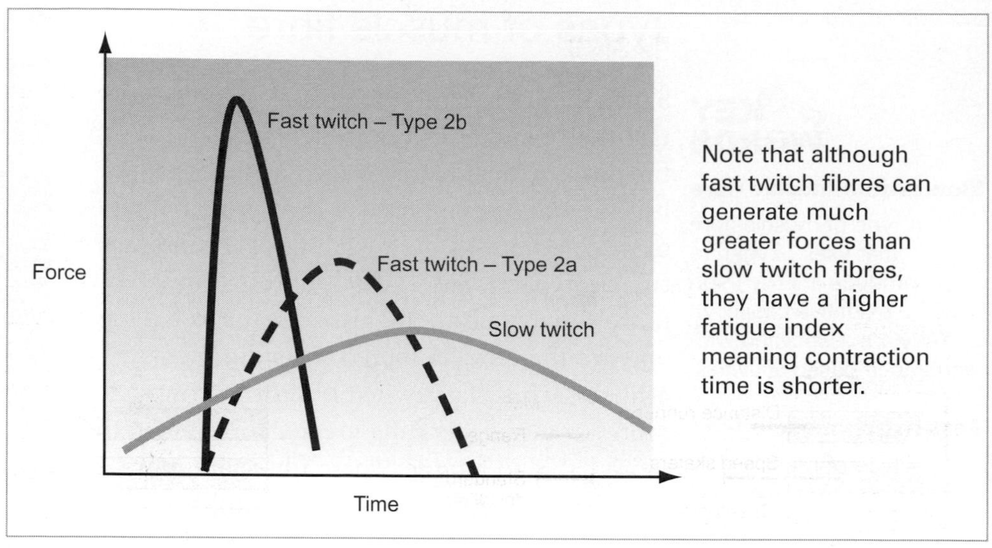

Fig 1.04 Muscle fibre contractile response

TASK 1

Draw up a continuum like the one shown below. Now collect as many sporting pictures from magazines, newspapers or the Internet as you can and place them along the continuun according to the fibre type predominantly used by the selected performer.

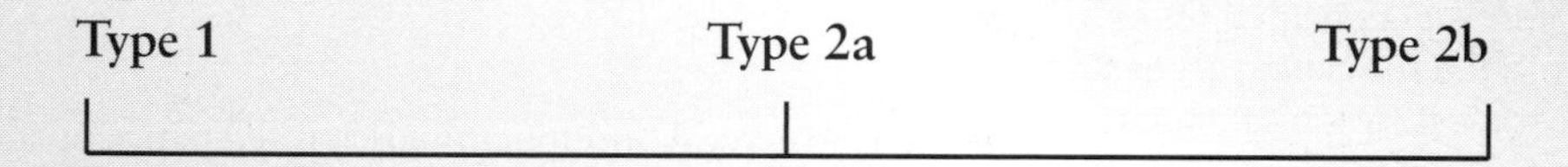

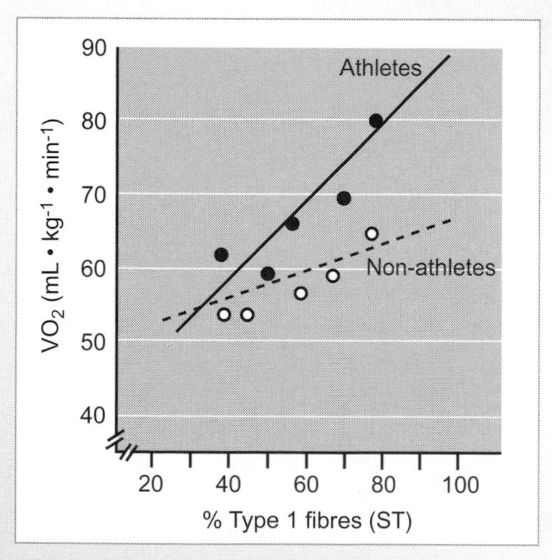

TASK 2

Use Figure 1.05 to help explain the relationship between VO2max and the per cent distribution of slow twitch muscle fibres in both athletes and non-athletes.

Fig 1.05 The relationship between aerobic capacity and per cent distribution of slow twitch fibres of trained athletes and non-athletes

TASK 3

Using Figure 1.06 explain the distributions of fibre types for each of the 'populations' identified.

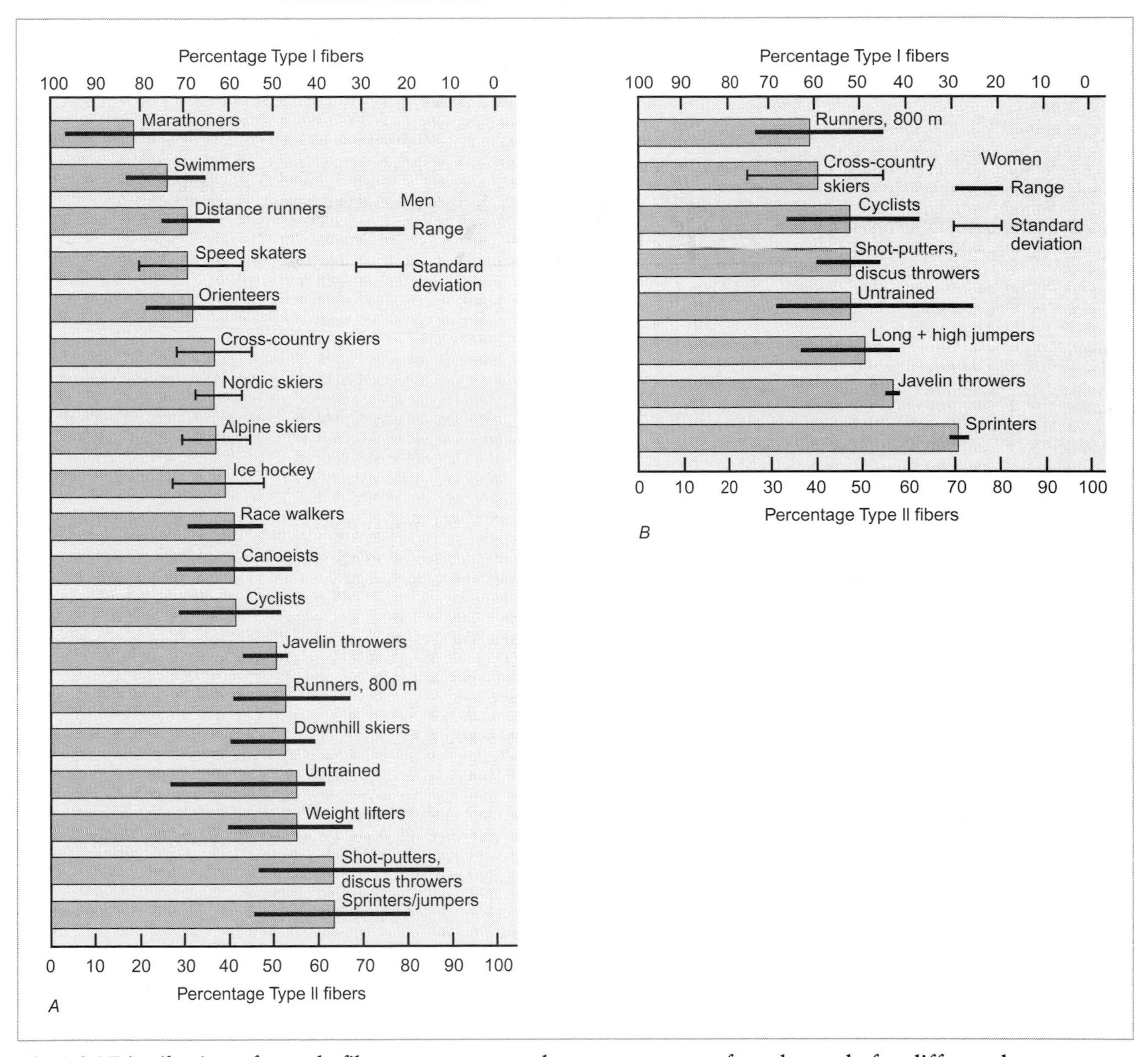

Fig 1.06 Distribution of muscle fibre types expressed as a percentage of total muscle for different human 'populations'

TASK 4

In a group, discuss the role of genetics in the determination of muscle fibre distribution. Can muscle fibre distribution predict success in certain sporting activities?

Muscle fibre recruitment

Motor unit
The motor neuron and the group of muscle fibres that it controls.

The primary function of skeletal muscle is to contract and facilitate movement of the body. Muscle contraction involves the interaction of the muscles with the nervous system. Individual muscles (such as the anterior deltoid, for example) are connected to the nervous system via a group of motor neurons. Each muscle fibre within the muscle belly is supplied by only one motor neuron. However, this neuron can innervate (stimulate) anything from just a few fibres to several hundred. The motor neuron plus the fibres it innnervates is known as the **motor unit.**

The motor unit

More motor units will be recruited when performing a bicep curl against a load of 10kg than of 5kg.

The motor unit is the basic functional unit of skeletal muscle. Stimulation of one motor neuron causes all the muscle fibres in that motor unit to contract simultaneously. Each individual muscle will be made up of a number of motor units (just like a school is made up of a number of forms or tutor groups). The number of motor units that are recruited at any one time in the muscle varies with the amount of strength required for a given movement. The more strength needed, the greater the number of motor units activated.

The number of fibres within a particular motor unit is dependent upon the control of movement required in that muscle. A small muscle that is required to perform fine motor control, such as those that enable the eye to focus, may only have one fibre per motor neuron. Large muscles responsible for gross movements, such as the quadriceps group when kicking a ball, may be innervated by a motor neuron supplying 500 or more fibres.

Motor units are usually made up of the same type of muscle fibre. Consequently both fast and slow twitch motor units are found in a muscle. Fast twitch motor units are generally recruited during high intensity activity such as sprinting or throwing the javelin, whilst slow twitch motor units are used during lower intensity exercise such as running a half marathon or cross-country skiing.

Innervation

The innervation of skeletal muscle is accomplished by a motor neuron transmitting a nerve impulse or action potential to the muscle fibre. How the muscle fibre responds is governed by the **'all or none law'**.

All or none law
If a motor impulse is of sufficient intensity, the motor unit is stimulated and all the muscle fibres within it will contract to their maximum possible extent.

The all or none law

The all or none principle essentially states that individual muscle fibres within a motor unit contract either fully or not at all. In other words, individual muscle fibres cannot partially contract. In order to activate these muscle fibres, however, a minimum amount of stimulation is needed (termed the threshold). If the stimulation equals or exceeds the threshold, all the fibres

APPLICATION

When kicking a conversion in rugby, the quadriceps muscle group will recruit more motor units the further away from the posts the kicker is.

within the motor unit will contract at the same time and to their maximum possible extent. If the stimulus falls short of the threshold, the muscle fibres do not respond and muscular contraction fails to occur.

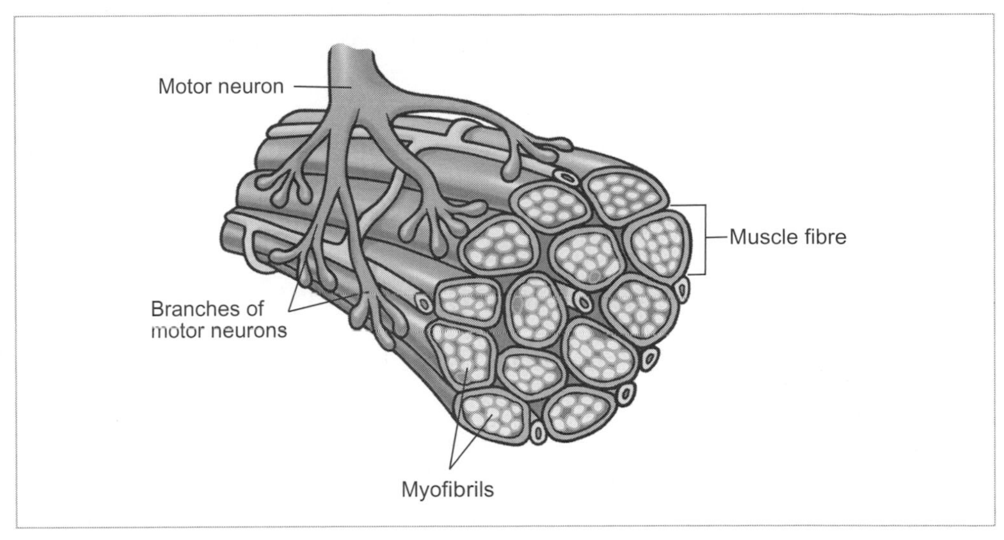

Fig 1.07 A motor unit of skeletal muscle

Variations in the strength of the muscle response

Sporting performance requires variations in strength or muscular force, from very weak efforts such as a short putt in golf to all out maximal efforts such as a shot put. How then does the body cope with these different requirements?

The strength of a muscle can be graded in several ways:

- multiple unit summation
- wave summation
- synchronicity of motor unit stimulation.

Multiple unit summation

The strength of a muscle contraction can be increased by recruiting more motor units. Maximal contractions will recruit all motor units within a particular muscle whilst weaker contractions will recruit fewer units. Fast twitch motor units will be recruited ahead of slow twitch units, for more powerful contractions.

Wave summation

KEY WORDS

Wave summation

A method of increasing the force of contraction of a muscle by adding together the effect of several motor impulses.

Wave summation considers the frequency with which impulses arrive at the motor unit. Typically the motor unit will respond to an impulse (innervation) by giving a twitch – a very short period of contraction followed by relaxation. If a second impulse arrives at the motor unit before it has had time to completely relax from the first twitch, the motor unit responds with a stronger contraction since the effect of the second stimulus is added to the first. They summate, creating greater tension within the motor unit. When a motor unit is stimulated many times in quick succession there is little or no time for relaxation. This produces the highest level of sustained tension,

Tetanus

A smooth and sustained contraction produced when a motor unit is stimulated by a series of impulses fired in quick succession.

referred to as **tetanus** or tetanic contraction, which will continue until fatigue ensues. This is illustrated in Figure 1.08 below.

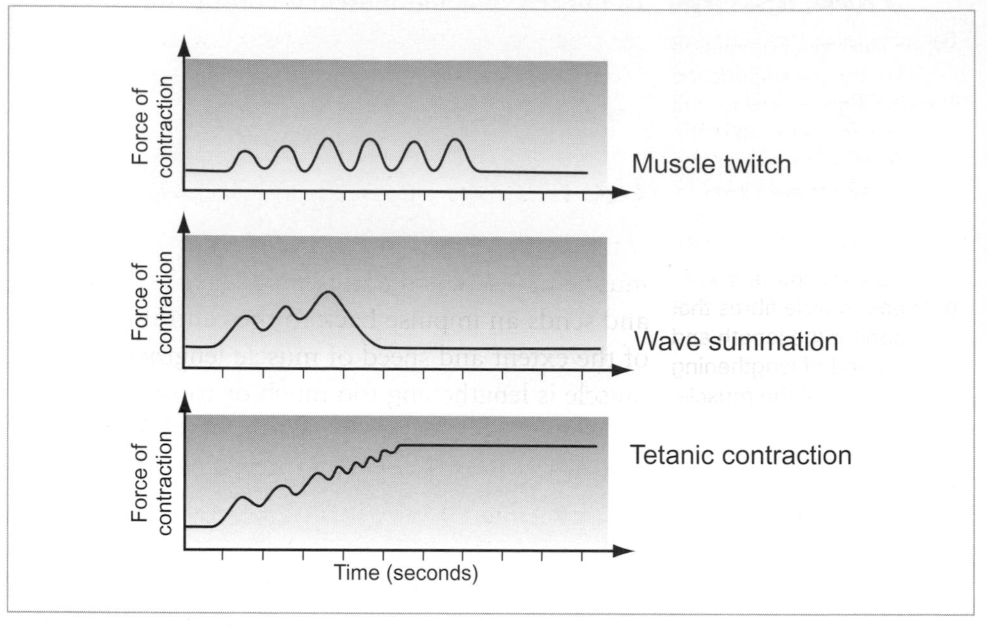

Fig 1.08 Varying the strength of muscular contraction by wave summation

Synchronicity of motor unit stimulation

We have already established that during a maximal contraction such as a weight lift, all motor units within a muscle will be synchronised to contract more or less simultaneously (synchronous contraction). However, with tetanus comes fatigue. On the other hand some athletes, such as a marathon runner, need to produce sub-maximal contractions within a muscle over an extended period of time. In this instance motor units will contract at different times (asynchronously) so that while some are contracting, others are relaxing and recovering. This helps the whole of the muscle share the workload and reduces the effects of fatigue.

TASK 5

Without using any words, draw a diagrammatic representation of the following passage.

'The motor unit will respond to a stimulus by giving a "twitch" – a brief period of contraction followed by relaxation. When a second impulse is applied to the motor unit before it completely relaxes from the previous stimulus, the sum of both stimuli occurs, increasing the total contraction. Sometimes rapid firing of stimuli occurs giving motor units little or no time for relaxation. This increases total contraction further ...'

Without looking at the passage, explain your diagram to a friend. How closely did your explanation match the passage? If it was fairly close this is a good indication that you understand this topic. Well done!

Proprioceptors
Sensory receptors found in muscles, tendons, joints and the inner ear that detect the motion or position of the body or a limb by responding to stimuli.

Muscle spindles
Sensory receptors that lie between muscle fibres that monitor the length and speed of lengthening of the muscle.

Stretch reflex
An automatic response that causes a muscle to shorten, thereby preventing it from being over-stretched.

The control of muscular contraction

The neuromuscular system is responsible for the control of muscular contraction in order for effective movement within sporting activity to occur. It does this through several **proprioceptors** located in the joints, muscles and tendons.

The muscle spindle apparatus

Muscle spindles are very sensitive proprioceptors that lie between skeletal muscle fibres. When a muscle is stretched, the spindle stretches along with it and sends an impulse back to the central nervous system (CNS) informing it of the extent and speed of muscle lengthening. If the CNS believes that the muscle is lengthening too much or too quickly then it will control the movement by initiating a **stretch reflex**. When performing the triple jump, for example, the quadriceps muscle group lengthens rapidly upon landing from the 'hop' stage. The muscle spindles detect the rapid lengthening and send sensory (afferent) impulses to the CNS. This then reciprocates by sending an efferent (motor) neurone to the quadricep muscles, initiating a stretch reflex causing a powerful concentric contraction. This drives the jumper into the next 'step' phase of the jump. In doing so the muscle spindles have prevented the quadricep muscles from over-stretching and causing injury.

Eccentric contraction
The lengthening of a muscle during contraction.

Elastic energy
Energy stored when a muscle is stretched or lengthened.

Concentric contraction
The shortening of a muscle during contraction.

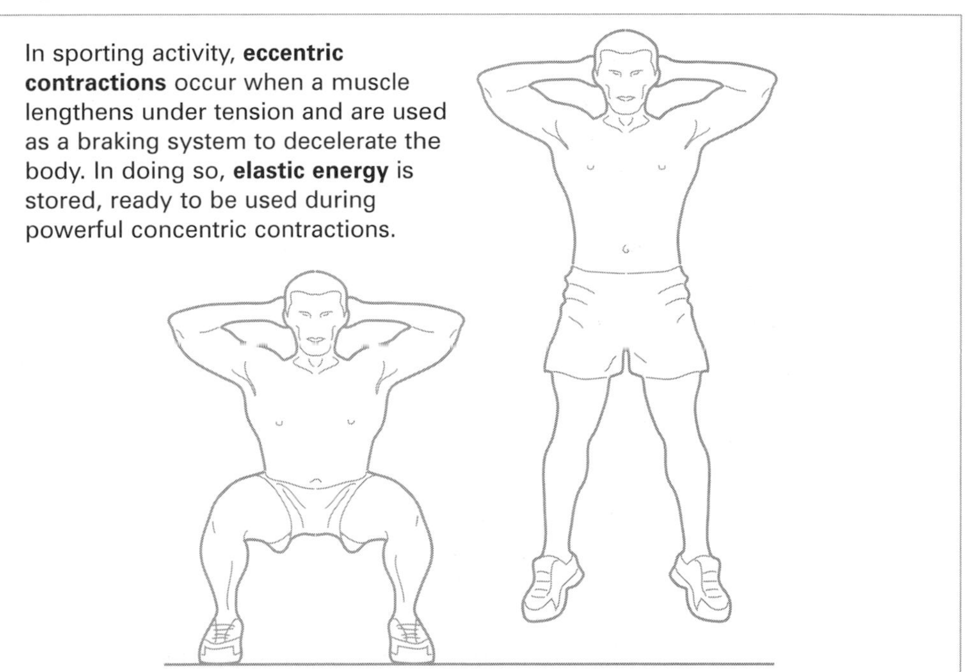

In many sporting skills, eccentric contractions are often followed by concentric contractions. When performing a squat jump, elastic energy is stored in the quadricep muscle group during the down phase. In this instance the quadricep group is lengthening, undergoing an eccentric contraction. Muscle spindles detect the lengthening of the muscle group and may initiate a stretch reflex, causing the quadricep muscle to contract concentrically enabling the performer to jump vertically upwards. It's like an elastic band!

Fig 1.09 The stretch reflex at work during a squat jump

Golgi tendon organs

KEY WORDS

Golgi tendon organ
A sensory receptor that exists within tendons and monitors the force of muscular contractions.

Golgi tendon organs are similar to muscle spindles in that they protect tendons and their connected muscles from damage which may result from extreme muscular forces. Tendon organs lie between tendon fibres and relay sensory impulses to the CNS regarding the state of tension within them. If tension or force becomes excessive, tendon organs will cause the muscle to relax.

Neuromuscular adaptations to resistance training

Neuro-muscular system
The interaction of the nervous system with the muscular system.

Muscle hypertrophy
A term used to describe the enlargement of individual muscle fibres or the whole muscle belly associated with resistance training.

Hyperplasia
The splitting of individual muscle fibres to create new fibres.

Resistance training will signal some long-term physiological responses to the **neuro-muscular system.**

- **Recruitment of more motor units**
  More motor units may be trained to act synchronously (together) so that greater forces can be generated therefore resulting in greater strength gains.
- **Muscle hypertrophy**
  The size of the muscle belly will increase due to an increase in the size of individual muscle fibres (**muscle hypertrophy**) and the possible splitting of fibres (**hyperplasia**).
- **Hypertrophy of fast twitch muscle fibres**
  As fast twitch fibres are predominantly recruited during resistance training, these fibres in particular will enlarge.
- **Hyperplasia of fast twitch muscle fibres**
  There is some evidence to suggest that muscle fibres split, particularly with heavy resistance training. This splitting will contribute to the general hypertrophy of the muscle.
- **Conversion of type 2b fibres to type 2a fibres**
  Some studies have shown that the percentage of type 2b fibres within a trained muscle actually decrease in favour of type 2a fibres. This could account for the delay in muscular fatigue associated with prolonged training.

Revise as you go!

1. Name the three types of muscle fibre and give a sporting example where each of these fibres prevail.
2. Give two structural and two functional characteristics of each type of muscle fibre.
3. Explain the role of motor units in controlling the strength of muscular contractions in sporting activity.
4. Name a muscle of the body that will contain motor units composed of several hundred fibres and a muscle which will contain motor units of relatively few fibres.

5 What types of training would cause hypertrophy (enlargement) of:
   a) slow twitch fibres
   b) fast twitch (type 2b) fibres?
6 Explain how the strength of muscle contraction can be varied in relation to a high jumper and a distance runner.
7 Explain the role of the muscle spindle apparatus during a plyometric training session.
8 What do you understand by the term stretch reflex? Explain this response in relation to a basketball player performing a slam dunk.
9 Give three neuromuscular adaptations to training.

Chapter 2: The sources and supply of energy in the body

Learning outcomes

By the end of this chapter you should be able to:
- provide a definition of energy
- explain the role of adenosine triphospate (ATP) in providing energy for movement
- compare the effectiveness of the ATP-PC, lactic acid and aerobic systems
- identify the chemical/food fuel used, the site of the reaction, the controlling enzymes, the energy yield and any by-products produced for each of the energy pathways
- identify the predominant energy system used related to the type, duration and intensity of exercise for a given activity
- explain the term 'energy continuum' in context of a range of physical activities.

Introduction

Energy
The capacity of the body to perform work.

Make sure you can give the correct units of measurement of energy. Energy can be measured in **calories (kcal) or joules (J).** 1 calorie = 4.184 joules.

Central to the study of exercise physiology is **energy**. As exercise physiologists we are interested in:
- where we get our energy to exercise from
- how we can optimise our energy usage during exercise
- how we can recover our energy stores following exercise.

In this chapter we will look at how the body converts energy from food into energy for muscular contractions which enable us to run, jump, throw or indeed perform any number of movements used in sporting activity. We will examine the energy requirements of a number of activities, from a gymnastic vault to marathon running, and determine how the intensity and duration of the activity affects the way in which the body provides energy. Perhaps most importantly, we will discover how a knowledge of energy supply can, help the coach and athlete to maximise performance.

Defining energy

Energy exists in a number of different forms. Electrical, heat and light energy are just a few types that we all use on a daily basis. Energy is never lost; it is constantly recycled, often being transferred from one form to another. When boiling a kettle, for example, electrical energy is transformed into heat energy. Similarly, energy found in the chemical bonds of food fuels that we eat are transformed into mechanical energy, enabling us to move and participate in sporting activity. It is this conversion of chemical energy into mechanical and heat energy that is of particular interest to the sports physiologist and which forms the basis of discussion for this chapter.

Sources of energy in the body

Adenosine triphosphate (ATP)

The energy currency of cells. ATP is the only direct source of energy for all energy-requiring processes in the body.

We have already established that for movement to occur, chemical energy must be transferred into mechanical energy. Chemical energy in the body is stored in an easy-access, energy-rich compound called **adenosine triphosphate** (ATP). ATP exists in all cells and consists of a number of atoms held together by high energy bonds. It is through breaking down these bonds that energy is released for all processes in the body that require energy.

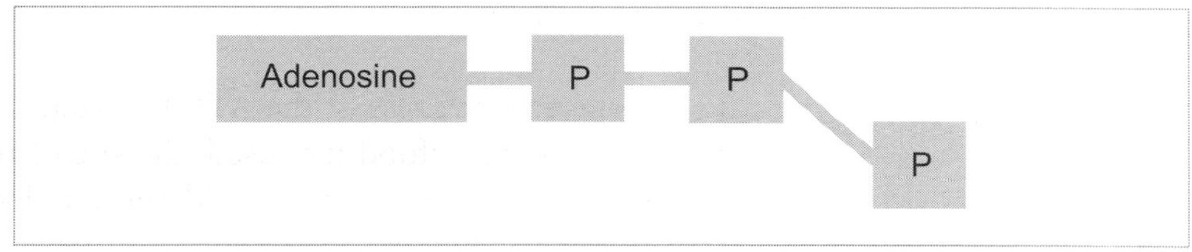

Fig 2.01 The structure of ATP

Through the breakdown of ATP, energy is released to enable the muscles to contract, the heart to beat and the brain to fire electrical impulses.

When energy is required, the enzyme ATPase is released which initiates the breakdown of ATP. It is the outermost bond of ATP that attracts ATPase, as it is this bond that stores most energy. Through the breakdown of ATP, energy is released leaving adenosine diphosphate (ADP) and an inorganic phosphate (Pi), which is illustrated in Fig. 2.02.

This reaction can be summarised as follows:

Adenosine triphosphate	→	Adenosine diphosphate	+	Inorganic phosphate	+	Energy
ATP	→	ADP	+	Pi	+	Energy

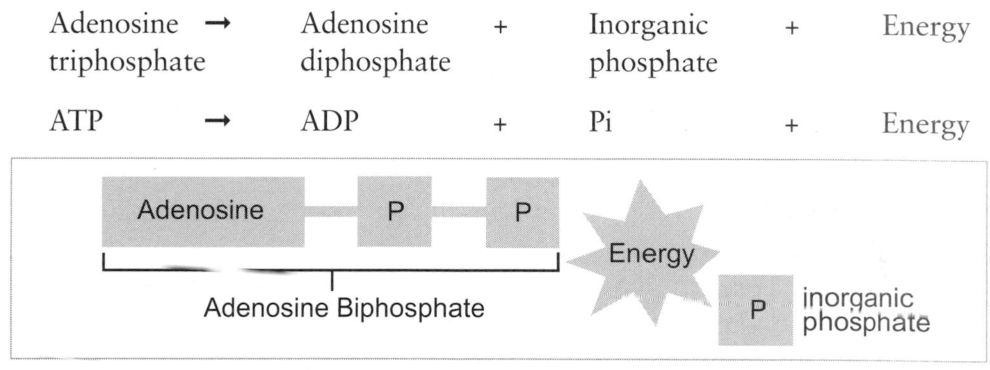

Fig 2.02 The breakdown of ATP by ATPase

Exothermic reaction

A chemical reaction that releases energy some of which is given off as heat.

Because some of the energy is given off as heat, this reaction is termed **exothermic.**

There is only sufficient ATP stored within the muscle cell to perform high intensity activity for two or three seconds.

There is a limited supply of ATP within the muscle cell, probably only enough to perform maximal exertion for two or three seconds, such as performing a maximal weight lift in the weights gym or for a sprint start. This is because if we were to have an unlimited supply of ATP, we would have to carry around a supply equivalent to our own body weight in order to meet the body's daily energy requirements! Obviously this is not very practical, so the body has adapted to become a recycling machine. ATP is constantly recycled to ensure a continuous supply of energy. However, recycling or resynthesising of ATP itself requires energy, and this energy is acquired from the food that we eat.

Phosphocreatine (PCr)
A high-energy compoud which exists in the muscle cells alongside ATP and provides the energy for ATP resynthesis during high-intensity exercise.

Glycogen
The form of carbohydrate stored in the muscles and liver.

Anaerobic metabolism
The release of energy through the breakdown of food fuels in the absence of oxygen.

Aerobic metabolism
The release of energy through the breakdown of food fuels in the presence of oxygen.

The fuels for ATP resynthesis are derived from the following sources:

- **Phosphocreatine**

Phosphocreatine (PCr) is used to resynthesise ATP in the first 10 seconds of intense exercise. To help facilitate this immediate resynthesis of ATP, PCr is stored within the muscle cell itself alongside ATP. Once again, however, stores of PCr are limited.

Fig 2.03 The body is a very effective recycling machine, as ATP needs constant recycling or recharging

- **Glycogen** (stored carbohydrate)

Glycogen is stored in the muscles (350g) and liver (100g). It is first converted to glucose before being broken down to release the energy for ATP resynthesis. During high intensity exercise, glycogen can be used without the presence of oxygen (**anaerobic metabolism**). However, much more energy can be released from glycogen during **aerobic metabolism**, when oxygen is available.

When exercising at higher intensities, the body will rely more upon glycogen as a source of fuel.

- **Triglycerides** (muscular stores of fat)

At rest, up to two-thirds of our energy requirement is met through the breakdown of **fatty acids.** This is because fat can provide more energy per gram than glycogen (1g of fat provides 9.1 kcal of energy compared to 4.1 kcal of energy for every 1g of glycogen). In spite of the fact that fat requires about 15 per cent more oxygen than glycogen to metabolise, it remains the favoured fuel source at rest and during endurance-based activity. Fats can only be used as an energy source when there is a plentiful supply of oxygen and must be used in conjunction with glycogen. This is because the transport of fatty acids in the blood is poor (and slow!) due to their low solubility. Consequently fatty acids do not arrive at the muscle cell in sufficient quantities to sustain muscle contraction on their own – glycogen must provide the supplementary energy.

Fatty acids
The component of fat used for energy provision.

- **Proteins**

Protein is the least favoured source of energy, only contributing five to ten per cent of the total energy yield. In the presence of oxygen, protein is used as an energy provider, usually when stores of glycogen are low. Protein's primary function is to facilitate the growth and repair of the body's cells, including muscle tissue.

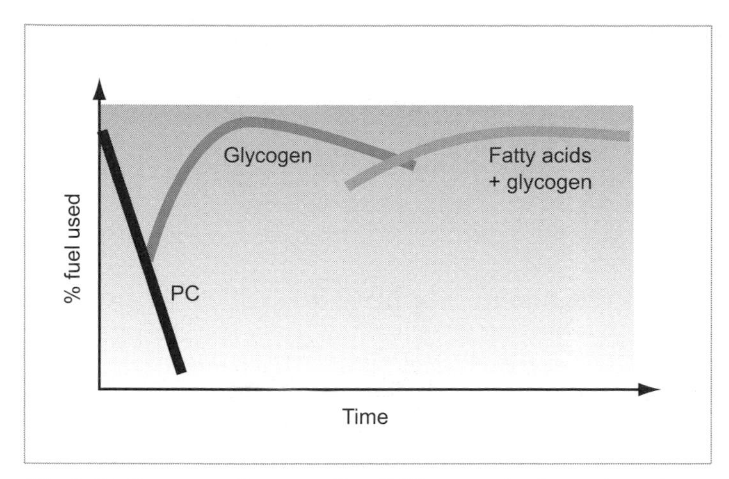

Fig 2.04 Sources of energy for ATP resynthesis against time

The conversion of these fuels into energy which can then be used to resynthesise ATP occurs through one of three pathways or energy systems. Don't forget that it is the intensity and duration of the exercise that dictates whether oxygen is present and ultimately which energy system predominates.

The three energy systems are:
1 **the ATP-PC or alactic system**
2 **the lactic acid system**
3 **the aerobic (oxidative) system.**

The more intense the activity (e.g. the harder the athlete is working, signalled perhaps by a higher heart rate), the more the performer will rely on the production of energy from anaerobic pathways such as the ATP-PC system or lactic acid system. As exercise intensity decreases and endurance increases, the more the athlete will rely on the aerobic system for providing the energy to resynthesise ATP.

The source of energy for ATP resynthesis is dependent largely upon the intensity and duration of the sporting activity.

TASK 1

Keep a diary of all the food and drink that you consume in one day. From the packaging calculate how much energy you have consumed in both calories (Kcal) and joules (J).

TIP – You may need to measure out quantities of foodstuffs to give an accurate picture of your energy intake.

The ATP-PCr (alactic) system

Sarcoplasm
Fluid that surrounds the nucleus of a muscle cell. It is the site for both anaerobic energy pathways.

Creatine kinase
The enzyme used to release energy from phosphocreatine.

We have established that muscular stores of ATP will have depleted after about three seconds of maximal activity. For high intensity activity to continue the immediate recycling of ATP is necessary. However, the rapid increase in activity has resulted in insufficient oxygen being available (an oxygen deficit) to sustain this ATP resynthesis. The body therefore relies upon a second energy-rich compound found alongside ATP in the muscle cells. This compound is phosphocreatine (PCr).

As with ATP, the breakdown of phosphocreatine takes place in the **sarcoplasm** of a muscle cell and is facilitated by the enzyme **creatine kinase.** The release of creatine kinase is stimulated by the increase in ADP and inorganic phosphates (both products of ATP breakdown).

PCr → Creatine + Pi + energy

Don't forget that for very intense activities lasting less than three seconds, such as a maximum weight lift, energy will be provided solely through the breakdown of ATP.

Unlike ATP, the energy released from the breakdown of phosphocreatine is not used for muscle contraction but is instead used to recycle ATP, so that it can once again be broken down to maintain a constant energy supply.

Energy (from PCr breakdown) + ADP + Pi → ATP

As energy is required for this reaction to take place it is known as an **endothermic reaction.**

KEY WORDS

Endothermic reaction
A chemical reaction that consumes energy.

Coupled reaction
A reaction where the product of one reaction is used in a linked (second) reaction. The ATP-PC system is an example of a coupled reaction.

The coupled reaction

Because PCr exists alongside ATP in the sarcoplasm of the muscle cell, as rapidly as energy is released from ATP during exercise it is restored through the breakdown of PCr. This linked reaction more or less occurs simultaneously. It takes one molecule of PCr to recycle one molecule of ATP.

The ATP-PC system is of particular use to athletes who compete at high intensity for about 10 seconds, such as a 100m sprinter or a gymnast performing a vault.

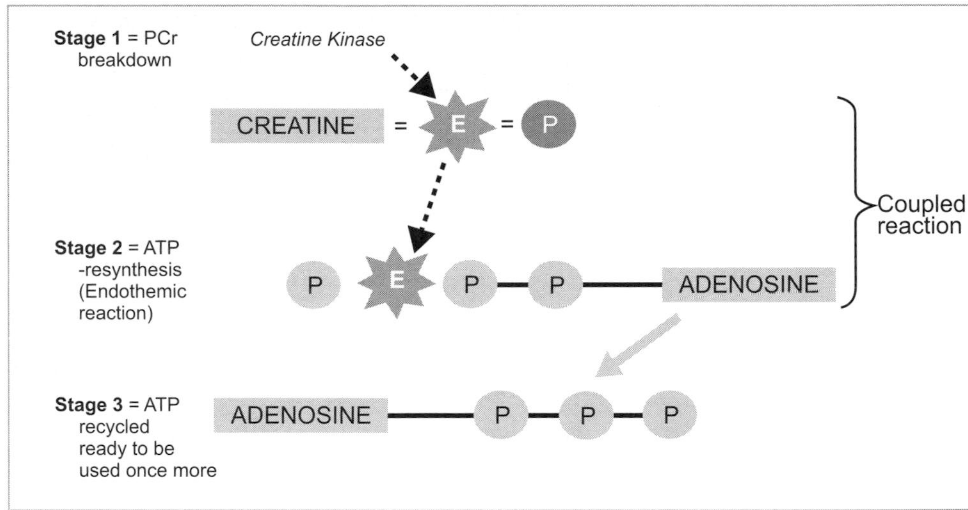

Fig 2.05 The ATP-PC system as a coupled reaction

Creatine suplementation – some athletes seek to extend the threshold of the ATP-PC system by ingesting creatine monohydrate. Some side effects by athletes have been recorded, such as abdominal cramps, bloating and dehydration.

Advantages of the ATP-PC system to the athlete

- The most important feature of this system is that ATP can be resynthesised very rapidly (almost immediately) by PCr.
- PCr stores are recovered very quickly, within two to three minutes of stopping exercise. This means that high intensity can once again ensue.
- It is an anaerobic process and does not need to wait for the three minutes or so for sufficient oxygen to be present.
- There are no fatiguing by-products which could delay recovery.
- Some athletes may seek to extend the time that they can use this system through creatine supplementation.

Drawbacks of the ATP-PCr system to the athlete

- The main drawback is that there is only a limited supply of PCr stored in the muscle cell. It is sufficient only to resynthesise ATP for approximately 10 seconds or so. Fatigue occurs when concentrations of PCr fall significantly and can no longer sustain ATP resynthesis.
- Resynthesis of PCr can only take place when there is sufficeint oxygen available – this is usually during resting conditions once exercise has ceased.
- Only one **mole** of ATP can be recycled through one mole of PCr.

KEY WORDS

Mole
An amount of a substance that contains a standardised number of atoms (6.0225 x 10^{23}, known as Avogadro's number).

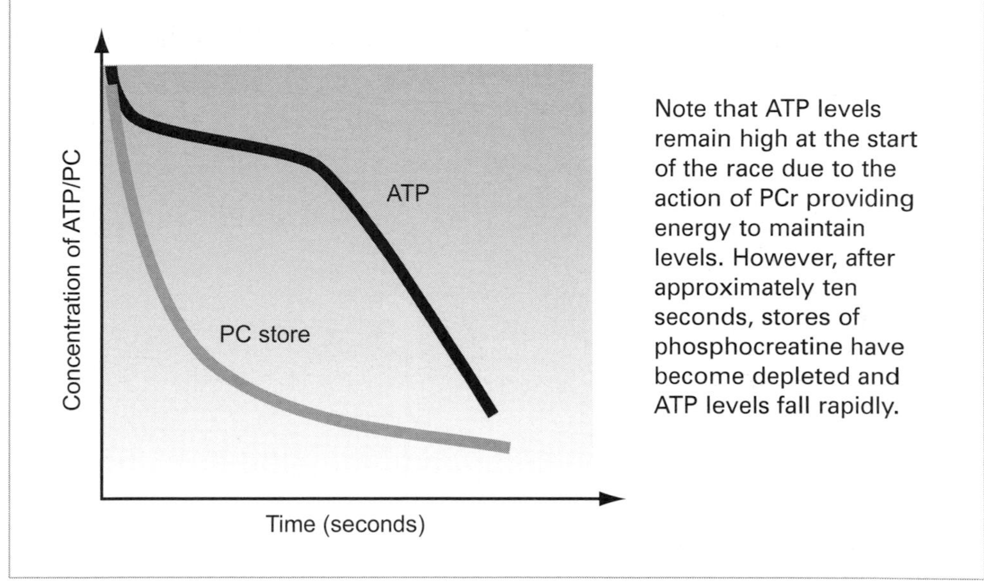

Fig 2.06 Muscle phosphagen depletion during a 100m sprint

TASK 2

During a 100m sprint ATP will initially split to enable the athlete to drive away from the starting blocks. PCr will then breakdown to maintain a constant supply of energy for the remainder of the race. Complete table 2.01 below with the required information.

Table 2.01 Key aspects of ATP splitting and the ATP-PC energy system

	Site of reaction	Fuel used	Active enzyme	Moles of ATP produced per mole of fuel
ATP splitting				n/a
ATP-PC system				

The lactic acid (lactate anaerobic) system

Threshold

The point where one energy system is exausted and another takes over as the predominant system. For example, the LA-O2 threshold represents the point where sufficient oxygen becomes available to enable the aerobic system to take over as the major energy provider.

Glycolysis

The breakdown of glucose to pyruvic acid.

Most activities last longer than the 10 second **threshold** of the ATP-PC system. If strenuous exercise is required to continue, ATP must be resynthesised from another fuel source. In fact, the body switches to glycogen (the stored form of carbohydrate) to fuel the working muscles once phosphocreatine stores have been depleted. The glycogen which is stored in the liver and muscles must first be converted into glucose-6-phosphate before it is broken down to pyruvate (pyruvic acid) by the enzyme phosphofructokinase (PFK) in a process known as **glycolysis**. It is during glycolysis (which takes place in the sarcoplasm of the muscle cell) that energy is released to facilitate ATP resynthesis. In fact, a net of two moles of ATP are gained for every mole of glycogen broken down. In the absence of oxygen, pyruvate is converted into lactate (lactic acid) by the enzyme lactate dehydrogenase.

$$C_6H_{12}O_6 \text{ (glycogen)} \rightarrow 2C_3H_6O_3 \text{ (lactic acid)} + \text{Energy}$$

$$\text{Energy} + 2ADP + 2Pi \rightarrow 2ATP$$

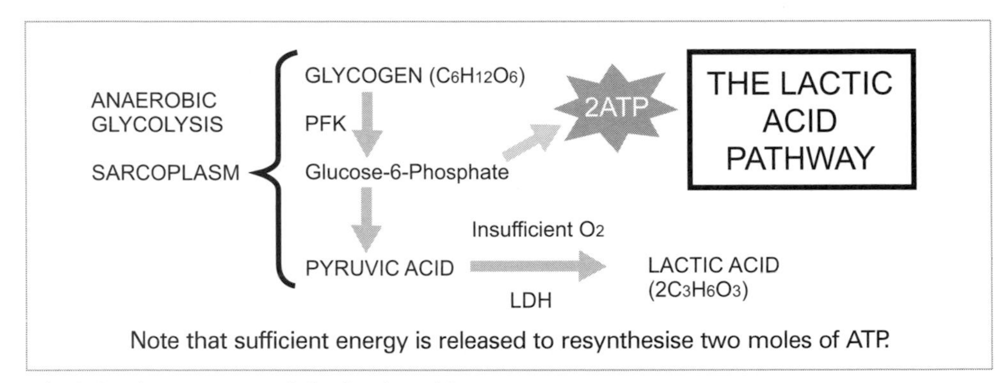

Fig 2.07 A summary of the lactic acid system

The lactic acid system is of particular use to athletes who need to perform high intensity exercise for a period of one to two minutes. A 400m runner is an obvious example, as is a squash player during a lengthy rally.

Fig 2.08 A 400m hurdler utilises the lactic acid system to provide energy for muscular contractions

Advantages of the lactic acid system to the athlete

- Because there are few chemical reactions, ATP can be resynthesised relatively quickly for activities or bouts of exercise that last between 10 seconds and 3 minutes.
- It is an anaerobic process and so does not need to wait for the three minutes or so for sufficient oxygen to be present.
- Any lactic acid that has accumulated can be converted back into liver glycogen or used as a metabolic fuel by reconversion into pyruvate and entry into the aerobic system.
- During aerobic activities such as a 10,000 km run, the lactic acid system can be called upon to produce an extra burst of energy during the race or a sprint finish.

Drawbacks of the lactic acid system to the athlete

Catalytic ability
The ability to increase the rate at which chemical reactions take place.

- The most obvious drawback of this system is the accumulation of lactic acid which can make glycolytic enzymes acidic. This causes them to lose their **catalytic ability** , inhibiting energy production through glycolysis. The intensity of the exercise must be reduced or, in the worst case scenario, stopped to enable the body to remove the lactic acid.
- Only a small amount of energy (approximately five per cent) locked inside a glycogen molecule can be released in the absence of oxygen. The remaining 95 per cent can only be released in the presence of oxygen.

TASK 3

During a 400m hurdles race the ATP-PC system will be used during the first 10 seconds or so and then the lactic acid system will provide the energy for ATP resysnthesis for the remainder of the race. Complete table 2.02 below with the required information.

Table 2.02 Key aspects of the lactic acid energy system

	Site of reaction	Fuel used	Active enzyme	Molecules of ATP produced
Lactic acid system				

The aerobic system

During resting conditions or exercise where the demand for energy is low, oxygen is readily available (hence the name aerobic system) to release stored energy from muscle glycogen, fats and proteins. The aerobic system is the body's preferred energy pathway as it is by far the most efficient in terms of ATP resynthesis. In fact the energy yield from aerobic metabolism is 18 times greater than anaerobic processes.

KEY WORDS

Mitochondria
The powerhouse of the cell. They are specialised structures within all cells that are the site of ATP production under aerobic conditions.

Under anaerobic conditions you will remember that pyruvic acid (pyruvate) is converted into fatigue-inducing lactic acid. However, when oxygen is in rich supply, pyruvic acid is instead converted into acetyl-coenzyme-A by combining with the enzyme pyruvate dehydrogenase. The site for energy release now moves to specialised parts of the muscle cell known as **mitochondria**. These industrious units are in abundance within the muscle. They manufacture energy for ATP resynthesis by facilitating the many chemical reactions required to completely break down stores of glycogen and fats, to ensure a continuous supply of energy. Figure 2.09 illustrates a mitochondrion. There are two key stages of the aerobic system that take place within the mitochondrion: the Kreb's cycle and the electron transport system.

APPLICATION

Slow twitch muscle fibres house many more mitochondria than fast twitch fibres, and hence are more suited to aerobic activity such as marathon running.

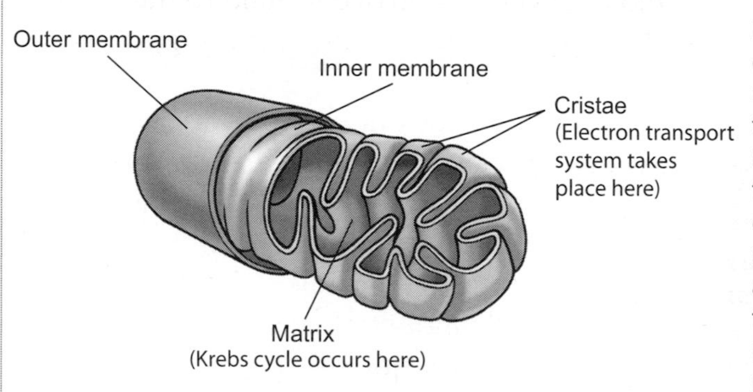

Mitochondria exist in all cells and are the ultimate destination of the oxygen that we breathe in. It is inside these 'factories' that all our aerobic energy is produced. The more aerobically 'fit' we are, the more and larger mitochondria we possess.

Fig 2.09 A mitochondrion

APPLICATION

The aerobic system is of particular use to athletes who need to perform relatively low intensity exercise for a long period of time. A triathlete or marathon runner are obvious examples.

Fig 2.10 A race walker will utilise the aerobic system to provide energy for muscular contractions

The Kreb's cycle

KEY WORDS

Kreb's cycle
A series of chemical reactions that occur in the matrix of the mitochondria yielding sufficient energy to resynthesise 2ATP and carbon dioxide. It forms part of the aerobic system.

The **Kreb's cycle** takes place in the fluid-filled matrix of the mitochondria, which has a rich supply of enzymes that are ready to perform the necessary chemical reactions to help release the remaining energy stored within the molecule.

Three significant events occur at this stage.

1 **Oxidation of acetyl-coenzyme-A.** This involves the removal of hydrogen atoms from the compound which then enter the final stage of the aerobic system; the electron transport system – (see below).
2 **Production of carbon dioxide (CO_2).** The removal of hydrogen means that only carbon and hydrogen remain. These combine to form carbon dioxide which is carried around to the lungs where it is breathed out.
3 **Resynthesis of ATP.** Sufficient energy is released at this stage to resynthesise two moles of ATP.

The electron transport system

KEY WORDS

Electron transport system
A series of reactions in the cristae of the mitochondria where the majority of energy is yielded for ATP resynthesis. Thirty four moles of ATP can be resynthesised from just one mole of glycogen at this stage of the aerobic system.

This final stage of glycogen and fat breakdown occurs in the cristae of the mitochondria. Hydrogen given off at the Kreb's cycle stage is carried to the **electron transport system.**

There are two important features of this stage of the aerobic pathway:

1 **Water (H_2O) is formed** when the hydrogen ions (H+) and electrons (e-) combine with oxygen through a series of enzyme reactions.
2 **Resynthesis of ATP.** The majority of energy is released here for the resynthesis of ATP. In fact, 34 moles of ATP can be resynthesised, making this by far the most efficient source of energy in the body.

Other fuels used in aerobic energy production

APPLICATION

During endurance exercise such as a triathlon, the body will use a mixture of both glycogen and fats. This is due to the low solubility of fats in the blood which means that they cannot be used on their own.

So far we have only focussed our attention on the aerobic breakdown of glycogen. However, fat and protein can also be metabolised under aerobic conditions to form CO_2, H_2O and energy for ATP resynthesis. Fats stored in the muscle as triglycerides must first be broken down into glycerol and free fatty acids (FFAs) before they go through the process of beta(ß)-oxidation (the fat equivalent of glycolysis). Following beta-oxidation fatty acids can enter the Kreb's cycle where they can then follow the same path of metabolism as glycogen. The main difference between fat and glycogen metabolism, however, is that substantially more energy (for ATP resynthesis) can be elicited from one mole of fatty acids than from one mole of glycogen. Consequently, fatty acids become the preferred fuel as the duration of exercise increases. This has important consequences for endurance performers as it enables them to spare their glycogen for later in the event or competition, when intensity of the exercise might increase.

HOT TIPS

One mole of fatty acid typically yields around 130 moles of ATP!

Glycogen sparing

A process by which performers become more effective at utilising fatty acids as a source of energy. This allows glycogen to be used more efficiently throughout the event or competition.

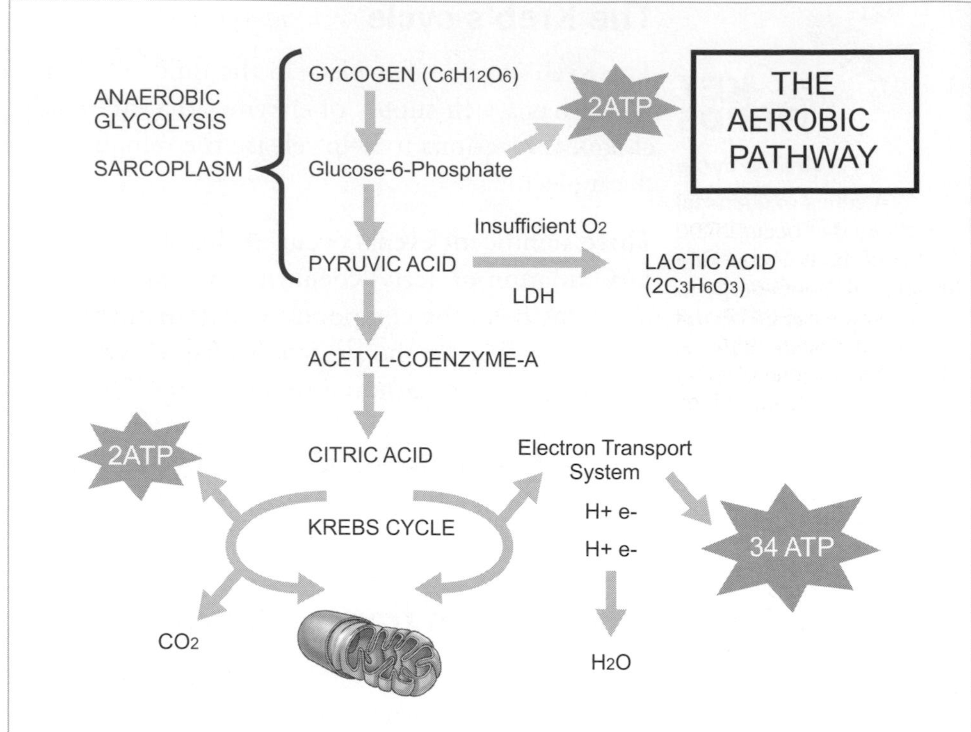

Fig 2.11 ATP resynthesis via the aerobic system

Advantages of this system to the athlete

- Significantly more ATP can be resynthesised under aerobic conditions than anaerobic (36 ATP aerobically compared to 2 ATP anaerobically – from one mole of glycogen).
- The body has substantial stores of muscle glycogen and triglycerides to enable exercise to last for several hours.
- Oxidation of glycogen and fatty acids do not produce any fatiguing by-products.

Drawbacks of this system to the athlete

- When we go from a resting state to exercise it takes a while for sufficient oxygen to become available to meet the new demands of the activity and enable the complete breakdown of glycogen and fatty acids. Consequently this system cannot provide energy to resysnthesise ATP in the immediate short term (unless the activity is of particularly low intensity) or during higher intensity activity.
- Although fatty acids are the preferred fuel during endurance events such as a marathon, the transport of fatty acids to the muscle is slow and requires about 15 per cent more oxygen than that required to break down the equivalent amount of glycogen.
- Due to the low solubility of fatty acids the endurance athlete will usually use a mixture of both glycogen and fatty acids to provide the energy for ATP resynthesis. When glycogen becomes depleted

The main enzyme used in the breakdown of fat is lipase.

Marathon runners often encounter the phenomenon of hitting the wall. This condition occurs when all the body's glycogen stores have been depleted and,to continue exercising, the body attempts to metabolise fat as a sole source of fuel.

and the body attempts to metabolise fatty acids as a sole source of fuel, muscle spasms may result. This is commonly known as 'hitting the wall'.

The complete breakdown of one mole of glycogen can be summarised as follows:

$$C_6H_{12}O_6 + 6O_2 \rightarrow 6CO_2 + 6H_2O + \text{Energy}$$

$$\text{Energy} + 38\text{ADP} + 38\text{Pi} \rightarrow 38\text{ATP}$$

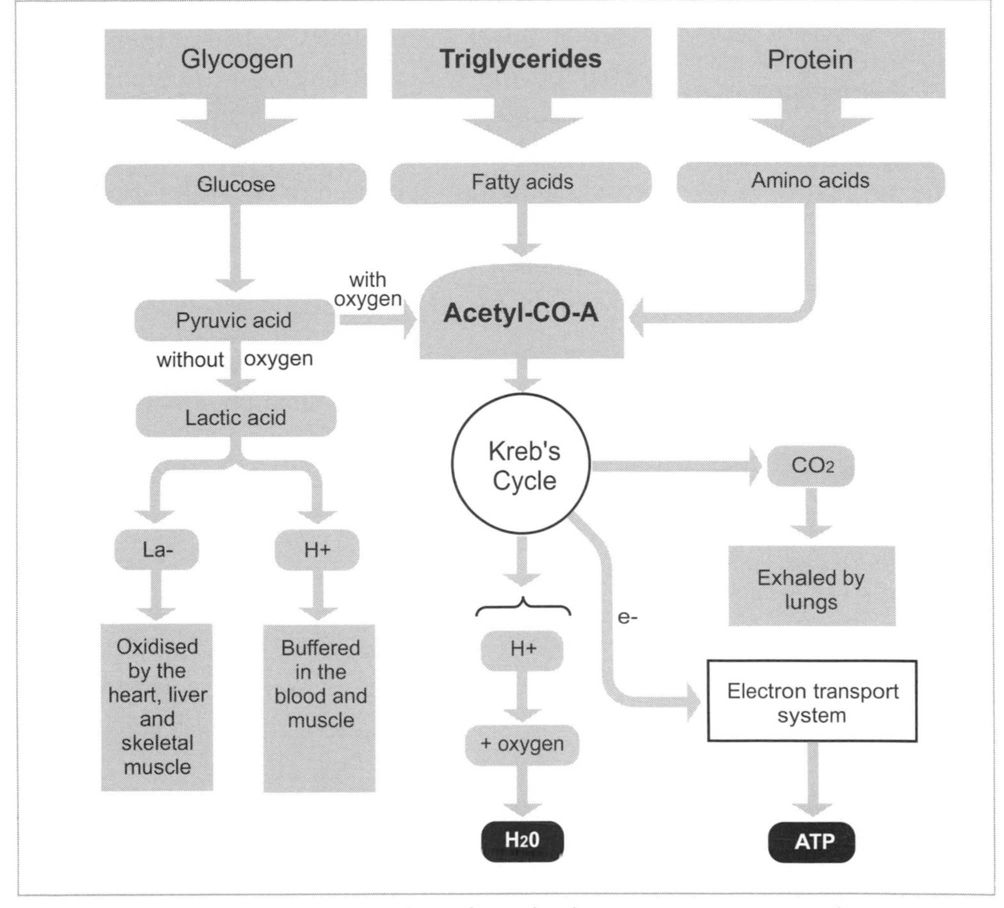

Fig 2.12 A summary of ATP resynthesis from the three main energy providing nutrients

TASK 4

During a 10,000m race the aerobic system will be used for the majority of the event to resynthesise ATP. Complete table 2.03 below with the required information.

Table 2.03 Key aspects of the aerobic energy system

	Site of reaction	Fuels used	Active enzymes	Molecules of ATP produced
Aerobic (oxidative) system				

Energy profiling and the energy continuum

Energy profiling
A representation of the importance of each energy system to a particular activity.

Energy continuum
An imaginary line which illustrates the relative contribution of each energy system to a particular activity.

Energy profiling considers the relative importance of each energy system to a particular activity. The reality is that all three energy systems work alongside each other, each contributing different amounts of energy to resynthesise ATP. A marathon runner, for example, whilst gaining most of his or her energy from the aerobic system, may need to draw upon the ATP-PC system at the very start of the race and upon the lactic acid system for a sprint finish. This will reflect where along the **energy continuum** a marathon runner is placed (obviously nearer the aerobic extreme). A midfielder in football may need to work for long periods of time in the lactic acid system, but will also have periods of less intense work when he or she can recover using the aerobic system or may need to sprint for a ball using the ATP-PC system. In this instance, as the football player spends more time in the lactic acid and aerobic systems than the ATP-PC system, he or she will be positioned in between the two (lactic acid and aerobic) along the continuum.

The position of each activity along the energy continuum is primarily governed by the intensity of the activity.

It may help to think of the energy sources in the body as a series of reservoirs, each with a stopcock controlling the amount of energy released from them. (See Figure 2.13.) For most activities all of the taps will be on at the same time but some of the taps may just be dripping whilst others will be open fully.

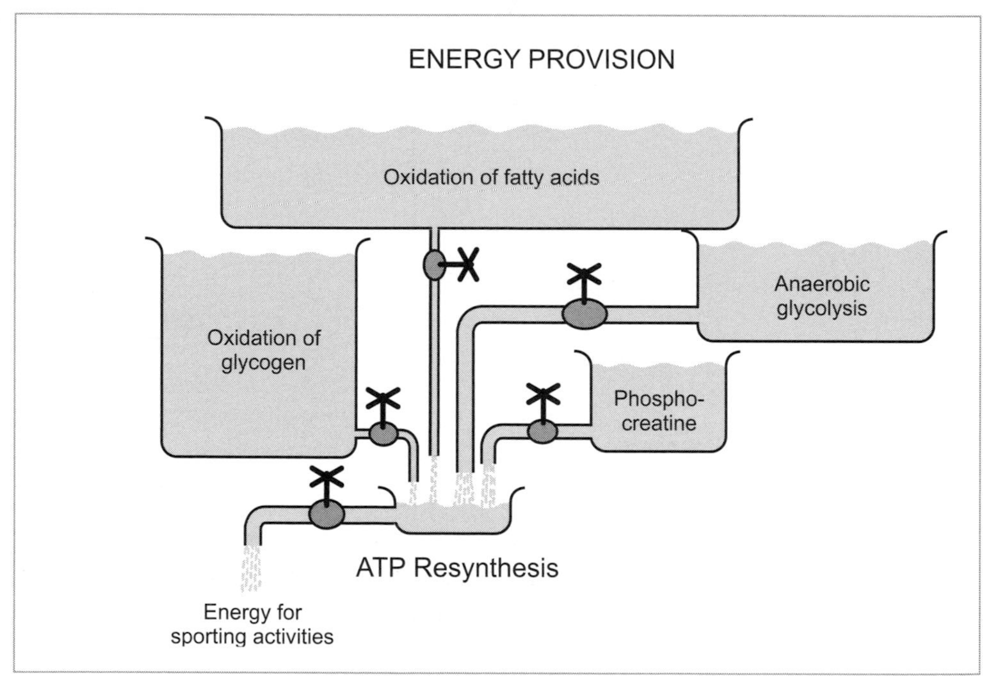

Fig 2.13 Sources of energy and the energy continuum

The energy profile can be illustrated as an energy block which represents the percentage contribution of each energy system to a particular activity. Figure 2.14 illustrates an energy block for a squash player. A squash player will largely use anaerobic systems during each point. However, the aerobic system will be called upon between points and games to ensure swift recovery. Study the profile on page 25 and then have a go at tasks.

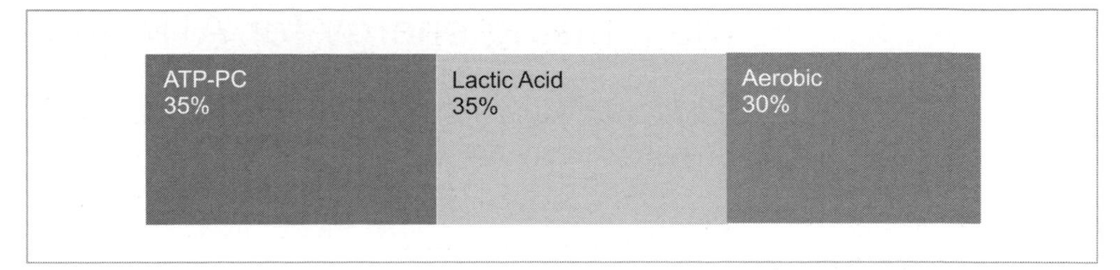

Fig 2.14 The energy profile of a squash player

TASK 5

The graph below (Figure 2.15) illustrates the amount of energy supplied from each of the energy systems against time. Copy out the graph labelling each line with the most appropriate energy system, i.e. ATP-PC, lactic acid or aerobic. Give a brief explanation to justify your labelling.

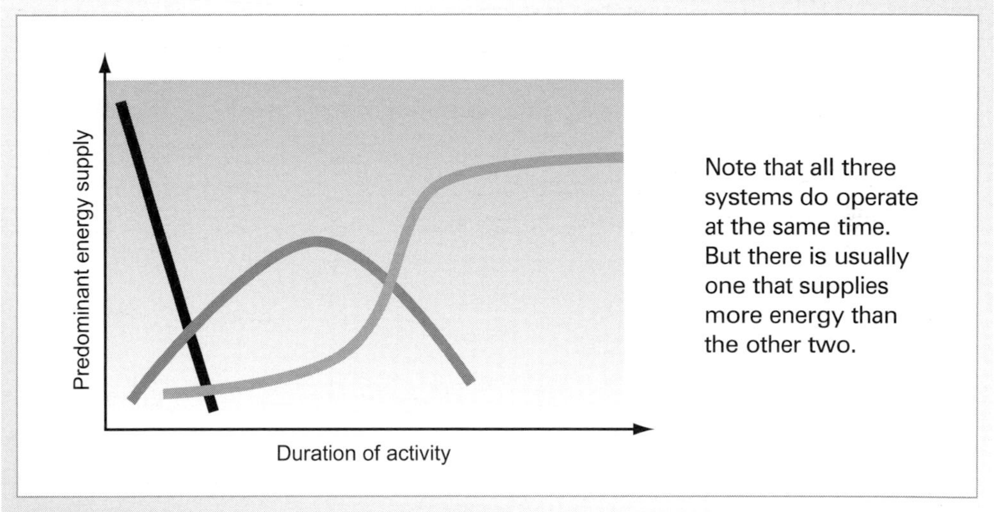

Fig 2.15 Energy system supplied against time

TASK 6

Draw a continuum with ATP splitting at one end and the aerobic system at the other, with the ATP-PC system and lactic acid system in between. Collect as many action pictures as you can from a wide variety of sports and activities and place them along the continuum depending upon the relative contribution of each system to the action illustrated. Beside each picture write a short commentary justifying its position along the continuum.

TASK 7

Construct an energy profile for each of the following activities:

- judo player
- 1500m runner
- basketball player
- hockey forward.

Maximising energy for ATP resynthesis

It is possible to enhance the production of energy from each energy system by following an apropriate diet and training programme.

Glycogen loading

The manipulation of dietary intake of carbohydrates prior to an endurance event in which performers try to maximise stores of glycogen.

Glycogen loading

The process of **glycogen loading**, favoured by endurance athletes, seeks to elevate muscle glycogen stores above their normal resting levels, to enable effective resynthesis of ATP via the aerobic pathway. Typically this practice involves depleting the glycogen levels seven days prior to the event through endurance-based training, followed by three days of a low carbohydrate diet whilst performing some kind of tapering exercise. On the remaining days leading up to the competition the athlete consumes a diet rich in carbohydrates whilst performing little or no exercise.

Table 2.04 A suggested glycogen loading method

Day 1	Long bout of exercise	Depletion of glycogen stores
Day 2	Tapering exercise	Low carbohydrate intake (200-300g)
Day 3	Tapering exercise	Low carbohydrate intake (200-300g)
Day 4	Tapering exercise	Low carbohydrate intake (200-300g)
Day 5	Tapering exercise	High carbohydrate intake (500-600g)
Day 6	Rest/little exercise	High carbohydrate intake (500-600g)
Day 7	Rest/little exercise	High carbohydrate intake of (500-600g)
Day 8	Competition	Pre-competition meal of moderate carbohydrate intake

Table 2.05 The advantages and disadvantages of glycogen loading to the athlete

Benefits of glycogen loading	Drawbacks of glycogen loading
Increased glycogen synthesis	Water retention and bloating
Increased muscular glycogen stores	Possible weight increase
Increased endurance capacity	Fatigue and muscle soreness
Delays fatigue/reduces risk of 'hitting the wall'	Irritability during the depletion phase

Studies have shown that following a carbohydrate regime like this can almost double muscular stores of glycogen.

Recent research indicates that the initial depletion stage of the glycogen loading process may not be necessary for trained athletes. Simply resting for the three days prior to competition and eating carbohydrate-rich meals may be sufficient to maximise glycogen stores.

However, whichever glycogen loading method you follow, it is important to increase the consumption of water as it helps to facilitate glycogen synthesis and storage. This will have the added bonus of preventing dehydration during the endurance race.

Creatine supplementation

Some athletes seek to extend the threshold of the ATP-PC system by ingesting creatine monohydrate, which ensures a readily available source of phosphocreatine in the muscle. Some side effects recorded by athletes include abdominal cramps, bloating and dehydration.

Soda loading

Soda loading

A method used by athletes to improve the buffering capacity of the body which entails drinking a solution of bicarbonate of soda.

Buffering

A process which helps in the removal of lactic acid and maintains blood and muscle pH (acidity).

By drinking a solution of bicarbonate of soda (something found in everybody's kitchen cupboard!) the pH of the blood increases, making it more alkaline. **Soda loading** enhances the **buffering** capacity of the blood, improving its ability to neutralise the negative effects of lactic acid. Consquently the threshold of the lactic acid system can be extended, enabling performers to work at higher intensities for longer. However, before you raid your kitchen cupboards, take a moment to consider the side effects: bloating, diarrhoea, stomach cramps and nausea are just a few that have been reported!

Training

You may remember from your Personal Exercise Programme in your AS course that there are a range of training methods at your disposal to improve performance. Table 2.06 suggests some training regimes that can be used to improve the efficiency of each of the three energy pathways. Whilst there are many adaptations that occur as a result of training, this table details only those that directly have an impact on ATP resynthesis. (See Chapter 5 for a more indepth investigation into all the structural and physiological adaptations of the body that follow a well planned training regime.)

Plyometrics

A type of training which typically takes the form of bounding and hopping. An eccentric muscle contraction is immediately followed by a powerful concentric contraction.

Interval training

An intermittent training regime that involves periods of alternating exercise and rest.

Fartlek

A form of continuous training where the intensity or speed of the activity is varied throughout the session.

Continuous training

Low intensity rhythmic exercise that uses large muscle groups and is used to develop endurance.

Table 2.06 Some training regimes to improve efficiency

Energy system	Duration of activity	Examples of activity	Training Method	Adaptation following training
ATP-PC	3 to 10 seconds	• 100m sprint • Gym vault	• Sprint interval training • **Plyometrics** • Weight training (80-95% 1RM/4-8 reps)	• Increased stores of ATP and PC • Increased activity of ATPase and creatine kinase
Lactic acid system	10 seconds to 3 minutes	• 400m run • 100m swim • Squash rally	• **Interval training** • **Fartlek** • Weight training (65-80% 1RM/ 8-15 reps) • Circuit training	• Increased stores of muscle glycogen • Increased number of glycolytic enzymes (PFK)
Aerobic system	Over 3 minutes	• Marathon • Triathlon • Recovery during team games	• **Continuous training** • Fartlek • Distance interval training	• Increased muscular stores of glycogen and triglycerides • Increased number of oxidative enzymes

Revise as you go!

1. Write out an equation which summarises each of the three energy systems.
2. Explain the specialist role of the mitochondria in the production of energy.
3. Draw a diagrammatic representation of each of the three energy systems.
4. Compare the three energy pathways with regard to their relative efficiency.
5. Explain the energy continuum in relation to a games player of your choice. Use specific examples from the game when each energy system is likely to be in use.
6. Explain what happens when a marathon runner 'hits the wall'.
7. What nutritional advice would you give to a marathon runner preparing for a major competition in the coming week?
8. Construct a food fuel graph which illustrates the predominant food fuel metabolised against time during a triathlon.
9. Why might performers take creatine supplements? What type of performer is likely to benefit from creatine supplementation?
10. Outline some methods of training you would use to develop and improve your ATP-PC system. For one of these methods give an example of a training session.

Chapter 3: Factors that contribute to successful endurance performance

Learning outcomes

Maximum oxygen consumption (VO_2max)
The maximum volume of oxygen that can be utilised or consumed by the working muscles per minute. It is usually measured in ml/kg/min.

By the end of this chapter you should be able to:

- define the term **maximum oxygen consumption (VO_2max)**
- outline at least three factors that contribute to a high VO_2max
- give at least one test of VO_2max
- explain what is meant by the onset of blood lactate accumulation (OBLA)
- explain the relationship between VO_2max and OBLA
- suggest at least one training regime that can be used to improve VO_2max
- outline the anatomical and physiological differences between males and females
- state the differences in fitness measures between males and females
- state the differences in fitness measures between trained and untrained subjects.

Introduction

You should be aware by now of the clear link that exists between

- the ability of the cardio-respiratory system to transport oxygen to the muscles
- the chemical ability of the muscle tissue to utilise this oxygen to break down fuels to release energy
- successful endurance performance.

HOT TIPS

VO_2max is expressed as a rate, either millilitres per kg of bodyweight per minute (ml/kg/min) for weight bearing activities such as running or litres per minute (l/min) for partial weight bearing activities such as rowing or cycling.

In this chapter we will investigate the factors that enable us to exercise under aerobic conditions and also consider the differences in fitness measures that we may expect between different population groups, such as males and females and the trained and untrained.

Maximum oxygen consumption (VO_2max)

Lance Armstrong's is reported as 83.8ml/kg/min, Paula Radcliffe's is an amazing 80ml/kg/min and Matt Pinsentt has the highest ever recorded in the UK at a staggering 8.5l/min. What do these figures represent? Well, it's their VO_2max of course! Indeed, if you visit the chat room of any marathon running web site, conversation soon turns to the size of your VO_2max.

APPLICATION

The average VO_2max score for an A-level student should be around 45-55ml/kg/min for males and 35-44ml/kg/min for females.

Your VO_2max or maximum oxygen consumption can be defined as:

the maximum volume of oxygen that can be utilised or consumed by the working muscles per minute.

A high VO_2max or maximum oxygen consumption is indeed one of the hallmark characteristics of great endurance performance in activities such as swimming, cycling, rowing and running. However, it is elite cross-country skiers that are considered the most powerful in oxygen uptake capacity. This is probably because cross-country skiing engages just about all of the major muscle groups of the body. But this is not the only determining factor of VO_2max.

Fig 3.01 Cross-country skiers reportedly have the highest VO_2max of all sports performers

The ability of the muscles to consume the greatest volume of oxygen possible is dependent upon two key things:

1 **An effective oxygen delivery system** that brings oxygen from the atmosphere into the working muscles.
2 **An aerobic–friendly muscle structure** which has a large amount of myoglobin and a high density of mitochondria which can be used to produce ATP via the aerobic energy system.

So for effective endurance performance we need a big and efficient pump to deliver oxygen-rich blood to the muscles and mitochondria-rich muscles to use the oxygen and enable high rates of exercise.

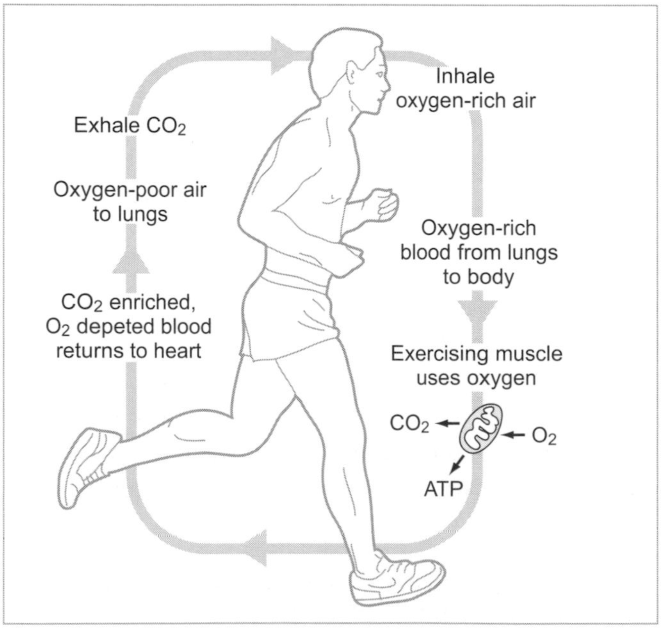

Fig 3.02 Oxygen transport and consumption during exercise

Measuring maximum oxygen consumption (VO_2max)

You will recall from your AS study that there are a number of tests of maximum oxygen consumption (VO_2max). These tests are listed below:

- the multi-stage fitness test
- Harvard step test
- PWC170 test
- Cooper 12 minute run test.

KEY WORDS

Direct gas analysis
The most valid and reliable method of measuring VO_2max. During the test, subjects are measured at progressively increasing intensities on a treadmill, cycle ergometer or rowing machine. Concentrations of oxygen and carbon dioxide inspired and expired are monitored.

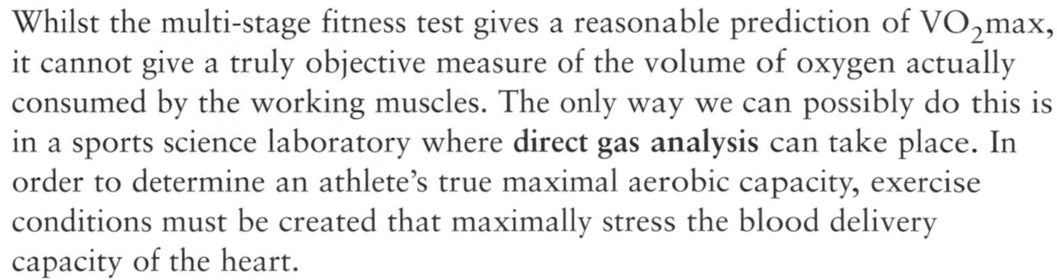

Whilst the multi-stage fitness test gives a reasonable prediction of VO_2max, it cannot give a truly objective measure of the volume of oxygen actually consumed by the working muscles. The only way we can possibly do this is in a sports science laboratory where **direct gas analysis** can take place. In order to determine an athlete's true maximal aerobic capacity, exercise conditions must be created that maximally stress the blood delivery capacity of the heart.

An example of a VO_2 max treadmill test now follows using Johnny, a typical A-level student, as a subject.

1 First of all, Johnny is weighed. This is so his VO_2 max can be given relative to his body weight. A simple reading of ml/min would ignore the fact that larger people have larger lungs and are capable of taking more oxygen into their bodies.

2 Following a warm up, Johnny places a mask over his mouth which is attached to the computer by a hose tubing. Johnny begins the treadmill test at a speed of 10km/h. Whilst running he breathes through a two-way valve system. The computer analyses the relative concentrations of oxygen and carbon dioxide inspired and expired respectively. From this it is possible to calculate the amount of oxygen extracted and consumed by the muscles and the amount of carbon dioxide produced over time. In order to reach an exhaustion point and get a maximum reading, the treadmill speed is increased by 1km/h every minute.

HOT TIPS

Make sure you are able to describe a test of VO_2max. You must be able to critically evaluate the test commenting on its validity and reliability.

3 After two minutes the speed of running has increased to 12km/h. Figure 3.03 overleaf shows an increase in the level of oxygen breathed in and carbon dioxide breathed out. The distance between the two values shows that Johnny is working aerobically with a good supply of oxygen to the muscles. He is in, a steady state where oxygen demand is being met by oxygen supply.

4 After seven minutes the speed has increased to 17km/h and Johnny's heart rate has increased significantly to 192bpm. His breathing rate has become faster as the levels of carbon dioxide increase further. Now the level of oxygen begins to level out. Johnny will have to call on more and more anaerobic energy to meet any other extra energy demands as his body struggles to get oxygen to his muscles.

5 After 10 minutes Johnny is racing along at 20km/h, his heart is doing overtime at over 200bpm and his lungs are working at their maximum to get oxygen into the body. This is the point where thc VO_2max is taken. His reading is 57.6ml/kg/min. After nearly 10.5 minutes Johnny is completely exhausted – he can no longer exercise and the test is stopped.

6 Johnny's reading of 57.6ml/kg/min is good and shows that he has some capacity to perform endurance-based activity.

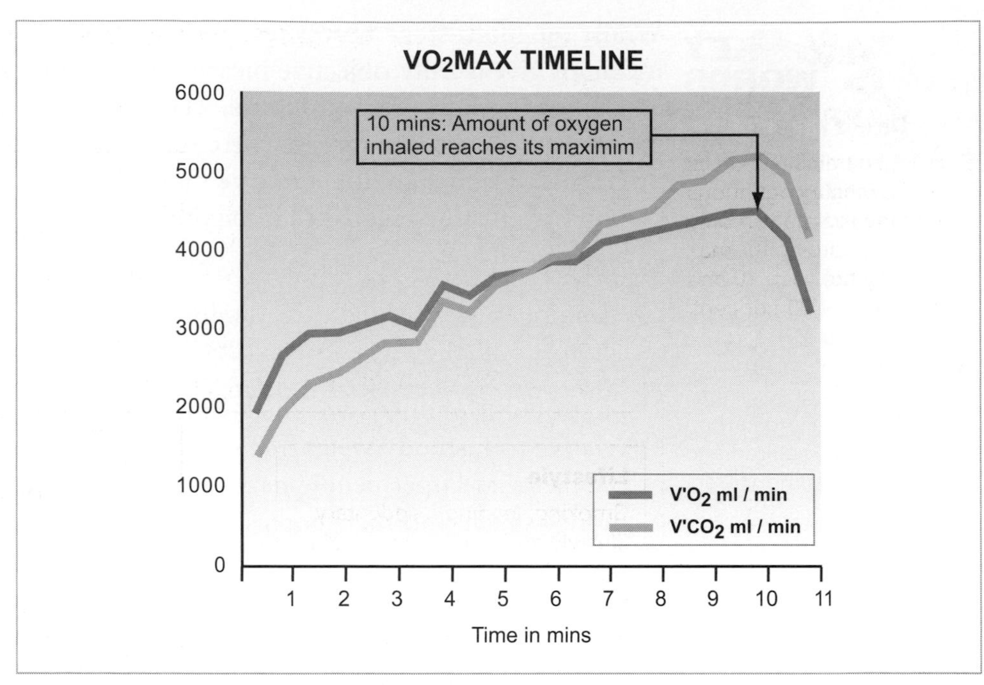

Fig 3.03 VO_2max timeline: Johnny's result

TASK 1

Use the following data in Table 3.01 to plot a bar graph illustrating the expected VO_2max scores for the activities shown.

Table 3.01 Typical VO_2max scores for a range of sporting performers

Activity	Male (ml/kg/min)	Female (ml/kg/min)
Triathlete	80	72
Marathon runner	78	68
Distance swimmer	72	64
Middle distance runner (800-1500)	72	63
Games player	66	56
Gymnast	56	47
Weightlifter	52	43

Absolute VO_2max
A VO_2max value given in litres/min.

Relative VO_2max
A VO_2max value that takes account of bodyweight and is measured in millilitres of oxygen per kg of bodyweight per minute (ml/kg/min)

TASK 2

If your **absolute VO_2max** was measured at 4.0l/min and you weighed 75kg, calculate your **relative VO_2max.**

TASK 3

Design a training programme aimed at improving the VO_2max of a performer. Make sure you prescribe appropriate methods of training and clearly state the expected intensity of training.

Factors affecting maximum oxygen consumption (VO_2max)

Endurance training such as following a continuous training regime can only improve VO_2max by between 10 and 20 per cent.

Physiology

The physiological make up of the body will almost certainly affect VO_2 max. Below are just a few physiological factors that contribute to a higher VO_2max score:

* a high percentage of slow twitch (type 1) muscle fibres
* high capillary density
* high mitochondrial density and myoglobin content
* high blood volume and haemoglobin content.

Lifestyle

Smoking, leading a sedentary lifestyle and having a poor diet can greatly reduce VO_2max values.

Age

Typically VO_2max will decrease with age. After the age of 25 years, VO_2max is thought to decrease by about 1 per cent per year. Regular physical activity can slow down the rate of this decline.

Genetics

Studies on identical and fraternal twins have suggested that genetics accounts for 25 to 50 per cent of VO_2max scores.

It appears that Olympic champions are born with a unique potential that is transformed into athletic performance through years of hard training.

Body composition

Research shows that VO_2max scores decrease as the percentage of body fat increases. This is because fat is non-functional weight that must be carried around. Typically males should aim for a body fat per cent of between 14–17 per cent whilst females should aim for a value between 24–29 per cent.

Gender

When we consider absolute VO_2max, the typical untrained male has a value of 3.5l/min whilst that of a female is approximately 2l/min – a 43 per cent difference! When we consider bodyweight to give a relative value this difference is reduced to 15 to 20 per cent.

Training

VO_2max can only be improved by 10 to 20 per cent following training. This is somewhat surprising given the vast improvement in the delivery and transport of oxygen resulting from long-term endurance training. The best methods of training to improve VO_2max include continuous training, Fartlek and aerobic interval training.

Fig 3.04 the main factors that affect an individual's maximum oxygen consumption

Onset of blood lactate accumulation (OBLA)

Onset of blood lactate accumulation (OBLA)
The point at which lactic acid begins to accumulate in the blood. Usually taken when concentrations of lactic acid reach 4mmol/litre of blood.

Millimole
A unit used to measure the amount of a chemical substance. It is equal to 1/1000 of a mole.

You may have heard of the lactate threshold and anaerobic threshold. Together with OBLA these essentially describe the same phenomenon.

Lance Armstrong can tap into an exceptionally high percentage of his VO_2max. His OBLA reportedly occurs at 88.6 per cent of his VO_2max.

We have established that a large VO_2max sets the ceiling for endurance performance: it is an indication of the size of our performance engine. However, it is the **onset of blood lactate accumulation (OBLA)** that determines the actual percentage of that engine power that can be utilised.

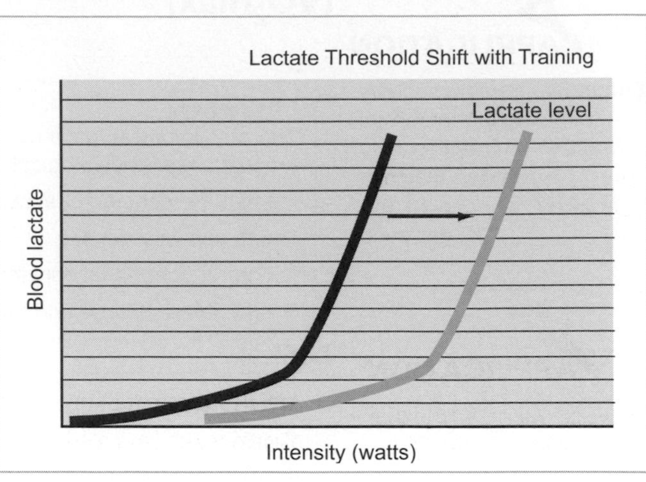

Fig 3.05 A comparison of the point of OBLA between trained (grey line) and untrained (black line) athletes when measured as a percentage of their VO_2max

The onset of blood lactate accumulation describes the point at which lactic acid starts to accumulate in the muscles. During normal resting conditions the normal amount of lactic acid circulating in the blood is 1–2 **millimoles/litre (mmol/l)**. This rises dramatically during intense exercise. Quite simply, the more intense the exercise the greater the extent of lactic acid production. The onset of blood lactate accumulation (OBLA) is said to occur when concentrations of lactic acid in the blood reach 4mmol/l.

Just like VO_2max, OBLA occurs at different intensities of exercise for different people. It is expressed as a percentage of VO_2max. For the average untrained individual, OBLA occurs at around 55–60 per cent of VO_2max, whilst trained endurance performers can delay OBLA until they have utilised 85–90 per cent of their VO_2max.

Measuring OBLA

OBLA can only truly be measured in a sports science laboratory. The test should be conducted using a mode of exercise most suited to the performer, usually a treadmill, bicycle ergometer, rowing ergometer or swimming bench. Typically the test is conducted in four to six stages. During the first stage the exercise intensity is set at about 50 per cent of VO_2max and increases in intensity at the start of each of the subsequent stages. Each stage generally lasts about five minutes. At the end of each stage, heart rate is recorded, oxygen consumption measured, and blood samples are taken by a small prick on the finger or earlobe and the concentration of blood lactate is analysed. The point at which blood lactate levels rise to 4mmol/l of blood usually signals OBLA. The exercise intensity, oxygen consumption and heart rate at this point can now be recorded and used to monitor progress and assess exercise intensity during training.

OBLA and training

Buffering

A process which helps in the removal of lactic acid and maintains blood and muscle pH (acidity).

Improvements in endurance capacity can be observed where lower lactate levels are recorded for any given exercise intensity. This shows that the body has adapted to cope with higher levels of blood lactate and speeds up removal through effective **buffering**. You will recall that untrained individuals usually reach OBLA at about 55–60 per cent of VO_2max. With training this figure can increase to 70 per cent or even higher. Elite endurance athletes such as Lance Armstrong have values approaching 90 per cent. Whist OBLA is a much greater product of training than VO_2max, it is still influenced by genetics.

APPLICATION

A cyclist during a time trial can use data from the OBLA test to determine her racing heart rate by calculating the percentage of HR max that leads to OBLA. If she had a HR max of 182bpm and OBLA occurred at a HR of 158bpm, this equates to about 87 per cent of HR max. Her racing heart rate should be somewhere just below this point.

TASK 4

Using the information from Table 3.02, plot a graph of blood lactate accumulation (mmol/l) (y-axis) against running speed (ms-¹) (x-axis).

Table 3.02

Blood lactate (mmol/l)	2.9	3.7	5.7	9.1
Running speed ms-¹	3.5	4.0	4.5	4.9

1 On your graph show the point of OBLA. Give a brief explanation as to why you have chosen this point on the graph.
2 At what running speed did OBLA occur?

HOT TIPS

The following equation can be used to calculate the percentage of VO_2max used by a performer:

$$\frac{VO_2 \text{ (amount of } O_2 \text{ used)}}{VO_2\text{max (max potential)}}$$

HOT TIPS

Although lactic acid and lactate are often used interchangeably, they are not in fact the same thing. Lactate is a salt of lactic acid and results when hydrogen is removed from the lactic acid molecule. When lactic acid is flushed from the muscle into the blood stream, hydrogen is attracted to the bicarbonate ion in the blood to form carbonic acid (H_2CO_3) which breaks down into CO_2 and H_2O.

A word on lactic acid

You will recall that lactic acid is produced when there is insufficient oxygen available to sustain a given exercise intensity. The pyruvic acid produced during glycolysis is converted into lactic acid by the enzyme lactate dehydrogenase. Once formed, lactic acid quickly dissociates into lactate and hydrogen ions (H+). It is the presence of hydrogen ions that make the muscle acidic and ultimately causes muscle fatigue. The acidic environment slows down enzyme activity and ceases the further breakdown of glycogen. High levels of acidity can also irritate nerve endings which can cause some degree of pain. The 'heavy legs' often associated with lactic acid can thus be blamed on the hydrogen ions.

However, lactic acid is not always the bad guy it is made out to be. The heart, the liver, the kidneys and inactive muscles are all locations where lactic acid can be taken up from the blood and either converted back into pyruvate and metabolised in the mitochondria producing energy or converted back to glycogen and glucose in the liver. Table 3.03 summarises what happens to the lactic acid once it has been removed from the muscle.

Table 3.03 The fate of lactic acid

Conversion into CO_2 and H_20	Up to 65%
Conversion into glycogen	Up to 20%
Conversion into protein	Up to 10%
Conversion into glucose	Up to 5%
Conversion into sweat and urine	Up to 5%

Factors influencing the rate of lactate accumulation

Exercise intensity

The higher the exercise intensity the greater the ATP demand, (type 2) muscle which can only be sustained using glycogen as a fuel. As fast twitch (type 2) muscle, fibres possess greater stores of glycogen (and therefore lactate dehydrogenase), pyruvate is soon converted to lactic acid.

Muscle fibre type

Slow twitch (type 1) fibres produce less lactate at a given workload than fast twitch fibres. As slow twitch muscle fibres possess greater amounts of mitochondria, pyruvate will tend to be converted into acetyl-coenzyme-A and move into the mitochondria with little lactate production.

Rate of blood lactate removal

If the rate of lactate removal equals the rate of production then blood lactate concentrations should remain constant. When the rate of lactate production exceeds the rate of removal then blood lactate will accumulate as OBLA is reached.

The trained status of the working muscles

If muscles are trained then they benefit from the associated **adaptive responses**. These include improved capacity for aerobic respiration due to higher mitochondrial and capillary density, improved use of fatty acids as a fuel (which do not produce lactic acid!) and increased stores of myoglobin.

Adaptive responses

The anatomical and physiological changes that occur to the body as a result of following a training programme.

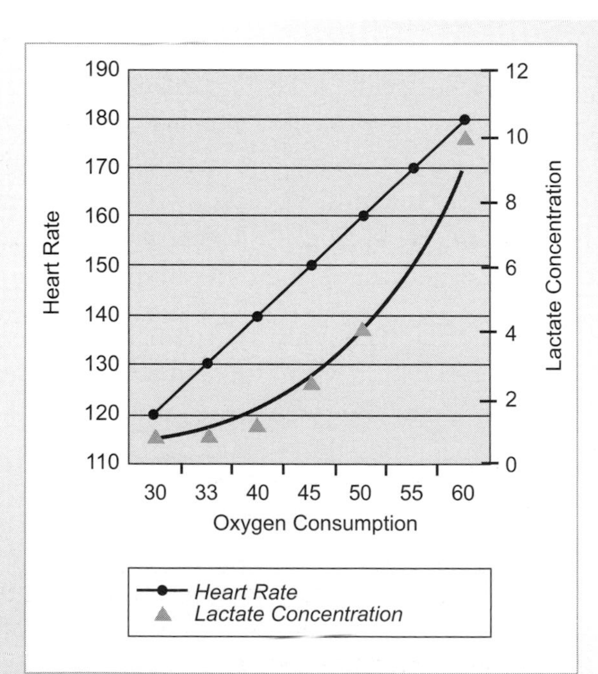

Fig 3.06 The relationship of oxygen consumption to heart rate and lactate concentration of a middle distance runner during a maximal test to exhaustion

TASK 5

The graph in Figure 3.06 provides data gained from an OBLA test on a middle-distance runner.

1 Use Figure 3.06 to calculate OBLA of the runner given that she has a VO_2max of 61ml/kg/min.

2 If her HR max is 182bpm, at what percentage of HR max does OBLA occur?

Gender differences in athletic performance – the battle of the sexes!

APPLICATION

When we consider absolute VO_2max the typical untrained male has a value of 3.5l/min whilst that of a female is approximately 2l/min – a 43 per cent difference! When we consider bodyweight to give a relative value this difference is reduced to 15–20 per cent.

For many years social issues, misunderstandings and presumptions concerning physical and medical issues excluded many females from participating in vigorous physical activity, leading to the slow development of female athletic performance. Thankfully those times are gone now and female athletes are rapidly closing the gap on their male counterparts.

Contrary to popular belief the following variables show very little or no difference between the sexes:

- distribution of muscle fibre types
- lactate threshold when measured as a percentage of VO_2max
- muscular concentrations of ATP and PC.

Having said that, we know that there are some anatomical and physiological differences between the sexes and we need to consider just how these differences affect fitness levels and competition performance.

Table 3.04 considers the major performance differences between the sexes that are of particular interest to the exercise physiologist and attempts to explain these differences using knowledge of anatomy and physiology.

Table 3.04 The major differences in fitness measures between males and females

Performance factor (females compared to males)	Anatomical/physiological explanation (females compared to males)
15–20% lower maximum oxygen consumption (VO_2max)	Lower haemoglobin content of the blood – this limits oxygen transport and delivery Lower blood volume – this limits oxygen transport and delivery Smaller heart size – this makes a less effective pump in the delivery of oxygen More body fat which increases the non-functional weight using up oxygen during exercise Smaller lung capacity which means less oxygen is entering the body and available for aerobic respiration
Up to 50% lower in measures of strength and power (although these differences are smaller when adjusted for fat-free mass)	Less muscle mass Lower capacity for anaerobic glycolysis
7–10% more body fat	The female hormone **oestrogen** promotes the deposition of subcutaneous fat which offers little benefit to women during endurance events
Biomechanical differences	A wider pelvis and forward orientation of the hips can hinder running and cycling efficiency

Revise as you go!

HOT TIPS

As a rule of thumb when VO_2max is measured in relative terms (taking bodyweight into consideration), female athletes have a score of approximately 10ml lower than comparable males of the same activity group.

1. Define VO_2max.
2. Suggest typical VO_2max values for the following:
   a) a healthy male A-level PE student
   b) a centre in netball
   c) an olympic rower.
3. The multi-stage fitness test or 'bleep test' is often used to determine the VO_2max of an athlete. Briefly outline this test and give reasons why this may not be the most accurate test to use.
4. Identify and explain the procedures of a more valid test that may be used to determine an athlete's VO_2max.
5. Outline the factors that could limit VO_2max.
6. Suggest a method to improve VO_2max
7. Explain why the VO_2max of women is typically 15–20 per cent lower than that of men from the same activity group.
8. Explain what you understand by the term OBLA.
9. OBLA and lactate threshold are often used interchangeably. How is the lactate threshold related to VO_2max?
10. At what point does OBLA typically occur? What might cause an athlete to reach OBLA?
11. Andrew Johns represents Great Britain in triathlon. Explain how knowledge of blood lactate levels during a triathlon might assist his performance.
12. Briefly outline the factors that affect the rate of lactate accumulation.
13. Explain what you understand by the term 'buffering'. How does the body buffer lactic acid?
14. What happens to lactic acid once it has been produced in the body?

Chapter 4: Causes of fatigue and recovery from exercise

Learning outcomes

By the end of this chapter you should be able to:
- identify at least four causes of fatigue during exercise
- explain how the body 'recovers' by returning to its pre-exercise state
- define EPOC
- explain the relationship between EPOC and oxygen debt
- identify the two components of EPOC
- define the term DOMS
- give two reasons why DOMS occurs and suggest one way to reduce the effects
- discuss how knowledge of the recovery process can help the coach and athlete in planning training sessions.

Introduction

A triathlon is an exceptionally demanding event. Triathletes must complete a significant volume of training in three different disciplines (swimming, cycling and running) which may require them to train more than once a day. How does the body cope with this? How long does it take the body to recover between training sessions and what causes the body to fatigue during training and competition? These are just a few key questions that this chapter seeks to address as well as discussing just how the coach and athlete can use knowledge of fatigue and recovery to their advantage.

Causes of fatigue

Fatigue
General feelings of tiredness often associated with inhibited muscular performance.

Acetylcholine
A neuro-transmitter that enables a nerve impulse to jump the synaptic cleft (the gap which separates the nerve ending and muscle fibre) and initiates muscular contraction.

Fatigue is a word often associated with exercising at near maximal levels together with the physical actions and feelings that go along with this, such as heavy or laboured breathing, and muscular pain and tiredness.

The causes of fatigue are many and varied and will depend largely upon the activity undertaken. The fatigue associated with running 800m to exhaustion, for example, are totally different to that experienced by the triathlete mentioned above. The former may fatigue due to lactic acid accumulation whilst the latter may tire through glycogen depletion.

Figure 4.01 summarises the six major causes of fatigue experienced through exercise:
- reduced rate of ATP resynthesis
- hydrogen ion accumulation
- reduced levels of **acetylcholine** at the neuromuscular junction

- glycogen depletion
- dehydration
- reduced levels of calcium for muscular contraction.

Reduced rate of ATP resynthesis

Depletion of ATP and PC may result in there being insufficient ATP to sustain muscular contraction, causing a deterioration in performance.

Glycogen depletion

The body only has sufficient glycogen stores to last for about 90 minutes of exercise. Once depleted the muscles are unable to sustain contraction as the body is unable to use fat as a sole source of fuel – as fat can only be used in conjunction with glycogen. Marathon runners often 'hit the wall' when glycogen stores have been depleted and the body tries to metabolise fat. This is often due to them running at too high an intensity earlier on in the event.

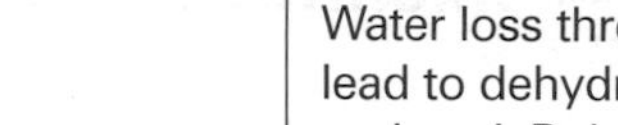

Dehydration

Water loss through sweating can lead to dehydration if it is not replaced. Dehydration of as little as 2 per cent of body weight can have an adverse effect upon performance. This is largely due to impairment of blood flow to the muscles and loss of electrolytes such as calcium which help in muscular contraction.

Accumulation of hydrogen ions (H+)

During intense exercise greater amounts of lactic acid will be produced which in turn releases hydrogen ions. These hydrogen ions increase the acidity of the muscle causing acidosis. This reduces muscular performance by inhibiting enzyme activity (PFK) and irritating nerve endings causing a degree of pain.

Reduced levels of calcium

The release of calcium is essential for effective muscular contraction. It is thought that increased levels of hydrogen ions (H+) decreases the amount of calcium that is released from the sarcoplasmic reticulum, interfering with muscle contraction.

Reduced levels of acetylcholine

Studies of fatigued muscles have highlighted that a deficiency in the levels of acetylcholine may be responsible. Acetylcholine is a neuro-transmitter responsible for helping a nerve impulse to jump the synaptic cleft (the gap which separates the nerve ending and muscle fibre) and initiate muscular contraction.

Fig 4.01 Major causes of fatigue during exercise

Thermoregulation
The process by which the body maintains body temperature within acceptable limits.

A marathon runner should use continuous type training as their favoured method whilst a sprinter should use sprint interval training.

One further consideration is that of **thermoregulation.** Whilst exercising in a hot environment, the muscles generate heat as a result of the metabolic pathways discussed in Chapter 2. The heat is transported to the surface of the body by the circulating blood where it is lost either by radiation and convection or by the evaporation of sweat. During prolonged exercise or when the body becomes dehydrated, total blood volume may decrease and more blood is redistributed to the skin, reducing the volume of blood (and therefore oxygen) available to the working muscles resulting in impaired performance. Both training and acclimatisation to hot environments can modify the control systems which regulate blood flow to the skin and sweating.

What steps can a performer take to reduce the likelihood of fatigue?

- **Train the relevant energy system and use the most appropriate method of training for the sport or activity.**

By training the relevant energy system the body adapts and becomes more efficient at maintaining ATP resynthesis through that pathway, thus delaying fatigue. Using the most appropriate training method for your activity will help achieve this.

- **Spare your glycogen!**

For endurance events (especially the marathon and triathlon) it is essential that the performer can spare glycogen throughout the entire duration of the event. You will remember that due to the hydrophobic nature of fat the body cannot metabolise it sufficiently quickly to maintain muscular contraction (when used on its own). Appropriate endurance training helps the body 'switch on' fat metabolism earlier and slow the rate of glycogen depletion. Furthermore, you will recall that the rate at which glycogen depletes is dependent upon the intensity of the activity being undertaken. A sprinter, for example, will use up glycogen 20 to 30 times quicker than a marathon runner. The marathon runner must therefore pace him or herself appropriately and not be tempted to run too fast early in the race as this will speed up glycogen depletion.

- **Undertake a period of glycogen loading prior to endurance competition.**

By manipulating the amount of carbohydrate consumed in the days leading up to competition, the body may be able to store more glycogen and enable endurance activity to continue for longer. An example of a suggested glycogen loading cycle is given in Chapter 2.

Hypertonic drinks
Drinks with a greater concentration of solid particles (such as carbohydrate) per unit of water.

- **Drink plenty of fluid to remain hydrated.**

During exercise it is advisable to drink fluid that has a carbohydrate content of no more than six per cent carbohydrate. This should give a small boost to blood glucose levels. It is also essential for these drinks to replace electrolytes lost through sweating, which helps to maintain the physiological processes of the body. **Hypertonic drinks** which have a much higher concentration of carbohydrate can be consumed following exercise to help restore muscle glycogen.

Recovery from exercise

KEY WORDS

Recovery

The return of the body to its pre-exercise state.

As recovery can only occur when there is sufficient oxygen available, it is often associated with the aerobic energy system.

The term oxygen debt was often used to explain the restoration of ATP and PC and removal of lactic acid during recovery. But this failed to explain the extra oxygen needed during recovery to restore muscle oxymyoglobin and to keep respiratory and heart rates elevated. EPOC is therefore the preferred term now and oxygen debt is viewed as one part of this process.

The **recovery** process is concerned with returning the body to its pre-exercise state so that heart rate, oxygen consumption, blood lactate levels and glycogen stores are at exactly the same levels as they were *before* the exercise commenced!

You will know from your own experience that whatever the exercise that you may have performed, whether it be a maximal lift in the weights room or a 5K run, the recovery period involves a period where breathing and heart rates are elevated. This occurs because all recovery is dependent upon the consumption of oxygen, and the elevated respiratory and heart rates ensure that adequate amounts of oxygen are taken into the body and delivered to the muscles to enable a swift recovery. The oxygen delivered to the muscles will help rebuild stores of PC and ATP as well as remove any lactic acid that may have accumulated during the activity.

TASK 1

Carry out an investigation to examine recovery heart rate response to varying intensities of exercise.

Equipment you will need includes: heart rate monitor, stop watch, gymnastics bench, metronome, a copy of Table 4.01 (on page 43) to record your results. (If you do not have access to a heart rate monitor then record your heart rate at the carotid artery for a 10-second count and multiply by six to convert to beats per minute.)

1 Record your resting heart rate at the beginning of the class.

2 Record your heart rate immediately prior to exercise.

3 Commence exercising by stepping onto and off the bench in time with the metronome that has been set at a low intensity.

4 Record your heart rate after one, two and three minutes of exercise. After the third minute of exercise stop the test. Continue to record your pulse each minute during recovery until it has returned to its resting value.

5 Once your heart rate has returned to its resting value (or within a few beats) repeat the test at a medium intensity. Record your results as before.

6 Repeat the exercise for a third time but at very high intensity. Once again record your results.

7 Now use your results to plot a graph for each of the three workloads. (Figure 4.02 will help to get you started.) Plot each graph using the same axes, placing heart rate along the y-axis and time along the bottom x-axis. Don't forget to show your resting heart rate values on the graph.

8 For each of your graphs explain the pattern of recovery heart rate.

Table 4.01

Time	Exercise intensity		
	Low	Medium	High
Resting HR			
HR prior to exercise			
Exercise 1 min			
Exercise 2 min			
Exercise 3 min			
Recovery 1 min			
Recovery 2 min			
Recovery 3 min			
Recovery 4 min			
Recovery 5 min			
Recovery 6 min			
Recovery 7 min			

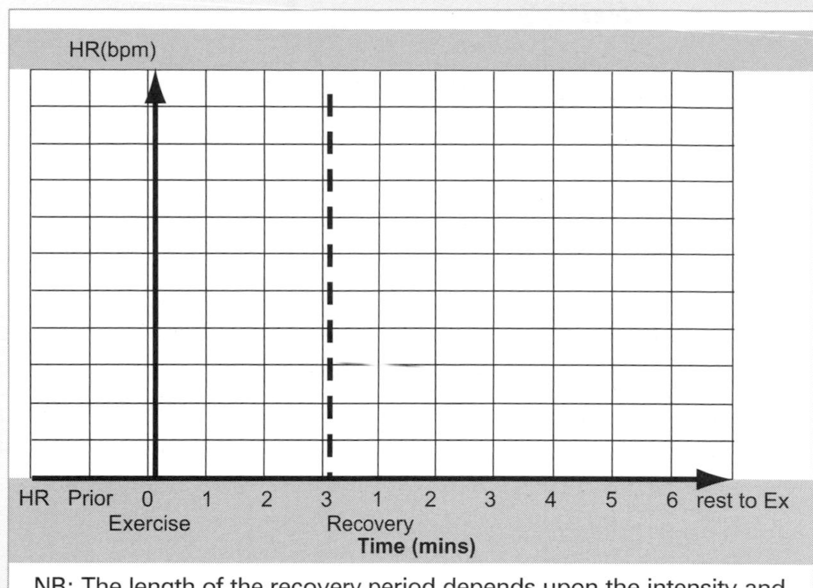

Fig 4.02 Example graph

Excess post-exercise oxygen consumption (EPOC)

KEY WORDS

Excess post-exercise oxygen consumption (EPOC)
The volume of oxygen consumed during recovery above that which normally would have been consumed at rest in the same period of time.

Oxygen deficit
The volume of extra oxygen required to complete an entire activity aerobically.

Fast replenishment
The first component of EPOC. Oxygen consumed is used to resaturate myoglobin and resynthesise ATP and PC. It takes approximately two to three minutes.

Excess post-exercise oxygen consumption (EPOC) represents the extra volume of oxygen consumed following exercise that enables the body to fully recover and return to its pre-exercise state.

At the very beginning of exercise (even at low intensities) or when exercise is of high intensity, it is likely that the body will need to work anaerobically for a period of time. This is because there may be insufficient oxygen available to use the aerobic energy system exclusively to provide the energy for muscular work. That is to say that a deficit in oxygen supply occurs. The **oxygen deficit** thus represents the amount of extra oxygen required to enable the entire activity to be completed using the aerobic energy system. Since it takes a while for the aerobic system to 'kick-in' and provide the muscles with energy at the beginning of activity, a deficit will always develop.

Researchers have identified two stages of recovery:

- **Stage 1:** the **fast replenishment** stage (formerly referred to as the alactacid debt).
- **Stage 2:** the **slow replenishment** stage (formerly known as the lactacid debt).

TASK 2

Examine your graphs drawn in task 1. Can you identify a fast and slow stage of oxygen consumption during the recovery period? If so, shade these stages on the graph and label them 'fast stage' and 'slow stage'.

Slow replenishment

The second component of EPOC. Oxygen consumed during this stage is largely used to remove lactic acid, which takes about one hour. In addition, oxygen is also used to maintain cardiac and respiratory rates and normalise body temperature.

You will note from Figure 4.03a that the volume of EPOC is greater than the volume of oxygen deficit. This is because the 'muscles' of recovery, such as the heart and respiratory muscles, require oxygen to keep breathing and heart rates elevated.

You will note from Figure 4.03b that the two stages of recovery are clearly visible following maximal or high intensity exercise. However, following sub-maximal or low intensity exercise only the fast stage may be evident. This is because the majority of the work has been completed aerobically and little lactic acid has accumulated during the exercise.

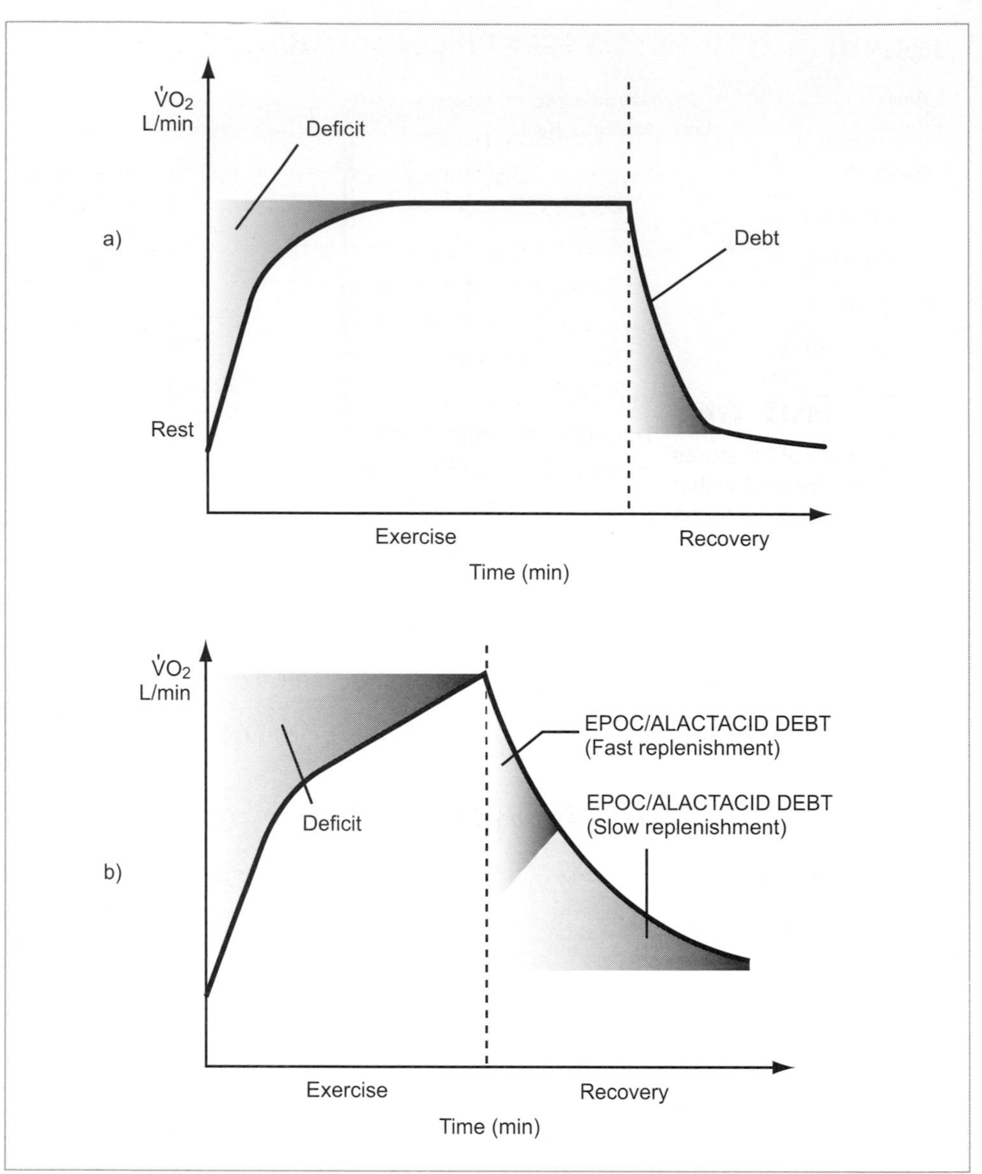

Fig 4.03 Oxygen consumption during and following a) a sub-maximal task b) a maximal task

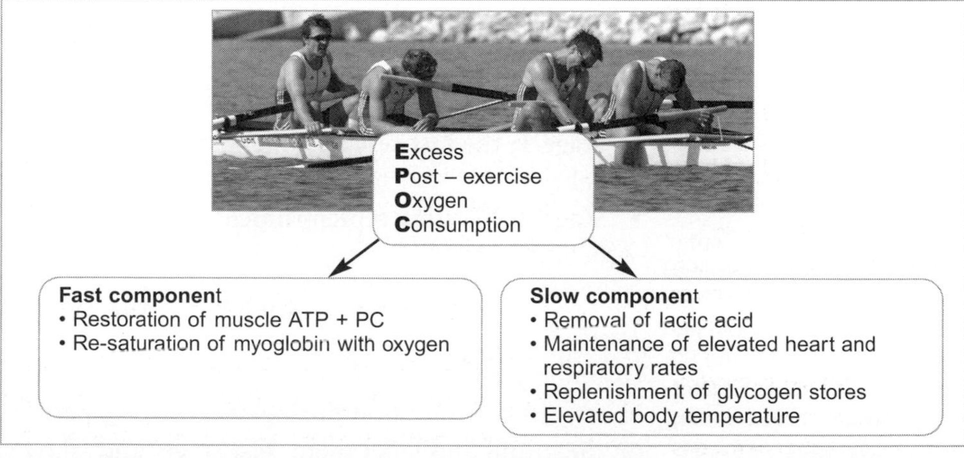

Fig 4.04 The components of excess post-exercise oxygen consumption (EPOC)

The fast replenishment stage

This is the first stage of the recovery process and relates to the immediate consumption of oxygen following exercise.
Its primary function is to re-saturate myoglobin with oxygen and provide aerobic energy to resynthesise adenosine triphosphate (ATP) and phosphocreatine (PCr).
The fast stage of recovery is usually completed within two to three minutes and utilises up to four litres of oxygen.

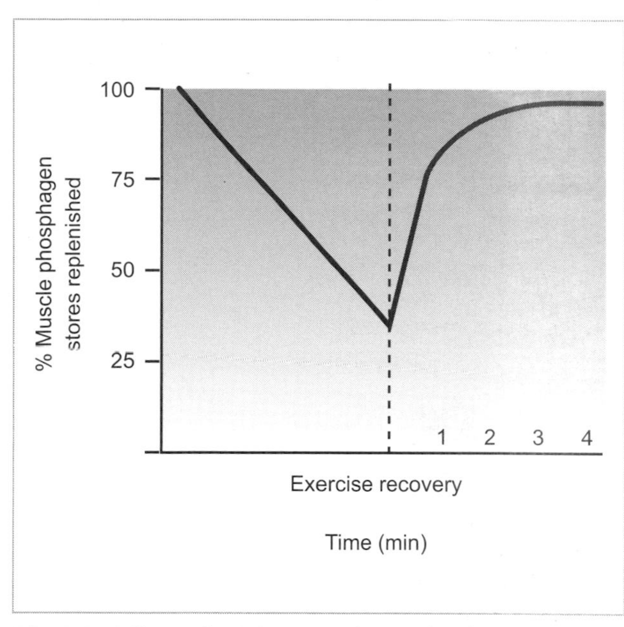

Fig 4.05 The replenishment of muscle phosphagens following maximal exercise

HOT TIPS

Fifty per cent of PC stores are restored within the first 30 seconds of recovery!

APPLICATION

The exercise intensity during a cool down that best removes lactic acid is between 30–45 per cent VO_2max for untrained subjects and 50–65 per cent VO_2max for trained performers.

The slow replenishment stage

The slow replenishment stage of EPOC can take up to two hours and utilises between 5–10 litres of extra oxygen depending upon the intensity of the preceding exercise. The oxygen consumed during the slow stage of recovery has several functions.

APPLICATION

A 400m runner will consume a large volume of oxygen during the slow replenishment stage as a large amount of lactic acid will have accumulated in the muscles.

Removal of lactic acid

Lactic acid accumulated during exercise must be removed if the body is to recover fully. You will recall from Chapter 3 that the majority of lactic acid is converted back into pyruvate and then into CO_2 and H_2O. The remainder is converted into muscle glycogen, blood glucose and protein. Much of the oxygen consumed during this stage is therefore used to provide the energy to enable this removal of lactic acid to take place. Typically the oxidation and removal of lactic acid during **rest recovery** takes about an hour, but this can be accelerated by performing a cool down. The cool down or **active recovery** helps keep the metabolic activity of the muscles high and the capillaries dilated, so that oxygen can be flushed through the muscle tissue oxidising and removing any lactic acid accumulated.

KEY WORDS

Rest recovery
A recovery period during which time the performer has rested passively.

Active recovery
A recovery period during which time light exercise is performed.

Maintenance of elevated heart and respiratory rates

Like all muscles, the muscles of the respiratory system and the heart require oxygen to provide energy for them to work continuously. During the recovery period extra energy is required to keep the heart and respiratory rates elevated above resting levels. This is so the lungs can take in plenty of oxygen which can then be pumped around the body by the heart to the working muscles, to re-saturate myoglobin, resynthesise muscle phosphagens (ATP and PC) and remove lactic acid.

Replenishment of muscle glycogen stores

Cori cycle
The process where lactic acid is taken to the liver for conversion into glucose and glycogen.

During all types of exercise it is likely that some of the body's muscle glycogen stores will become depleted. It is in the interests of the performer to replete these stores as soon after exercise as possible.

The replenishment of muscular stores of glycogen is largely dependent upon two key factors:

1 the type of exercise that has been performed
2 the amount and timing of carbohydrate consumption following exercise.

The best time to consume a post-exercise meal is as soon as is practical following the activity. The rate of muscle glycogen replacement is significantly quicker during the first 45 minutes to an hour. This is known as the carbohydrate window.

First of all, let us consider the type of exercise performed. Studies have suggested that following continuous, endurance-based activity, little glycogen is restored in the period immediately following activity. Complete muscle glycogen repletion can take up to 48 hours in this instance. During high intensity, short duration activity, however, a significant amount of muscle glycogen can be resynthesised within the 30 minutes to one hour immediately following exercise (probably due to conversion of lactic acid back into glycogen via the **cori cycle**). Complete resynthesis requires a 24-hour recovery period.

The second key factor concerns the amount of carbohydrate consumed following exercise. Muscle glycogen repletion occurs more rapidly when a high carbohydrate meal is consumed within the first 45 minutes to one hour following exercise. This is commonly known as the carbohydrate window. A high carbohydrate meal should consist of 200–300g of carbohydrate.

An elevated body temperature

APPLICATION

The body strives to maintain body temperature within the 'normal' range – even during exercise the normal range is 36.1–37.8 °C (97–100°F). Some marathon runners have experienced body temperatures approaching 41°C (105°F).

You have probably experienced the increase in body temperature that accompanies all exercise whether it is a maximal all-out effort on the bench press or a 5K run. This increase in body temperature generally results from the increased metabolic activity of the body which provides the energy to perform work. However, with every 1° increase in body temperature the metabolic activity of the cells increase by 10%. Oxygen is needed to feed this increase, even during the recovery period, and continues to do so until the body has cooled back down to normal resting temperatures. The oxygen for this comes through the slow replenishment stage of EPOC.

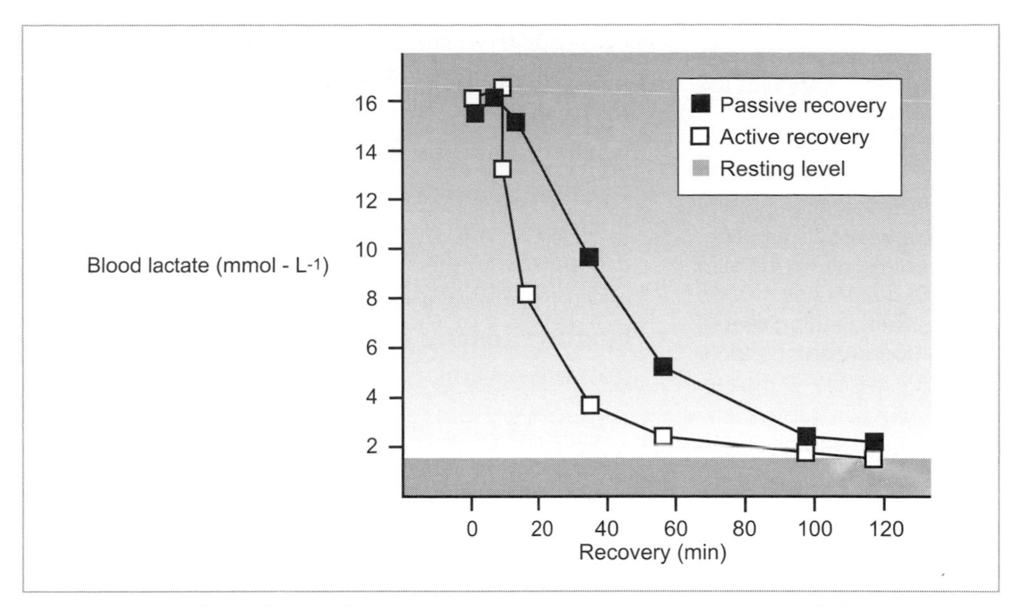

Fig 4.06 The effect of cool down or active recovery on recovery time following a bout of high intensity work

TASK 3

Figure 4.07 opposite is often used to illustrate EPOC.

1. From the graph, state what each of the letters A to E represent.
2. For what is the oxygen consumed during part D used?
3. Which letters can be used to determine EPOC?

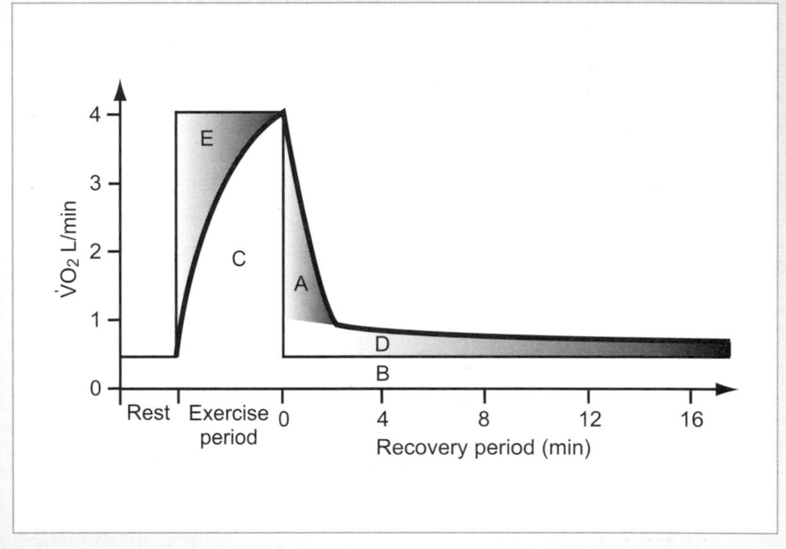

Fig 4.07 Oxygen consumption during exercise and recovery

A word about DOMS

KEY WORDS

Delayed onset of muscle soreness (DOMS)
The painful and tender muscles often experienced 48 hours following exercise.

DOMS or **delayed onset of muscle soreness** is a term used to explain the feelings of muscle stiffness and tenderness often experienced in the days (usually 48 hours) following exercise. It is perhaps more common in those embarking upon a new exercise regime or when performing **eccentric muscle contractions,** such as those experienced when lowering weights or running downhill.

It is thought that DOMS occurs as a result of microscopic tears to the muscle fibres and surrounding connective tissue, along with the associated swelling. Although DOMS is an annoying hindrance, symptoms are usually temporary

Eccentric muscle contraction
The lengthening of a muscle whilst contracting, for example, as happens in the quadriceps muscle group when landing during the hop phase of a triple jump.

and disappear within a couple or days or so once the muscle fibres have repaired themselves. There are a few tips that can be followed to prevent and avoid DOMS:

- warm up thoroughly before exercising and cool down completely following the activity
- during the training session, progress from lower intensity bouts of work through to higher intensity periods
- when beginning a new activity start gradually and build up intensity slowly
- limit the amount of eccentric contractions performed early in the training session.

DOMS are most likely to occur when performing eccentric muscle contractions. These might occur in physical activity when running downhill, lowering weights and during the downward phase of squats or press-ups.

TASK 4

1 Interval training involves alternating periods of exercise and recovery (relief). Sketch graphs to represent the following aspects of recovery during the interval training session:
   a) the pattern of PC depletion and restoration (during the work and rest periods respectively) for a set of 5 x 40m sprints
   b) the pattern of muscle lactic acid accumulation and removal (during the work and active recovery periods respectively) for a set of 3 x 300m sprints.

2 Draw the pattern of glycogen depletion during an interval training session for a swimmer completing 10 work intervals of two minutes. Sketch on your graph the pattern of muscle glycogen restoration after the session.

Some useful guidelines for recovery!

Knowledge of EPOC and the recovery process can help the coach and athlete in several ways to ensure that training and competitive performance are at optimal levels. The coach should make sure that:

- **Athletes warm up thoroughly before training.** This can help 'kick start' the aerobic system and reduce oxygen deficit. It will also help reduce DOMS.
- **The athlete is training at the correct intensity.** This is particularly important for endurance-based activities where OBLA should be avoided. In doing so the slow component of EPOC will be reduced.
- **When stressing the ATP-PCr system** (during sprint interval training, for example) **full recovery is allowed.** This should take a maximum of 2–3 minutes depending upon duration of the work period. (Remember, 50 per cent of PC stores are recovered within the first 30 seconds!)
- **Athletes undergo active recovery by performing a cool down.** This will speed up lactate removal and reduce the slow component of EPOC. This is particularly essential if athletes are performing in more than one event or training several times a day!
- **A meal high in carbohydrates is consumed as soon as possible** (and definitely within 45 minutes to one hour) **following training or competition.** This will speed up the restoration of muscle glycogen stores.

TASK 5

The data in Table 4.02 relates to the rate of lactate removal during recovery from exhaustive exercise following:
i) active recovery
ii) rest recovery.

1 Draw a graph using the data in the table. Briefly explain what the graph shows.
2 On your graph mark off the times for each type of recovery when 50 per cent of blood lactate had been removed. What does this suggest?
3 What type of activity would you suggest a performer undertake during a period of active recovery?
4 What intensity of exercise (measured as a percentage of VO_2max) would you suggest is completed for the active recovery period for:
a) an untrained subject
b) a trained performer?

Table 4.02

% lactate removed	Recovery time (mins) (rest recovery)	Recovery time (mins) (active recovery)
20	8	4
40	20	8
60	35	15
80	55	25
100	180	70

TASK 6

Copy out Table 4.03 opposite and complete the approximate recovery times for each factor.

Table 4.03

Recovery process	Recovery time
Re-saturation of myoglobin with oxygen	
Resynthesis of muscular stores of ATP & PC	
Repayment of fast component of EPOC	
Removal of lactic acid: a. with active recovery b. with rest recovery	
Repayment of slow component of EPOC	
Restoration of muscle glycogen stores	

Revise as you go!

1 Outline four factors that can cause fatigue.
2 Describe the possible causes of fatigue during:
a) a gymnastic floor routine
b) a marathon run in a hot environment.
3 Define the following terms:
a) recovery
b) oxygen deficit
c) EPOC.
4 How long does it take the fast component of EPOC to recover?
5 How is lactic acid removed from the muscle following a 400m run? What organs and tissues are involved in the removal of lactate?

6 Explain the terms active recovery and rest recovery. How do these different types of recovery influence the speed of lactate removal?

7 Explain the replenishment of muscle glycogen stores with reference to:
a) the type of exercise performed
b) the post-event meal.

8 Outline the recovery patterns for the following performers:
a) a gymnast performing a vault
b) an 'iron-man' triathlete
c) a 200m butterfly swimmer.

9 Swimmers are often required to compete in several events during a swimming gala. What advice would you give a swimmer concerning recovery between events?

10 Explain what is meant by DOMS.

11 Give two suggestions as to how a performer could reduce the likelihood of DOMS occuring.

12 Briefly explain why EPOC is often larger than the oxygen deficit.

13 How can knowledge of the recovery process be of use to the coach and athlete when designing training programmes?

Chapter 5: Planning training regimes for elite performers

Learning outcomes

By the end of this chapter you should be able to:
- briefly outline the general principles of training and apply them in the design of a training programme
- briefly outline the different methods of training available to the coach and athlete
- apply the most appropriate methods of training to particular sporting performers
- explain the term 'periodisation' in the context of designing training programmes
- outline a typical periodised year for a 100m sprinter and a games player
- explain the process and physiological reasons behind altitude training
- identify and explain the immediate or short-term responses of the body to exercise
- identify and explain the long-term physiological adaptive responses of the body to a period of training.

Introduction

Kelly Holmes was at the peak of condition during the Athens Olympics in 2004. Her training and preparation for the championships was wholly effective and she was rewarded with two gold medals and a place in the record books for a British female athlete. This chapter will examine how coaches and athletes apply training theory when designing training programmes for elite performers. Designing effective training programmes is a science and we will look at the specialised training regimes that coaches can use and how they structure the training year so that the performer can peak at the right time.

You will recall from your study at AS the key factors to consider when designing a training programme.

Fig 5.01 To become an Olympic champion, a physiological and psychological 'peak' must be reached

TASK 1

Take a moment to reflect upon the stages you went through when designing your Personal Exercise Programme. (You may wish to revisit Chapter 15 in the *AS PE for AQA* student text book.)

Table 5.01 Applying the principles of training

Principle of training	Explanation	Application
Specificity	All training must be relevant to the activity or sport. For example, a cyclist must perform most of his or her training on a bike. There is, of course, some value in other forms of training, but the majority must be performed on the bicycle. Actions from the activity should also be replicated during training.	Be sure to train the: • relevant muscles • energy systems • relevant fibre types • fitness components. Use appropriate technique
Overload	If training is to have the required effect, then the performer must find the training taxing. The level of training must be pitched at a level greater than the demands regularly encountered by the player. The old adage 'no pain, no gain' can be applied here!	• Use heart rate to gauge how hard you are working • Work at an appropriate percentage of max heart rate or 1RM • Increase the duration of the activity if needed
Progression	As the body becomes better with coping with the training over time, greater demands must be made if improvement is to continue. This is often linked to overload and is known as 'progressive overload'.	Increase: • percentage HR max • percentage 1RM • duration • frequency of training
Reversibility	Use it or lose it! If the training load decreases or if training stops altogether, then the benefits of the prior training can be lost.	Unless injured, training should continue
Moderation (adequate recovery)	Sufficient recovery time must be built into the training programme to prevent over-training. Rest allows the body to overcompensate and adapt to the training, leading to improved performance. Overtraining is characterised by muscular fatigue, illness and injury.	Heavy training sessions should be followed by lighter sessions or even rest days. The ratio of 3:1 is often used to express the number of hard sessions to easy sessions within a week's training cycle
FITT	F (frequency) = how often we train I (intensity) = how hard we train T (time) = how long we train for T (type) = what type of training we use	• Train 3–6 days per week • Percentage HR max or percentage 1RM • 30 minutes to 2 hours session • Use the principle of specificity!
W		
I		
M		
P		

Table 5.02 An overview of the different types of training

Type of training	Brief description	Major components of fitness stressed	Example of a session
Continuous training	Low intensity rhythmic exercise that uses large muscle groups. The intensity of the training should be between 60–85% HR max, and the duration of the session between 30 minutes and 2 hours. Distance running, swimming and cycling are good examples of this,	• Cardiorespiratory endurance • Muscular endurance	5–10K steady runs at 65% HR max
Fartlek training	A form of continuous training where the intensity or speed of the activity is varied throughout the session – from sprinting to walking. The beauty of this type of training is that it develops both aerobic and anaerobic fitness. It is ideal for games players.	• Cardiorespiratory endurance • Muscular endurance • Speed	Jog at 60% HR max for 15 minutes Sprint × 50m, jog × 150m Repeat 10 times Walk for 90 seconds Jog at 70% HR max for 5 minutes Sprint × 200m Jog gently to finish
Sprint interval training	An intermittent training regime that involves periods of alternating exercise and rest. Widely used in athletics and swimming, the main benefit of this training method is its versatility, since there are many variables that can be altered in order to stress the required components of fitness. These variables include: • distance of work period • intensity of work period • the number of sets • the number of reps • duration of rest period.	• Speed • Power	3 sets × 10 reps × 30m sprints (wbr) 5-minute rest between sets
Anaerobic interval training		• Speed • Power • Muscular endurance	2 sets × 4 reps × 300m runs (90-second rest, work relief)
Aerobic interval training		• Cardiorespiratory endurance • Muscular endurance	3 × 1000m runs (125% personal best time) Work:relief ratio = 1:1/2
Weight training	An intermittent training method that uses free weights or resistance machines to overload the body. The resistance is determined by working as a percentage of your one rep max (1RM) and the session is divided into sets and repetitions, which can be manipulated to stress the required aspect of strength.	• Maximum strength • Power • Muscular endurance	**Maximum strength** Heavy weights, low reps 5 sets × 6 reps × 85% 1RM **Elastic strength** (must be rapid contractions) 3 sets × 12 reps × 75% 1RM **Strength endurance** Light weights, high reps 3 sets × 20 reps × 50% 1RM
Circuit training	A general conditioning activity in which a series of exercises are used to work different muscle groups. Exercises can be made activity- or game-specific.	• Muscular endurance • Cardiorespiratory endurance	Circuit A = 8 exercises × 30 seconds Circuit B = 8 exercises × 30 seconds Circuit C = run for 4 minutes Total = 12 minutes Repeat 2 or 3 times
Plyometrics	A type of training that involves an eccentric muscle contraction followed immediately by a concentric contraction. When the quadriceps lengthen, for example, when jumping down from a box top, it pre-loads the muscle and initiates the stretch reflex, which causes a rapid and forceful concentric contraction.	• Power • Strength • Speed	A plyometrics circuit to include depth jumping, hopping, skipping, press-ups with claps, throwing and catching a medicine ball

Proprioceptive neuromuscular facilitation (PNF)

A stretching technique that overrides the stretch reflex to enable a performer to achieve a greater range of movement at a joint.

Specialised training regimes

In addition to those methods of training outlined in Table 5.02, there are two further training practices often undertaken by elite performers that you are required to be familiar with for your examination:

1 **proprioceptive neuromuscular facilitation (PNF)**
2 altitude training.

Proprioceptive neuromuscular facilitation (PNF)

Fig 5.02 PNF in action

PNF is an advanced stretching technique used to improve the flexibility and mobility of elite performers. PNF training is the most effective form of stretching activity as it takes full advantage of the muscles' safety mechanisms. You will recall that a muscle contains stretch receptors known as muscle spindles (that lie adjacent to muscle fibres) which detect changes in the length and the rate of change of length of muscle fibres. When a muscle is stretched so is the muscle spindle. If the muscle has been stretched too far sensory information is sent to the central nervous system which triggers a stretch reflex. Other receptors are sensitive to tension developed within a muscle when it contracts. These are called **Golgi tendon organs (GTOs)**. If the critical tension threshold is exceeded within the muscle, Golgi tendon organs initiate muscle relaxation, something known as autogenic inhibition. Because the GTOs override the stretch reflex, the window of relaxation allows PNF to be very effective. Table 5.03 describes a simple method of PNF.

KEY WORDS

Golgi tendon organ (GTO)

Proprioceptors found at the attachment of muscle and tendon fibres that are sensitive to changes in muscle tension.

APPLICATION

For improvements in flexibility and mobility to occur, PNF stretching should be undertaken at least three times each week and, for maximum benefit, take place when the muscles are fully warmed up.

Table 5.03 A simple method of PNF

Method	• With the aid of a partner, move the body part to the limit of its range of movement (ROM) and hold in position for several seconds. • The performer should now isometrically contract the target muscle for between 6–10 seconds. This can be done by pushing against a resistance offered by the assistant. • The muscle is then relaxed. • The target muscle is moved once again to the limit of its ROM by the partner (which should be further!).
How it works	• When the target muscle is contracted isometrically, inhibitory signals from the Golgi tendon organ (GTO) override excitory signals from the muscle spindles which delay the stretch reflex. This causes further relaxation of the target muscle allowing it to be stretched further.
Adaptation	• With regular practice of PNF, the range of movement (ROM) is increased due to increased length of muscle and connective tissues such as tendons and ligaments.

Altitude training

APPLICATION

Paula Radcliffe spends four months in Albuquerque (1600m or 5250 ft above sea level) in the USA when preparing for marathon events and three to four weeks in Font Romeau, France (1980m or 6500 ft above sea level) where she undertakes higher-intensity training runs ready for her 5000m and 10,000m events on the track.

When we think about the best endurance athletes in the world today, many originate from countries that have an altitude of 1000m (3300 ft) or more (Morocco, Ethiopia and Kenya, for example). No wonder then that training at high altitude has been favoured among elite endurance performers when preparing for major competitions. So why does training at altitude work? Or does it?

Fig 5.03 Paula Radcliffe regularly undertakes a period of altitude training as part of her preparation for competition

The reasoning behind training at altitude is based around the fact that the concentration of oxygen in a given volume is reduced at altitude. In fact the partial pressure of oxygen decreases by about 50 per cent at an altitude of 5000m (16,400 ft)so the body compensates by breathing more quickly and deeply in an attempt to increase blood-oxygen concentrations to normal levels. Heart rate also increases in order to deliver more oxygen to the tissues. These responses occur immediately whereas others may take up to 30 days to complete. These other adaptations include an increased production of red blood cells resulting in an increase in the haemoglobin concentration of the blood. Upon returning to sea level these increased concentrations of red blood cells and haemoglobin remain for a period of six to eight weeks and greatly enhance the oxygen-carrying capacity of the blood.

KEY WORDS

Detraining
The reversal of positive training effects.

The major problem with training at altitude is that because of the decreased availability of oxygen, training becomes very hard and it becomes very difficult to train at the same intensity as you would normally do at sea level. Additionally, lactate levels at a set speed increase and VO_2max is reduced. Together, these factors may lead to a **detraining** effect.

Because the beneficial effects of living at altitude can be offset by the negative effects of training (exercise performance impairment) it is now argued that the best solution is for athletes to live at altitude and train at sea level. In fact athletes have simulated low oxygen environments (hypoxic) at sea level through the use of altitude tents and hypoxic apartments.

Table 5.04 Benefits and drawbacks of altitude training

Perceived benefits	Likely drawbacks
• Increased haematocrit (concentration of red blood cells) • Increased concentration of haemoglobin • Enhanced oxygen transport	• Expensive • Altitude sickness • Due to the lack of oxygen, training at higher intensities is difficult • Detraining • Any benefits are soon lost on return to sea level

Periodisation

Peaking
The planning and organisation of training so that a performer can be at the height of physical and psychological conditioning during major competitions.

Effective planning is crucial when designing a training programme. Periodisation is simply the organisation of training into blocks or 'cycles' which each have a particular focus and enable an optimal physiological and psychological **peak** to be reached during major competition. Essentially periodisation involves the manipulation of specificity (type), intensity and volume of training, and whilst the general principles of periodisation are common to all sports, they must be adjusted to suit the needs of different sports and individual performers.

Periodising the training programme is based around three distinct periods, more commonly referred to as cycles:

- **Macrocycles**

The long-term performance goal. In games such as football the macrocycle will usually correspond to the year-long season. For other performers, who perhaps have the ambition of competing in the Olympics, it could be as long as four years.

- **Mesocycles**

Typically mesocycles are sub-divisions of a macro cycle which may last between two to eight weeks. A mesocycle will usually have a particular focus, e.g. the development of speed during the pre-season phase of training.

- **Microcycles**

Microcycles are sub-divisions of a mesocycle which are usually a week in duration. They provide more detailed information regarding the specific intensity and volume of training.

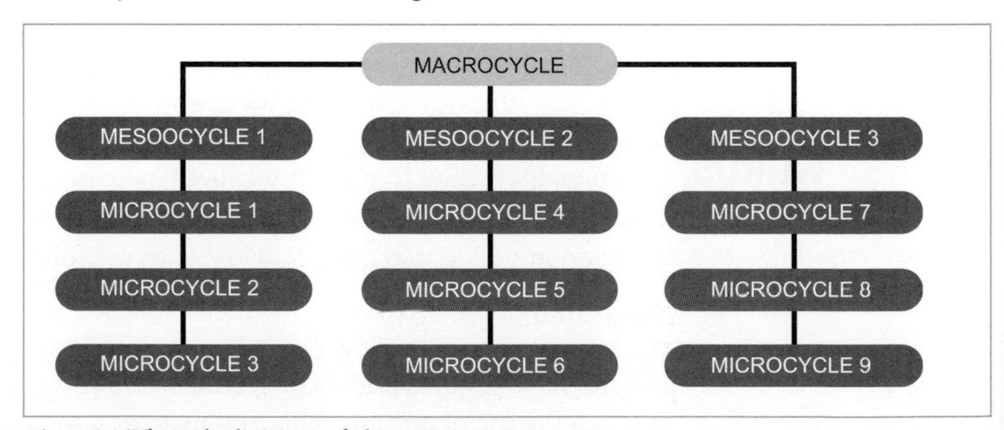

Fig 5.04 The sub-division of the training year

A further important component of the periodised year is (of course) the individual training session, which in this case is referred to as the training unit.

A macrocycle – the long-term training goal

The planning of the macrocycle should be focused around peaking for major competitions or important games on the fixture card. The basic structure of a macrocycle will be the same whatever the sport or activity, whether it be a four-year Olympic cycle, a two-year world championship cycle, or an annual or seasonal cycle. In its simplest form the macrocycle will be made up of three distinct periods:

1 preparation period (subdivided into two phases)
2 competition period (sometimes subdivided into three phases)
3 transition or recovery period (one phase).

The preparation period (phases 1 and 2)

The preparation is perhaps more commonly referred to as pre-season training and is typically divided into two phases:

- general conditioning training (phase 1)
- competition specific training (phase 2).

Even those athletes using anaerobic sources of energy, such as 100m sprinters or 400m hurdlers, need to develop a sound aerobic endurance base during the general conditioning stage of the preparation period.

The general conditioning stage of the preparation period is characterised by high volume, low intensity work. The key theme or focus should be on the development of a solid endurance base upon which to build future training. A good general conditioning programme should aim to develop aerobic and muscular endurance, general strength and mobility.

The competition specific training sees an increase in the intensity of training. This is the time when much of the strength and speed work should be undertaken. The performer should therefore be working at higher speeds or working against greater resistances (e.g. by lifting heavier weights). In addition to competition specific fitness requirements, technique and tactical appreciation should also be developed now so that the performer is fully prepared and finely tuned for the first day of the competitive season

The competition period (phases 3, 4 and 5)

The main goal of the competition period is to develop optimal competition performance. Maintaining levels of fitness and conditioning is essential during this stage as is the continued development of competition specific aspects of training. During this stage the overall extent or volume of training is decreased but the intensity of the training is increased. During a long season or where an athlete may need to peak on more than one occasion, the competition period may be subdivided into the following phases:

Phase 3 (6 to 8 weeks)
The typical competition period. There should be a reduction in the volume of general training but an increase in intensity of competition specific training. Trials and qualifying competitions should fall within this phase.

Phase 4 (4 to 6 weeks)

During a long competitive season it is recommended to introduce a period where competitions are eliminated altogether and the level of competition specific training is reduced. It can be likened to a mini transition period where the body can recover and prepare for phase 5, in which major competitions or cup finals occur.

Phase 5 (3 to 4 weeks)

Effectively this is the culmination of the training year! The major events of the performer's calender will fall during this phase, e.g. Olympic finals, cup finals, etc. Competition specific training is maintained and **tapering** for peak performance should take place. Tapering involves the manipulation of training volume and intensity to promote peak performance.

KEY WORDS

Tapering
A reduction in the volume of training prior to major competition. It enables an athlete to reach peak performance.

Fig 5.05 Swimmers will often taper their training prior to competition

The coach's task is to manage training so that peak performance can occur in a window between the removal of training-induced fatigue and the reversal of the training effect. A typical taper will last between 10 and 21 days but will vary between sports and different performers. The two key ingredients to a successful taper are:

1 increase training to, or maintain training at, competition intensities
2 decrease the volume of training by approximately one-third.

APPLICATION

An athlete may only ever be in peak condition for one or two days during a season. It is essential therefore that the peak occurs during the final of the major competition or ultimate training goal.

The application box suggests how a swimmer might taper ahead of a major competition.

APPLICATION

Two to three weeks prior to competition a swimmer may gradually taper from 4,000m to 2,500m a day whilst maintaining the same high intensity. Many male swimmers will also shave their body hair at the end of their taper period to reduce drag and give them a psychological boost during the competitive swim.

Table 5.06a An example of a single periodised year

<table>
<tr><td>Month</td><td>1</td><td>2</td><td>3</td><td>4</td><td>5</td><td>6</td><td>7</td><td>8</td><td>9</td><td>10</td><td>11</td><td>12</td></tr>
<tr><td rowspan="2">Periodisation (phase)</td><td colspan="4">Preparatory 1</td><td colspan="3">Preparatory 2</td><td colspan="4">Competitive</td><td>Trans</td></tr>
<tr><td colspan="4">General Preparation</td><td colspan="3">Specific preparation
PC</td><td colspan="3">Competition Maintenance</td><td>Taper</td><td>Light recreative activity</td></tr>
</table>

Legend:
T - transition phase: 4 - 5 weeks long
PC - pre-competitive, or exhibition competitions/games/matches
Taper unloading/tapering for the major competition of the year

The transition or recovery period (phase 6)

The transition period is the final stage of the periodised year yet perhaps the most important phase of all! Crucially it helps the performer recover from the previous year of training and competition and prepare for the next. Following a hard season of training and competition a period of three to six weeks of active recovery is needed. This is to allow the performer to fully recharge his or her physical and psychological batteries so that he or she is injury free and highly motivated for the forthcoming season. This active recovery should take the form of general exercise where performers engage in a variety of fun activities.

TASK 2

Consider the following stages of a swimmer's training programme and place them in the correct order as they would appear in the periodised year:

- Swim 6000–7000m. High intensity sprints. Speed training.
- Swim less than 5000m. Tapering.
- Swim 7000m. Introduce anaerobic training. High distance, high intensity. Technique and skill work.
- Swim 7000–8000m. Low intensity, long distance. Aerobic training.

TASK 3

a) Copy out the 'training pyramid' shown in Figure 5.06. For a games player of your choice, write down the focus of training in each of the four periods of the macrocycle. Be sure to give examples of specific components of fitness training together with the intensity and volume of training in each stage. Write your training guidelines actually *in* the relevant section of the training pyramid.

b) Study Table 5.05. For each of the mesocycles 1–8 give examples of a specific training unit or session that we might expect to see.

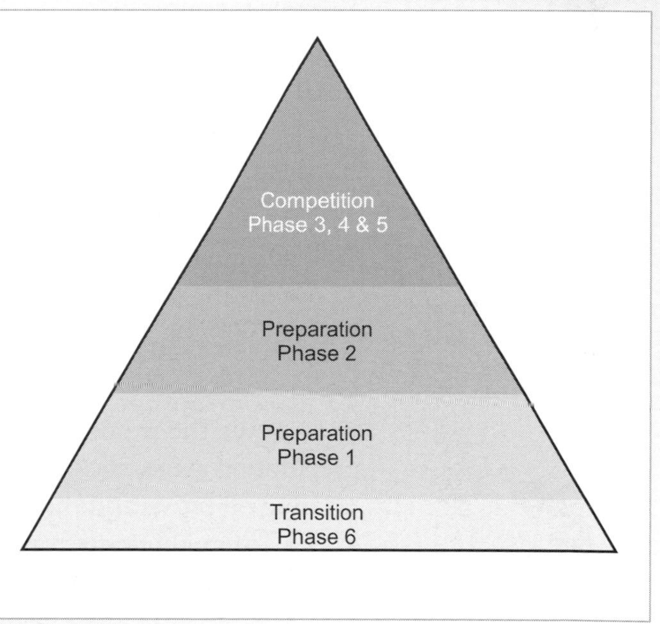

Fig 5.06 Training pyramid

A mesocycle – the short-term training goal

The macrocycle is sub-divided into blocks of training known as mesocycles. The mesocycles are typically two to eight weeks in duration and are usually closely related to the performance goals of the particular cycle. They have as their focus a particular component of fitness, e.g. aerobic endurance, strength, power or active rest, etc.

Table 5.05 An example of a macrocycle or periodised year for an elite netball player

	Jun	Jul	Aug	Sept	Oct	Nov	Dec	Jan	Feb	Mar	Apr	May
Mesocycle	Prep 1		Prep 2		Competition							Tran
	8 / 1	2	3	4	5		6		7			8

↑ Pre-season starts here

The season finishes here ↑

A microcycle – the training week

The weekly training plan is referred to as a microcycle. Microcycles are planned around the objectives of the mesocycle but should contain more detail concerning the intensity, volume and sequence of training programmes. It is especially important to plan the appropriate ratio of training to recovery sessions to enable effective **adaptation** of the body. A balance between training and recovery must be struck so that the performer is not faced with several successive sessions that are of very high intensity. A coach will often apply a 3:1 ratio where a rest unit is given following three training units within a particular microcycle.

In many team games the microcycle is based around a weekly competitive fixture. A small taper or rest day will therefore be needed immediately prior to the competition.

The training unit – the training session

The training unit is a single training session. The main section of the session should have as a focus the key training objective. For example, if the coach and swimmer seek to improve lactate tolerance then the training unit may look something like this:

- 5 x 100m on 4 minutes, maximum effort, aim for a personal best (PB) on all
- 3 x 200m on 5 minutes, maximum effort, aim for a PB on all
- 8 x 75m on 3 minutes, maximum effort on all.

If, however, the training unit forms part of a mesocycle in phase 1 of the preparation stage, then it is likely that aerobic endurance may be the main training objective and the session may look something like this:

- 3 x 800m alternate front crawl/choice stroke (45 seconds rest) (even pace, target pulse = HR max-50)
- 8 x 400m individual medley (30 seconds rest) (increase pace, target pulse = HR max-50)

Adaptation

The long-term structural and physiological responses of the body to training that explain the improvements in performance.

In order to prevent over-training the coach may adopt a 3:1 ratio. During a microcycle the performer may have three hard sessions followed by one easier session, or in a mesocycle the athlete may undergo three hard weeks of training followed by an easier week!

Double periodisation

Some sports require a performer to peak on more than one occasion throughout the year. Consider the athlete who needs to peak for cross-country competitions in the winter and track championships in the summer, or the tennis player wishing to peak for each of the four Grand Slam competitions. In this instance the coach and performer must follow a double (or even multi-!) periodised year. Table 5.06b illustrates the double periodised year for a swimmer wishing to peak for both short course and long course championships.

Fig 5.07 Track and field athletes will often follow a double periodised year so that they can peak for both indoor and outdoor competitions

TASK 4

Using Table 5.06b as a guide, construct a chart that illustrates a double periodised year for a sprinter wishing to compete in both indoor and outdoor championships.

Table 5.06b An example of a double periodised year

Month	1	2	3	4	5	6	7	8	9	10	11	12
Periodisation (phase)	Preparatory 1			Competitive 1				Preparatory 2		Competitive 2		T2
	General Prep.		PC	Specific preparation	Taper	M	General Prep.	Comp-etitve	PC		Taper	

Legend: T - transition phase: the first one of only two weeks, while the second one

TASK 5

Copy out Table 5.07 (a blank periodisation template). For an activity of your choice attempt to design a year-long training programme. On your periodisation chart you will need to identify the following:

- the major competitions for peaking
- an example of a microcycle and training unit for each mesocycle
- a taper.

Table 5.07 The periodisation of an annual plan

Training Phases	Preparatory Phase					Competitive Phase				Transition
mesocycles										
Microcyles										

Short-term responses of the body to exercise

You may recall that during your study of anatomy and physiology at AS level you examined how the different physiological systems of the body responded to exercise. Tables 5.08, 5.09 and 5.10 summarise the key points.

Table 5.08 Short-term cardiovascular responses to exercise

	Explanation	Diagram
Heart rate	During sub-maximal exercise HR increases rapidly at first but then plateaus into steady state where oxygen demand is being met by supply. During maximal exercise HR increases proportionally with exercise intensity until a maximum level is reached. This will also be the point of VO_2max. It is the release of hormones such as adrenaline and noradrenaline that cause HR to increase from 60–80 bpm at rest to 160–180 bpm during exercise.	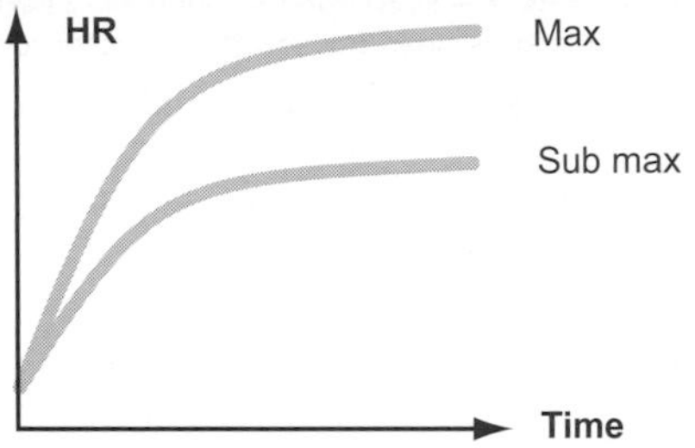 HR; Max; Sub max; Time
Stroke volume	Stroke volume increases as exercise intensity increases. From 80–110 ml at rest to 160–200 ml during exercise for a trained athlete. This is largely due to Starling's Law which suggests that increased stroke volume is a result of increased venous return and increased elasticity of cardiac muscle fibres.	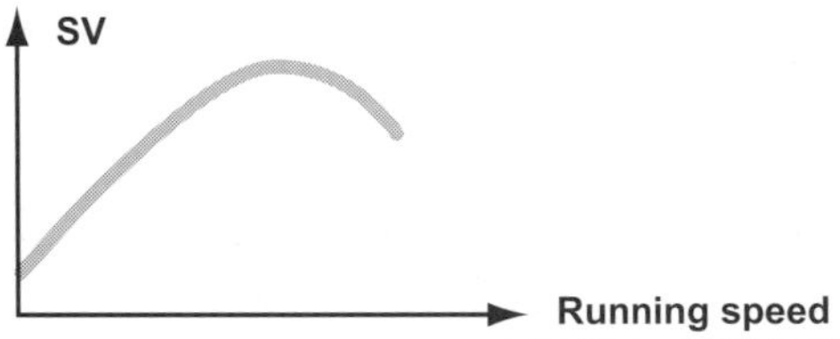 SV; Running speed
Cardiac output	Cardiac output increases as a direct result of the increases in both heart rate and stroke volume. (Q = HR x SV) Cardiac output increases from 5l/min to up to 40l/min for a trained performer during maximal exercise.	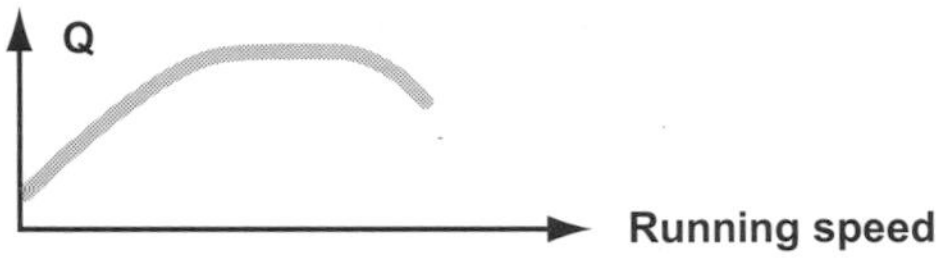 Q; Running speed
Blood pressure	During exercise, blood pressure changes are dependent upon the type and intensity of the activity performed. During low intensity aerobic exercise systolic pressure increases slightly (or even remains the same) whilst diastolic pressure remains unchanged. During activities that are of high intensity, such as weight lifting, both systolic and diastolic pressure increase significantly.	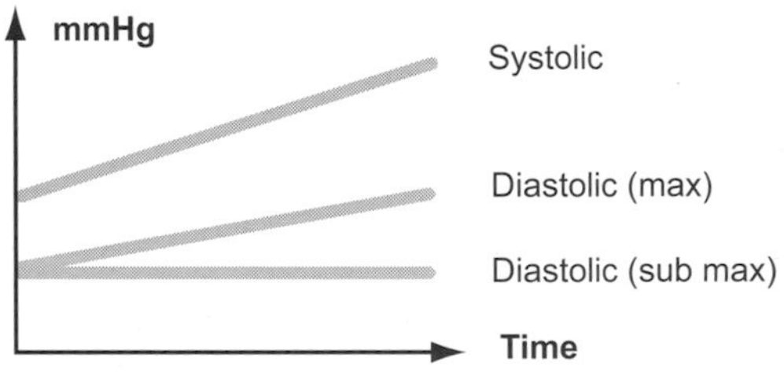 mmHg; Systolic; Diastolic (max); Diastolic (sub max); Time
Vascular shunt	Blood flow to the working muscles increases dramatically during exercise from 20 per cent to 88 per cent. This is due to the vascular shunting of blood. Blood flow to inconsequential muscles and organs (such as the intestines and kidneys) is reduced through vaso-constriction of blood vessels and contraction of the pre-capillary sphincters. This enables more blood to be diverted to the active muscles via blood vessels which vasodilate.	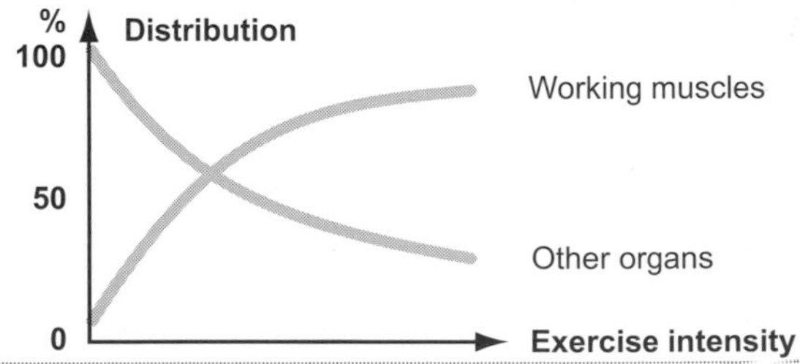 %; Distribution; 100; 50; 0; Working muscles; Other organs; Exercise intensity
Blood acidity	During exercise the metabolism increases which increases the production of the associated by-products such as carbon dioxide and lactic acid. Both of these products increase the acidity of the blood and therefore reduce blood pH from resting values of 7.5 down to 6.5 during exercise.	 Blood pH; Exercise intensity

Table 5.09 Short-term muscular responses to exercise

	Explanation
Energy production	The increased energy demand is met through the greater breakdown of phosphocreatine and the oxidation of fatty acids and glycogen. This provides the energy for ATP resynthesis.
Lactic acid production	Greater amounts of lactic acid are produced as a result of the increase in glycolysis. During intense bouts of exercise, lactic acid accumulation may lead to OBLA.
Oxy-myoglobin	Levels of oxymyoglobin decrease in the muscle cell as oxygen is used for aerobic energy production.
Carbon dioxide	With increased levels of metabolism comes a greater production of carbon dioxide. This causes the pH of the muscle to fall (acidity to rise).
Temperature	As energy is given off in the form of heat during metabolic activity, body temperature rises. To counteract this, the body's sweating response increases during exercise.

Table 5.10 Short-term respiratory responses to exercise

	Explanation
Minute ventilation	Increased ventilation occurs due to the increased production of carbon dioxide and lactic acid resulting from muscle metabolism (as well as the demand for more oxygen). Maximal exercise ventilation can exceed 200l/min in male athletes. This is due to both an increase in breathing rate and tidal volume.
Oxygen consumption	As the demand for oxygen increases during exercise, more is extracted from the blood and consumed.
a-VO_2diff	At rest only 25 per cent of the oxygen inspired is actually consumed. During exercise the muscles extract more oxygen which increases the difference in oxygen content between arterial and venous blood.

a-VO_2diff (arterio-venous oxygen difference)

A measure of how much oxygen has been extracted and utilised by the muscles. It is measured by analysing the difference in oxygen content of the blood in the arteries leaving the lungs and the mixed venous blood returning to the lungs.

Long-term physiological adaptive responses to training

Responses to aerobic training

Table 5.11 below highlights some of the physiological adaptive responses of the body we might expect to see following a period of aerobic training. In essence all the physiological responses outlined contribute to improving maximal aerobic power or VO_2max.

Table 5.11 Responses to aerobic training

Structural adaptation	Physiological consequence
Increased heart size (cardiac hypertrophy)	The heart adapts by increasing the volume of the ventricular cavities in response to aerobic training (such as continuous training). This enables greater diastolic filling of the heart which increases stroke volume both at rest and during exercise. Resting heart rate will fall as a consequence (bradycardia). Although resting cardiac output remains the same it will increase dramatically during exercise.
Increased capillary density	With capillarisation comes increased gaseous exchange. More oxygen can reach the exercising tissues and removal of carbon dioxide and lactic acid improves.
Enhanced elasticity of blood vessels	Enhanced elasticity enables more effective vasoconstriction and vasodilation, which improves the redistribution of blood via the vascular shunt and helps to control blood pressure.
Increased blood volume	Increased blood volume facilitates the transport of oxygen and carbon dioxide. An increase in plasma content decreases the viscosity of the blood, speeding up blood flow.
Increased red blood cell volume	An increase in red blood cell volume means that there is more haemoglobin available to transport oxygen around to the working muscles.
Hypertrophy (and hyperplasia) of slow twitch muscle fibres	Enlargement of slow twitch fibres (by up to 22 per cent) and some fibre splitting provide more opportunity for aerobic respiration to take place and provide the energy needed to fuel the muscles during aerobic activity.
Increased mitochondrial density	Endurance training signals an increase in the size (by up to 40 per cent) and number (up to 120 per cent) of mitochondria. As these are the factories of aerobic respiration, more and larger factories quite simply means that more energy for the working muscles is produced.
Increased myoglobin volume	An increase (up to 75 per cent) in the myoglobin content of muscle cells means that more oxygen can become available to the mitochondria for the production of aerobic energy.
Increased muscle glycogen stores	Increased muscular stores of glycogen provide a larger source of fuel to draw upon during endurance-based exercise.
Increased number of oxidative enzymes	This improves the aerobic breakdown of glycogen and fat which releases more energy to resynthesise ATP. In particular the increased oxidation of fat, the preferred fuel during endurance activity, leads to the sparing of glycogen and a decrease in the **respiratory exchange ratio**.
Increased maximum pulmonary ventilation	A larger tidal volume and use of available alveoli allows a greater diffusion rate of respiratory gases (O_2 and CO_2).

Respiratory exchange ratio

A method of determining which metabolic fuel is predominantly in use during exercise. It is calculated by analysing oxygen consumption and carbon dioxide production =

$$\frac{VCO_2 \text{ expired/min}}{VO_2 \text{ uptake/min}}$$

The closer the value is to 1.0 the more likely it is that the body is using glycogen as a fuel. If the value is nearer 0.7 then fatty acids are the likely fuel. Also known as the respiratory quotient.

Responses to anaerobic training

Table 5.12 below highlights some of the physiological adaptive responses of the body we might expect to see following a period of anaerobic training.

Table 5.12 Responses to anaerobic training

Structural adaptation	Physiological consequence
Increased heart size (cardiac hypertrophy)	The heart adapts by increasing the thickness of the ventricular walls in response to anaerobic training such as weight lifting. This enables a more forceful contraction which increases stroke volume both at rest and during exercise. Resting heart rate will fall as a consequence (bradycardia).
Hypertrophy (and hyperplasia) of fast twictch muscle fibres	Enlargement of fast twitch fibres (by up to 22 per cent) and some fibre splitting provide more opportunity for the ATP-PC system and anaerobic glycolysis to take place and provide the energy needed to fuel the muscles during anaerobic activity. This will lead to greater speed, strength and power.
Increased levels of ATP and PC within muscle cells	Stores of ATP and PC have been shown to increase by approx 25 per cent and 40 per cent respectively. This allows a greater energy yield from the ATP-PC system which provides more energy more rapidly and delays the point when the lactic acid system 'kicks in'.
Increased activity of ATP-PC energy system enzymes	The activity of ATPase and creatine kinase both increase following a period of anaerobic training. This ensures the quick release of energy via the ATP-PC system.
Enhanced buffering capacity	Improves the removal of lactic acid from the muscles and can delay the lactate threshold or OBLA. This enables the performer to achieve higher work rates before the arrival of fatigue.
Increased number of glycolytic enzymes	The activity of the enzyme PFK can double following a period of anaerobic training. This facilitates the release of energy from glycogen under anaerobic conditions.

Revise as you go!

1. Describe the method commonly used in proprioceptive neuromuscular facilitation (PNF).
2. With reference to Golgi tendon organs and muscle spindles, explain why PNF stretching can produce better results in terms of increased flexibility than other forms of stretching.
3. What are the arguments for and against altitude training?
4. Explain how the coach of a triple jumper may sub-divide the training year.
5. Give a definition and a practical example for each of the following:
   a) macrocycle
   b) mesocycle
   c) microcycle
   d) training unit.
6. Using the example of a swimmer, explain what you understand by the term tapering.

7. Describe five structural adaptations that may result from a period of continuous training and explain how these give a physiological advantage to the trained performer.
8. Describe five structural adaptations that may result from a period of weight training and explain how these give a physiological advantage to the trained performer.
9. Briefly outline and explain the responses of the cardiovascular system during a period of exercise.
10. How can a coach use the respiratory exchange ratio to gauge how hard a performer is working?

Chapter 6: Applying mechanics to sporting activity

Learning outcomes

By the end of this chapter you should be able to:
- define and give units of measurement for quantities of linear motion
- apply each of Newton's three laws of motion to sporting activity
- describe the application of forces in sporting activities
- explain the concept of impulse in sprinting
- explain the relevance of momentum to sporting techniques
- use high jump to demonstrate the concept of net forces
- identify the nature of forces acting on a sports performer
- sketch free body diagrams identifying the type, size and application of forces acting on a sports performer or object at a particular moment in time
- explain the factors that govern the flight of projectiles, using shot put as a reference
- apply each of Newton's three laws to angular motion
- define and give units of measurement for quantities of angular motion
- identify the three major axes of rotation and give examples of sporting movements that take place around them
- explain the concept of angular momentum and its conservation during flight
- explain the relationship between moment of inertia and angular velocity when somersaulting and spinning.

Fig 6.01 A hammer thrower uses biomechanics to maximise efficiency of technique

Introduction

Aspects of biomechanics touch all sports performers, from the club sprinter wishing to improve technique to the Olympic ski jumper aiming to stay in flight for longer. At the heart of our study will be Newton's laws of motion and we will establish how these can be applied to sporting activity to help develop and enhance performance.

Linear motion

Linear motion occurs when a body moves in a straight or curved line with all parts moving the same distance in the same direction at the same speed.

The following are quantities of linear motion that are useful in your study of the mechanics of motion:

- vector quantity
- scalar quantity
- inertia
- acceleration
- mass
- speed
- displacement
- momentum.
- weight
- velocity
- distance

Vector versus scalar quantity

KEY WORDS

Scalar quantity
Quantities which are fully described by magnitude alone.

Vector quantity
Quantities which are fully described by both a magnitude and a direction.

Some quantities of linear motion are only considered in terms of their size or magnitude. These are known as **scalar quantities**. Other quantities are described in terms of both a magnitude and a direction. These are termed **vector quantities**.

Consider the following scenario: a car is travelling at 30mph. From this statement we have information regarding the magnitude or speed of the car but no information regarding its direction; in this instance a scalar quantity has been described. Now consider this same car travelling at 30mph in a north-easterly direction. We now have information with respect to both magnitude and direction; a vector quantity (velocity) has just been described.

KEY WORDS

Gravity
The force of attraction between all masses in the universe. The gravitational attraction of the earth causes objects to fall to the ground when dropped at an acceleration of $10ms^{-2}$

Mass versus weight

Mass is the quantity of matter a body possesses. The greater the density and volume of the body, the greater is the matter and the bigger the mass. A shot put therefore has a greater mass than a table tennis ball, as it is higher in both density and volume.

Mass and weight of an object are often confused. Mass of an object remains the same always at any place. Weight on the other hand is the force which a given mass feels due to **gravity**. For example, if you go to the Moon your mass remains the same, e.g. 60kg, but your weight becomes less by one-sixth of the amount since the Moon's gravity is one-sixth that of Earth's. Weight is a force and as such is measured in newtons (the units of force).

APPLICATION

To work out the perpendicular resolution of a vector or the resultant force, a parallelogram of forces can be constructed.

As weight always acts downwards from the centre of mass it has a direction as well as a magnitude. Weight is therefore a vector quantity. Mass on the other hand only has size (no direction) and so is a scalar quantity.

Calculating your weight force

If your mass is 60kg, then your weight is:

60 x 10 = 600 newtons

HOT TIPS

Force is measured in newtons (N). A newton is the force required to give a 1kg mass an acceleration of $1ms^{-2}$.

This is because:

Force = Mass x Acceleration (from Newton's Second Law)

Thus:

Weight = Mass x Acceleration due to gravity

TASK 1

Find your mass using a pair of bathroom scales. Use your mass to calculate your weight force.

Inertia

Inertia

The reluctance of a body to move or change its state of motion.

If equal force is applied to a cricket ball and a shot put, the acceleration of the cricket ball will be greater as it has lower inertia.

Inertia is the reluctance of a body to move or change its state of motion. The bigger the mass of an object the harder it is to move or change its motion, and therefore the larger the quantity of inertia it has. A sumo wrestler has a large amount of inertia and is therefore difficult to move. Moving objects or bodies that have high inertia will need a large force to change the state of motion. Consider two rugby league players running with the ball at the same speed. The larger, heavier player will have greater inertia and will therefore be more difficult to stop than the smaller, lighter player.

Distance versus displacement

The quantity of **distance** refers to the amount of ground an object covers during its motion. **Displacement** considers how far the position of the object has changed as a result of the motion, and is usually measured 'as the crow flies' from the starting to the finishing position. For example, consider a 400m runner who has just completed a race. She has just covered a distance of 400m but because the start and finish line are in the same position her displacement is in fact zero.

Distance

A measure of the path a body takes in moving from one position to another. Measured in metres (m).

Displacement

The shortest possible route between the starting and finishing point of a body that has moved. This will normally be in a straight line 'as the crow flies'. Measured in metres (m).

Since distance is the length of path taken by a body in moving from one place to another, it is a scalar quantity. Displacement, however, is a vector quantity because it has a direction as well as size. The Great North Run is an annual half-marathon event. The route of the run (the distance) is shown in Figure 6.02; the displacement is shown by the vector arrow.

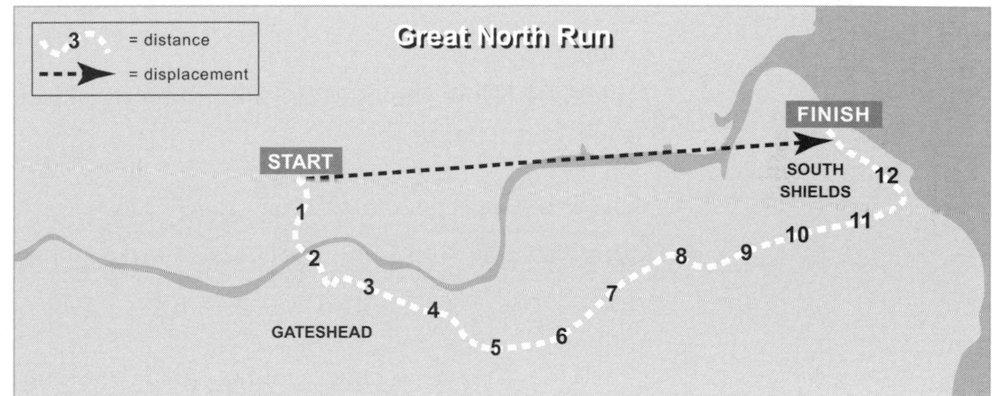

Fig 6.02 Route of the Great North Run

Speed

A body's movement per unit of time with no consideration for direction. Measured in metres/second (ms^{-1}).

Velocity

The rate of change of displacement. The speed of a body in a given direction. Measured in metres/second (ms^{-1}).

Speed versus velocity

Speed and **velocity** are terms that are often used interchangeably. They are, however, very different with regard to biomechanical analysis.

Speed is the rate of change of distance, or a body's movement per unit of time, and has no consideration for direction. Speed is therefore a scalar quantity.

$$\text{Speed } (ms^{-1}) = \frac{\text{Distance (m)}}{\text{Time (secs)}}$$

Fig 6.03

Velocity is a vector quantity and as such is 'direction-aware'. When evaluating the velocity of an object we must therefore keep track of direction. It would not be enough to simply say that an object has a velocity of 30mph, we must include directional information in order to fully describe the velocity of the object. We should therefore say that the car was travelling at 30mph in an easterly direction.

$$\text{Velocity (ms}^{-1}\text{)} = \frac{\text{Displacement (m)}}{\text{Time (secs)}}$$

Acceleration and deceleration

Acceleration or deceleration is the rate of change of velocity of an object. Just like velocity, acceleration and deceleration are 'direction-aware' and are therefore vector quantities. Acceleration is the rate of increase in velocity and deceleration is the rate of decrease in velocity.

Acceleration

The rate of change of velocity. Measured in metres/second/second (ms^{-1}).

$$\text{Acceleration (ms}^{-2}\text{)} = \frac{\text{Change in velocity (ms}^{1}\text{)}}{\text{Time (secs)}} = \frac{vf - vi}{t}$$

Where:

vf = final velocity (ms^{-1}), vi = initial velocity, (ms^{-1}), t = time taken (s)

A high jumper accelerates in an upwards direction at take off!

TASK 2

Kelly Holmes won the 800m gold medal at the 2004 Athens Olympics in a time of 1 minute 56.38 seconds.

a) Calculate Kelly's average speed during the race.
b) Calculate Kelly's average velocity during the race.

TASK 3

Table 6.01 below shows 100m split times of Maurice Greene in an Athens Grand Prix event in 1997.

Table 6.01 100m split times of Maurice Greene

10m	20m	30m	40m	50m	60m	70m	80m	90m	100m
1.71	2.75	3.67	4.55	5.42	6.27	7.12	7.98	8.85	9.73

a) Under the following headings, give the required information for each 10m section of the race.

Distance	Time	Time for 10m section	Average speed ms-1	Average acceleration ms^{-2}
10m				

b) Plot a graph of average speed (ms^{-1}) against time (sec).
c) Using your graph, highlight the point where Greene reaches maximum velocity.
d) Calculate Greene's average acceleration between 0.5 and 1.5 seconds.

TASK 4

Decide whether the following are vector or scalar quantities: mass, distance, velocity, inertia, acceleration, weight, displacement, force, air resistance, speed, deceleration. Add your answers to a two column chart.

Momentum

Momentum is the amount of motion a body possesses and is the product of mass and velocity:

Momentum = Mass (kg) x Velocity (ms^{-1})
The standard unit of measurement of momentum is kilograms per metres per second ($kgms^{-1}$).

The momentum of a 90kg prop travelling at a velocity of $10ms^{-1}$ is therefore $900kgms^{-1}$. Interestingly, because the mass of an object or performer tends to remain constant during sporting activity, any changes in momentum must be as a result of a change in velocity (i.e. acceleration or deceleration). Furthermore, when we consider an object or performer in flight, such as in the long jump, neither mass nor velocity can be altered so momentum is said to be conserved. The long jumper therefore tries to maximise his or her velocity during the run up and at take off since it cannot be changed once in the air. This relates to Newton's First Law of Motion and is referred to as the law of conservation of momentum.

HOT TIPS

The law of conservation of momentum is closely linked to Newton's First Law of Motion.

Fig 6.04 Jonah Lomu was so successful because he could produce a large momentum

TASK 5

Table 6.02 below considers the momentum of a variety of projectiles used in sport. Complete the blanks in the table.

Table 6.02 Momentum of a variety of projectiles used in sport

Ball	Mass	Velocity ms^{-1}	Momentum kgms-1
Hockey	0.16kg	20 ms^{-1}	
Table Tennis	0.0024kg	20 ms^{-1}	
Tennis	0.067kg		0.3
Tennis		50 ms^{-1}	3.0

Newton's Laws of Motion

Newton's laws go some way in helping to explain the principles of movement within the sporting arena.

Newton's First Law (the law of inertia)

Earlier in this chapter you discovered that inertia is the reluctance of a body to move or change its state of motion. Newton's First Law relates to this notion:

'Every body at rest, or moving with constant velocity in a straight line, will continue in that state unless compelled to change by an external force exerted upon it.'

KEY WORDS

Reaction force

A force that acts in opposition and is of equal magnitude to an action force. Reaction forces will occur whenever two bodies are in contact with one another.

In pursuit of an explanation of Newton's First Law, consider a golf ball at rest on a tee. There are two forces acting upon the golf ball. One force is the Earth's gravitational pull which exerts a downward force through the centre of mass of the ball. The other force is the **reaction force** from the tee which pushes back onto the ball. Since these two forces are of equal magnitude and in opposite directions (see Newton's Third Law), they balance each other out. The golf ball is said to be at equilibrium and therefore remains at rest. The golf ball will remain on the tee motionless, until it is struck by the golf club which transfers an 'action force' causing it to overcome inertia and to change its state of motion. Similarly, once the golf ball has been struck it will continue to travel with constant velocity in a straight line as long as forces remain balanced.

Fig 6.05 Newton's First Law in action

Fig 6.06 Newton's Second Law can be seen in action when teeing off in golf

Newton's Second Law (the law of acceleration)

Newton's Second Law states that the acceleration of an object or body is directly proportional to the force acting upon it. It is formally stated as:

'The rate of change of momentum of a body (or the acceleration for a body of constant mass) is proportional to the force causing it and takes place in the direction in which the force acts.'

HOT TIPS

Sometimes Newton's Second Law is stated as F=ma. This suggests that if mass of the body or object remains constant then acceleration is equal to the size of the force causing it. It also tells us that assuming the action force remains constant, acceleration will be greater for lighter bodies or objects.

This therefore implies that in order to produce a greater acceleration, an athlete must generate proportionally greater forces. Using golf as an example once more, when teeing off, the golf ball receives a greater change in velocity (i.e. acceleration) than during a putt. In both instances the golf ball will accelerate in the direction of the force. This law also tells us that the greater the mass, the greater the force required to give the same acceleration.

Newton's Third Law (the law of action/reaction)

'For every force that is exerted by one body on another, there is an equal and opposite force exerted by the second body on the first.'

Or more simply:
'For every action, there is an equal and opposite reaction.'

The statement means that in every interaction, there is a pair of forces acting. The size of the force on the first object is equal to the size of the force on the second object, and the direction of the force on the first object is opposite to the direction of the force on the second object. To help explain this law further, think of what happens when you step off a boat that is floating on water onto dry land. As you move onto the land, the boat tends to move in the opposite direction (leaving you face down in the water, if you're not careful!). Returning to golf this implies that the golf club receives from the golf ball an equal and opposite force to that imparted by the golf club onto the ball.

Fig 6.07 Newton's Third Law in action

TASK 6

Apply Newton's three laws of motion to the following sporting situations:

a) a high jumper at take off
b) a high diver performing a dive
c) a gymnast performing a vault
d) a football player taking a penalty.

The role of force in sporting activity

One key factor in any kind of sporting performance is force. Without force we would not be able to jump, kick, throw or even move! Force can be a push or a pull, and more force is needed to move a larger object than a smaller one. When a force is applied to an object, the velocity of that object changes. This change in velocity constitutes an acceleration. So, forces are tied to accelerations. Forces can therefore cause:

- a body at rest to move
- a moving body to accelerate
- a moving body to decelerate
- a moving body to change direction
- a body to change shape.

Understanding net force (balanced versus unbalanced)

Net force

The resultant force acting on a body having considered all other forces acting. If all forces cancel each other out then there is zero net force.

Balanced forces occur where two or more forces are in operation that are of equal size but opposite in direction. All the forces cancel each other out so that there is zero **net force**. In this instance an object or body will either remain stationary or, if moving, continue to do so at constant velocity. A sprinter running at constant velocity does so because there is zero net force acting.

Unbalanced forces on the other hand, occur where a force acting in one direction is larger than that acting in the opposite direction, so that the object or body will start to move or accelerate/decelerate in the direction of the bigger force. If we consider the high jumper in Figure 6.8, he is able to accelerate upwards because the reaction force is greater than the weight force, i.e. reaction force = weight force + applied muscular force.

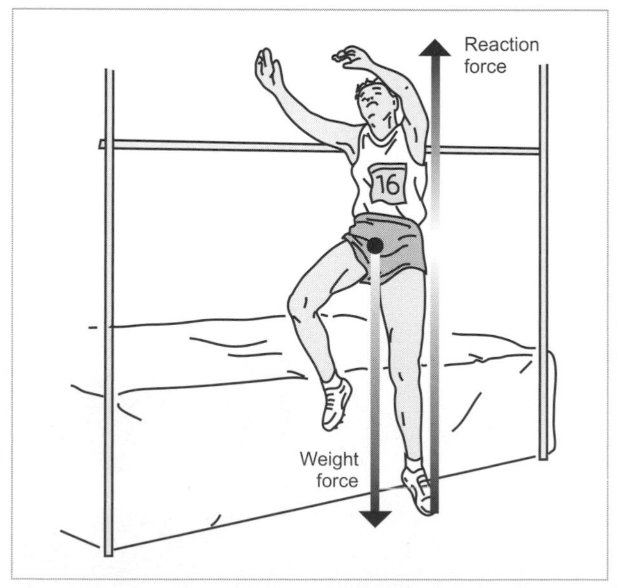

Fig 6.08 The high jumper accelerates upwards as the reaction force is greater than the weight force.

Types of force

HOT TIPS

When describing a force make sure you state or show:

- a point of application
- a direction
- a magnitude or size.

By understanding the role of force in sport, the coach and athlete can manipulate technique to use force to best effect. Although there are many different forces at play, the following are those that you are required to know for your examination:

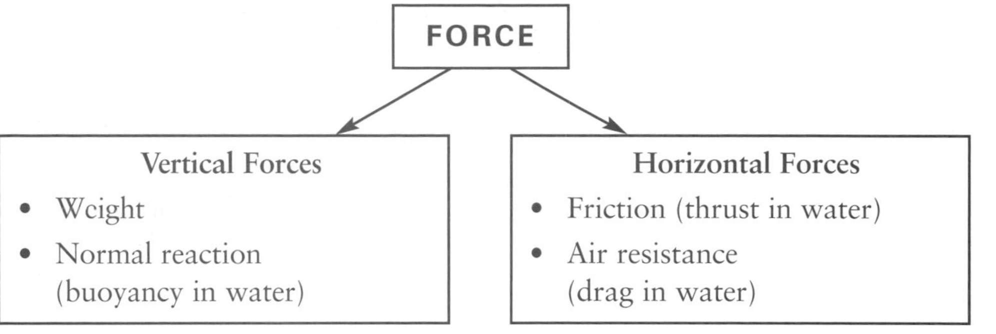

Vertical forces

Weight

We discovered earlier that mass and weight are not the same. A weight force is equal to the mass of an object or body and the acceleration due to gravity.

Weight = Mass x Acceleration due to gravity ($10ms^{-2}$)

Weight always acts downwards (from the centre of mass of an object or body) towards the centre of the Earth.

Reaction force

You will remember from Newton's Third Law that every action has an equal and opposite reaction. Reaction forces will therefore always occur whenever two bodies are in contact with one another. Reaction forces will always act at right angles (90°) to the contacted surface (this is an important rule when drawing free body diagrams). Figure 6.09 illustrates the reaction forces that might occur on a tennis player playing a forehand drive.

Fig 6.09 Reaction forces occur whenever two bodies are in contact with each other

Horizontal forces

KEY WORDS

Friction
A resistive force encountered when two or more bodies in contact move past one another.

Friction

Some see **friction** as the 'evil' of all motion. It seems as if nature has given us friction to stop us from moving anything. Regardless of which direction something moves in, friction pulls it the other way. In simple terms, *friction opposes motion.*

But friction is not all bad. In fact, it has a lot to do with our sporting lives. Without it, we wouldn't be able to walk, run or play the majority of sports as we know them. Everything would just keep slipping and falling all over the place.

Friction is actually a force that appears whenever two things rub against each other or slide over one another. Although two objects might look smooth, microscopically they're very rough and jagged. As they slide against each other, their contact is anything but smooth. They both grind and drag against each other and this is where friction comes from.

Factors affecting friction include:

- **The roughness of the surfaces in contact** – the rougher the surfaces the greater the friction. For example, football studs or spikes worn by athletes are designed to increase friction. Hard courts with a rough surface will also increase friction.
- **The greater the downforce or mass of an object the greater the friction.** A mountain biker will sit back over the driving wheel when riding up a muddy slope in order to gain a better grip of the tyre on the surface.
- **Warmth of surfaces** – dependent upon the surface this will either increase or decrease friction. Consider the metal blade of an ice skate moving over the ice, for example. This will heat up and create a thin film of water which decreases the friction between the two surfaces.

Air resistance

Air resistance

The force of air pushing against a moving object. It is a form of fluid friction that acts on something moving through the air.

Air resistance is a form of fluid friction and therefore opposes motion. The degree of air resistance (often referred to as drag) experienced by sports performers such as swimmers, cyclists, motor racers and skiers very much depends upon the following:

- **The velocity of the moving body** – the faster an object is moving the more it is subject to the effects of air resistance.
- **The frontal cross-sectional area of the moving body** – the larger the frontal cross-sectional area the greater the effects of air resistance.
- **The shape and surface characteristics of the moving body** – the less streamlined and rougher the surface of the moving body the more it will be affected by air resistance and drag.

TASK 7

Discuss with your classmates how sports performers such as swimmers, cyclists, motor racers and skiers try to reduce the effects of air resistance and drag.

Free body diagrams

In your examination you may be required to draw or interpret free body diagrams. Free body diagrams are diagrams used to show the relative magnitude and direction of all the forces that are acting upon an object or body in a given situation. The length of the arrow in a free body diagram reflects the magnitude of the force and the position of the arrow head reveals the direction in which the force is acting.

The shaded area below the graph (-ve impulse) represents a body landing on the ground. The +ve impulse above the graph represents the impulse of a body due to the ground reaction force.

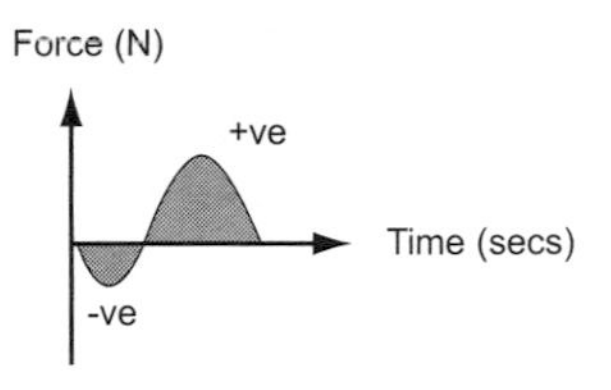

a) An accelerating body (+ve > -ve)

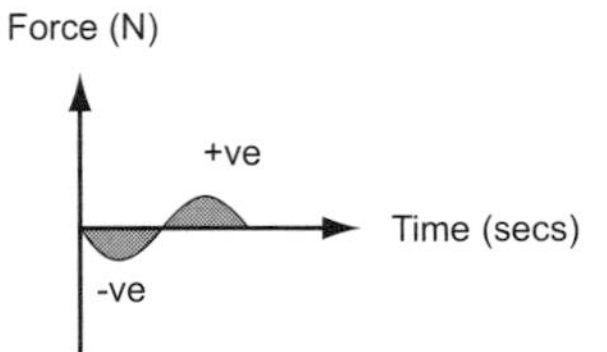

b) A body moving at constant velocity (+ve = -ve)

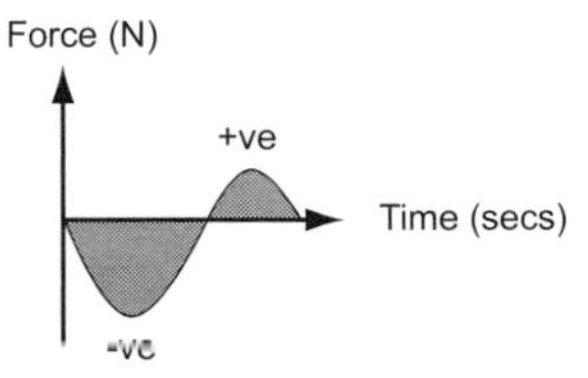

c) A decelerating body (+ve < -ve)

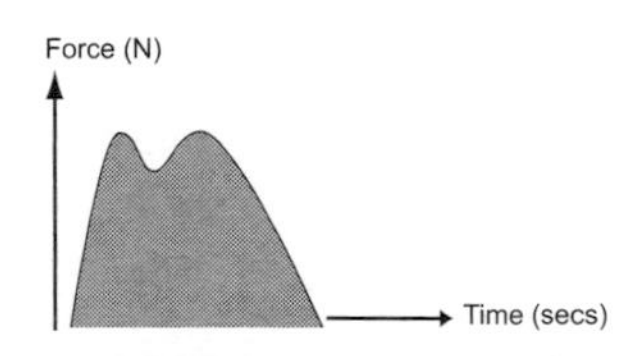

d) A large +ve impulse is generated by a sprinter as he or she drives away from the blocks.

Fig 6.11 Graphs showing the effects of +ve and -ve impulse on a body

Figure 6.10 below summarises the main guidelines to follow when constructing or interpreting free body diagrams.

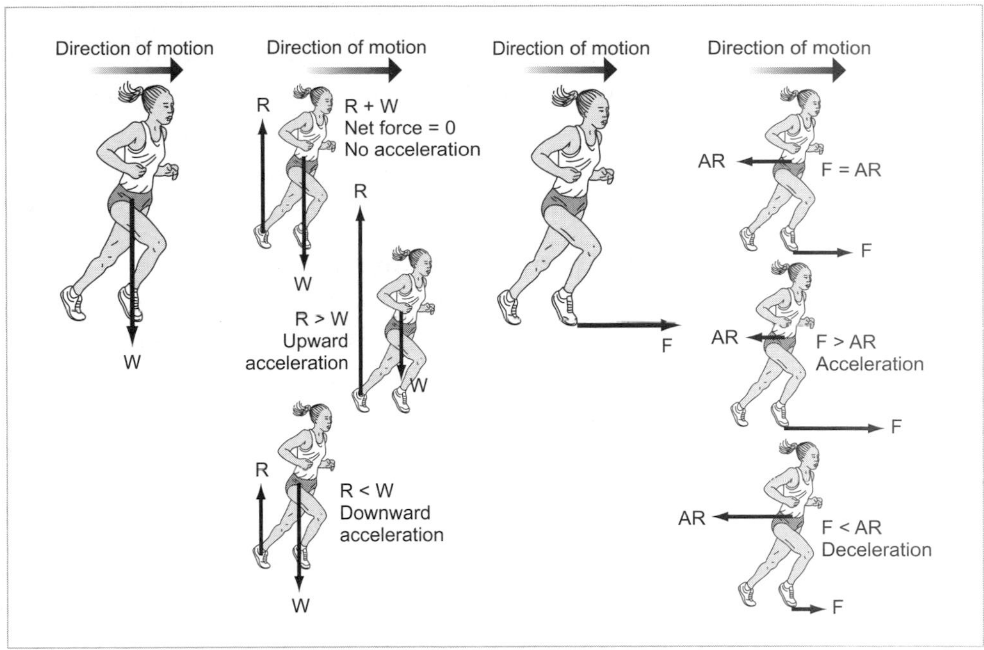

Fig 6.10 Key points to remember when drawing free body diagrams

Impulse

Another way of thinking about force is in terms of impulse. Impulse is concerned with the length of time a force is applied to an object or body and relates to a change in momentum that occurs as a consequence.

Impulse = Force x Time

A change in momentum is synonymous with a change in acceleration, therefore:

$$F = ma \longrightarrow a = \frac{vf - vi}{t}$$

$$\downarrow$$

$$F = m\frac{(vf - vi)}{t}$$

$$\longleftarrow$$

$$Ft = mvf - mvi$$

(change in momentum)

Impulse can therefore be used in sporting activity to:

- add speed to a body or object
- slow down moving bodies slowly on impact.

For example, the O'Brien technique whereby a shot putter performs a one-and-three-quarter turn before release is designed to maximise the time over which a force is applied to the shot, increasing outgoing acceleration. Similarly, a follow-through is used in racket and stick sports to increase the time the racket or stick is in contact with the ball, which will also increase the outgoing momentum of the ball (as well as giving direction).

A fielder in cricket will cradle a fast-moving cricket ball by meeting the ball early and withdrawing the hands in the direction of the ball's motion. This increases the time over which the player's hands are in contact with the ball, cushioning the impact and preventing the ball from bouncing off uncontrollably.

Similarly, a gymnast landing from a vault or dismount will flex at the hip and knee to extend the time over which the impact force is imparted to the body. In doing so they can reduce the likelihood of impact injuries.

Projectile motion

Projectile motion is central to the performance of many sporting activities. Objects and implements are used as projectiles in basketball, tennis and athletics whereas it is the human body that acts as a projectile in high jump, ski jumping and gymnastic events. Once in the air projectiles are only subject to the forces of gravity and air resistance. As gravity always remains constant (approximately $10ms^{-2}$) any changes to the velocity of the projectile can be explained by the effects of air resistance. For some projectiles such as a shot or the human body, the effects of air resistance are minimal and the flight path will be symmetrical or parabolic. For others such as a shuttlecock or table tennis ball, the effects of air resistance are great which causes the projectile to veer away from the normal parabolic path to form an assymetrical or distorted parabola.

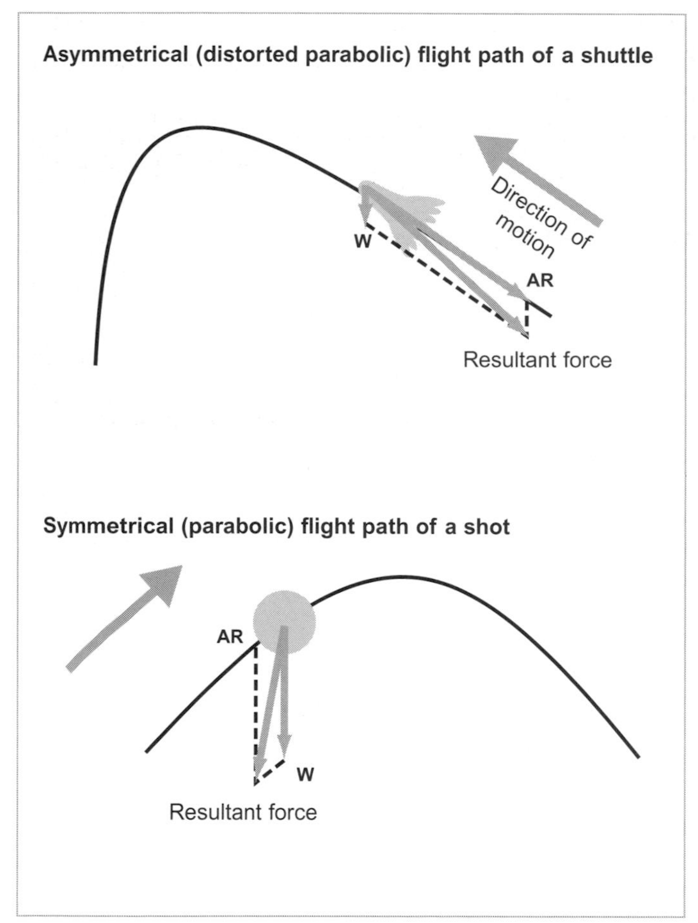

Fig 6.12 A comparison of the flight paths of a shot and shuttlecock

Three factors determine the horizontal displacement of a projectile such as a shot:

- velocity of release
- height of release
- angle of release.

Generally, an increase in the velocity of the shot at release and an increase in the height of release will increase the horizontal displacement of the shot. However, for any given velocity and height of release there is an optimal release angle which maximises the horizontal displacement.

The velocity of release

An increase in the release velocity will increase the horizontal displacement of the projectile. Throwing events in athletics are very technical. The shift or rotation of a shot putter is designed to ensure that the shot leaves the performer's hand at maximum velocity.

The height of release

An increase in the release height will increase the horizontal displacement of the projectile. We can conclude therefore that taller shot putters have an advantage over shorter ones! That is not to say that shorter shot putters can never win – they simply need to manipulate the angle of release to suit them best!

The angle of release

The optimum angle of release of a projectile is dependent upon the relative heights of release and landing. Where release height and landing height are the same, such as when performing the long jump, the optimum angle for take off is 45°. Where release height is greater than landing height, for example, when putting the shot, the optimum angle of release is less than 45°. Where release height is below the landing height, such as when performing a free throw in basketball (the landing height in this instance is the hoop and not the floor) the optimum angle of release is greater than 45°.

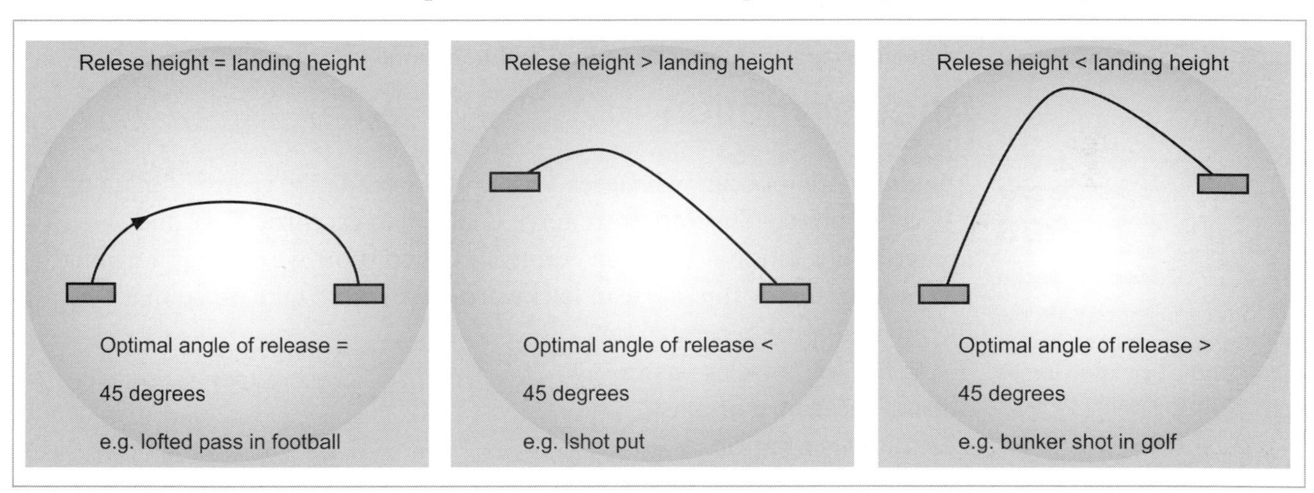

Fig 6.13 Optimal angles of release relative to release and landing heights of projectiles

TASK 8

Video a member of your class performing several of the following skills. (Make sure you are at right angles or side-on to the performer.)

- Free throw in basket ball
- Drop kick in rugby
- Shot put
- Penalty flick in hockey
- Shooting in netball
- A tennis serve

In each situation study the angle of release and sketch the flight path of the projectile. Share your findings with others in your class and between you come up with the optimum angle of release for each situation.

TIP – You may need to consider the horizontal displacement of each projectile as well as the accuracy of the skill performed!

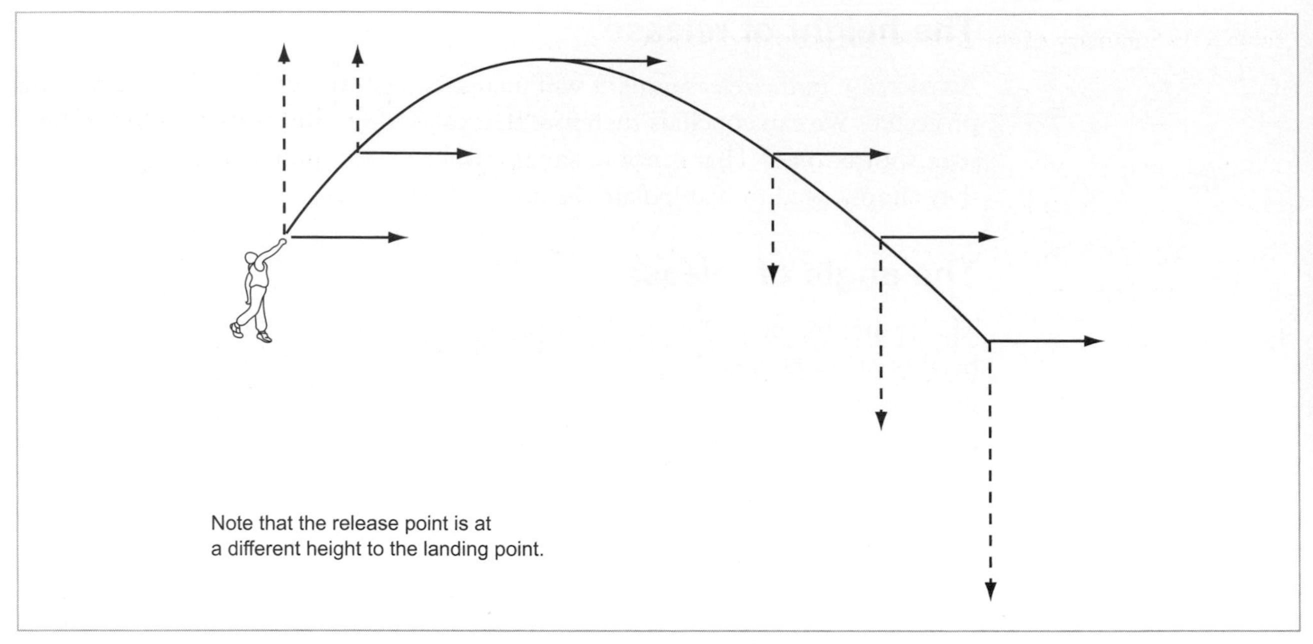

Fig 6.14 The flight path of a shot showing the changes in vertical and horizontal velocity

Angular motion

KEY WORDS

Eccentric force
A force applied outside the centre of mass of an object or body. Eccentric forces cause angular motion.

Angular motion occurs whenever a force acts outside the centre of mass of a body or object. This off-centre force is called an **eccentric force** and is necessary if rotation is to occur. Applying this to sport we see that a gymnast performing a back flip will lean backwards just before take off so that the internal force generated by his or her leg muscles passes outside the centre of mass and initiates rotation. Likewise, a footballer taking a free kick may kick the ball slightly off-centre so that the ball spins and follows a curved flight path around the defensive wall.

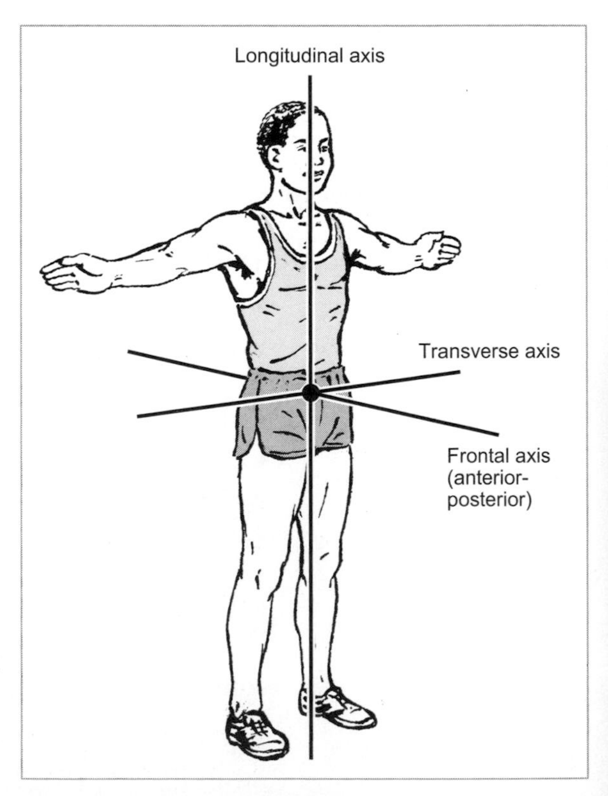

Fig 6.15 Principal axes of the body

Rotational movements

Axes of rotation

You will recall from your AS studies that the body has three imaginary poles running through the body that are the axes of rotation. Table 6.03 summarises the actions that occur about each axis.

Table 6.03 Summary of the actions that occur about each axis

	Position	Angular movements possible at joints	Sporting examples
Longitudinal axis	Runs through the body or joint from top to bottom	Rotation, pronation and supination	Spinning ice skater
Horizontal or transverse axis	Runs through the body or joint from side to side	Flexion and extension	Front/ backward somersaulting high diver
Frontal axis	Runs through the body or joint from front to back	Abduction and adduction	A gymnast performing a cartwheel or side somersault

Torques or moments of force

Torques are the turning effects or rotational consequences of a force. The torque caused by a force depends upon the size of the force and the distance that the force acts from the axis of rotation (referred to as the moment arm):

Torque = Size of force (F) x Moment arm (d)
(perpendicular distance from the fulcrum)

The standard unit of measurement of a torque is Newton metres (Nm).

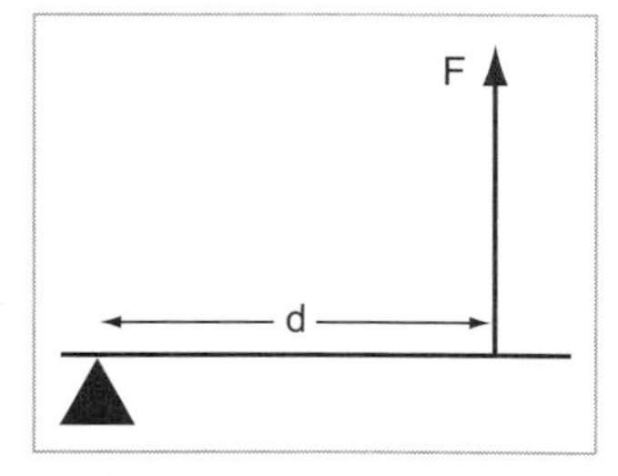

Fig 6.16 A torque in the body is the product of force multiplied by the distance the force acts from the joint

Angular distance
The angle turned about an axis. Measured in degrees (°) or radians (rads).

Angular displacement
The smallest angle between starting and finishing positions. Measured in degrees (°) or radians (rads).

Angular speed
The angular distance travelled in a specified time.
Angular distance (rads) / Time taken (secs)
Measured in rads/sec.

Angular velocity
The angular displacement travelled in a specified time.
Angular displacement (rads) / Time taken (secs)
Measured in rads/sec.

Angular acceleration
The rate of change of angular velocity.
Angular velocity (rads/sec) / Time taken (rads).
Measured in rads/sec^2.

Quantities of angular motion

All the quantities of linear motion have angular counterparts. The following measurements should aid your understanding of angular motion:

- angular distance
- angular displacement
- angular speed
- angular velocity
- angular acceleration.

TASK 9

It will be useful for you to know a definition, an equation and a unit of measurement for each of the quantities of angular motion. Revise the definitions used in linear motion and see if you can work out their angular equivalents.

TIP – If you get stuck have a look in the margin at the key words!

Angular analogues of Newton's laws

Linear and angular motion are pretty close bed fellows! What goes for linear motion also goes for angular motion. Consequently, Newton's laws that govern linear motion also underpin rotational movement.

HOT TIPS

Angular distance and angular displacement are usually measured in radians. A radian is a measurement of angle. 1 radian = 57.3 degrees.

Newton's First Law:

A rotating body will continue to turn about its axis of rotation with constant angular momentum unless an external or eccentric force is exerted upon it.

Newton's Second Law:

The rate of change of angular momentum of a body is proportional to the torque (force) causing it. Also, the change takes place in the direction in which the torque acts.

Newton's Third Law:

For every torque that is exerted by one body on another, there is an equal and opposite torque exerted by the second body on the first.

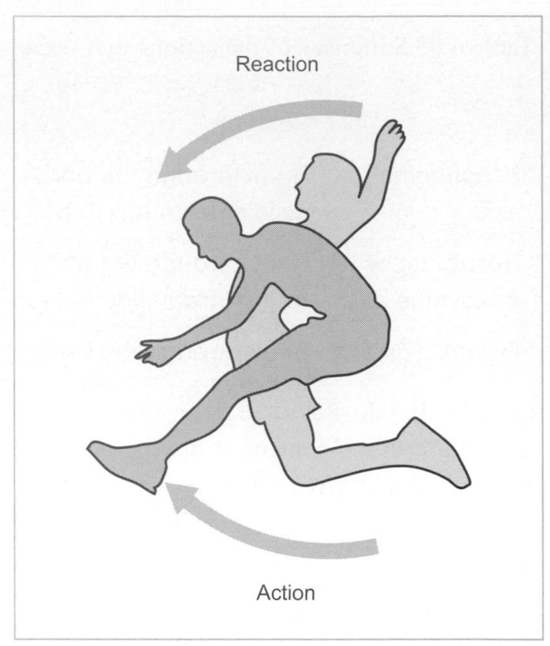

Fig 6.17 An angular analogue of Newton's Third Law of Motion

Moment of inertia (MI)

KEY WORDS

Moment of inertia (MI)

A measure of the resistance of a body to change its state of angular motion. Measured in kgm^2.

The **moment of inertia** (MI) is a measure of the resistance of an object to rotation and the desire of a body to want to continue to rotate once it has been set in motion. It is dependent upon two key factors – the mass of an object or body and the distribution of its mass around the axis of rotation.

The mass of the object

The greater the mass of an object the greater its moment of inertia. A ten-pin bowling ball is therefore more difficult to roll along the ground than a volleyball.

The distribution of the mass from the axis of rotation

The further the mass is distributed away from the axis of rotation the greater the moment of inertia. A 4kg medicine ball should have a higher moment of inertia than a 4kg shot as its mass is spread further away from the axis of rotation. The shot has its mass concentrated about the axis so the moment of inertia is therefore lower and the shot will rotate faster. We can apply this to rotating humans too!

Applying moment of inertia to sport

Take, for example, a trampolinist. When performing a tucked back somersault the speed of rotation is much quicker than when performing a straight back somersault. This is because the mass of the trampolinist is spread further away from the axis of rotation when performing the straight back, which in turn increases the moment of inertia and reduces angular velocity.

Fig 6.18 A slalom skier initiates the turn in a low tucked position. Moment of inertia (MI) is high and angular velocity (AV) is low. As he rounds the gate he straightens up, effectively halving MI and doubling AV. As he comes out of the turn he tucks once more, returning to a state where MI is high and AV low. This enables him to prepare for the next gate

Fig 6.19 An ice skater speeds up rotation by pulling body parts in towards the axis of rotation

By altering body shape it is possible to change the moment of inertia of the performer and either speed up or slow down rotation. Nowhere more do we see this than when an ice skater performs a spin. Initially the skater may have arms outstretched so that the moment of inertia is large; as the skater brings his or her arms in closer to the body, the mass is brought in closer to the axis of rotation and the angular velocity increases.

This same principle is used by swimmers when swimming front crawl. After the propulsive phase, the arm exits the water and flexes at the elbow. This reduces the moment of inertia and helps increase the speed of the recovery phase so that the arm can enter the water as quickly as possible, ready for the next arm pull.

Angular momentum

The relationship between angular velocity and the moment of inertia is inversely proportional: So that when one goes up the other goes down proportionally. This means that angular momentum must remain constant when an object or body is in flight, and cannot change until an external force is applied. This is known as the law of conservation of angular momentum and is related to Newton's First Law.

The law of conservation of angular momentum

Angular momentum cannot be changed during flight. This has important implications for sporting activities that require many rotations to be performed, such as high diving and figure skating. Currently many figure skaters are attempting quadruple jumps in their routines. To ensure maximal angular momentum at take-off the skater prepares for the jump so that at take-off arms are out to the side and one leg extended behind. The idea is to generate as great a torque (turning moment) as possible. The larger the force or the further the force is from the axis of rotation, the larger the torque. The larger the torque, the greater the angular momentum. Once in flight the skater pulls his or her arms and legs in as close to the longitudinal axis as possible, which decreases moment of inertia and increases angular velocity, enabling the skater to rotate very quickly. Upon landing the skater spreads his or her arms out once again to increase moment of inertia and decrease angular velocity.

Fig 6.20 A sprinter can use the concept of moment of inertia to improve leg technique

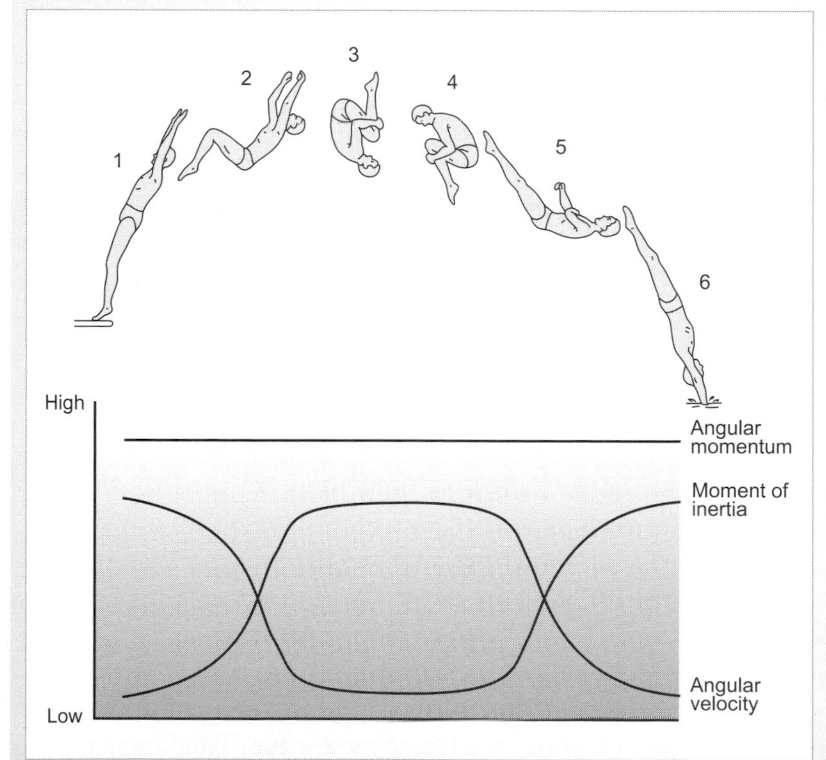

Fig 6.21 The relationship between angular velocity, moment of inertia and angular momentum during a dive

TASK 10

Perform a full twisting jump using the following methods:

a) arms by side at take-off
b) arms outstretched at take-off and brought in close to the body during flight.

In which jump could you perform the most rotation? Use your understanding of angular momentum to explain your observations.

TASK 11

Use Figure 6.20 to explain how a sprinter can use the concept of moment of inertia to improve technique and sprint times.

TASK 12

Use Figure 6.21 to explain how a diver can use knowledge of moment of inertia and the law of conservation of momentum to help maximise performance.

Revise as you go!

1. Use Newton's three laws of motion to explain the motion of a high jumper at take off.
2. Draw a stick figure diagram showing the vertical forces acting on a high jumper at take off. With reference to your diagram explain what is meant by a net force.
3. Define momentum. Calculate the momentum of a downhill skier who has a mass of 85kg and is travelling at a velocity of 42m/s.
4. Air resistance is a force that acts against a moving body. How might a track cyclist attempt to reduce the size of this force?
5. Sketch a diagram to show the flight path of a shot from the moment it leaves the putter's hand to the moment it lands. Add arrows to the sketched flight path to represent the horizontal and vertical components of the shot at the following points:
   a) as it leaves the shot putter's hand
   b) the highest point of the flight path
   c) the point of the flight path that is level to release
   d) the point just before landing.
6. How does the angle of release, height of release and velocity of release affect the horizontal distance travelled by a shot?
7. The follow-through is an important aspect of the stroke in all racquet sports. Sketch a graph of the force applied by a squash racquet against time:
   a) with no follow-through
   b) with a follow-through.
8. Name the three axes of rotation. Give an example of a skill from sport where rotation about each of these three axes occurs.
9. Define the moment of inertia. With reference to a bent leg recovery, explain how a long jumper uses the concept of moment of inertia during the run up.
10. Trampolinists are now regularly performing triple front somersaults in their optional routines. State the relationship between angular momentum, moment of inertia and angular velocity. Sketch a graph to demonstrate this relationship during a tucked back somersault.
11. How does an ice skater maximise angular momentum at take-off?

Section 2: Psychological factors

Introduction

During the AS course you studied the nature of skilled performance, methods to optimise the learning of skills and how a performer processes the information available to him or her in order to produce an efficient performance. The psychological aspect of the course for A2 builds on that knowledge but focuses on the factors which influence an elite performer during competition.

The aim of this theoretical section is to develop your understanding of how an elite performer prepares him or herself mentally for intense competition. In the modern world of sport, where events are won by the narrowest of margins, it is often the performer who can consistently control his or her emotions and concentration levels most effectively who will emerge victorious. There may be the odd occasion where a performer may find him or herself in the 'zone', allowing the performer to produce the performance of a lifetime, but the ultimate champions are those who can repeat that level of performance again and again when under pressure.

The vast majority of elite performers now have access to high quality preparation including: state of the art facilities, funding, high quality coaching, technology allowing detailed analysis of movement, physiologists, physiotherapists and a variety of other resources at their disposal. As a result there may only be minor differences in the physiological capabilities of the athletes. The margin between winning and losing is minimal but the consequences of victory are enormous, both in terms of recognition and rewards.

The relatively new field of 'sports psychology' is one way in which performers can attempt to gain an advantage over their opponents. Many elite athletes now employ various aspects of psychological techniques as an integral aspect of their preparation, and devote time to mastering those techniques in a competitive environment.

Think how often you have heard coaches and performers refer to their mental ability or the need to win using the 'top two inches'. The mind exerts a powerful influence during competition: it can either allow you to be full of confidence, totally focused and ready or it can cause you to feel anxious, worry about the consequences of failure and ultimately *be* the major factor causing failure.

In order to answer the examination questions, each topic should be approached in a similar manner. After studying each topic you should

be able to answer questions which focus on the following areas:
- What are the various theories linked to this area?
- How might this information affect my performance?
- How can this knowledge be used and what strategies can be employed to improve performance?

Section 2 will attempt to answer some of the following questions:
- Is a certain personality needed to be an elite performer?
- How can aggressive behaviour be controlled?
- How can a performer reach their optimum level of arousal?
- How is motivation maintained?
- What are the effects of people watching a performer?
- What is the best way to form an effective team?
- What makes a good leader?
- How do we control stress?

As you can see, the topics are varied and can all be applied to your own sporting experiences, allowing you to become a better performer.

Chapter 7: Personality

Learning outcomes

By the end of this chapter you should be able to:
- understand the term personality and outline its relationship to sport
- outline the trait approach and explain its limitations
- outline the interactionist approach and explain its relationship to performance
- discuss the various methods used to measure personality and evaluate their effectiveness
- explain the profile of mood states, or iceberg profile, and evaluate its relationship to performance.

Introduction

Many psychologists have completed research in an attempt to find the most suitable personality to be an elite performer. Often as a component of a talent identification programme, some form of psychological testing may take place. This may be helpful to determine levels of motivation, reaction to pressure situations, suitablity towards specific forms of training and the ability to deal with failure. In order to be successful, are certain traits required such as competitiveness, self-confidence and the ability to deal with crowds and media attention? If they are, can they be identified? Do certain sports benefit from a performer having a specific personality? If they do, can this allow us to predict a person's personality and his or her subsequent behaviour? This may help us when attempting to identify potential elite performers.

Understanding the personality of a performer also allows the coach, other team members and anyone linked with him or her to better identify potential weaknesses when placed in a competitive situation and implement strategies to overcome those deficiencies.

This section will focus on two basic prepositions – that of nature versus nurture. In other words, are we born with the innate **traits** which allow us to be successful or do we develop personality based on our experiences?

Trait
Innate, enduring characteristics possessed by an individual that can be used to explain and predict behaviour in different situations.

Definitions of personality

Before we study the different theories in more depth, we need to develop an understanding of the term personality.

TASK 1

With a partner, devise a definition of personality and attempt to describe the characteristics of your own personality. Discuss with other students and compare your definition to those on page 89.

There are numerous definitions of personality suggested by different psychologists but many have common characteristics, as illustrated below.

Gross:
'Those relatively stable and enduring aspects of individuals which distinguish them from other people, making them unique but at the same time permit a comparison between individuals.' (1992)

Eysenck:
'Personality is the more or less stable and enduring organizations of a person's character, temperament, intellect and physique, which determines the unique adjustment the individual makes to the environment.' (1995)

Hollander:
'Personality is the sum total of an individual's characteristics which make him unique.' (1971)

The key factor in each of the definitions is that personality is unique to the individual. The work of Hollander (1967) provides an easy structure which allows a clear understanding of personality. He sub-divided personality into three separate but inter-related levels:

- *Psychological core* – this is the inner core of your personality; it can be described as 'the real you'. It comprises your beliefs, values, attitudes and self-worth, all of which are relatively permanent and tend to be resistent to change.
- *Typical responses* – as the term suggests, this layer of the model represents our usual response to a situation, which is often learned. Such responses can be a good indicator of the psychological core. For example, one player may react to a defeat by training harder and viewing the experience in a positive manner, whilst another may feel that her or she is unable to improve and give up easily.
- *Role-related behaviours* – refers to our behaviour at any given time depending on the specific circumstances and our perception at that time. This is the most changeable aspect of our personality. In other words, our behaviour alters to suit the situation and at times may appear 'out of character' and may not be a true reflection of our psychological core. For example, a player may normally be controlled during a game but may resort to an aggressive act if provoked.

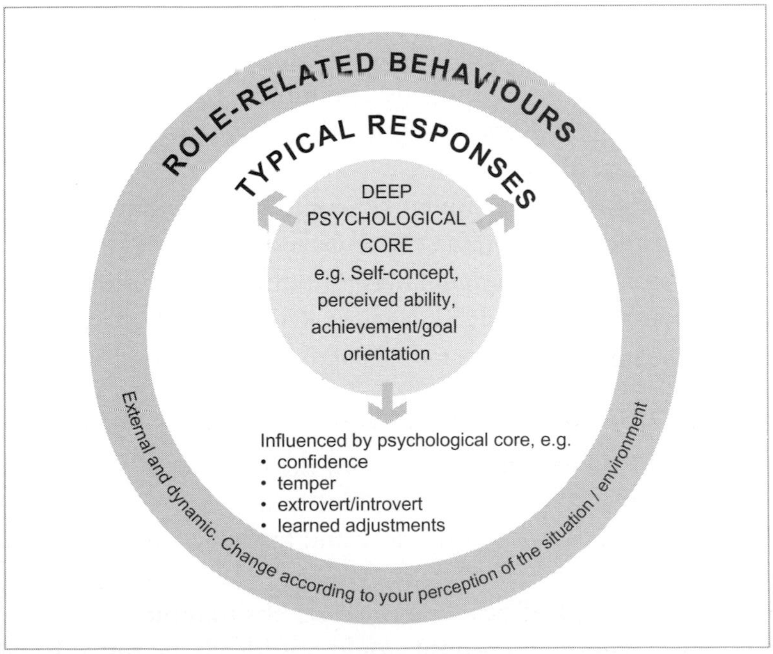

Fig 7.01 The structure of personality (Hollander)

Trait theories

Trait theories of personality represent the 'nature' approach. They suggest we are born with inherited characteristics which do not alter over time and which cause us to react in a similar fashion irrespective of the situation. Traits are seen to be stable, enduring and consistent. For example, if a person has an aggressive nature then he or she will be aggressive in all situations or may display behaviour patterns of extreme competitiveness.

HOT TIPS

Make sure you can outline the various theories of and evaluate their strengths and weaknesses.

If the concept of the trait theories is correct it would allow us to predict behaviour patterns in all situations. This would obviously be useful in terms of sporting performance as it would help identify potential performers who could cope with the pressure of intense competition without becoming over-aroused or aggressive. Similarly, potential leaders or captains could be identified if they possessed the necessary traits required to fulfil such roles of responsibility.

The measurement of traits using questionnaires provides a quick and straightforward assessment of personality (measurement of personality traits will be covered in more detail later). However, as you may gather from your own experiences, behaviour patterns may alter from one situation to the next and as a result merely using traits to predict behaviour is unreliable. Also, despite numerous attempts to classify the characteristics required to perform at elite level, there are no common traits, with many performers displaying wide-ranging differences in personality despite being highly successful.

Eysenck's personality dimensions

Hans Eysenck suggested that individuals possess stable traits based on two broad dimensions based on biological factors.

Extrovert–Introvert dimension

KEY WORDS

Extrovert
Sociable, outgoing, talkative, active and optimistic.

Introvert
Quiet, passive, unsociable, reserved and careful.

Stable
Calm, even-tempered, reliable, controlled and logical.

Neurotic
Moody, anxious, touchy, restless and aggressive.

This dimension is based on the assumption that individuals attempt to maintain a certain level of stimulation or arousal suitable for them. The level of stimulation is controlled by the Reticular Activating System (RAS), which is located in the central cortex of the brain.

- **Extroverts** need more arousal and stimulation as the RAS inhibits or dampens down information received via the sensory system. In other words it needs extra stimulation to maintain optimum levels of attention.
- **Introverts** need less arousal and stimulation as their RAS is already stimulated and additional excitement will cause the individual to become over-aroused.

Stable–Neurotic dimension

The second dimension is based on emotionality and the reaction of the Autonomic Nervous System (ANS) to stressful situations.

- **Stable** individuals tend to possess a fairly slow and less vigorous response to stressful situations.
- **Neurotic** individuals have a rapid reaction to stressful situations. Obviously a performer with this response would not ideally be suited to the high pressure environment of the modern day sporting arena.

The two personality dimensions are independent of each other and an individual can be a combination of the differing traits. For example, overall personality may lie in any one of the four quadrants shown in Figure 7.02.

A third dimension of Psychotism–Intelligence (the P-Dimension), relating to how far a person was prepared to conform to society's rules and conventions, was added later, in 1976.

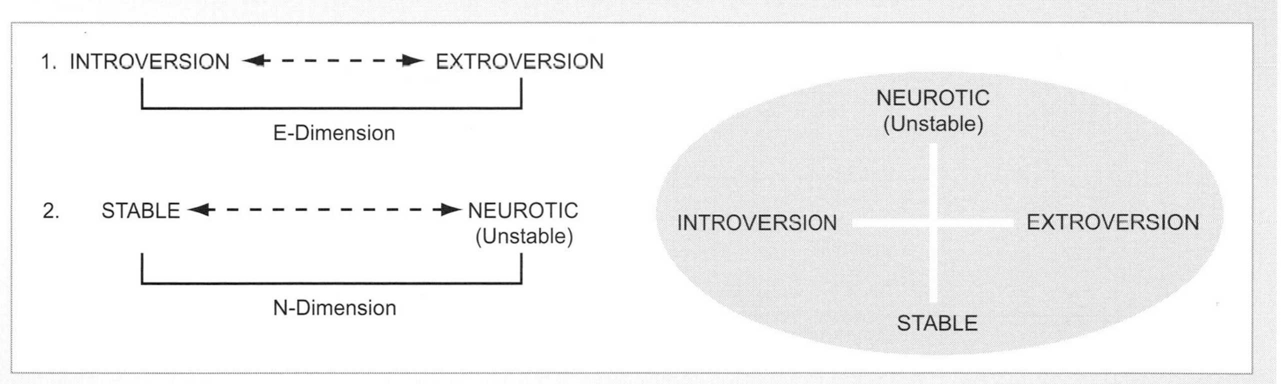

Fig 7.02 Eysenck's personality dimensions

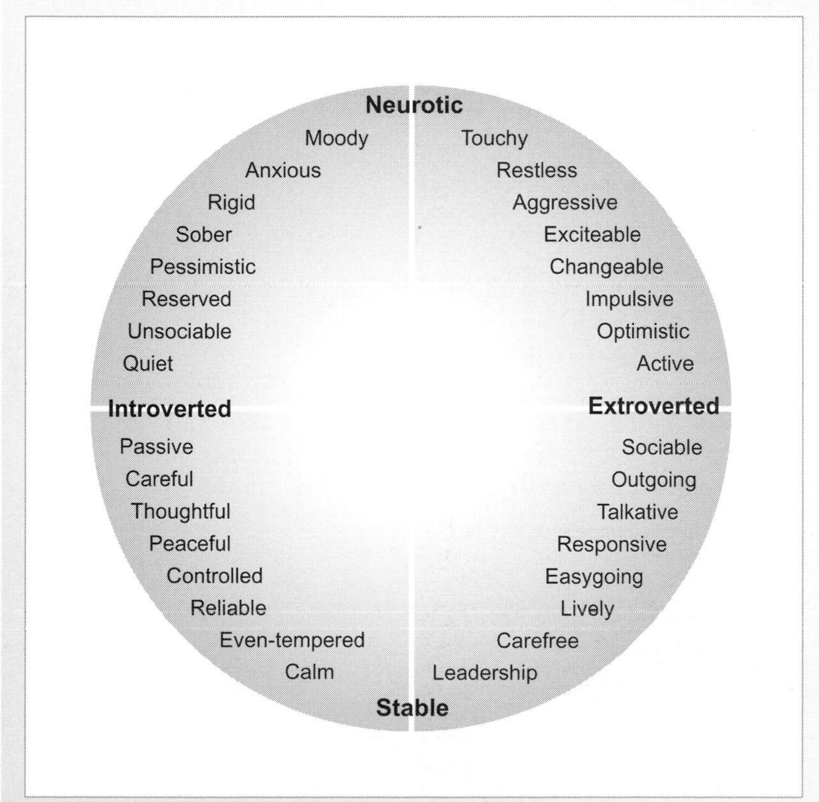

Fig 7.03 Eysenck's circular diagram

TASK 2

1 Copy Figure 7.02 and place a cross in the section which you feel best matches your personality based on the characteristics listed in Figure 7.03.

2 Complete Eysenck's Personality Inventory (EPI) in Table 7.01 and plot your results on the graph.

3 Compare your results with a partner and discuss the relationship between your personality and choice of sports.

Table 7.01 Eysenck's Personality Inventory (EPI)

Complete the questions below answering either Yes or No.	Yes	No
1 Do you often long for excitement?		
2 Do you often need understanding friends to cheer you up?		
3 Are you carefree?		
4 Do you find it hard to take 'no' for an answer?		
5 Do you stop to think things over before doing anything?		
6 If you say you will do something do you always keep your promise, no matter how inconvenient it might be to do so?		
7 Does your mood often go up and down?		
8 Do you generally do things quickly without stopping to think?		
9 Do you ever feel 'just miserable' for no good reason?		
10 Would you do anything for a dare?		
11 Do you suddenly feel shy when you want to talk to an attractive stranger?		
12 Once in a while do you lose your temper and get angry?		
13 Do you often do things on the spur of a moment?		
14 Do you often worry about things you should not have said or done?		
15 Generally do you prefer reading to meeting people?		
16 Are your feelings rather easily hurt?		
17 Do you like going out a lot?		
18 Do you occasionally have thoughts and ideas that you would not like other people to know about?		
19 Are you sometimes bubbling over with energy and sometimes very sluggish?		
20 Do you prefer to have a few but special friends?		
21 Do you daydream a lot?		
22 When people shout at you do you shout back?		
23 Are you troubled by feelings of guilt?		
24 Are all your habits good and desirable ones?		
25 Can you usually let yourself go and enjoy yourself a lot at a lively party?		
26 Would you call yourself tense or highly strung?		
27 Do other people think of you as being lively?		
28 After you have done something important, do you often come away feeling you could have done better?		
29 Are you mostly quiet when you are with other people?		
30 Do you sometimes gossip?		
31 Do ideas run through your head so that you cannot sleep?		
32 If there is something you want to know about, would you rather look it up in a book than talk to someone about it?		
33 Do you get palpitations or jumping in your heart?		

		Yes	No
34	Do you like the kind of work that you need to pay close attention to?		
35	Do you get attacks of shaking or trembling?		
36	Would you always declare everything at customs, even if you knew that you could never be found out?		
37	Do you hate being in a crowd who play jokes on one another?		
38	Are you an irritable person?		
39	Do you like doing things in which you have to act quickly?		
40	Do you worry about awful things that may happen?		
41	Are you slow and unhurried in the way you move?		
42	Have you ever been late for an appointment or work?		
43	Do you have nightmares?		
44	Do you like talking to people so much that you never miss a chance of talking to a stranger?		
45	Are you troubled by aches and pains?		
46	Would you be unhappy if you could not see lots of people most of the time?		
47	Would you call yourself a nervous person?		
48	Of all the people you know are there some who you definitely do not like?		
49	Would you say you were fairly self-confident?		
50	Are you easily hurt when people find fault with you or your work?		
51	Do you find it hard to really enjoy yourself at a lively party?		
52	Are you troubled by feelings of inferiority?		
53	Can you easily get some life into a party?		
54	Do you sometimes talk about things you know nothing about?		
55	Do you worry about your health?		
56	Do you like playing pranks on others?		

Follow the instructions below to assess you answers:

1 Obtain a score out of 13 for the Extrovert–Introvert dimension (E):
- 1 point for answering 'yes' to questions 1, 3, 17, 39, 44, 46, 49 & 53
- 1 point for answering 'no' to questions 15, 29, 32, 41 & 51

2 Obtain a score out of 3 for the Neurotic–Stable dimension (N):
- 1 point for answering 'yes' to questions 19, 35 & 55

3 Obtain a Lie score (L):
- 1 point for answering 'yes' to questions 6 & 24, and 'no' to questions 42 & 52

4 Plot your results on Figure 7.02. Extreme extrovert = 13; Extreme introvert = 0; Extreme neurotic = 3; Extreme stable = 0. If your 'lie' score is 3 or 4 your answers for the test will not be valid. Look at those questions again and think why this might be the case.

TASK 3

Discuss the strengths and weaknesses of using a self-report questionnaire such as the EPI to evaluate personality.

Eysenck later included a third dimension of Psychoticism–Intelligence, which indicted how tough-minded or tender a person may be. This was measured by using a modified version of the questionnaire known as the Eysenck Personality Questionnaire (EPQ).

Based on these claims it was suggested that certain personality types would be suited or drawn towards specific activities. It was generally claimed that most elite performers possessed stable, extrovert characteristics. Other claims included:

- Extroverts would be more likely to play high-action sports such as rugby and football.
- Stable individuals were more likely to participate in sport compared to the general population.
- Introverts would be drawn to individual activities, such as running.

Be able to give the advantages and disadvantages for all methods of personality testing.

However, despite these claims, numerous other researchers have been unable to prove conclusively that a particular personality type is required to participate in particular sports or needed to reach elite standard.

Cattell's theory: 16 personality factors

Raymond Cattell (1965) also suggested that personality was based on stable traits but thought Eysenck's theory to be too simplistic. He proposed that personality could be profiled into 16 categories which give a more accurate picture of people's characteristics and behaviour patterns. He measured these traits using the 16PF questionnaire, but accepted that responses may be different each time depending on motivation, mood and situational factors.

Whilst this allowed for a more dynamic approach to personality there was still no clear evidence to suggest particular personalities were more likely to be successful performers than others.

Evaluation of trait theories

The research completed by psychologists such as Eysenck and Cattell was widely criticised but provided a framework for further study and debate. Numerous studies have attempted to find correlations between choice of activity and personality type and, whilst there may be some evidence, there is no conclusive proof that particular traits are drawn to certain sports. However, there are some serious criticisms, some of which you may have already thought of and discussed based on your completion of the EPI.

Criticisms of the trait theories include:

- too simplistic

- they do not account for personality changing over time
- they do not fully account for environmental or situational factors
- they fail to allow for individuals actively shaping and understanding their own personality
- they are not an accurate predictor of sport preference
- they have limited value as a predictor of sporting success.

However, the identification of personality traits may be useful to a coach in order to highlight potential difficulties an individual might encounter and employ strategies to reduce any negative behaviour patterns that may occur.

Interactionist theories

HOT TIPS

Ensure you can outline the most commonly used personality tests and critically evaluate them.

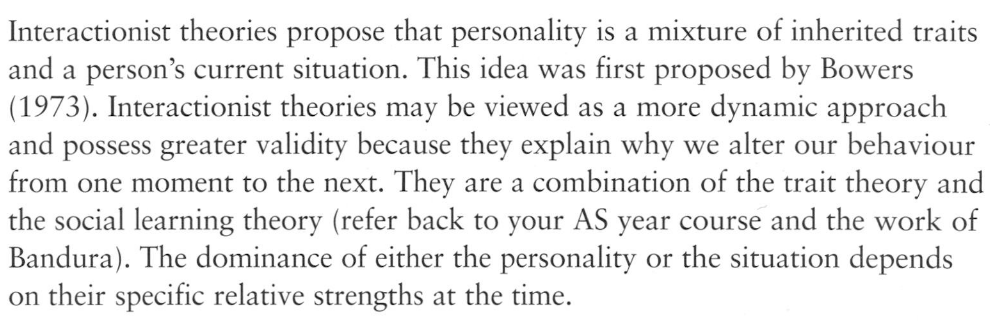

Interactionist theories propose that personality is a mixture of inherited traits and a person's current situation. This idea was first proposed by Bowers (1973). Interactionist theories may be viewed as a more dynamic approach and possess greater validity because they explain why we alter our behaviour from one moment to the next. They are a combination of the trait theory and the social learning theory (refer back to your AS year course and the work of Bandura). The dominance of either the personality or the situation depends on their specific relative strengths at the time.

For example, if the situational factors are strong, such as in a highly competitive match with a high extrinsic reward for success, these factors may be more influencial on behaviour than personality. However, if the situational factors are not strong, such as a recreational game, personality is more likely to control behaviour.

A common equation used to understand this approach was put forward by Lewin:

B = f (PE)

Where:

B = Behaviour, f = function, P = Personality and E = Environment.

The work of Hollander outlined earlier in the chapter is an example of the interactionist theory.

Consider similar situations in which you have found yourself and think how your behaviour may have altered as a result of differing factors. For example, has your behaviour changed if:

- a crowd or **significant other** has been watching
- the match is against an old adversary or a derby match
- the final outcome is of great importance or you have been provoked by the opposition?

KEY WORDS

Significant other

A person that is held in high esteem by the individual. Significant others may include family, peer group, teachers, coaches and role models.

The coach or sports psychologist can use this dynamic approach and attempt to identify characteristic behaviour patterns in specific situations. For example, if a player becomes over-aroused or aggressive in the final stages of a match if the result is close, various stress management strategies can be developed. Similarly, if the performer can pinpoint specific situations that have a negative impact on his or her performance, attempts can be made to alter behaviour patterns. However, this does mean the coach must recognise that each performer is unique, must devote time to developing an understanding of each person, and must treat them accordingly.

Measurement of personality

As you may have found from completion of the EPI, measuring personality is not straightforward. The two main forms of evidence collection used are self-report questionnaires and observation.

Self-report questionnaires such as the EPI, Cattells 16PF, and the Athletic Motivation Inventory (AMI) developed by Ogilvie and Tutko, are widely used because they are easy to administer, collection of data is straightforward and large numbers can be accommodated in a short space of time. However, they have all been criticised on several counts:

- their validity may be questioned as there is no agreed definition of personality
- their reliability may be questioned as the results may vary when the test is repeated
- participants' responses may be affected by their mood, situation and attitude towards the test
- respondents may lie or not answer accurately as they may be tempted to give socially acceptable answers
- participants may not fully understand the questions as they may be ambiguous or be interpreted differently
- possible response options, for example, 'yes' or 'no', may be too limited to provide a complete picture of the individual to emerge
- the ethics of personality testing have been questioned. Respondents should be fully informed of the purpose of the test and have the right to withdraw at anytime.

Many sports psychologists now utilise more sport-specific objective questionnaires, such as the Sport Competition Anxiety Test (SCAT) and the Competitive State Anxiety Inventory (CSAI–2), as they provide more reliable evidence. (These tests will be covered in detail in Chapter 17.)

Observation techniques involve the performer's behaviour being recorded in specific situations over a period of time. Similarities of behaviour are noted and a personality profile can be constructued. Whilst this method is useful as it observes relevant behaviour, it is time consuming and, subjective, and the recorder must ensure that her or she collects the data using the same criteria on each occasion.

Interviews can also be used, with a series of questions devised to reflect behaviour patterns in different situations. The questions could be similar to those found in the EPI and other questionnaires. The major problems associated with this method are the same as for questionaires.

Profile of Mood States (POMS)

The personality of a performer can change from moment to moment, but it has been suggested by Morgan (1979) that mood states are more useful in the identification of successful athletes. Rather than stable personality traits being the most important factor, mood states are temporary and change with the situation. Consequently this might be seen as a better predictor of performance and behaviour.

McNair, Lorr and Droppleman (1971) developed the Profile of Mood States (POMS), which measures six mood states:

- tension
- depression
- anger
- vigour
- fatigue
- confusion.

Iceberg Profile

On Profile of Mood Status (POMS) score successful athletes were above the waterline (population norm) on vigour but below the surface on the more negative moods, thus creating the profile of an iceberg.

Morgan compared the mood states of successful and unsuccessful athletes and suggested that to be a successful performer the score for vigour should

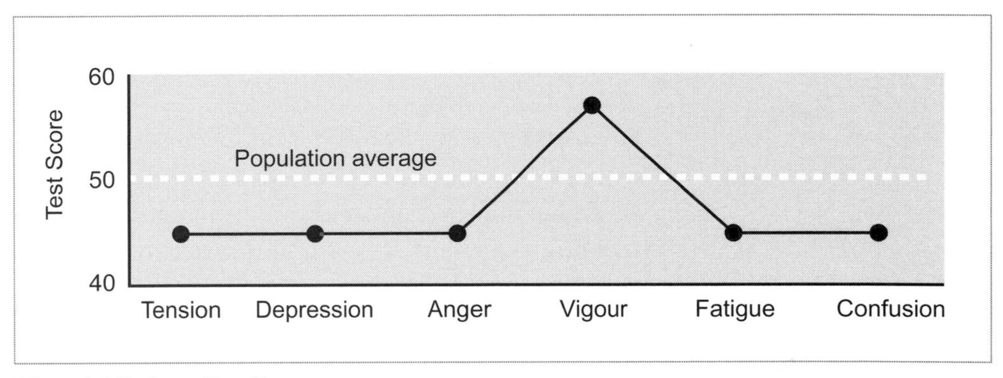

Fig 7.04 Iceberg Profile

be high, whilst the tension, depression, fatigue and confusion scores should be lower. This pattern is known as the **Iceberg Profile** as shown in Figure 7.04. The more pronounced the profile, the more successful the individual.

Sceptical approach

Based on the approach which questions the link between personality and sports performance

Credulous approach

Based on the approach which supports the link between personality and success in sport.

Whilst there has been extensive research to support this suggestion, there has also been evidence to demonstrate it is possible to reach elite level without displaying the Iceberg Profile. Some psychologists have also put forward the notion that as success is achieved this contributes to a positive self-image, high confidence levels and positive mood states, rather than this being a prerequisitive for success initially.

Personality and sporting performance

Based on the research evidence, is it possible to identify links between personality and sporting performance? Many of the theories appear to contradict each other. Some psychologists adopt the **sceptical approach,** which questions the link between the two, whilst other adopt the **credulous approach,** believing there is a link between success and personality type.

Some key factors have emerged:

- there is no clear link between personality type and success in sport
- there is no clear link between personality and choice of sport
- personality can be affected by the situation and the environment.

Revise as you go!

1. What is a trait?
2. What do trait theories suggest about personality and choice of sporting activity?
3. Interactionist theories propose that specific personality types are suited to particular sports – true or false?
4. Explain the characteristics of the deep psychological core as suggested by Hollander.
5. What does Hollander suggest influences the outer layer of his model (the role-related behaviour)?
6. Trait theories are a good predictor of sporting success – true or false?
7. Explain the formula B = f (PE).
8. How can a coach use the knowledge gained from observing particular behaviour patterns?
9. Name the three most common methods used to measure personality.
10. Outline Eysenck's Personality Inventory (EPI).
11. Suggest two advantages of using self-report questionnaires.
12. Suggest two disadvantages of the observational method of data collection.
13. The POMS for a performer with positive mental health is commonly known as the I____________ P_____________.
14. All successful elite athletes display a positive profile – true or false?
15. Which aspect of mood states gives the shape of the POMS graph in Figure 7.04 the distinctive peak?

Chapter 8: Attitude

Learning outcomes

By the end of this chapter you should be able to:
- explain what is meant by the term attitude
- describe the components of an attitude
- understand the importance of developing positive attitudes towards specific attitude objects and the impact a negative attitude can have on performance
- describe the methods used to assess attitudes and evaluate their effectiveness
- outline the factors influencing the formation of an attitude
- explain the methods used to change an attitude.

Introduction

The development of a positive attitude in an elite performer is vital if he or she is to achieve success. All athletes are motivated to win but they must also possess a positive approach and consistent behaviour pattern to training, preparation and competition, to compete at the highest level (see Achievement Motivation and Approach Behaviour in Chapter 10). Whilst an individual may strive to produce his or her maximum performance in the competitive environment, he or she may not be so committed to training. It is the role of the coach to ensure the high level of motivation is maintained in all aspects of the individual's training programme. If the performer has a positive attitude and this can be maintained, he or she is more likely to engage in activities enthusiastically and display persistent behaviour patterns in order to master the skills being developed. It is therefore vital that the factors influencing the formation of an individual's attitude can be identified and, if required, systems implemented to modify that attitude, thereby leading to more productive behaviour.

Definitions of attitude

As with many aspects of psychology there are numerous definitions of attitude, but they all have common elements.

TASK 1

With a partner devise a definition of attitude and attempt to describe the characteristics of your own attitude. Discuss with other students and compare your definition to those on page 100.

Several definitions of attitude are outlined below:

Aronson et al (1994):
'An enduring evaluation – positive or negative – of people, objects and ideas.'

Triandis (1971):
'Ideas charged with emotion (positive or negative) which pre-disposes a class of actions to a particular social situation.'

Allport (1935):
'A mental and neural state of readiness, organized through experience, exerting a directive or dynamic influence upon the individual's response to all objects and situations with which it is related.'

Based on these three definitions there are common threads:
- attitudes can be positive or negative
- they are generally stable and enduring
- they are focussed to a particular item or situation (see attitude object)
- attitudes are evaluative, subjective or beliefs.

Consider your own attitudes are they all positive? The truthful answer is probably not. It is important to realise that we possess both positive and negative attitudes and that they are each the focus of specific attention. Attitudes influence our behaviour towards certain situations; are based on our evaluation or beliefs our thoughts towards an **attitude object**. Our attitude may alter dramatically from one attitude object to another. For example, we may have a positive attitude towards sport in general but a negative attitude towards sports which involve physical violence. Similarly, it may be argued that just because a performer has a positive attitude towards a particular activity and regularly participates, it does not mean that he or she will always display a fully committed behaviour pattern in training or competition; other factors may have a more influential effect at that particular time. Therefore, we can say that whilst generally a positive attitude can lead to positive behaviour patterns, this cannot be guaranteed.

Attitude object
The focus of an individual's attitude. The object may be training, people, events, ideas or specific objects.

Make sure you can explain: how an attitude is formed: its components; methods to measure an attitude; implications for the coach; and methods to alter a negative attitude.

TASK 2
Discuss with a partner specific attitude objects to which you have a positive and negative attitude. Select an activity for which you have a positive attitude. Have there been occasions when you displayed a negative attitude? Why did this occur and how did your behaviour alter?

Components of attitude

Attitudes often form our beliefs and values, which in turn may influence our behaviour (though not always). To illustrate this it is useful to study Triandis' proposal that our attitude comprises three components: cognitive, affective and behavioural components. This is known as the Triadic Model.

Cognitive component

This aspect of attitude reflects our beliefs, knowledge, thoughts, ideas and information we have regarding an attitude object. For example, based on information received from our parents and physical education lessons, we may think swimming is good for us in terms of our health and safety.

Affective component

This involves our emotional response or feelings to the attitude object. For example, in the past we may have enjoyed swimming lessons and visited a local pool with friends. This may have led to positive feelings towards future participation. However, if the experience has been negative (possibly due to feelings of fear for personal safety) then future participation may be affected.

Behavioural component

The final component involves our intended or actual behaviour towards an attitude object. This is often based on our evaluation of the first two components. For example, due to positive beliefs and experiences about swimming, we actually participate regularly.

Whilst this structural analysis of attitude is a good starting point for discussion, it also shows that cognitive and affective components are not always an accurate predictor of behaviour. For example, how many of you think swimming is good for you and enjoy going but fail to actually visit a pool on a regular basis and complete a worthwhile exercise session?

Stereotype
A standardised image or conception shared by all members of a social group.

Discrimination
To make a distinction or to give unfair treatment because of prejudice.

Predjudice
A formed opinion, especially an unfavourable one, based on inadequate facts, often displaying intolerance or dislike towards people of a certain race, religion or culture that may be different from their own.

Formation of attitudes

An understanding of how attitudes are formed is vital if we are to develop desirable positive attitudes and suppress negative attitudes. This not only helps to create an environment in which healthy attitudes are created but can also break down the negative **stereotyped** opinions which may restrict participation and lead to **discrimination** and **prejudice**.

TASK 3

Discuss with a partner the reasons how you know you have a positive attitude towards your chosen practical activity (refer to the three components of attitude). Suggest how this attitude has developed.

From your discussion many of you will have mentioned that the major factor in attitude development is your past experiences. Those situations which have been enjoyable and successful will undoubtedly have meant your future participation, whilst those that have involved failure, disappointment or possibly injury will have had the opposite effect.

The majority of attitudes are developed through learning, either socialisation/social learning (watching others) or operant conditioning (positive reinforcement). (For each of these refer back to your AS studies to remind yourself of their full meaning.) Linked to these areas, other influences may have included parents, family, peer group, teachers, coaches, the media and role models. Some of these factors will be more influential than others and may change over time.

TASK 4

Discuss with a partner reasons how you know you have a negative attitude towards an attitude object. Suggest why this attitude has developed.

An understanding of how attitudes are formed allows us to identify areas which may develop negative attitudes. Some examples are listed below:

- negative experiences/failure
- fear of failure
- fear of injury/personal safety
- negative role models
- high task difficulty
- low self-confidence
- lack of support from family and friends/peer group
- cultural beliefs
- low status of activity in society
- stereotypical images.

Later in the chapter we will use this information to look at how a negative attitude can be changed.

You will need to know the names of different methods of measuring attitudes and evalute their effectiveness, but you do not need to know how to construct a specific type of questionnaire.

Measurement of attitudes

It is important for psychologists to ascertain the attitude of an individual in order to understand his or her beliefs and emotions. If these do not meet the expectations, required strategies may have to be implemented in an attempt to change negative aspects and to ensure positive behaviour patterns. There are several direct and indirect methods in which a person's attitude may be measured. The former includes interviews and questionnaires, whilst the latter involves observation of behaviour and physiological responses. The most popular methods are interviews and self-report questionnaires, as they are less subjective and therefore less interpretation is required on the part of the researcher.

Validity
The confidence we may have that the test or measurement produces the results that it is designed to do.

Reliability
If the findings of a test can be repeated, it is said to be reliable.

Whichever method is utilised, the **validity** and **reliability** of the data is important to identify specific issues and monitor future changes.

The three major types of self-report questionnaires are:

- Thurston Scale (1931)
- Likert Scale (1932)
- Osgood's Semantic Differential Scale (1957).

Thurston Scale

The questionnaire is made up of a number of statements covering a range of opinions towards an attitude object. Initially about 100 statements are issued to a panel of judges. Each statement is given a rating on their favourableness or unfavourableness on an 11-point scale. The statements with scores which vary widely are rejected until there are 11 favourable and 11 unfavourable items left. The remaining statements form the attitude scale. The average of the judges' rating becomes the scale value for the statement. Therefore, a statement with a value of 6 shows a neutral opinion, whilst a statement with a score of 10 indicates a favourable opinion and a score of 2 indicates an unfavourable opinion. This type of scale allows comparisons with other individuals but:

- is time consuming
- requires a large number of experts to construct the scale initially
- because the average show is used it can hide extreme attitudes.

Likert Scale

This is a simplified version of the Thurston Scale but still provides valid and reliable data. As a result this is the most frequently used form of attitude scale. A series of statements are constructed showing both favourable and unfavourable opinions towards the attitude object. The participant is required to respond to a statement on a 5-point scale, for example where:
5 = strongly agree, 4 = agree, 3 = undecided, 2 = disagree, 1 = strongly disagree.
Favourable statements score 5 for 'strongly agree' with unfavourable statements 1 for 'strongly disagree'. The scores are then totalled to provide an overall attitude score.

For example:
Gymnastics is good for you.
5 strongly agree, 4 agree, 3 undecided, 2 disagree, 1 strongly disagree

Gymnastics is dangerous.
1 strongly agree, 2 agree, 3 undecided, 4 disagree, 5 strongly disagree

Advantages of using scales such as these include:

- allows for a range of answers
- easy to administer
- cheaper and easier to construct
- produces reliable results.

Osgood's Semantic Differential Scale

The participant is required to give the attitude object a 7-step rating based on two opposing adjectives. The individual has to select a point which best reflects his or her feeling.

For example:
Rate how you feel about the safety of performing gymnastics.
Dangerous +3 +2 +1 0 -1 -2 -3 Safe

Whilst this is a quick and simple method to use, the selection of the word pairs may not allow the individual much choice and could be interpreted differently.

TASK 5

Construct an attitude questionnaire on a topic of your choice, for example, value of exercise or media portrayal of sport. Ask a group to complete it and evaluate the results and its effectiveness.

Evaluation of attitude scales

These types of questionnaires are useful but the results must be viewed cautiously as there can be several problems with collection of the data. These include:

- individuals not responding truthfully
- people providing socially acceptable answers
- misunderstanding of the question/ambiguous questions
- attitudes may be difficult to express in words
- wording of the statement may lead to respondents answering in a certain manner.

Changing attitudes

If changing an attitude, a measurement of the original attitude should be made to assess the impact of the attempted change.

It is important that we understand how to change an attitude if this will lead to a more positive approach and behaviour. If a performer has a positive attitude the coach generally has fewer problems to overcome in terms of motivation and task persistence. The two most commonly used methods are:

- persuasive communication
- cognitive dissonance.

Persuasive communication

The topic of changing attitudes is questioned regularly. Ensure you know the theoretical basis and be able to apply it to a practical situation.

This method involves the attitude being altered by persuasion. There are four factors which need to be considered in order for this to be effective:

- The messenger or person delivering the new ideas. If this person has certain characteristics then he or she is more likely to be successful. For example, the person should be of high status/a significant other, seen as an expert, likeable with good intentions and be attractive to the individual.
- The message should make the individual want to change his or her attitude. Therefore it should be clear, unambiguous, appeal to the recipient's sense of fear/failure, and be presented in a confident and logical manner. The higher the quality of the message the more likely the chance of success.
- The characteristics of the recipient can influence the degree of resistance to change. Factors to consider include original formation of the attitude, the strength of current belief and the level of education.

- The situation or context in which the message is being delivered. Different situations require different approaches, for example, when considering the formality of the environment, the level of support from other people, and the time and resources available.

For example, a performer may enjoy competing but is not focussed on training because she feels that she has sufficient talent to succeed (success has been achieved relatively easily to date). She may listen more favourably to a high profile athlete who visits her during a training session and who explains the value of a dedicated approach whilst recounting his own experiences. The performer is more likely to listen to the athlete than her current coach who has no experience of competing at elite level.

Consider how often the media use role models to promote positive messages of healthy lifestyle, fair play and sportsmanship, and to advertise sporting goods and numerous other products.

TASK 6

Select a high profile sports performer who has been used in an attempt to promote a positive attitude. Using the variable factors listed above, identify how this has been achieved. Discuss your findings with a partner. Has one advertising campaign been more successful than another?

Cognitive dissonance

Dissonance
An emotional conflict.

Triadic model
An attitude that consists of three components – affective (emotions) behavioural (actions) and cognitive (thoughts).

Festigner (1957) proposed that an individual's beliefs and thoughts have a direct influence on his or her behaviour. If these ideas or cognitions are challenged with new information then a person will experience a sense of psychological discomfort and will attempt to restore the balance of harmony. Such a conflict of beliefs is known as **dissonance**.

The aim of this method to change an attitude is based on the assumption that one of the components of the **Triadic model** (see pages 100–1) can be manipulated to create dissonance. After reviewing the new information or experience the individual either then develops a new attitude or retains the existing approach. If dissonance does occur the feelings of discomfort can be dispelled by following three stages:

- making the cognition/thought less important
- changing the cognition
- replacing the cognition.

Be able to apply the methods of changing an attitude to actual practical situations with relevant examples.

To alter the cognitive component of an attitude, new information can be provided. For example, the performer who thinks training is not required is given detailed benefits of adopting a more committed approach in terms of skill, fitness levels and possible future extrinsic rewards; he or she may be shown examples of others who have comparable ability but have wasted their talents by not training, or discuss the consequences of his or her actions with a respected significant other.

The affective component may be changed by giving a different experience, which may be viewed as more positive. For example, the performer is given more praise during training, set challenging targets, the activities are made more enjoyable and possibly less repetitive. Also, he or she may be given feedback based on knowledge of performance rather than being compared to others or focusing on the outcome. If the performer is concerned about his or her safety, manual or mechanical guidance may be used to alleviate such fears. Other methods may include giving roles of responsibility and encouraging the peer group to be supportive or apply pressure to conform, i.e. a sense of group/shared responsibility.

The behavioural component can be altered by ensuring the skill is simplified, success is achieved and subsequently reinforced, thus causing a positive affective component of attitude.

Often negative attitudes to an attitude object can be altered dramatically by the change of opinion within the peer group or society generally. For example, people's attitudes towards a sport which has declining interest due to indifferent results, lack of role models or stereotypical images can quickly change if:

- the team is successful
- high profile stars emerge
- non-stereotyped performers are involved.

Such a case can be found with the England cricket team. In 2005 the team were involved in a high quality Ashes series against Australia which gained huge amounts of media coverage. Subsequently there was an increase in the number of players and spectators from all sections of society.

TASK 7

With reference to the cognitive dissonance theory, explain how you would change the attitude of a group of young people who have a negative attitude towards swimming. Include practical examples to illustrate your suggestions.

Revise as you go!

1. Explain the term attitude object.
2. Name two common forms of questionnaires used to measure the attitude of an individual.
3. Attitudes can be used to predict behaviour – true or false?
4. List the three components of Triandis' model.
5. Give three factors that may influence the formation of an attitude.
6. Outline the term stereotype.
7. Explain the cognitive dissonance theory.
8. Suggest three strategies to improve the attitude of a performer.
9. How can the effectiveness of the persuasive communication technique be maximised?
10. Give two reasons why a performer's attitude may need to be changed.
11. Suggest strategies to control reactive aggressive behaviour.

Chapter 9: Aggression

Learning outcomes

By the end of this chapter you should be able to:
- differentiate between an aggressive and an assertive act
- understand the difference between hostile/reactive aggression and channelled/instrumental aggression
- outline the reasons why performers may become aggressive with specific reference to the Instinct theory, the Frustration–Aggression hypothesis, the Cue Arousal theory/Aggressive Cue hypothesis and the Social Learning theory
- explain the consequences of aggressive actions
- suggest strategies to control reactive aggressive behaviour.

Introduction

The term aggression is commonly used during modern sports commentary, but for the purpose of your studies it is often used in the wrong context. A performer is often said to be 'aggressive in their tackle' or 'playing aggressively in order to exert his dominance'. In fact the performer may actually just be displaying forceful behaviour rather than being aggressive. There is a grey area between acceptable and unacceptable behaviour and it is the role of the officials to determine when a player's behaviour has crossed this boundary. Many of these decisions are subjective and have to be made in a split second, the consequence of which may have a significant impact on the final result and manner in which the remainder of the contest takes place. It is also important to realise that acts of aggression may be interpreted differently depending on the nature of the sport. For example, during a tennis match punching an opponent is clearly unacceptable, but within a boxing match it is an integral aspect of the sport.

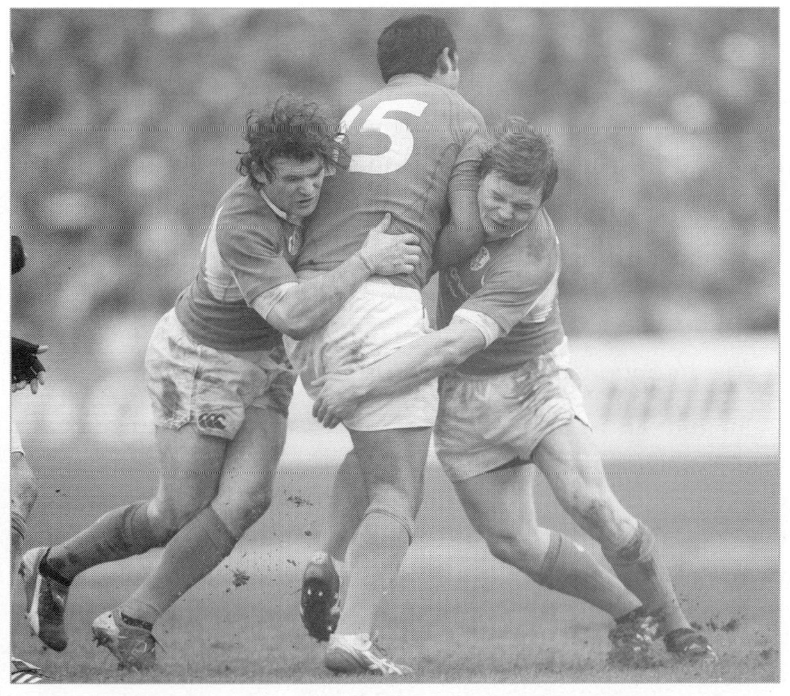

Fig 9.01 The term aggression is often used in the wrong context

The ability of the performer to control his or her aggressive behaviour is vital, not only for his or her own performance but because it may directly affect others if involved in a team activity. As a result it is important to identify potential causes of aggressive behaviour and implement appropriate strategies to deal with over-arousal.

Definitions of aggression

There are numerous definitions of aggression but they all have similar characteristics, as shown below:

Baron:
'Aggression is any form of behaviour directed toward the goal of harming or injuring another living being who is motivated to avoid such treatment.' (1977)

Bull:
'Any behaviour intended to harm another individual by physical or verbal means.' (1991)

Fig 9.02 Aggressive acts have common characteristics

Gill (1986) identified key features for an act to be aggressive:

- It must actually happen (behavioural), either physically or verbally. The mere act of thinking you may hurt someone is not enough.
- It must harm another person either physically or emotionally, for example, kicking a ball in anger or smashing a racket would not be classed as aggressive.
- It must be intentional, for example, an accidental collision which causes an injury is not deemed to be aggressive.
- Other psychologists also suggest that an aggressive act is outside the rules of the activity.

Sporting actions which possess these characteristics can be classified as hostile or reactive aggression.

Channelled aggression – instrumental aggression
The actions of the performer are within the laws of the game, with no intention to harm another player and are goal-directed.

Assertive behaviour
A form of aggression where the aim is to achieve a goal and any injury which may be caused is incidental.

The terms commonly used to describe actions that are acceptable are **channelled aggression** or **instrumental aggression** and **assertive behaviour**. However, there are subtle differences between these terms.

Channelled (or instrumental) aggression involves behaviour that is within the rules of the activity and aims to successfully complete the skill but has the side-effect of inflicting harm or physical pain. For example, a rugby player will attempt to tackle an opponent legally but also as physically as possible.

In contrast, Husman and Silva (1984) suggested that **assertive behaviours**:

- are not intended to cause injury or harm
- are goal-directed
- are within the rules, laws and spirit of the game
- only use legitimate force.

For example, a rugby player competing for a 50-50 ball on the ground who collides with another player would be assertive, as would a basketball player driving for a lay-up. As a result these actions would not be classed as aggressive.

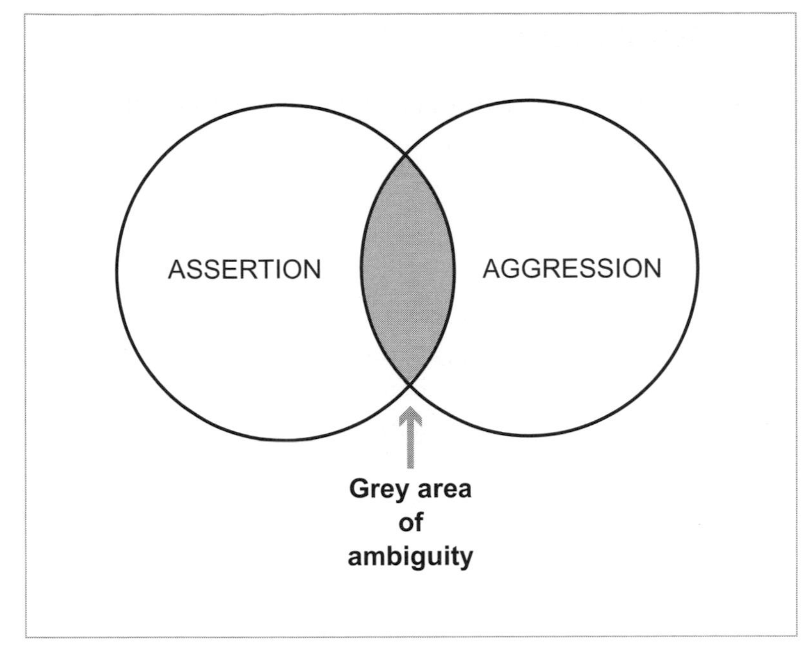

Fig 9.03 Aggression or assertion? – an area of doubt

TASK 1

For a sport of your choice, list two acts of reactive aggression, two acts of instrumental aggression and two assertive acts.

As you can see there are clear differences between the terms aggression and assertion. However, in many sporting situations there is an area of doubt involving intention and this increases if the nature of the sport involves physical contact. The subjective decisions of the officials are important if the sport is to be played in the correct spirit, allowing the players to participate fairly, safely and to the best of their ability.

Be able to give examples of aggressive and assertive acts and justify your reasons for each.

TASK 2

Watch a sporting event which involves physical contact, e.g. a rugby or football match, and list:

1 possible acts of aggression
2 possible causes
3 consequences of aggressive acts
4 acts of assertion.

Causes of aggression

When question

Before studying the theoretical basis of aggressive behaviour we should consider the specific causes within a competitive situation. The list below is not exhaustive and might not apply to all performers. It might also vary depending on the situational factors. Compare your list from Task 1 and your own experiences of sport to the factors listed below:

- nature of the sport – contact or non-contact
- rivalry between teams or players, e.g. local derby match
- high arousal levels
- importance of the event and expectation from peers, coaches, managers, the media
- nature and proximity of the crowd
- venue – home or away
- frustration at personal performance or that of others
- score line – large difference may lead to more aggression
- poor officiating
- copying other players, especially role models/significant others
- extrinsic rewards – financial gain, status, fame, selection to higher level team.

Theories of aggression

Many of the causes of aggression listed on page 109 can be applied directly to the theories outlined below. As with your study of personality, discussions focus on the nature versus nurture debate.

Instinct theory

As the name suggests, this theory is based on the nature approach. It argues that aggressive behaviour is innate, genetically inherited and, as a result, inevitable. Freud proposed aggression is due to our evolutionary development; our need to dominate and our death instinct (a trait directed towards self-destruction but balanced by our life instincts). The energy that builds up within us has to be released to maintain our well-being, and sporting participation allows this to occur in an acceptable manner – it is a cathartic release.

It is also suggested that displacement may occur via sport. Rather than display aggression in an inappropriate situation, such as the workplace, an individual will wait for a more suitable time, such as during a sporting contest.

Evaluation of the instinct theory

Numerous psychologists have criticised the theory because:

- human aggression is often not spontaneous
- aggression is often learnt and linked to culture – cultural norms can influence the levels of acceptable aggression displayed by individuals
- levels of aggression tend to increase during sporting participation rather than decrease
- performers in sports of an aggressive nature do not tend to display similar characteristics away from the sporting environment
- no biological innate characteristics have been identified
- rather than being warriors, early humans were hunter-gatherers.

Frustration–Aggression hypothesis

Dollard (1939) suggested an interactionist approach to aggression (see also page 95). He argued that individuals display aggressive behaviour due to innate characteristics and learning from others, becoming aggressive when their goal is blocked leading to frustration. He proposes that frustration will always lead to aggressive behaviour and aggression will always be caused by frustration. Figure 9.04 shows that if the performer is able to release his or her frustration via an aggressive act, it has a cathartic effect. However, if the aggressive act is punished the frustration levels are increased.

The performer's drive may increase due to a number of factors (as outlined previously), such as an opponent playing well against him or her. This causes an increase in frustration and a bad tackle may be the result. As the frustration has been released the player feels satisfied, but if he or she is punished, further aggressive acts may follow.

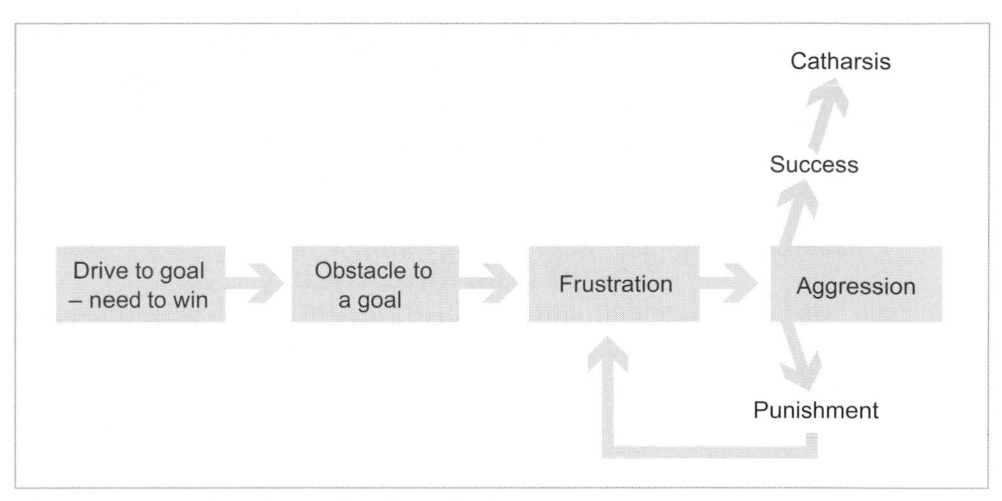

Fig 9.04 Frustration–Aggression hypothesis

Evaluation of the Frustration–Aggression hypothesis

- Not all frustration leads to aggression.
- Not all aggression is caused by frustration – it can be learnt.
- It does not account for situational factors or individual differences.

Cue Arousal theory/Aggression Cue hypothesis

Arousal
The energised state of readiness of the individual to perform a task, motivating him or her to direct his or her behaviour in a particular manner.

Cue
Signal, action or situation which will act as a trigger to perform a specific type of behaviour.

The work of Dollard formed a basis for other research and Berkowitz (1969) proposed the Aggressive Cue hypothesis, also known as the Cue Arousal theory, which incorporates learning and arousal into the explanation for aggressive behaviour. The theory suggests that frustration will cause **arousal** to increase but aggression will only occur if there are socially acceptable **cues** present. For example, a player may commit a dangerous tackle if the player's team or coach reinforces such behaviour. Similarly, a player may commit such an act if he or she thinks the official is not watching.

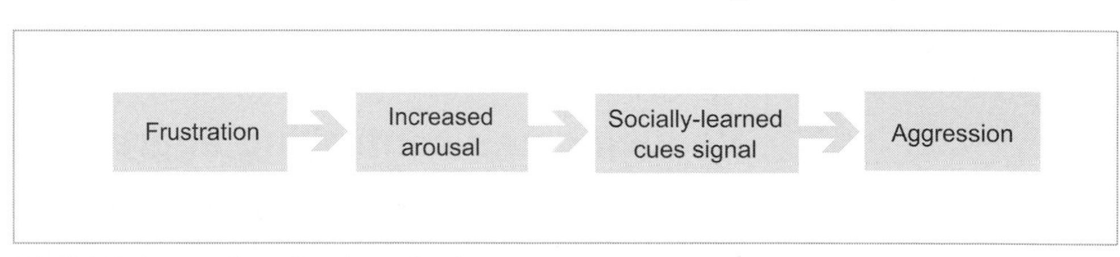

Fig 9.05 Aggression Cue hypothesis

Some sports-related cues are more likely to lead to aggression than others; for example:

- people associated with aggressive acts (a coach, player or fans)
- sports associated with aggression (contact sports)
- places associated with aggression (a venue linked to previous experience of violent acts)
- objects associated with aggression (bats, boxing gloves, etc).

If this theory is correct it may explain why some players are able to maintain their composure and control their arousal levels and not act aggressively.

HOT TIPS

Be able to outline the various theories of aggression and comment on their validity.

Evaluation of Cue Arousal theory/Aggressive Cue hypothesis

Berkowitz's theory is a more valuable explanation of aggression than earlier theories. Rather than simply being an innate response to an external stimulus, aggression is actually linked to learning and will occur only when suitable environmental cues are present.

Social Learning theory

KEY WORDS

Vicarious experience
The process of watching other performers and copying their actions. More likely to be successful if the model is a significant other or similar standard to the observer.

Bandura's Social Learning (1966) theory adopts the nurture approach, rejecting the idea that aggression is innate. It proposes that aggressive behaviour is learned through observation of others and copying their actions. If reinforced, the copied actions are repeated in similar situations. This is known as a **vicarious experience.**

There are many examples of vicarious experience in modern day sport. Due to the extensive media coverage of sport, many players see their role models or significant others displaying acts of aggression. Often such behaviour is not punished and consequently others copy their actions believing it is acceptable to act in this manner. The player may receive many forms of reinforcement which encourage such behaviour, from spectators, coaches, team mates and parents.

Fig 9.06 Social Learning theory suggests that referees should punish aggressive acts and ensure they apply the rules consistently

Whilst there are negative aspects to this proposal, it should also be viewed that if players can be taught unacceptable behaviour they can also be taught acceptable behaviour. If this is the case it is possible to control arousal levels and modify behaviour if the correct reinforcement is provided.

Evaluation of Social Learning theory

Whilst it is clear that many aggressive actions are copied from significant others and are more likely to be repeated if reinforced, the Social Learning theory does have some critics. It does not fully explain how some people may be aggressive without observing others if placed in a particular situation.

Reducing and controlling aggressive behaviour

As we have seen there are numerous causes of aggressive behaviour and each may be specific to the individual. As a result the strategies outlined below may not be suitable for all performers but must be applied differently depending on the situation. The responsibility for eliminating aggressive behaviour should be shared between the player, team mates/peer group, coaches, officials, spectators, the media and even sponsors.

Possible solutions to reduce aggressive behaviour include:

- Punish aggressive acts using penalties such as booking, sin bins, sending-off, bans and fines.
- Increase peer group pressure and highlight responsibility to the team.
- Remove the offending player from the situation by the coach (either a substitution or a change of position).

HOT TIPS

Be able to give practical examples of methods to control aggressive players and comment on the implications these methods may have on their performance.

- High quality officials who offer consistent interpretation of the laws.
- Positive reinforcement and rewards for non-aggressive play, e.g. fair play awards.
- Highlight non-aggressive role models.
- Reduce the importance of the event and the emphasis on winning.
- Increase personal fitness levels to delay the effects of fatigue.
- Set performance goals rather than outcome goals.
- Develop effective stress management techniques, such as positive self-talk, thought-stopping and imagery (see Chapter 17, pages 160–1).
- Lower levels of arousal via relaxation methods.
- Educate players on the difference between aggression and assertion.

TASK 3

Observe either a live or televised match. Note any instances when a player becomes aggressive. Outline strategies used by various people to limit aggressive behaviour and evaluate their effectiveness. Suggest alternative strategies which could have been used.

Revise as you go!

1. What is the difference between an aggressive and an assertive act?
2. Outline the Instinct theory of aggression.
3. Explain how an act of catharsis may influence aggression.
4. The Frustration–Aggression hypothesis suggests frustration will always lead to aggression – true or false?
5. Outline two criticisms of the Frustration–Aggression hypothesis.
6. How does the Aggressive Cue theory differ from the Frustration–Aggression hypothesis?
7. Explain the Social Learning theory of aggression.
8. Give three practical examples of possible causes of aggression during a game.
9. Suggest three strategies a coach may use to limit the aggressive acts committed by a player.
10. Outline how officials can limit aggressive acts.

Chapter 10: Achievement motivation

Learning outcomes

By the end of this chapter you should be able to:
- explain the concept of achievement motivation
- outline the characteristics of the personality types classified as 'need to achieve' and 'need to avoid failure'
- suggest factors which contribute to the adoption of each behaviour pattern
- discuss the effect that approach behaviour and avoidance behaviour has on performance
- suggest strategies to develop approach behaviour.

Introduction

Sports performers have to endure many hardships in order to be successful. Their innate ability and high skill levels will be insufficient to guarantee them a place on the victory podium. Throughout their training there will be times when motivation will be low because progress is not as fast as they initially hoped. During competition, results may be poor or emotions may have taken over causing a sub-standard performance. The following pages will study aspects of sports psychology which help to explain the reasons why this may occur and also outline strategies to deal effectively with emotional problems which the performer may encounter.

During your studies at AS level the topic of motivation was covered. Refer back to this area and refresh your memory about the importance of developing intrinsic motivation and the considerations which must be taken into account when using extrinsic motivation. This knowledge will help to develop a greater understanding of the topics discussed in the following pages.

Theory of Achievement Motivation
A theory which proposes that the behaviour of an individual is based on his or her interaction with the environment and desire to succeed.

The motivation level of an individual is a key factor in his or her desire to strive for success and directly affects his or her behaviour. It influences the performer in many ways; it ensures he or she persists even if he or she fails or finds tasks difficult, and may also encourage challenges to be taken even if the attempt is not successful. The **theory of achievement motivation** attempts to link personality with competitiveness and to explain why a performer may behave in a specific manner when faced with a particular task.

Theory of Achievement Motivation

McCelland and Atkinson (1964) viewed achievement motivation as a stable aspect of personality. They suggested we all have two underlying motives when placed in a situation in which some form of evaluation takes place:

n.Ach
Abbreviation for 'need to achieve'.

- The motive to succeed/need to achieve (**n.Ach**) – performers display the following characteristics:
  - a sense of pride and satisfaction from competing
  - perserverance
  - quick completion of the task
  - they welcome feedback
  - optimism
  - confidence
  - they take responsibility for their own actions
  - they attribute performance to internal factors (see Attribution theory, Chapter 13)
  - they are prepared to take risks and face challenges
  - they enjoy performing in front of others and being evaluated
  - they do not mind if they fail as it is seen as a learning experience.

n.Af
Abbreviation for 'need to avoid failure'.

- The motive to avoid failure/need to avoid failure (**n.Af**) – performers display the following characteristics:
  - attempt to avoid shame and humiliation
  - worry about failure
  - avoid situations with a 50–50 chance of success
  - choose tasks which are very easy or very hard
  - dislike personal feedback
  - attribute performance to external factors (see self-serving bias on page 133)
  - their performance tends to deteriorate when being evaluated
  - they give up easily.

Be able to explain, with the aid of practical examples, how the different types of personality will approach a specific situation.

When faced with a competitive situation we make a decision based on the relative strengths of each aspect of our personality. This can be expressed as:

Achievement motivation = desire to succeed – fear of failure

To put these characteristics into context, consider the following example. A club standard tennis player with a motive to achieve is given the opportunity to play someone of a similar or better ability. He will rise to the challenge and use the experience he may gain in the future, irrespective of the result. However, a player with a motive to avoid failure will tend to choose opponents who are better or worse than himself, because he is not expected to win or should do so easily. As a result, the outcome will not be a reflection of the player's ability.

Interactionist
The behaviour of an individual is a combination of his or her personality and the environment or situation at the time.

The theory of achievement motivation, an **interactionist** perspective, also takes into account the situation in which the performer finds him or herself. Our level of achievement motivation is a combination of personality and an evaluation of the situational factors. The evaluation assesses two aspects:

- the probability of success (this relates to the difficulty of the task)
- the incentive value of the success (this relates to the relative feelings of pride or shame following the final result).

This can be expressed as:

$$(Ms - Maf) \times (Ps \times \{I - Ps\})$$

Where:

- Ms = motive to succeed
- Maf = motive to avoid failure
- Ps = probability of success
- I = incentive value of success.

KEY WORDS

Approach behaviour
The performer is motivated to attempt a challenging situation even if he or she may fail.

Avoidance behaviour
The performer is motivated to protect his or her self-esteem and may not place him or herself in a situation where he or she may be evaluated.

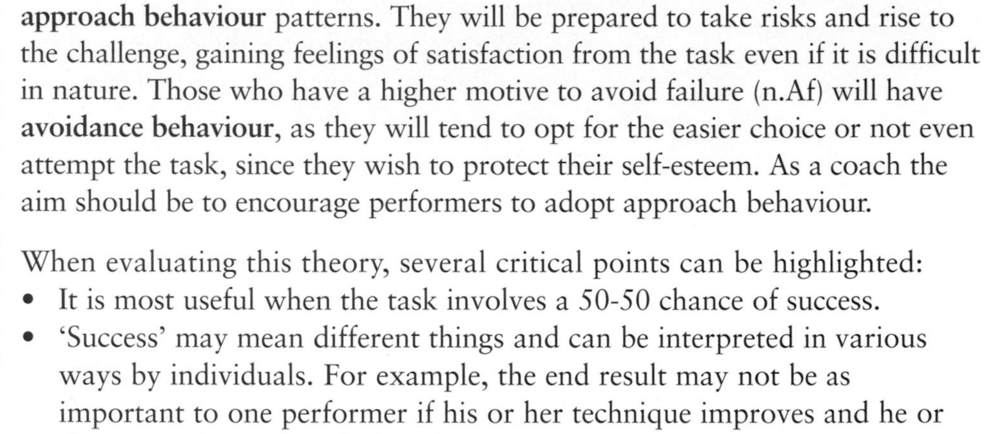

Performers who have a higher motive to achieve (n.Ach) will tend to have **approach behaviour** patterns. They will be prepared to take risks and rise to the challenge, gaining feelings of satisfaction from the task even if it is difficult in nature. Those who have a higher motive to avoid failure (n.Af) will have **avoidance behaviour**, as they will tend to opt for the easier choice or not even attempt the task, since they wish to protect their self-esteem. As a coach the aim should be to encourage performers to adopt approach behaviour.

When evaluating this theory, several critical points can be highlighted:

- It is most useful when the task involves a 50-50 chance of success.
- 'Success' may mean different things and can be interpreted in various ways by individuals. For example, the end result may not be as important to one performer if his or her technique improves and he or she meets the goal set before the event.
- Measuring achievement motivation using attitudes and anxiety scales may be unreliable.
- Achievement motivation is not a global concept – performers may react in different ways depending on the sport-specific situation and it may be more appropriate to consider an individual's level of competitiveness.
- No clear relationship between achievement motivation and performance has been established. However, it is useful when attempting to predict long-term motivation.

Fig 10.01 Performers with a high need to achieve will be prepared to challenge themselves in highly competitive situations

TASK 1

Explain with reference to Achievement Motivation theory the decision of each of the players in the following scenario:

'In a cup final the scores are level at the end of full-time. The coach asks different players to participate in a penalty shoot-out. Some agree and others refuse.'

Achievement Goal theory

More recently sports psychologists including Duda (1993) and Roberts (1993) have proposed the Achievement Goal theory that suggests that a performer's level of achievement motivation will differ and is dependent on the reasons for his or her participation, the goals set and the relative meanings of those goals. The performer may be set different types of achievement goals such as:

- **Outcome goal** – a goal that is set to judge the performance of the individual against others and the end result. For example, a cyclist may be set the goal of either winning the race or finishing in the top three places to qualify for the next round. The efficiency and manner of the performance is not relevant, only the final result. If the goal is realistic and within the performer's capability, and he or she achieves the aim, motivation and feelings of pride and self-esteem are increased. However, it can be demotivating if the performer is unsuccessful, especially after repeated attempts. The performer may feel shame and attribute the failure to his or her own ability, causing him or her to adopt avoidance behaviour patterns in the future.

Learn the characteristics of each personality type and how it may influence the type of goal setting to be used.

- **Task-orientated goal** – a goal that is used to judge the performance of the individual against his or her own standards, rather than in comparison with competitors. For example, a cyclist may set a number of goals for a race including:
  - applying the tactics as agreed with the coach
  - using effective slipstreaming behind another rider
  - comparing how close he or she rode to a personal best time, rather than the finishing position.

Be able to outline the different types of goals that can be used with practical examples. Be able to state which is the most appropriate with each type of personality.

If the goal of the coach is realistic, the performer can evaluate his or her own actions and not worry about comparison with others. This helps to reduce anxiety, allowing the cyclist to remain motivated wherever he or she finishes. This type of goal may be an effective method of developing a performer's approach behaviour and encouraging a positive motive to succeed. (For more on goal setting, see Chapter 17.)

TASK 2

You are the coach of a team for a sport of your choice. Give examples of team and individual goals you may set at the start and mid-way through the season. For each you should set both outcome and task-orientated goals. Discuss your goals with a partner.

Self-efficacy

The degree of self-confidence experienced by a performer when placed in a specific situation.

Learned helplessness

Feelings experienced by an individual when he or she believes that failure is inevitable because of negative past experiences.

Attributions

The perceived reasons a performer gives for his or her performances, both success and failure.

Development of approach behaviour

The aim of the coach must be to develop performers who possess a high level of achievement motivation, with a high motive to succeed and approach behaviour. There are various strategies which can be used to fulfil this aim including:

- providing positive childhood experiences and encouraging feelings of pride and satisfaction through success
- reducing punishment and negative feelings
- gradually increasing the task difficulty but ensuring that challenging tasks are set
- catering for all levels of ability
- raising levels of **self-efficacy** and avoiding **learned helplessness**
- setting appropriate outcome or task-orientated goals
- considering cultural differences
- using **attributions** correctly
- providing encouragement from significant others.

TASK 2

Copy the table below and place each of the following characteristics in the appropriate column, either Need to Achieve (n.Ach) personality or Need to Avoid Failure (n.Af) personality.

- a sense of pride and satisfaction from competing
- quick completion of the task
- optimistic
- perseverance
- attempt to avoid shame and humiliation
- avoid situations with 50–50 chance of success
- take responsibility for their own actions
- dislike personal feedback
- attribute performance to external factors
- performance tends to deteriorate when being evaluated
- welcome feedback
- confident
- worry about failure
- choose tasks which are very easy or very hard

Need to Achieve	Need to Avoid Failure

TASK 3

Complete the following passage using the words provided.

avoidance approach satisfaction easier choice
self-esteem risk

Performers who have a higher motive to achieve (n.Ach) will tend to have ____________ behaviour patterns. They will be prepared to take____________ and rise to the challenge, gaining feelings of ____________ from the task even if it is difficult in nature. Those who have a higher motive to avoid failure (n.Af) will have ____________ behaviour, as they will tend to opt for the ____________ or not even attempt the task, as they wish to protect their ____________ .

Revise as you go!

1 Name the two factors that influence a performer's achievement motivation.
2 List five characteristics of a need to achieve (N.ach) performer.
3 What are the two types of achievement goal suggested by the Achievement Goal theory?
4 Suggest why it is important to develop N.ach performers with approach behaviour.
5 Suggest two strategies a coach could employ to improve the N.ach characteristics of a performer.

Chapter 11: Arousal

Learning outcomes

By the end of this chapter you should be able to:
- explain the term arousal
- outline and evaluate different theories of arousal, including the Drive theory, Inverted-U theory and Catastrophe theory
- discuss the relationship between arousal levels and sporting performance
- explain the term attentional narrowing
- suggest strategies to control arousal levels.

Introduction

The key to success in sport is often linked to the effective ability of an athlete to control the emotions experienced when faced with extreme pressure. The perceived pressure may be due to a number of factors, many of which you will be able to associate with. For example, the pressures may include:
- an audience
- the expectations of team mates, the coach or parents
- the importance of the event and personal aims.

Often the performer will become anxious and this in turn will hinder his or her performance. The ultimate champion will usually be the one who is able to control feelings of negativity and focus his or her attention on the task at hand. Arousal affects individuals in different ways: some need to reduce their levels to perform at their best, whilst others need to be more 'psyched up'. During this section we will explore the concept of arousal and outline strategies that can eliminate its negative effects on performance.

What is arousal?

Arousal
The energised state of readiness of the individual to perform a task, motivating him or her to direct his or her behaviour in a particular manner.

Somatic
Refers to the physiological changes which the performer experiences.

Arousal should be thought of as a multi-dimensional state. It has been defined as:

Gould & Krane (1992):
'A general physiological and psychological activation of the organism (person) that varies on a continuum from deep sleep to intense excitement.'

From this definition we can see that arousal may be cognitive, involving thought processes, or **somatic**, causing a change in the body's response such as an increase in heart rate or sweat production. Arousal also involves a variety of states, ranging from sleeping to normal everyday responses and highly energised states with high levels of excitement, such as the feelings created by taking part in competitive sporting events. If we become over-aroused this usually has a negative effect on performance, caused by anxiety and stress (see Chapter 17 for more information). The level of arousal is controlled by the **reticular activating system (RAS)**, which interprets the level of stimulation entering the body and initiates an appropriate response. The primary aim of the performer is to control his or her arousal to an optimal level suitable for the activity undertaken, so that concentration and decision-making are not impaired.

Recticular Activating System (RAS)

A cluster of brain cells located in the central part of the brain stem, which maintains levels of arousal.

Theories of arousal

Ensure you are able to draw each of the arousal graphs and label them correctly.

There are three theories of arousal with which you need to be familiar:

- Drive theory (Hull (1943), Spence and Spence (1966))
- Inverted-U theory (Yerkes and Dobson (1908))
- Catastrophe theory (Hardy and Fazey (1987)).

Drive theory

Drive theory

A theory suggesting a linear relationship between arousal and performance.

The original **Drive theory** (Hull, 1943) suggested a linear relationship between arousal and performance. Figure 11.01 shows that as the level of arousal increases, the level of performance also increases. Therefore the more aroused a performer becomes, the better the performance.

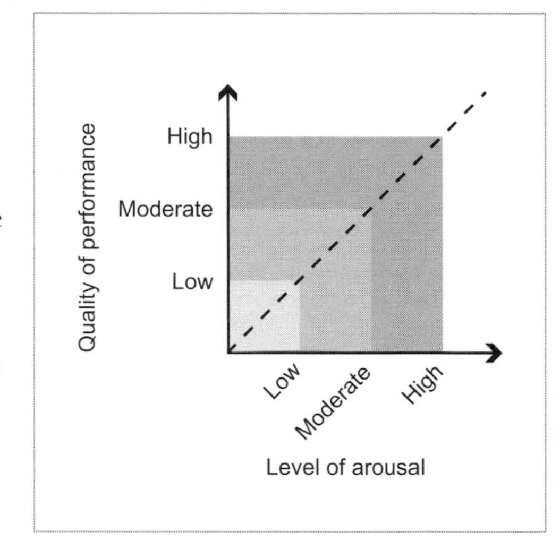

Fig 11.01 Original Drive theory

Dominant habit or response

The typical behaviour pattern of an individual, either skilled or non-skilled, in the execution of a task.

Later research by Spence and Spence adapted the theory, proposing that the performer's **dominant habit or response** would be more evident as his or her arousal level increased. This relationship is expressed as:

$$P = f\,(H \times D)$$

Where:

P = performance
f = function
H = dominant habit or response
D = drive or level of arousal

The effect of arousal on performance is therefore linked to the task and the experience of the performer. It is suggested that as arousal increases the following will occur:

- An experienced performer will complete the skill well because his or her dominant habit is well learnt.
- An inexperienced performer will execute the skill poorly as his or her dominant habit is not well learnt.

When discussing the Drive theory do not confuse 'performance' with 'dominant habit'.

KEY WORDS

Social facilitation
The influence of the presence of others on performance, which may be positive or negative.

Autonomous phase of learning
Stage reached by an athlete when he or she has learned a skill so that it becomes automatic, involving little or no conscious thought or attention when performing the skill.

Somatic or cognitive anxiety
A negative stress response which affects a performer's physiological responses, such as heart rate, or thoughts.

Inverted-U theory
A theory proposing that as arousal levels increase so does the performance, but only up to an optimum point after which performance deteriorates.

For example, during training a young badminton player has learnt the technique of a smash shot and is able to execute the skill reasonably well in practice. During a game situation, the pressure increases and the new skill that is not yet fully learnt is unsuccessful. However, an experienced player's smash would be executed properly during a match. The Drive theory is closely related to the concept of **social facilitation** (see Chapter 12). If this suggestion is accepted, novices must be able to develop their skills during practice situations with lower levels of arousal if learning is to be optimised.

Critics of Drive theory question some of the proposals as they do not explain the reasons why skilled performers in the **autonomous phase of learning** often fail to complete skills in situations of high arousal. For example, consider how often a professional player appears to make an easy mistake, such as missing a penalty or dropping a catch. According to the theory, an increased level of arousal should help the player's performance not cause it to deteriorate. The theory also takes no account of different types of arousal which may occur, such as **somatic or cognitive anxiety**.

Inverted-U theory

The Inverted-U theory (Yerkes and Dobson, 1908) counters some of the problems of the Drive theory by proposing that as arousal levels increase, so does the level of performance, but only up to an optimum point. The optimum point of arousal is usually reached at moderate levels of arousal. After this point further increases will cause the performance to deteriorate, as shown in Figure 11.02 below:

- **A: Under-aroused** – performer may show a lack of concentration and attention.
- **B: Moderate level of arousal** – optimal level of arousal, good selective attention and level of concentration.
- **C: Over-aroused** – performer may lose focus, miss cues, become anxious, experience muscle tension, make poor decisions and possibly display aggressive behaviour.

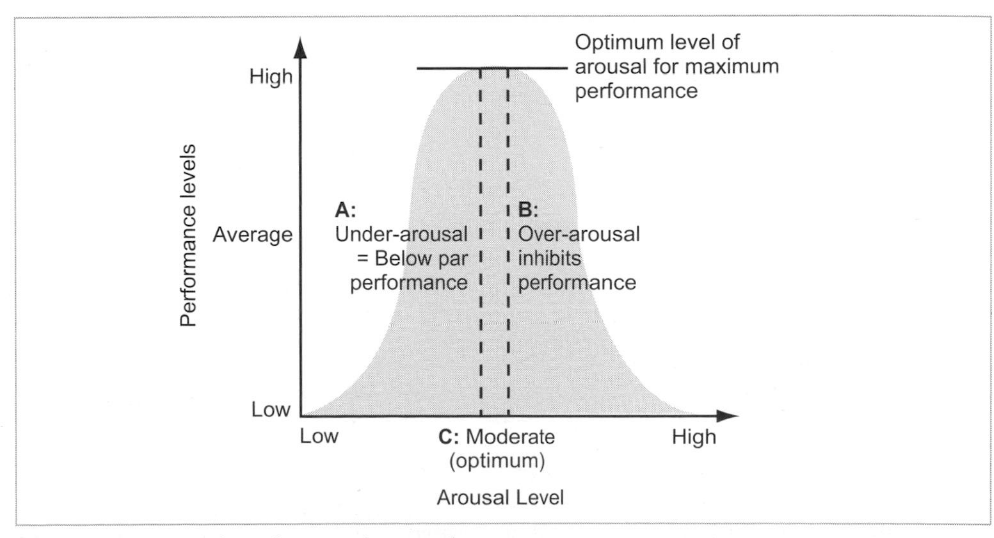

Fig 11.02 Inverted-U theory of arousal

Make sure you understand that the optimum level of arousal can alter for each performer, depending on his or her experience, personality, the task and the situation. Reinforce your answers with practical examples.

Each individual will have a different optimal level of arousal. Several factors need to be considered when attempting to determine the personal optimum level of arousal, including:

- **Nature of the task** – skills that are classified as complex or involve fine muscle movement (such as snooker, golf putting and archery) require a lower level of arousal than those of a gross or simple nature, for example, running, weight lifting or contact sports such as rugby.
- **Skill level of the performer** – performers who are experienced may be able to cope with higher levels of arousal as their movements are autonomous; in comparison, novice performers need to focus more carefully on relevant cues. For example, a novice basketball player will need to concentrate on the basic shooting action and may become over-aroused when faced with a defender, whereas an experienced player will be able to execute the skill under such pressure.
- **Personality of the performer** – performers who are more extrovert tend to be able to cope more effectively with higher levels of arousal and excitement when compared to introverted individuals.

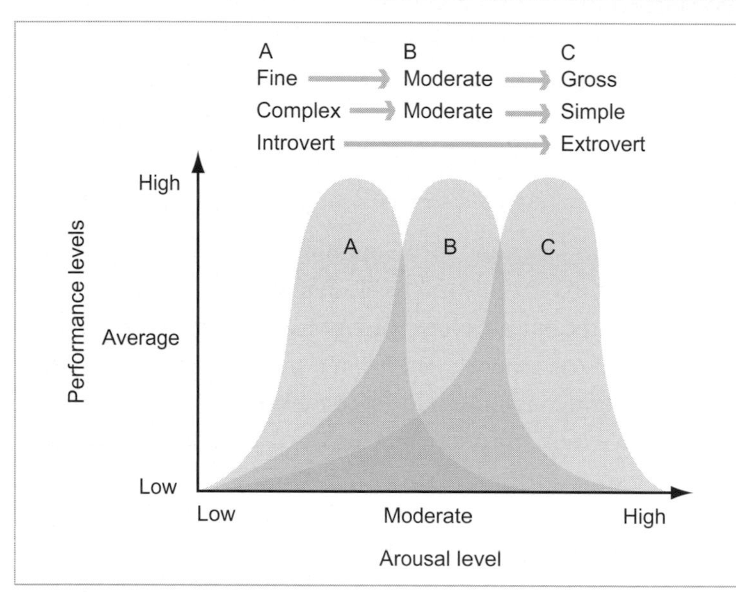

Fig 11.03 Relationship between arousal levels, the task, skill level and personality of the performer

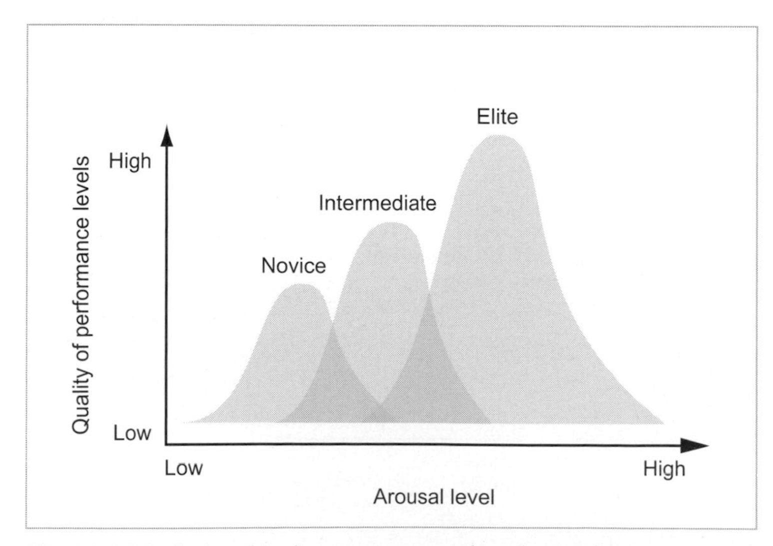

Fig 11.04 Relationship between arousal and experience

The coach must take all these factors into account and attempt to ensure the learning conditions are suitable for development to occur. The coach must also work with the performer to ensure that he or she recognises how different levels of arousal are required at various times during competition. For example, a rugby player may have to change his level of arousal from moment to moment as he may be required to execute a tackle and immediately afterwards attempt a penalty kick. As you can see, each skill requires a different level of arousal and unless the performer can make these adjustments, his or her performance may deteriorate.

A weakness of Inverted-U theory is that it does not explain how an individual may become over-aroused at some point during the performance yet still recover sufficiently to compete effectively. It assumes that when over-arousal occurs performance will continue to deteriorate.

Zone of optimal functioning

The unique level of arousal for each athlete, which allows the athlete to perform with maximum concentration and effort.

Hanin (1980) developed the work of Yerkes and Dobson and proposed that each individual has a **zone of optimal functioning**, commonly referred to as 'being in the zone'. Rather than occurring at the mid-point of the arousal continuum and at a specific point, there is an optimal band-width or area in which the performer achieves his or her maximum attention capacity.

When 'in the zone' the athlete often experiences:
- the feeling of the movement being effortless, without conscious control
- the ability to select the correct cues and make decisions quickly and effectively, in addition to remaining focused on the task without being distracted by other players or the audience.

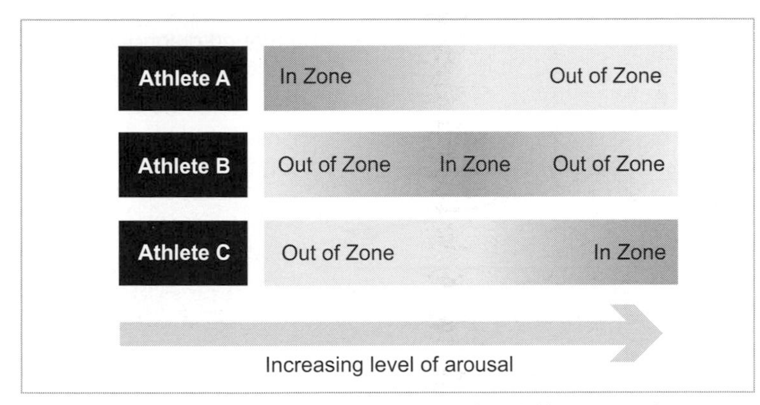

Fig 11.05 Zone of optimal functioning for different performers

It must be remembered that each individual will have his or her own zone of optimal functioning, as illustrated in Figure 11.05.

Critics of the theory claim it does not differentiate between cognitive and somatic anxiety. Also some studies have found that there is no significant difference in performance whether the athlete is in their zone or not.

TASK 1

Rank the following activities in order (1 to 10) of importance for high levels of arousal. Justify your decision.

- golf putt
- high jump
- hockey penalty flick
- boxing
- archery
- 100m sprint
- rugby
- pistol shooting
- weight lifting
- gymnastic vault

Catastrophe theory

A theory suggesting an increase in arousal levels will have a positive effect on performance, and that over-arousal may cause deterioration in performance but the individual may recover his or her optimum levels of arousal.

Catastrophe theory

The **Catastrophe theory** (Hardy and Fazey, 1987) suggests an increase in cognitive arousal will improve performance (as in the Inverted-U theory), but if over-arousal occurs one of two options may take place:
- If arousal levels drop slightly, caused by an increase in cognitive anxiety, a performer could recover sufficiently and regain his or her optimal arousal level. This may be achieved using supportive words from a coach or team mates, as well as the implementation of effective stress management techniques.
- If arousal levels continue to increase, both in terms of cognitive anxiety and somatic anxiety (physiological responses), the performer will not be able to recover and a catastrophe will occur. In other words, his or her performance will continue to decline and the performer will not be able to recover.

For example, during training a tennis player will have low levels of arousal and complete shots successfully, but in a competition she may become over-aroused causing a dramatic reduction in performance, including loss of concentration, ineffective decisions and poor execution of shots. The player may take time to recover from this position and return to an optimum level of arousal or her performance may continue to deteriorate. This is illustrated by Figure 11.06.

HOT TIPS

You will need to be able to sketch a graph of Catastrope theory and interpret its shape when linked to a practical example.

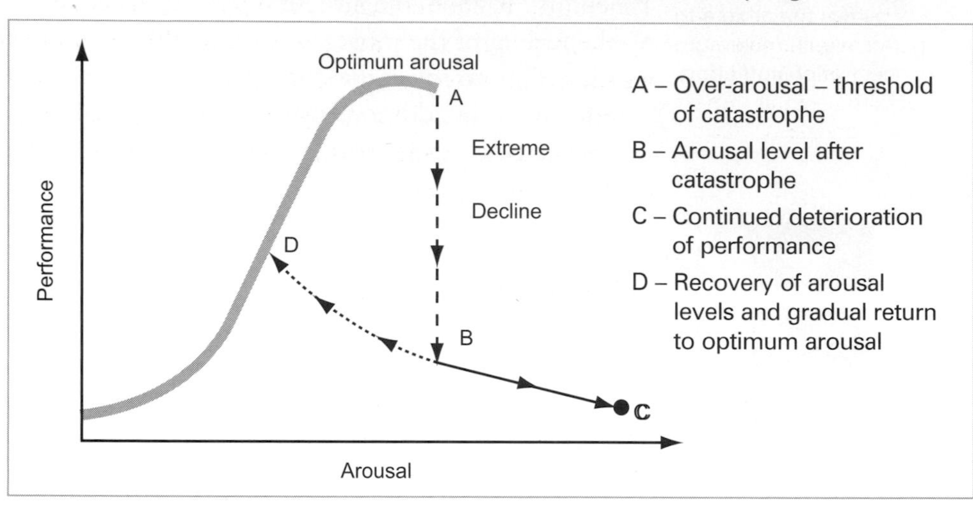

Fig. 11.06 Catastrophe theory

HOT TIPS

You need to understand the relationship and limitations of the different theories of arousal and be able to outline methods to control arousal levels.

TASK 2

In pairs, discuss a sporting situation in which you have participated where you performed well. Explain how you felt performing and identify how you maintained your correct level of arousal. Compare this situation to one when you became over-aroused. Discuss if you were able to recover and if so explain how this was achieved.

KEY WORDS

Cue-utilisation theory
This involves the use of relevant cues to focus the performer's attention as arousal levels increase in order to complete the task successfully.

Attentional narrowing
This links arousal theories directly to the individual's ability to focus on relevant cues.

Attentional wastage
This occurs when the performer's concentration is misdirected to cues that are irrelevant, causing a decrease in performance.

Attentional narrowing

During competition the aim of every performer is to ensure they select the appropriate cues and make the correct decisions as quickly as possible. When optimal arousal levels are reached the performer should be able to detect the correct stimuli easily. The **cue-utilisation theory** suggests that we detect the cues required to complete the task successfully. However, if arousal increases, the performer may actually begin to miss vital cues and signals which will lead to a reduction in his or her performance level.

Attentional narrowing links arousal levels directly to the individual's ability to focus on relevant cues and stimuli. If the performer reaches his or her optimal arousal level, he or she will identify the appropriate cues, but over-arousal will hinder the process. As attentional narrowing continues, vital cues will be missed, known as **attentional wastage**, leading to a decrease in performance. For example, a basketball player may not detect a team mate in an open shooting position or may fail to see a defender closing down his space as he moves in to shoot.

You need to understand the relationship between attentional narrowing and arousal theories, explain when it occurs and the impact on performance.

The attentional wastage occurs when the performer's concentration is misdirected to cues that are irrelevant, causing a decrease in performance. For example, as the performer becomes over-aroused during a game of basketball, he may listen to shouts from the crowd rather than focus on the position of players on court.

To ensure the correct level of arousal is reached and maintained, the performer and coach must work together to identify potential causes of weakness and over-arousal. They must then implement various stress management techniques (see Chapter 17) and other psychological strategies (as outlined throughout this section) to minimise the factors which may lead to over-arousal.

Revise as you go!

1. Explain the term arousal.
2. What is the purpose of the RAS?
3. Explain how the RAS differs depending on the personality of the performer.
4. What does Drive theory suggest will happen as arousal levels increase?
5. With reference to Drive theory, how will increased arousal levels affect the performance of experienced and novice performers?
6. What is the main criticism of Drive theory?
7. What are the characteristics of a performer who is over-aroused?
8. What is the term given to the optimal level of arousal that will produce the best performance?
9. According to the Inverted-U theory, at what level of arousal does optimal performance occur?
10. How does the skill level of a performer affect the optimum arousal level?
11. Explain how the personality of a performer may influence the optimum level of arousal.
12. How does the Catastrophe theory differ from the Inverted-U theory?
13. How can a performer recover his or her arousal levels and avoid catastrophe?
14. Explain the term attentional narrowing.
15. When does 'attentional wastage' occur during a performance?

Chapter 12: Social facilitation

Learning outcomes

By the end of this chapter you should be able to:
- explain the term social facilitation
- outline the different groups which affect performers
- discuss the relationship between social facilitation, arousal levels and performance
- explain the term evaluation apprehension
- suggest strategies to minimise the adverse effects of social facilitation.

Introduction

As we have discussed, the margin between success and failure at elite level is often very small. The nature of modern day sport means the actions of players are closely monitored by large crowds at the event, commentators and often a huge number of spectators via numerous media avenues. As you will know from your own experiences, when being observed arousal levels often increase. The ability of the performer to cope with the pressure of competing in front of an audience is another contributory factor to his or her overall effectiveness. Consider how often a performer becomes over-aroused because of the crowd and his or her performance deteriorates. However, a performer can also be motivated by people observing his or her performance, allowing the performer to produce a level of skill execution that he or she may not have thought possible. The concept of **social facilitation** attempts to explain why this happens.

Social facilitation

The influence of the presence of others on performance, which has a positive effect.

When participating in physical activity, the presence of other people, who may not be directly watching, may affect arousal levels. For example, there may be other competitors or other performers practising or even competing in the immediate area. All of these people may influence your arousal levels and affect performance.

Make sure you understand the relationship between the Drive theory and social facilitation. Do not get confused and think that as arousal increases so does performance – it depends on the experience of the performer.

Zajonc's model

Robert Zajonc (1965) suggested that:
'the influence of the presence of others on performance, may be positive or negative'.

If the presence of others, either in the form of spectators or other athletes, has a positive effect on performance, it is classed as social facilitation. If it has a negative effect it is known as **social inhibition**.

Social inhibition

Negative influence on performance caused by the presence of others during performance.

Zajonc's theory is closely related to the Drive theory of arousal. He suggested that as the level of arousal increases due to the presence of others, the dominant habit is more likely to occur. If this is the case we would expect the

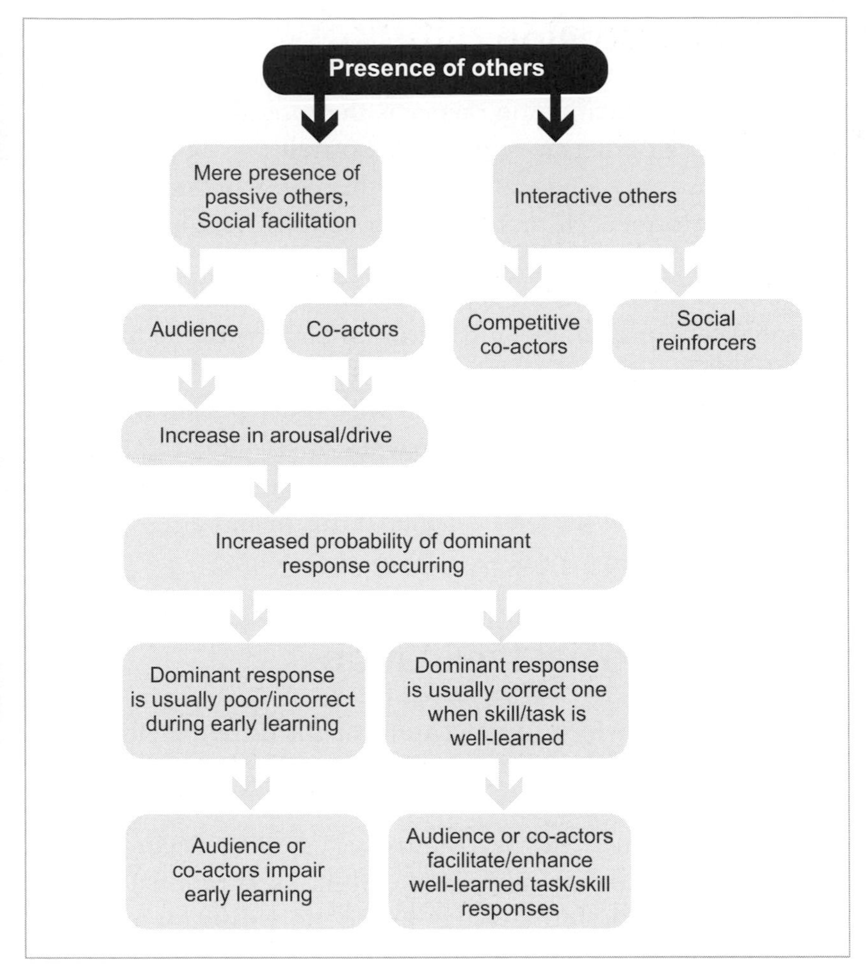

Fig 12.01 The effect of an audience will vary depending on the level of experience

performance of an experienced player to improve and that of a novice to decrease if they were being observed.

Figure 12.01 outlines the relationship between the different groups and the effect on performance.

As you can see, the 'others' are subdivided into four categories:

- **Audience** – those watching either as spectators at the event or at home via the different forms of media, including television, the radio or the Internet.
- **Co-actors** – those performing the same task but not in direct competition, e.g. another player on a badminton court.
- **Competitive co-actors** – those in direct competition with the performer, e.g. another badminton player in a game.
- **Social reinforcers** – those with a direct influence, e.g. a coach.

Within a sporting context, the 'passive others' are the important factors for us to consider. For example, the performance of an experienced badminton player when competing in front of an audience will improve as arousal levels increase. However, an inexperienced player is more likely to become over-aroused, causing him to execute his skills poorly as they are not yet well-developed.

HOT TIPS

Give clear explanations and examples of the different types of 'others' as suggested in Zajonc's model. Be aware of strategies to reduce the effects of social facilitation if performance is deteriorating because of the presence of others.

Other research suggests that the learning of complex skills can be hindered if an audience is present, and the execution of fine skills may also be adversely affected. However, if the skill is simple or gross in nature, co-actors may actually help to improve the final performance.

TASK 1

1. Observe a sporting event of your choice. Identify each of the 'others' as proposed by Zajonc and explain how they influence the performance of an individual performer.
2. Consider an event in which you have participated and explain how the presence of others affected your performance.
3. With reference to Drive theory, explain how your arousal levels influence your performance.

Evaluation apprehension

Evaluation apprehension
A sense of anxiety experienced by a performer, caused by the feeling that he or she is being judged by those in the audience.

Be able to give strategies with practical examples to reduce the negative effects of evaluation apprehension.

One weakness of the social facilitation theory is that not all performers are affected by the presence of others as suggested. Cottrell's work (1968) developed this initial proposal and stated that others only had an effect on arousal levels if the performer felt that his or her actions were actually being evaluated. This is known as **evaluation apprehension.** If this were the case there would be an increase in anxiety levels and a corresponding decline in performance. For example, a badminton player may be highly capable in the training environment and execute skills successfully. However, when placed in a competitive match with other people watching, she may worry about what the spectators, coaches or selectors think about her performance. This results in a deterioration in the performer's skill levels. If the observers were of perceived higher status or more knowledgeable, their presence may be even more threatening.

Factors affecting social facilitation

Trait anxiety
The general tendency of an individual to view situations as threatening.

Information processing
The process of gathering data, processing the relevant stimuli to form a decision and transferring the details to the muscular system.

There are numerous factors which may account for the differing effects on individual arousal levels, including:

- **trait anxiety** levels (see Chapter 17)
- personality of the performer (extrovert, introvert, stable or neurotic)
- previous experience (success or failure and current expectations)
- age and gender (younger performers may find it more difficult to be exposed to large crowds)
- knowledge of the watching crowd
- status of the observers
- nature of the audience (noise levels, hostile in nature, supportive, etc)
- proximity of the audience
- size of the audience and their surroundings – for example, a small crowd in a large stadium will have less influence than a small crowd in a small stadium.

Baron's Distraction-Conflict theory

HOT TIPS
Make sure you understand the relationship between social facilitation and evaluation apprehension.

Baron (1986) proposed that athletes must focus their attention on the demands of the task in hand, and anything which may distract them will hinder their performance. Think back to your studies of **information processing** and the suggestion that we can only process a limited amount of information at any time. When discussing the concept of social facilitation, the audience creates this effect. If the task is simple or well-learned, the effect of the audience on it will be less than that exerted on a complex or new skill. The implication for a performer has to be that he or she directs his or her attention to the task and attempts to ignore the distraction created by the crowd.

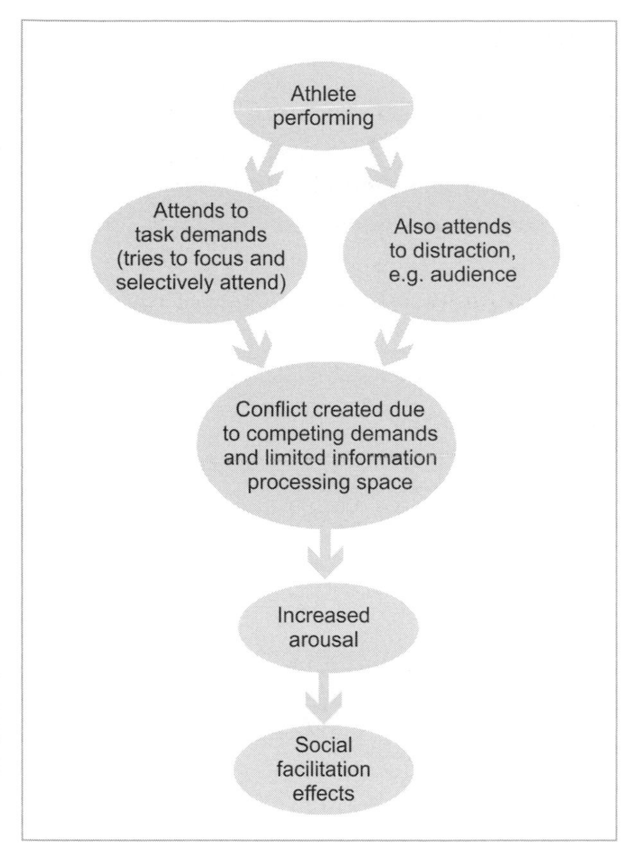

Fig 12.02 Baron's Distraction–Conflict theory

Home and away: advantages and disadvantages

We generally assume that a team playing at their home venue will have an advantage over their opponents. This may be due to a number of factors including:

- a larger number of home supporters
- familiarity of the surroundings
- a lack of travel required prior to the game.

Recent history has provided us with many examples of the home team performing well, especially at national level, and winning World Cup events even when they have not started out as favourites. For example, France won the football World Cup in 1998 and South Africa the rugby World Cup in 1999. Historically, more medals are won at major championships, such as the Olympics, by the host nation when compared to their results before or after.

However, this is not always the case and the performer must be aware of potential difficulties that may occur and impinge on his or her performance.

Key research concerning the 'home and away' advantage has found that:

- In the USA, more home matches are won than away matches.
- During the early rounds of competition, home advantage is helpful.
- As competitions progress, playing at home may hinder performance due to the increased expectations of the home supporters. This also applies to a team who are defending champions.

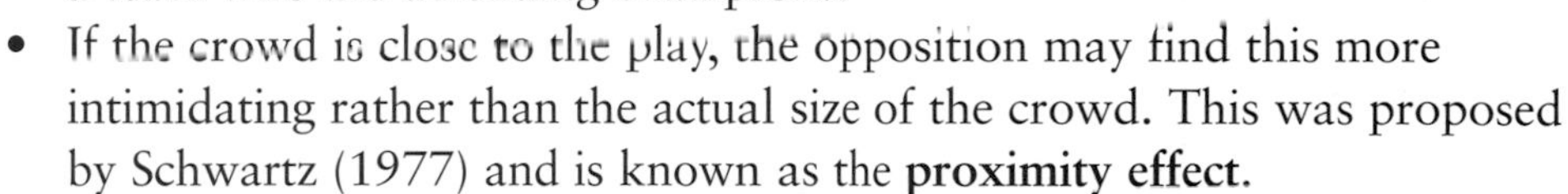

- If the crowd is close to the play, the opposition may find this more intimidating rather than the actual size of the crowd. This was proposed by Schwartz (1977) and is known as the **proximity effect**.
- More fouls are committed by the away team.

KEY WORDS

Proximity effect
The influence of a crowd is more marked when it is close to the play, rather than its size being the key factor.

Combating social inhibition

It is important the coach and the athlete work together to minimise the adverse effect of social facilitation. Outlined below are some of the strategies which can be used to help control arousal levels and prepare the performer for a competitive situation:

- develop the use of mental rehearsal
- train in front of others and gradually increase the numbers
- improve selective attention and cut out the effect of the audience

- reduce the importance of the event
- avoid social comparison with others
- encourage team mates to be supportive
- increase **self-efficacy**
- teach/coach in a non-evaluative environment initially
- use stress management and relaxation techniques
- use **attributions** correctly
- ensure skills are over-learned to encourage the dominant habit to occur as the levels of arousal increase.

Self-efficacy
The degree of self-confidence experienced by a performer when placed in a specific situation.

Attributions
The perceived reasons a performer gives for his or her performance, both success and failure.

Revise as you go!

1. What different effects might social facilitation have on novice and experienced performers and why?
2. The effect of social facilitation is caused by others. Name the four categories of 'others'.
3. Suggest three strategies a coach may employ to reduce the effects of social facilitation and improve performance.
4. How does evaluation apprehension differ to social facilitation?
5. How can the nature of the crowd influence evaluation apprehension?
6. Suggest two strategies to reduce the effects of evaluation apprehension.

Chapter 13: Attribution theory

Learning outcomes

By the end of this chapter you should be able to:
- explain the term attribution
- the implications for the correct use of attributions
- discuss different types of attribution with specific reference to Weiner's model
- explain the term self-serving bias
- outline the importance of attribution re-training.

Introduction

Whenever we play sport, after the event we will analyse and evaluate our performance. The reasons we give for our performance may influence our levels of motivation and future behaviour patterns. For example, if we feel the game was lost because of bad luck rather than our own lack of ability, motivation levels are likely to be higher and participation is more likely in the future. The manner in which a coach evaluates a performance and then provides feedback is vital if the individual is to adopt an approach behaviour in the future.

Attribution

The perceived reasons for the success or failure of an event or pattern of behaviour.

The perceived reasons we give for our performance, both success and failure, are known as **attributions**. The correct use of attributions is a crucial factor in maintaining a performer's:
- level of performance
- task persistence
- satisfaction of performance
- future expectations.

Attribution process

The attribution process is outlined below and explains the stages we go through when evaluating our performance.

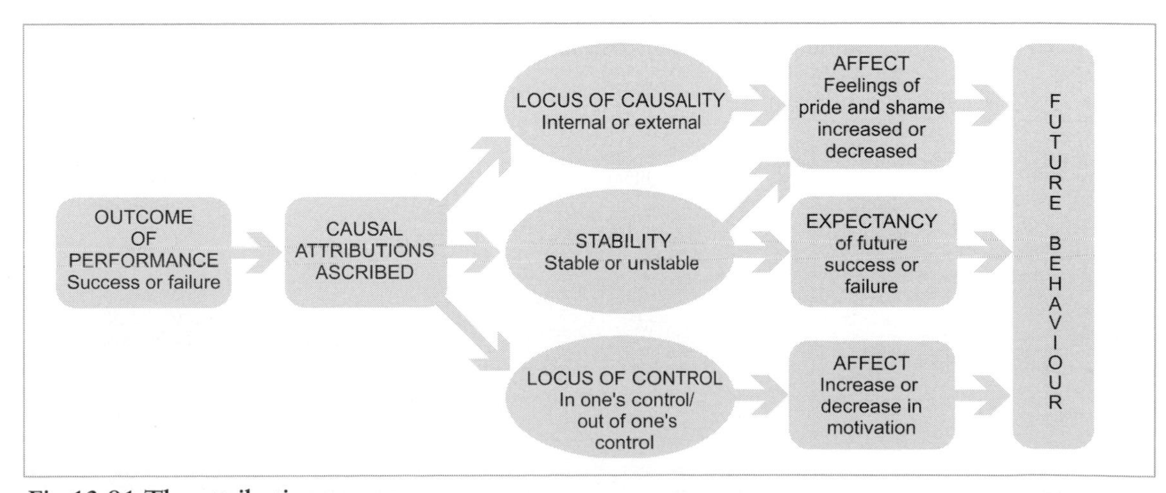

Fig 13.01 The attribution process

Weiner's Attribution theory

Attribution theory
This theory suggests that the perceived reasons given by a perfomer or coach after an event to explain the outcome, can affect future levels of motivation.

Locus of causality
To pinpoint the cause of the final outcome as being due to internal or external factors, i.e. those within or beyond the performer's control.

Locus of stability
Identified attributing factors which may have influenced the final result, and which may or may not change in nature over or short period of time.

Locus of control
Identified attributing factors based on the level of control the performer is able to exert on the final outcome.

Weiner's **Attribution theory** (1974) proposed that causal attributions (the factors affecting the result) tend's to fall into four areas:

- ability
- effort
- luck
- task difficulty.

He suggested this **locus of causality** could be sub-divided into two broad categories:

- **Internal causes** – factors within our control, such as ability and effort.
- **External causes** – factors outside our control, such as task difficulty and luck.

As seen in Figure 13.02, the second dimension in the model refers to the **locus of stability**. The relates to the changeable nature of the factor being discussed. For example, the ability of the performer would not change markedly from one week to the next, whereas his or her level of effort may well change dramatically depending on the situation. The stability dimension, therefore, is also sub-divided into:

- **Stable factors** – such as the level of individual ability, skill, coaching experience and the nature of the opposition.
- **Unstable factors** – such as the individual level of motivation and effort, arousal levels, refereeing decisions, quality of teamwork, imposed tactics, injury, form and pure luck.

Weiner's later work (1986) included a third dimension, the **locus of control**. This is also sub-divided into:

- **Personal control** – areas of performance over which an individual can take control, for example, effort, concentration or commitment to training. Based on Weiner's original model, effort is the only factor which can be classed as controllable.

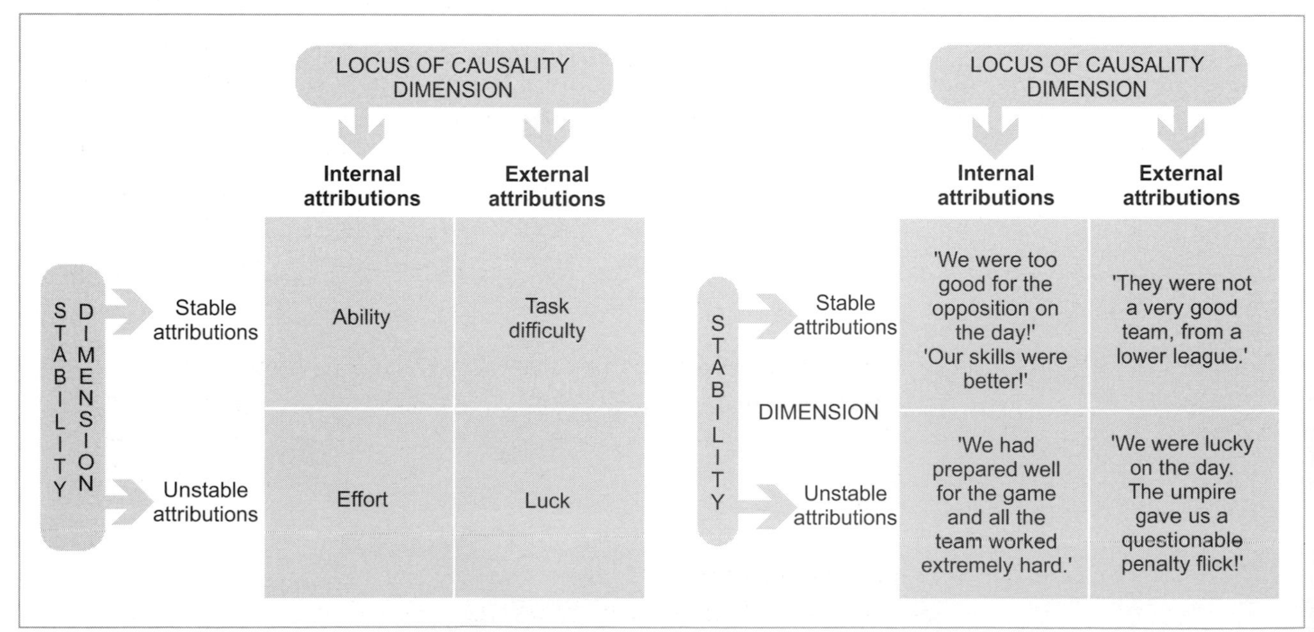

Fig 13.02 Weiner's two-dimensional Attribution model

Be able to draw or interpret Weiner's model and make sure it is labelled correctly with appropriate examples.

Be able to explain the attributions you would give to individuals or teams following a variety of results. Give practical examples and justify your reasons for each.

- **External control** – areas of performance over which an individual has little control, for example, the referee, tactics used by the coach or the quality of the opposition.

Attribution was seen to have an influential effect on the performer's level of pride or shame after the event. If he or she felt that success was due to internal factors such as ability or effort rather than external factors, the performer's level of pride increased along with his or her motivation. Similarly, if failure was attributed to internal factors, this resulted in a sense of shame and a corresponding decrease in motivation. Controllability also affects moral judgement and reaction to other people. A coach will often base his or her judgements on controllable factors. For example, praise is given to someone who has tried hard, even if the result was not as good as it could have been. However, the coach will be much more critical of a performance which is poor due to laziness or poor concentration.

TASK 1

Discuss with a partner two sporting events in which you have recently participated: one in which you were victorious and the other in which you experienced defeat.

1 List the reasons for the eventual outcome.
2 Draw Weiner's two-dimensional model and place each of the named reasons into the different categories.
3 Discuss your findings with your partner.

Effective use of attributions and self-serving bias

To maintain a performer's motivation you can attribute loss or failure to any factors other than internal stable factors.

Self-serving bias
The tendency of a performer to attribute his or her success to internal factors, such as effort and ability, while failure is attributed to external influences, for example, luck and task difficulty.

To use attributions effectively the coach must know how the performer is likely to react. This may depend on his or her personality, level of experience and current level of motivation. Generally, success is attributed to internal factors. This allows the performer to gain feelings of satisfaction, increasing his or her motivation and task persistence. However, failure should never be attributed to internal factors. In these situations the coach must use either external or unstable factors. This allows the athlete to believe changes can be made to improve his or her performance and it therefore protects his or her self-esteem. The use of attributions in this way is known as **self-serving bias**. This allows the individual to maintain his or her level of motivation and increase task persistence.

The use of attributions can be seen regularly after sporting events. Consider the statements below and observe how the respective managers use attributions to maintain the motivation level of their team. The following reasons for success and failure were given by two football managers during a post-match interview:

Victorious manager (away team):

- *'The striker took the goal well, despite the goalkeeper trying to put him off and hoping for the offside decision.'*

- *'We came away from home and won against the odds.'*
- *'The team worked hard and concentrated for the whole match.'*
- *'We learnt from the previous match, which we lost 3-1, and adjusted the tactics, which worked well.'*

Defeated manager (home team):

- *'The referee didn't award a penalty in the first half.'*
- *'The referee didn't play enough stoppage time.'*
- *'Rugby matches played on the ground previously have ruined the surface and affected our style of play.'*
- *'Strikers had a bad day and missed chances they normally would have scored.'*

Learned helplessness
Feelings experienced by an individual when he or she believes that failure is inevitable because of negative past experiences.

Attribution re-training
The process by which a performer is taught to attribute failure to changeable, unstable factors rather than internal, stable factors, i.e. lack of ability.

As we can see the correct use of attributions is important to develop self-esteem, maintain motivation and avoid **learned helplessness.**

Attribution re-training

Attribution re-training involves the coach or teacher developing and changing an individual's perception of failure, allowing him or her to deal with it effectively and improve future performances. For example, a talented runner may not believe that she has the ability to succeed, but the coach emphasising a slight variation in her technique will produce considerable improvement. This information may be sufficient to ensure that the runner will persevere with the task. Figure 13.03 outlines how attribution re-training may occur.

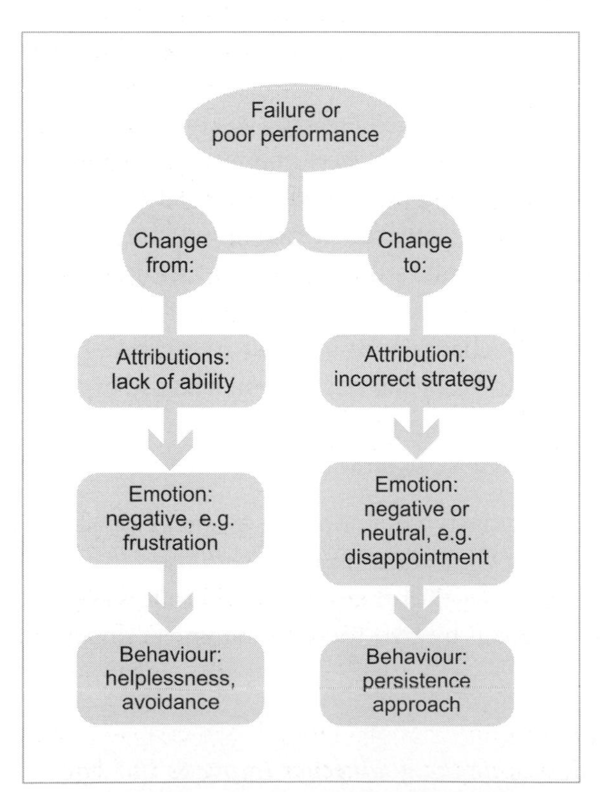

Fig 13.03 The process of attribution re-training

Revise as you go!

1. Why is it important to use attributions correctly?
2. Failure should be attributed to internal stable factors – true or false?
3. Explain the term 'self-serving bias'.
4. List the four categories of causal attributions and give an example of each.
5. Attributing failure to unstable factors minimises negative feelings – true or false?
6. What is attribution re-training?

Chapter 14: Self-efficacy

Learning outcomes

By the end of this chapter you should be able to:
- explain the term self-efficacy
- discuss the factors which contribute to the development of self-efficacy
- outline the concept of learned helplessness
- suggest strategies to develop high levels of self-efficacy and avoid learned helplessness.

Introduction

The potential performance of an athlete can be greatly enhanced if he or she has a high level of self-confidence in his or her own abilities. Similarly, if the performer enters a competitive environment with doubts concerning his or her ability, he or she is more likely to experience increased levels of arousal and possible anxiety. The role of the coach is not only to develop the physical skills of an individual but to ensure the performer approaches the event believing that he or she can perform successfully.

Self-efficacy
The degree of self-confidence experienced by a performer when placed in a specific situation.

Bandura (1977) proposed the concept of **self-efficacy**. He suggested the self-confidence level of an individual varies depending on the situation and it could actually alter from moment to moment.

There are numerous examples within sport of one unsuccessful attempt leading to a loss of confidence and a rapid decline in performance. There are also examples of one successful action boosting a person's confidence levels, allowing the performer to believe in him or herself and produce outstanding results. For example, a batsman in a cricket match may have never reached the milestone of scoring 100 runs and repeatedly loses his wicket after scoring between 80 to 90 runs. Each time this occurs the batsman may become anxious and lose confidence. However, after scoring his first century of runs, his level of confidence when placed in a similar situation may be higher and he may have a greater belief in his ability to repeat the feat.

Similarly, a young player may perform well in training but when faced with the prospect of competing in front of a large audience in a major event for the first time, may feel less confident.

Develop knowledge of how to improve the self-efficacy of a performer and use specific examples to highlight your understanding.

TASK 1

Reflect on your own experiences and consider situations in which you have felt very confident and not so confident. You may find if you experienced high self-efficacy your motivation levels and your task perseverance were higher.

The concept of self-efficacy does not only apply to individuals: it is of equal importance to teams. Consider how many teams appear to play to a higher level and with more consistency if they have high levels of self-confidence.

Often, cup-winning teams will quote a high level of self-confidence as a major influence and contributory factor in their success. Managers and coaches frequently make reference to the time taken to adjust to the demands of playing in a new environment or type of competition, and for the team to develop their self-confidence. When victory is achieved, it is often used to motivate the team by highlighting the fact that they have done it once, so therefore they should be able to repeat the performance. For example, during the build-up to the 2003 Rugby World Cup Finals, the England team had recorded victories over all their major competitors. This raised their level of self-efficacy and contributed to their positive attitude and approach to the competition.

The individual performer's level of self-efficacy can affect the:

- **choice of activity** – high levels will ensure the athlete participates
- **amount of effort applied** – high levels will ensure the athlete is highly motivated and applies him or herself fully
- **level of persistence** – high levels will ensure the athlete works hard and maintains his or her effort and commitment.

TASK 2

1 List six different sports in which you have participated.
2 Rank order them (1 being the highest) according to your personal level of self-efficacy.
3 Give reasons why you have a higher level of self-efficacy in the first two compared to the last two.
4 For your top-ranked activity, list three specific situations in which you have high levels of self-efficacy and explain why this is the case.

Development of self-efficacy

HOT TIPS

Learn the sections of Bandura's development of self-efficacy model and apply each to practical examples.

Bandura suggested that five key factors contribute to the development of self-efficacy, as illustrated in Figure 14.01.

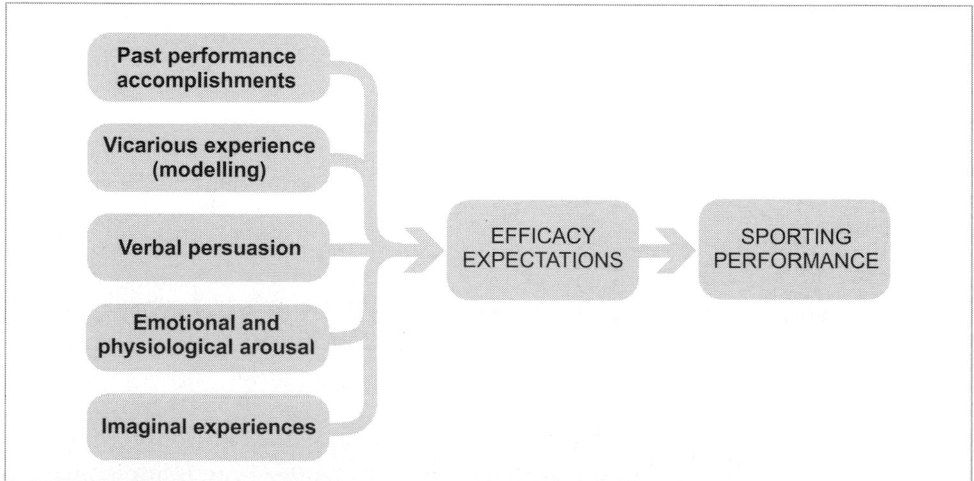

Fig 14.01 Bandura's model of self-efficacy development

While each factor is important, four are seen to be more influential:

- **Past experiences/past performance accomplishments** – a performer who has experienced success and enjoyment is more likely to develop high levels of confidence. For example, a cricket batsman who has developed a particular shot in training and scored runs regularly using the skill in a game will gain confidence and continue to use it when appropriate.
- **Vicarious experiences (modelling)** – a performer who has watched others achieving the task will feel that he or she is able to do so as well, especially if the model is of similar ability. For example, the cricketer watching one of his peer group successfully playing the shot is more likely to think that he too can achieve success.
- **Verbal persuasion** – a performer who receives encouragement about his or her abilities and actions, especially from significant others, will feel more confident about his or her actions or attempts. For example, the coach saying to the batsman 'well done, that was a great shot', or 'try to play the shot, but don't worry if it doesn't work this time'.
- **Emotional arousal** – a performer who is encouraged to perceive his or her physiological and psychological arousal before participation in a positive manner is more likely to develop high self-efficacy. For example, an increased heart rate, respiratory rate and cognitive anxiety should be viewed positively, in terms of being ready to compete, rather than being ill-prepared. For example, the batsman should be encouraged to remember occasions when he has been successful and to view any increases in arousal levels as an opportunity to improve his selective attention and anticipatory skills.

Developing high levels of self-efficacy

The coach has to consider each of the four components above and attempt to ensure that all are encouraged in a positive manner. Possibly the most influential factor is past performance accomplishments. Consequently success, no matter how small, is a key priority in the development of a performer.

Outlined below are a number of strategies to help develop positive expectations:

- experience early success
- observe demonstrations by competent others of similar ability
- set realistic but challenging goals
- set performance goals rather than outcome goals
- offer verbal encouragement and positive feedback
- develop effective stress management techniques
- use mental rehearsal
- avoid social comparison with others and limit the effects of social facilitation
- use attributions correctly by attributing failure to controllable, unstable factors.

Learned helplessness

As we can see, the development of high levels of self-efficacy is an important factor in the psychological preparation of an athlete. If the confidence level of the performer lowers this can lead to self-doubt and the performer may question his or her ability to complete the task, which in turn may lead to anxiety.

Learned helplessness
Feelings experienced by an individual when he or she believes that failure is inevitable because of negative past experiences.

Dweck (1975) proposed the concept of **learned helplessness**, in which performers attribute failure to internal, stable factors such as ability. Consequently they feel that when faced with particular situations they are unlikely to be successful and failure is the only viable outcome.

Learned helplessness is defined as:
'An acquired state or condition related to the performer's perception that he or she does not have any control over the situational demands being placed on him or her and that failure is therefore inevitable.' (Dweck, 1975)

There are many reasons which may contribute to this acquired psychological state other than inappropriate attributions, including negative feedback, criticism and a lack of success. As you can see the factors contributing to self-efficacy discussed in the previous section have a direct bearing on the likelihood of a performer thinking in this manner.

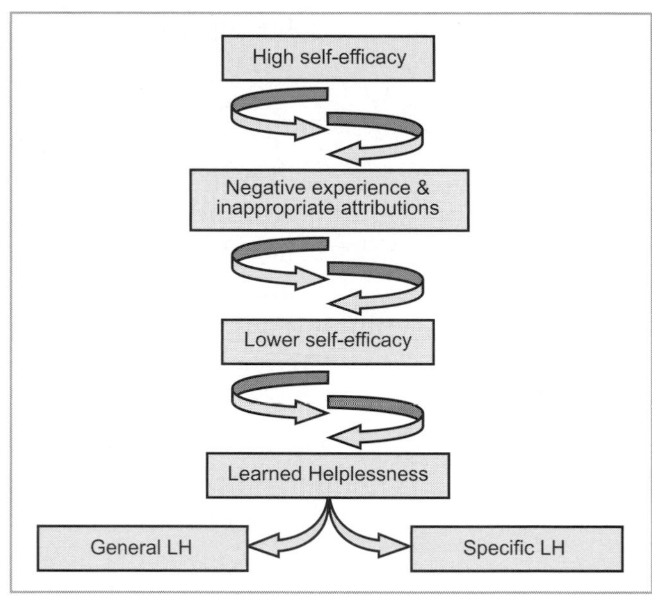

Fig 14.02 Performers may lose self-efficacy and develop learned helplessness

Learned helplessness can be sub-divided into two types:

- **General/global learned helplessness** – this suggests that the performer will think failure is inevitable in all sports or types of sport. For example, an individual may feel that she is unable to be successful in all water-based sporting activities because she has had previous negative experiences whilst swimming.

- **Specific learned helplessness** – this suggests that the performer will not necessarily be concerned about all water-based activities but certain sports. For example, when canoeing she may have capsized several times and been unable to control her movement. As a result the performer lacks confidence

Be able to explain the difference between specific and general learned helplessness, the causes and methods for avoidance or elimination.

and feels unable to attempt canoeing again for fear of failure.

There are a variety of strategies a coach can employ to avoid this condition and boost self-efficacy, including:

- all the strategies outlined to improve self-efficacy (see page 137)
- one-to-one attention
- attribution re-training
- highlight performance goals
- use correct attributions, i.e. attribute failure to external factors.

Research has shown the most effective methods to use are the final three. Even though the individual may achieve some success if the task is simplified, ultimately he or she must still believe that he or she is in control of the situation and must attribute reasons for that achievement to his or her own abilities.

TASK 3

In pairs, discuss how you could raise the level of self-efficacy of the following performers. Support your answers with practical examples.

- A gymnast entering a competition for the first time.
- A basketball player taking free-throws.
- A team playing in a cup final.
- A group of novice swimmers.

Revise as you go!

1. Why is it important to develop a performer's self-efficacy?
2. How does self-efficacy differ from self-confidence?
3. Name the four main factors which contribute to an individual's level of self-efficacy.
4. Why are performance accomplishments important to develop self-efficacy?
5. Explain the term vicarious experiences.
6. Suggest two methods to develop self-efficacy.
7. Suggest two reasons why learned helplessness may occur.
8. Explain the difference between general and specific learned helplessness.
9. Outline two strategies to reduce the effects of learned helplessness.
10. How might the inappropriate use of attributions contribute to learned helplessness?

Chapter 15: Group dynamics

Learning outcomes

By the end of this chapter you should be able to:
- explain the definition of a group and describe its characteristics
- outline the stages of group formation
- discuss the importance of cohesion within a group
- explain the term group productivity, identify reasons for poor group performance and suggest strategies to eliminate those factors
- explain the terms Ringelmann effect and social loafing
- describe strategies to overcome social loafing.

Introduction

Within all sports, individuals have to work together if success is to be achieved. The partnerships that have to be developed differ in nature depending on the sport, the number of people involved, the expected individual roles and the outcome expectation. The task of bringing together a collection of performers and moulding them into an effective team is a key priority in many sports. Consider how highly valued a good manager or coach can be and the consequences for them when it comes to winning and losing. There are numerous examples in sport where the most talented group of players has lost to a more co-ordinated team. Within this chapter we will look at how to maximise the effectiveness of each player and develop a cohesive team.

What is a group?

Fig 15.01 A group is different from a crowd

At first the term 'group' may appear straightforward but some clear distinctions must be made between this term and a 'crowd'. The definition below may help to clarify the difference:

McGrath (1984):
'Groups are those social aggregates that involve mutual awareness and the potential for interaction.'

Carron (1982) suggested that groups have the following unique characteristics:
- two or more people interacting
- all the individuals have a common or shared goal
- they all share a collective identity
- there are structured forms of communication.

Group dynamics
The process in which a group is constantly developing and changing when interaction takes place.

As the process of working together develops, the roles and norms of individuals within the team may alter. This is commonly known as **group dynamics** and it is important to recognise that change is inevitable and must be managed effectively if the group is to be successful.

Stages of group formation

The task of developing a team is not easy. There are many factors which may hinder the process, including differing abilities amongst the players, motivation, personality and attitude, in addition to the possible restriction of preparation time, coaching knowledge and effective leadership.

Be able to apply the stages of group formation to a practical situation, outlining the characteristics of each stage.

Tuckman (1965) suggested that there are four key stages which all groups must go through as part of their development:

- **Forming**, which involves the development of relationships within the group as individuals get to know each other. This often entails a player assessing where he or she may fit into the group structure based on others' strengths and weaknesses. It also provides a player with an opportunity to find out if he or she feels that he or she actually belongs within the group.
- **Storming** which often involves some form of conflict within the group as individuals attempt to establish their position, status and role within the group structure. It may involve confrontation with the leader until different roles are established.
- **Norming.** Once the structure has been established the group gains stability and starts to become cohesive. Players start to co-operate and work towards their common goal, accepting the agreed norms of the group.
- **Performing.** The final stage involves all the players working together towards their common goal. Each individual accepts his or her role and supports other group members accordingly.

Fig 15.02 A team working together

The time to complete the process of group formation can vary enormously depending on the complexity of the task, the attitude and the ability of the players, and the time available. Consider the task faced by an international manager/coach who has the most talented players to work with. Often his or her job may be more difficult than that of a club manager because of:

- limited preparation time
- players who are more familiar with other strategies and tactics
- higher levels of expectation.

Remember that once the final stage is reached there will be times when the whole process is repeated. This may occur due to an evaluation of the group's performance which leads to changes being introduced. Alternatively, a new player may join the team bringing different skills and abilities.

TASK 1

Devise and complete a task as a group with one person acting as an observer. The task must involve between four to eight students. For example, make up a game using specific pieces of equipment, construct a basic gymnastic routine or devise a group balance.

After completing the task discuss the effectiveness of the group and attempt to identify Tuckman's four stages of progression.

Cohesion

Cohesion

The extent to which a group works together to achieve a common goal.

Be able to evaluate the effectiveness of each form of cohesion and the relationship between the different forms.

The term **cohesion** refers to the dynamic process and tendency of a group of individuals to stay together whilst combining their efforts in order to achieve their goal. If a group is to be successful there has to be an element of cohesion; very few teams win if the players do not co-operate with each other. It has been suggested that cohesion develops as a direct result of success, whilst others feel cohesion is a pre-requisite. However, it is generally assumed that the more cohesive a group, the better the chance of victory.

Different forms of cohesion may be needed depending on the activity. For example, a netball team relies on players doing different things, such as fulfilling specific positional requirements (co-interacting), whilst rowers rely on everyone completing the same action (co-acting).

There are numerous factors (antecedents) which may contribute to the cohesiveness of a group. Carron (1982) suggested that these include:

- **Environmental/situational factors** – for example, the size of the group, the time available, training facilities, etc. The larger the size of the group the more interactions and potential co-ordination problems there will be between individuals.

Fig 15.03 The 2004 winning Olympic rowing team

- **Member characteristics** – including ability, motivation, affiliation to the group, similarity of opinions and status, satisfaction of other team members, etc.
- **Leadership style** – the involvement of the individuals in decision-making and expectations of the group.
- **Team elements** – for example, the desire of the whole team for success and, the nature of shared experiences either victorious or in defeat. Generally, the more success the group experiences, the higher the cohesiveness.

Other factors that may also affect the cohesiveness of a group include:

- **Nature of the sport** – interactive sports such as basketball and hockey rely heavily on cohesion, whereas in co-active sports (such as athletics and gymnastics) cohesion is not so important.
- **Stability of the group** – the longer the group is together with minimal changes, the greater the chance of cohesion.
- **External threats** – those who threaten the group may actually help to eliminate internal sub-groups and force the team to work together. For example, criticism from the media may encourage greater cohesiveness and a show of group loyalty.

Task cohesion
The interaction of group members and how effectively they work together to achieve a common goal.

Social cohesion
The interaction of individuals and how well they relate to each other.

Group cohesion can be sub-divided into two categories:

- **Task cohesion** – this refers to the interaction of individuals and how well they work together to achieve their common goal. For example, each player understands and fulfils his or her positional role effectively, allowing everyone else to do the same.
- **Social cohesion** – this refers to the interaction of individuals and how well they relate to each other, the level of support offered and the degree of trust. For example, the players enjoy each other's company and may socialise away from the sporting situation.

Each type of cohesion may help to develop an effective team, but it is generally agreed that task cohesion is vital for success and has greater importance than social cohesion. For example, a rugby team may be well drilled and highly skilled, allowing them to win the majority of their games, but may include groups of players that do not socialise with each other. A rival team may socialise very well but lack a co-ordinated approach to their game and as a result rarely win a match.

Fig 15.04 Effective task cohesion is essential if the team is to perform well

Social cohesion often develops as task cohesion improves, but it can undermine the effectiveness of the group. For example, a reluctance to question tactics or strategies for fear of conflict may disrupt the natural development of the group. Also, cliques may form and lead to problems of co-operation. If something like this happens, it is the role of the coach or captain to recognise it and to implement strategies to tackle such issues. This ensures that the task cohesiveness of the group is not jeopardised.

Strategies to develop an effective group and cohesion

HOT TIPS

Understand and explain strategies to improve the cohesion of a group with practical examples.

As we can see, developing a cohesive team is vital for success and there are numerous strategies which can be employed to achieve this, including:

- practice and training drills
- an explanation of roles and expectations within the group
- the setting of specific targets – individually and as a group
- giving individual players responsibility
- developing social cohesion away from the training or competitive situation
- creating a group identity (e.g. via clothing or a motto)
- encouraging peer support (using constructive advice rather than negative criticism)
- creating an open environment for discussion
- avoiding social cliques
- minimising the difference in status between players
- attempting to maintain stability and avoiding unnecessary changes
- identifing **social loafers** (see p.age 145).

KEY WORDS

Social loafer

Individual who attempts to 'hide' when placed in a group situation and does not perform to his or her potential.

Group productivity

The effectiveness of a group when completing a task.

Steiner's model of group productivity

The skill of the coach or manager is evident when he or she is able to mould a collection of individuals into an effective cohesive unit. However, this is not always an easy task even with a group of highly skilled performers. Steiner (1972) suggested that **group productivity** could be measured using the following equation:

Actual productivity = Potential productivity – Losses due to faulty processes

Where:

- **Actual productivity** is the performance of the group at a given time.
- **Potential productivity** is the quality and quantity of the group's resources relevant to the task. This is dependent upon skill level, the ability of the opponents, task difficulty and the expected outcome. For example, the manager of a national team is able to select the best players and in theory should have the best team. But there are numerous instances where players have underperformed or not been able to apply the strategies correctly. As a result they have not achieved their optimum performance level. It may be the case that in order to achieve the most co-ordinated approach the best player may have to be dropped from the team as others may contribute more to the overall team performance.
- Faulty processes are any factors which interfere with the group reaching its full potential. These are sub-divided into:
  - *Co-ordination losses* – caused by factors such as a lack of teamwork, poor execution of tactics, ineffective communication or misunderstanding of positional role.
  - *Motivational losses* – caused by factors such as a player losing concentration, under- or over-arousal, loss of motivation due to feelings

of not being noticed or valued, low self-confidence, reliance on other players or avoidance behaviour if the task is perceived as too difficult.

Ringelmann effect

KEY WORDS

Ringelmann effect
The performance of an individual may decrease as the group size increases.

As the group size increases there is an increased likelihood of co-ordination problems occurring and the performance of an individual decreasing. This is known as the **Ringelmann effect**. Ringelmann's research was completed nearly 100 years ago and was originally based on the amount of force exerted during a tug-of-war pull. The force exerted by a team of eight was not eight times as much as a solo pull. This is caused by a mixture of factors including a lack of co-ordination and a loss of motivation caused by being within a group.

Social loafing

Another factor which may cause a faulty process to occur is that of social loafing. This can be seen when a performer attempts to hide when placed in a group situation, often 'coasting' through the game and not performing to his or her potential. The performer may feel that his or her contribution to the team is not being recognised, evaluated or valued. He or she may also simply be relying on others to cover his or her lack of effort.

Strategies to minimise the effects of social loafing

If a player is loafing he or she is obviously being detrimental to the team performance and strategies to overcome the problem should be implemented immediately. Such methods may include:

- giving the player specific responsibility
- giving feedback; evaluating the performance; praising and highlighting an individual's contribution
- using video analysis
- setting challenging but realistic targets
- introducing situations where it is difficult for social loafing to occur (e.g. playing small-sided games)
- developing social cohesion and peer support
- varying practice to maintain motivation
- developing higher levels of fitness to avoid hiding to take a break
- highlighting the individual's role within the team and his or her responsibility to other players.

HOT TIPS

Give examples of faulty processes that may occur within a team and suggest strategies to eradicate or minimise them.

HOT TIPS

Be able to explain why social loafing and the Ringelmann effect might happen and the implications they have on group productivity.

TASK 2

Select a successful team and analyse its performance in terms of:

1 effectiveness of task cohesion
2 effectiveness of social cohesion
3 examples of poor cohesion and faulty processes
4 explanation of how cohesion was restored
5 strategies used to reduce social loafing.

Revise as you go!

1. Outline Tuckman's four stages of group formation.
2. How does a group differ from a crowd?
3. Explain the terms social cohesion and task cohesion.
4. List three factors which may determine the cohesiveness of a group.
5. Outline three methods a coach may employ to improve group cohesion.
6. Name two common faulty processes that may reduce group productivity.
7. Suggest three methods a coach may use to reduce faulty processes.
8. Suggest why the Ringelmann effect may occur.
9. Why might a group member lapse into social loafing?
10. Outline two methods a coach may use to reduce the effects of social loafing.

Chapter 16: Leadership

Learning outcomes

By the end of this section you should be able to:
- explain the term leadership
- outline the characteristics of a good leader
- evaluate theories of how leaders are developed: nature versus nurture
- identify different types of leadership styles and highlight situations where they are most effective.

Introduction

From your studies of group dynamics it should be obvious that, in order for a collection of individuals to be successful, clear guidance and leadership is required. Consider the importance in the modern world of sport of the coach, manager and captain. Often they are praised for their qualities and contribution to success but they are also the first to be singled out for criticism if the team fail to reach their potential. From your own experiences of watching sport, you will be able to highlight some effective leaders.

Definitions and characteristics of an effective leader

HOT TIPS

Be able to outline the characteristics of a good leader.

The definitions below explain the process of leadership:

Moorhead and Griffin (1998):
'The use of non-coercive influence to direct and co-ordinate the activities of group members to meet a goal.'

HOT TIPS

Questions may focus on evaluation of the theories of leadership.

Barrow (1977):
'The behavioural process of influencing individuals and groups towards set goals.'

Therefore, leaders play a vital role not only in co-ordinating the interaction between players but in inspiring them, maintaining their motivation levels, setting realistic targets and eliminating faulty processes immediately.

Fig 16.01 As captain, Martin Johnson led the England rugby team to World Cup success

TASK 1

Identify someone whom you consider to be a good leader. List the qualities that make him or her effective in the role and explain why you think he or she is a good leader.

The best player does not always make the best leader and specific qualities are needed to complete this role effectively. Outlined below are some of the characteristics which contribute to effective leadership:

- good communication skills
- interpersonal skills
- empathy with individuals
- approachable
- perceptual skills
- highly knowledgeable
- vision
- effective decision-making
- inspirational
- determined
- confident
- organised.

Theories of leadership – nature versus nurture?

HOT TIPS

Be able to suggest which form of leadership style is best suited to a specific situation and explain what the advantages and disadvantages may be for using a particular style.

As with other aspects we have studied, the psychological debate of 'nature versus nuture' is again relevant. Are leaders born or are they developed through the process of socialisation? Two contrasting theories are outlined below.

Great Man theory

This was proposed by Carlyle in the early twentieth century, who suggested that leaders inherit specific personality traits which enable them to be effective. According to this trait theory (which Carlyle only applied to men), leaders possess intelligence, self-confidence, assertion, good looks and a dominating personality. If this theory were correct, an individual would be an effective leader irrespective of the situation. Whilst there may be some similarities between leaders from different backgrounds, there is no conclusive evidence to support this theory. Consequently the trait approach has little credence today as there are many other factors of more relevance, such as how leaders emerge, the situation and the nature of the group being led.

KEY WORDS

Social Learning theory

This proposes we learn by observing others and then copying their actions. This theory has been covered in detail in several sections of your course already and you should be familiar with the different phases suggested by Bandura.

Social Learning theory

Social Learning theory outlines an alternative approach to the development of leaders. This suggests that all behaviour patterns are learnt due to environmental influences. For example, a player may observe his captain dealing with a difficult situation, such as maintaining discipline of the team during the final stages of an important match. In the future the player may be faced with a similar scenario and copy the captain's actions. It is a vicarious experience. A criticism of this theory is that it makes no allowance for any aspect of the trait approach and natural personality characteristics.

KEY WORDS

Interactionist theory

This theory proposes that leadership is formed due to a combination of innate traits and interaction with the environment.

Interactionist theory

The **Interactionist approach** combines both the trait theory and the influences of the environment. As a result it takes into account the need for differing behaviour patterns or leadership styles depending on the situation, the characteristics of the group and the required outcome.

Fig 16.02 David Beckham – a prescribed leader

Selection of leaders

An individual may become the leader of a group in two ways:

- **Prescribed leader** – an individual is appointed to lead the group by a higher authority from an external group. For example, often the captain of a national team is announced by the manager or the governing body.
- **Emergent leader** – an individual becomes a leader based on support from within the team. Emergent leaders are often nominated and elected based on ability, interpersonal skills and expertise. For example, many local club teams appoint their captain annually at their Annual General Meeting based on nominations and votes.

Leadership styles and their effectiveness

The term leadership style refers to the manner in which a leader decides to interact with the group. This may depend on the situation and the nature of the group. If the most appropriate style is adopted the group are more likely to be successful in their task. Lewin (1939) researched the effect that different styles of leadership would have on similar tasks with similar groups. The three styles and their effects are outlined below.

Authoritarian or autocratic leader

This leader dictates to the group what actions to take, with very little or no input from the members in terms of decision-making. This type of leader is generally not concerned with interpersonal relationships within the group is task-orientated, but with the primary focus being to complete the goal as soon as possible. The group works hard when this leader is present, but can become aggressive and independent when left alone. This style is most useful when the task needs to be completed quickly, is complex or dangerous.

Democratic leader

This leader encourages the group to discuss ideas and become involved in the decision-making process. However, he or she will make the final decision and oversee the completion of the task. This style of leadership is generally more informal and relaxed within the group. When left alone the group continues to work and co-operate to complete the set task. It is useful when working with more experienced or individual performers.

Laissez-faire leader

This leader tends to leave the group to their own devices, allowing them to make their own decisions and offering them little help with the decision-making process. He or she generally adopts a passive role and as a result the task is less likely to be completed. If the group is left alone they usually become aggressive towards each other, do little work and give up easily.

For effective leadership to take place, a leader should be able to adopt any one of the three leadership styles.

Whilst there are three different approaches, it is not suggested that a leader should choose one style and adhere to it. A leader should actually assess the situation and required outcome, then use this information to tailor his or her behaviour towards the group in the most appropriate way.

There has been extensive research into the most effective style of leadership to adopt and numerous theories have been proposed. Your studies have to focus on two approaches:

- Fiedler's Contingency model
- Chelladurai's Multi-dimensional model

Fiedler's Contingency model

This theory suggests the effectiveness of a leader is dependent on (contingent on) a combination of personality traits and the situation. Fiedler (1967) identified two types of leadership styles:

- **Task-centred/task-orientated leader,** who concentrates on efficiency, setting goals and completing the task as quickly as possible. This leader would adopt an autocratic approach. Such an approach would be desirable in dangerous situations, when time is limited, where there are large group numbers and when quick decisions are required.
- **Relationship-centred/person-orientated leader,** who concentrates on developing interpersonal relationships within the group. This leader would adopt a democratic approach. This approach would be useful when time is not such a crucial factor, when consultation is required and when personal support may help develop interpersonal relationships within the team.

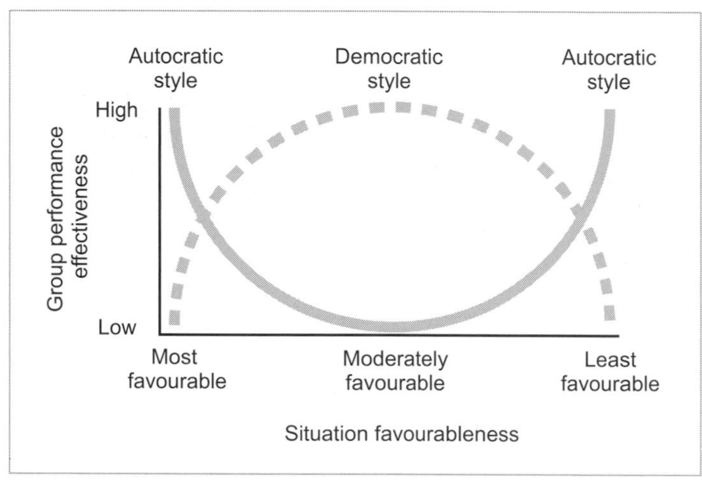

Fig. 16.03 Fiedler's Contingency model of leadership

Table 16.01 Characteristics of different situations relating to favourableness

Favourable situation	Moderately favourable situation	Unfavourable situation
Good leader/ student relationship	Friendly leader/ student relationship	Poor relationship with the group/hostile
Leader highly respected by group	Group prefers to consult with leader prior to decision	Leader's position is weak
Group of high ability	Reasonable ability level	Group of low ability
High motivation levels within group	Moderate motivation levels	Low motivation levels/ poor discipline
Good support networks, e.g. parents, community, etc.	Some support offered	Weak support networks, e.g. lack of community support
Task is simple or unambiguous	Task has no definite task-orientated outcome	Task is complex with no clear structure

The effectiveness of each style depends on the favourableness of the situation, which is dependent on:

- the relationship between the leader and the group
- the leader's position of power and authority
- the task structure.

Fiedler proposed the task-orientated style would be effective in very favourable or unfavourable conditions, whereas a person-orientated style would be better employed in moderately favourable conditions.

For example, the situation would be favourable if the coach of a team had the clear objective of winning the league, had good facilities and well-motivated players. In comparison, the situation would be unfavourable if a local team had a poor relationship with their coach, poor facilities and no clear objectives for the group. For both of these scenarios a task-oriented style could be used. A third rival team with a moderately favourable situation might have a reasonable relationship with their coach, limited facilities and a mid-table position in the league. In this instance a person-oriented style may be the most appropriate to develop task and social cohesion in preparation for next season.

Chelladurai's Multi-dimensional model

Familiarise yourself with the Multi-dimensional model. Be able to explain the different components and apply them to a practical situation.

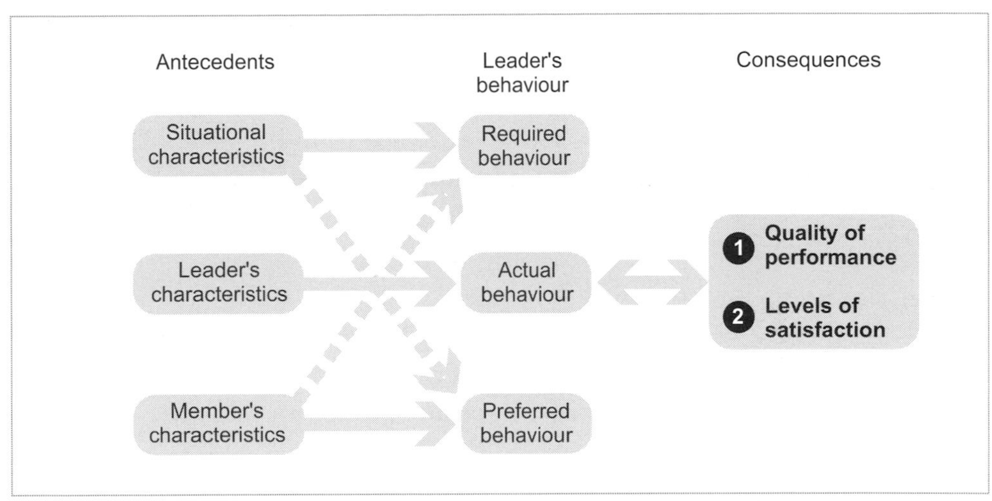

Fig 16.04 Chelladurai's Multi-dimensional model of leadership

Chelladurai's Multi-dimensional model (1980) suggests that before a leadership style can be chosen, three characteristics or antecedents must be considered:

- **Situational characteristics**, including factors such as the task difficulty, the nature of the opposition, the group size, the nature of the activity and the time available.
- **Leader characteristics**, including factors such as personality, experience, skill level and preferred leadership style.
- **Group members' characteristics**, including factors such as ability, motivation, age, gender and personality.

When these have been assessed the next stage involves consideration of the three types of leader behaviour:

- **Required behaviour** – depending on the situation and task, e.g. the coach may need to give instructions quickly during a timeout as time is limited.
- **Actual behaviour** – the leader's action in a situation, e.g. the coach issues directions in an effective, clear manner. This is often determined by the experience of the coach.
- **Preferred behaviour** – what the group want depending on their skill and goals, e.g. a team which is goal-orientated will want clear instructions, but

a team which merely plays for recreational reasons may simply want a rest and not necessarily want to be given detailed tactical ploys.

The more closely related the three types of leader behaviour are to the situation, the greater the chance of the group members' satisfaction. This in turn should lead to a more positive outcome.

For example, when a novice basketball team is preparing to play their first competitive game, the situational characteristics are to have fun and enjoy the game with no pressure to win. Therefore the leader's required behaviour is to help the players to use their skills in a team situation. The member characteristics are inexperienced and youthful players, therefore the required behaviour has the aim of ensuring they enjoy the experience irrespective of the result. The leader's preferred behaviour would involve providing support and encouragement to implement the player's skills. If the leader's actual behaviour does this, the team will enjoy the game and perform well in the match. However, as the team become older, more experienced and skilful, a different leader approach needs to be taken if the performance is to be effective and enjoyable.

TASK 2

Copy Chelladurai's Multi-dimensional model of leadership and complete it applying each of the following scenarios. How might the chosen leadership style differ to ensure group satisfaction?

1 The instructor of a group of novice climbers attempting an abseil for the first time.
2 The captain of an international team.

Revise as you go!

1 What is a leader?
2 List five qualities required to be an effective leader.
3 List the characteristics of an autocratic leader.
4 Explain how a democratic leader would interact with the group.
5 Name the three factors Chelladurai suggest need to be considered when adopting a particular leadership style.
6 Explain the term required behaviour.
7 How do the terms 'actual behaviour' and 'preferred behaviour' of the leader differ?
8 Explain the term favourableness and describe how it affects the style of leadership.
9 What characteristics might a group possess that would make the democratic leadership style most suitable?
10 When might an autocratic style of leadership be most appropriate to use?

Chapter 17: Stress and stress management

Learning outcomes

By the end of this chapter you should be able to:
- identify the characteristics and causes of stress
- understand the impact of stress on sporting performance
- explain the different forms of anxiety
- outline methods to measure anxiety levels for individual performers
- suggest strategies to combat anxiety and control arousal levels
- outline how to use goal setting effectively to help reduce levels of anxiety.

Introduction

HOT TIPS

Throughout this chapter think about your own experiences whilst participating in sport and attempt to relate the theoretical explanations to your own feelings and actions.

During your studies of sports psychology a key element in most topic areas is the ability of the performer to control his or her emotions, which then allows him or her to execute the appropriate skills and tactics to the best of his or her ability. In the modern world of sport the difference between success and failure is measured in hundredths of a second or a moment of inspiration from a player. All performers are physically well prepared and there is little to separate individuals. Coaches often highlight the importance of emotional control as a key factor in victory or defeat. The ability to manage stress levels can make the significant difference in the final result.

Definitions of stress

KEY WORDS

Stress
The perceived imbalance between the demands of the task and the individual's ability to complete the task.

The term **stress** is often used to describe the negative feelings a person experiences when placed in a potentially threatening situation. However, a clear distinction must initially be made between stress which has a positive effect and stress which has a negative effect on the individual.

The definitions below explain in broad terms the reaction of an individual:

Seyle (1956):
'The non-specific response of the body to any demand made on it.'

According to McGrath (1970) stress occurs due to:
'A substantial imbalance between demand (physical and/or psychological demands) and response capability, under conditions where failure to meet the demands has important consequences.'

Therefore, if we are placed in a situation in which we feel pressurised, unable to meet the task or worried about the consequences, we may experience a stress reaction. This may differ from one person to another.

Stressor
Any demands that are placed on the performer that initiate stress.

Cognitive response
Any change in the performer's thoughts (which are often negative), e.g. worry or feelings of failure.

Somatic response
Any change in the physiological response experienced by the performer, e.g. an increase in heart rate.

Because individuals react differently we have to recognise this fact and implement specific strategies to allow them to cope.

The stress experience, which is initiated by a **stressor**, may be positive or negative, as outlined below:

- Eustress is a positive form of stress which performers actively seek to test their abilities to the limit and provide them with an adrenalin rush. It can enhance their performance and heighten their emotions; if successfully completed it can lead to intrinsic satisfaction and boost confidence levels. Examples of eustress may include participation in adventurous activities or performing in front of significant others. You may have experienced this form of stress when preparing to ride on a roller-coaster at a theme park or when playing in an important match.
- Anxiety is the negative form of stress which can lead to an increase in arousal and a potential decrease in performance levels. Often performers experience loss of concentration, feelings of apprehension or an inability to cope, attentional narrowing and fear of failure (**cognitive responses**). They may also suffer from sweating, increased muscle tension, feelings of nausea, increased heart rate and other physiological reactions (**somatic responses**).

When the performer is placed in a stressful situation, McGrath (1970) suggested that he or she responds by progressing through four stages, as outlined in Figure 17.01.

Stage 1: Environmental demands – this involves the individual having to cope with either a physical or psychological demand. For example, performing a difficult skill in front of a large audience.

Stage 2: Perception of the demands – the individual then makes a judgement about the specific requirements of the task and his or her ability to deal with them. For example, more anxiety will occur if the performer has never competed in front of a large crowd (social facilitation).

Stage 3: Stress response – once a judgement of the situation has been made the individual experiences a specific reaction as outlined above, which may be physical (somatic) or psychological (cognitive). For example, the performer becomes apprehensive, worries about failure and doubts his or her ability to complete the task.

Stage 4: Behaviour – the performer then attempts to execute the skill. The performer's behaviour will often reflect his or her psychological attitude to the task. For example, the performer is worried and as a result suffers from muscle tension and poor selective attention, causing him or her to execute the skill poorly.

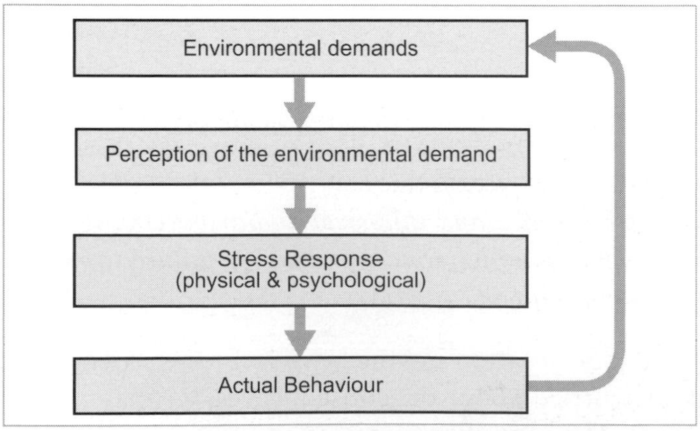

Environmental demands
Perception of the environmental demand
Stress Response
(physical & psychological)
Actual Behaviour

Fig 17.01 The stress process

Causes of stress

There are numerous causes of stress and different people will perceive each one differently. Any factor which initiates the stress response is known as a stressor. Within sport there are many such stressors, as outlined in Table 17.01. There may also be other stressors which you may have experienced or can identify.

Table 17.01 Types of stressor

Nature of the game – conflict	Fear of failure (N.af/avoidance)
Injury or fear for personal safety	Naturally high trait anxiety
Importance of the event	Attitude of coach
Status of the opposition	Parental pressure
Extrinsic rewards	Media pressure
Climate	Personal expectations
Frustration with own performance or that of others or officials	Nature of the crowd, e.g. size, proximity, knowledge

TASK 1

Select an event in which you have participated and identify potential stressors that may have affected you. Watch a professional sporting event and make a similar list. Compare the potential stressors and consider what the differences may be.

Stress response: General Adaptation Syndrome

HOT TIPS

You need to be able to explain the General Adaptation Syndrome and make reference to practical examples in your answer.

When stress is experienced, either positive or negative, the body responds in a similar manner. Seyle (1956) proposed that whatever the stressor may be, all individuals have the same physiological reaction. This is known as the General Adaptation Syndrome (GAS). Seyle outlined three main stages of the GAS, as shown in Figure 17.02.

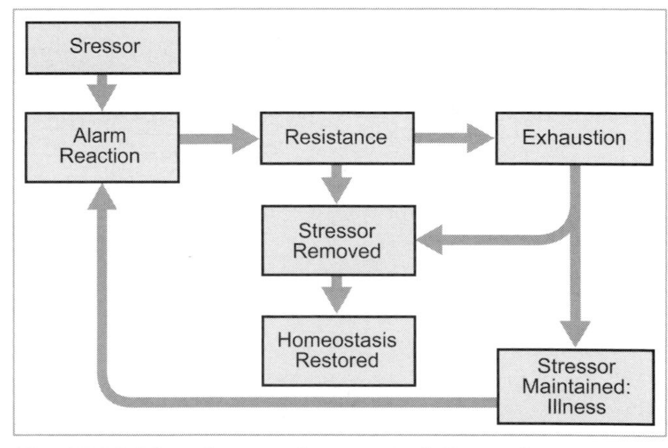

Fig 17.02 The three main stages of General Adaptation Syndrome

KEY WORDS

Autonomic nervous system (ANS)

The ANS works automatically to co-ordinate the body. The sympathetic branch of the ANS is stimulated by strong positive or negative emotions.

Homeostasis

The process by which the body maintains its constant internal physiological state.

- **Alarm reaction stage** – this is initiated when the perceived stressful situation occurs. The sympathetic branch of the **autonomic nervous system** (ANS) is activated causing increases in heart rate, blood sugar level, adrenaline and blood pressure. This is also linked to the emotional experiences of the 'fight or flight' response.
- **Resistance stage** – the body systems attempt to cope with the stressors if they are not removed by reverting to normal functioning levels if possible or a state of **homeostasis**. The body will attempt to resist the effect of the sympathetic nervous system.
- **Exhaustion stage** – the continued presence of the stressors will prove too much for the body to cope with, causing heart disease, stomach ulcers and high blood pressure. The body fails to deal with the continued demands placed upon it and is unable to fight infection and ultimately death may occur.

Anxiety

You need to understand the differences between the different forms of anxiety, and be able to explain the characteristics of each and how they influence performance.

There are several specific types of anxiety which affect a performer and each may influence performance in a different way. There are two broad categories of anxiety:

- Cognitive anxiety involves the performer's thoughts and worries concerning his or her perceived lack of ability to complete the task successfully. The individual will often experience feelings of nervousness and, apprehension, and have difficulty concentrating before and during competition. Cognitive anxiety is usually experienced prior to the event – even several days beforehand.
- Somatic anxiety involves the individual's physiological responses when placed in a situation where he or she perceives an inability to complete the task successfully. The performer may experience an increase in heart rate, sweating, blood pressure, muscle tension and feelings of nausea. All of which could hinder performance initially; however, these symptoms often reduce when the event has started.

Figure 17.03 below illustrates how a performer's cognitive and somatic anxiety levels may vary before, during and after competition. This graph does not apply to all performers but is an example of how anxiety levels may alter depending on the situation.

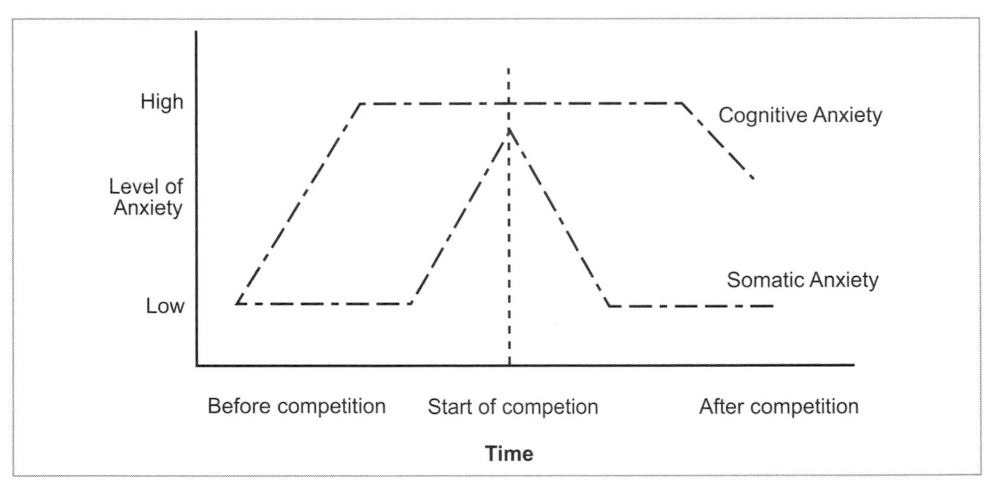

Fig 17.03 Cognitive and somatic anxiety levels may vary before, during and after competition

Individuals may react differently depending on the situation and their personality. Speilberger (1966) identified two types of anxiety which may account for such differences:

- Trait anxiety refers to the general disposition of an individual to perceive situations as threatening. As with other traits this disposition is stable and genetically inherited. If a performer possesses this characteristic he or she is more likely to become anxious in a wide variety of situations, experiencing a higher state of anxiety than those with low levels of trait anxiety. This is also referred to as 'A-trait'.

- **State anxiety** is a form of anxiety which occurs when the performer is placed in a particular situation. It is linked to the performer's mood and can literally alter from moment to moment. At times anxiety may be high, such as before the event, but may reduce when the event has started and increase again when faced with a new challenge, such as taking a penalty. Both cognitive and somatic anxiety may be experienced during this time. This form of anxiety is also known as 'A-state'.

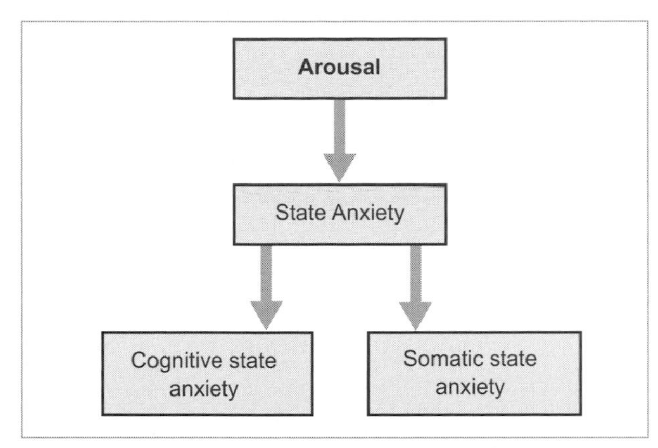

Fig 17.04 Relationship between types of anxiety

Further research by Martens (1977) also suggests there may be a specific trait named competitive trait anxiety. This involves the tendency of the performer to perceive competitive situations as threatening and to respond with feelings of apprehension or tension. An individual with high trait anxiety is more likely to experience a high state of anxiety when faced with stressful situations, such as competition, where he or she feels others may evaluate his or her performance (evaluation apprehension). The same person may not become as anxious in training as the performer may feel that he or she is not being judged and evaluated.

The causes of stress as previously outlined contribute to state anxiety levels prior to and during competition. This interactionist approach to anxiety is illustrated in Figure 17.06.

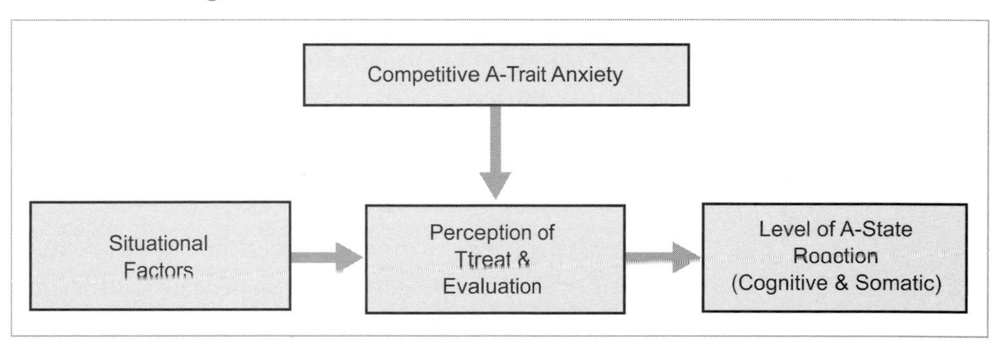

Fig 17.05 The interactionist approach to anxiety

Measurement of stress levels

Familiarise yourself with the most commonly used methods of stress measurement. Be able to explain the techniques, their methodology, and evaluate their effectiveness.

The measurement of stress levels is an important aspect of a performer's preparation. If patterns of behaviour can be identified and linked to specific situations, the coach can implement various strategies to reduce the performer's anxiety, control arousal levels and allow the athlete to operate in his or her zone of optimal functioning.

There are three methods generally used to gather such information:

- observation
- biofeedback
- self-report questionnaires.

Understand the value and limitations of the different techniques of measuring stress and be able to explain the most appropriate time they may be employed.

Observation

Observation of performance, whilst subjective, does allow the performer to be assessed in the actual performance situation. The observer will record two types of data:

- **Individual behaviour**, i.e. those behaviours usually associated with nervous actions, such as fidgeting, changes in speech patterns, acts of increased aggression, etc.
- **Aspects of performance**, i.e. execution of skilled actions such as accuracy of passing, decision-making, speed of reaction, etc.

The information is analysed and repeated behaviour patterns are noted. Detrimental aspects of performance are highlighted during specific situations and relevant stress management techniques are implemented.

There are several drawbacks to using this method. In order to fully assess the performer, several observers should be watching to ensure all actions are noted. Also, the performer should be well-known to the observers, allowing them to identify any unusual and uncharacteristic behaviour patterns.

Biofeedback

Biofeedback involves monitoring the physiological responses of the performer. Data is collected on changes in heart rate, muscle response, respiration rate, sweat production and levels of hormone secretion.

Whilst this provides accurate data there are several drawbacks including the difficulty of recording information during an actual competitive performance (as the athlete has to be 'wired-up' to obtain the results). The potential changes caused as a natural reaction to being evaluated and the replication of the competitive environment is difficult in the laboratory situation.

Self-report questionnaires

These involve performers answering a series of questions concerning their emotions in specific situations. There are numerous advantages to using this method including:

- ease of administration
- large numbers can be assessed quickly
- cheap to administer.

However, there are some drawbacks too:

- misinterpretation or lack of understanding of the questions
- the respondents may not answer honesty as they may wish to appear in a positive light or they may give the answers they think are required or socially desirable
- inappropriate questions may be used, which may lead to biased results
- the actual time of completion may influence the responses
- the available responses may not cater for the exact emotions being experienced.

Sport Competition Anxiety Test (SCAT)

Martens (1977) developed the Sport Competition Anxiety Test (SCAT) which is used to measure the competitive trait anxiety of a performer when placed in a pre-competitive sporting environment. The questionnaire consists of 15 statements and the performer is required to state how he or she generally responds to each. Examples of the statements are shown below:

1	Before I compete I feel uneasy.	Hardly	Sometimes	Often
2	Before I compete I am calm.	Hardly	Sometimes	Often
3	Before I compete I get a queasy. feeling in my stomach	Hardly	Sometimes	Often
4	Before I compete I am nervous.	Hardly	Sometimes	Often

Psychologists can then use this information to assess if the performer is prone to experiencing high levels of anxiety before the competition. To obtain a more accurate prediction, the performer should complete the SCAT several times before competing in different events, to develop a clear pattern of emotions.

To identify the type of anxiety a performer may experience, Martens (1990) refined the SCAT and developed the Competitive Sport Anxiety Inventory (CSAI-2). It is used to assess an individual's state anxiety and corresponding behaviour patterns. This questionnaire measures levels of both cognitive anxiety and somatic anxiety as well as self-confidence in a sporting situation. It is completed up to an hour before the start of the event. As you can see from the examples below, each question specifically refers to either a cognitive or somatic stress response.

1 I have self-doubts.
Not at all Somewhat Moderately Very much so

2 My body feels tense.
Not at all Somewhat Moderately Very much so

3 I feel at ease.
Not at all Somewhat Moderately Very much so

4 My heart is racing.
Not at all Somewhat Moderately Very much so

5 I am concerned about reaching my goal.
Not at all Somewhat Moderately Very much so

After evaluating the data the coach is able to identify trends in a performer's stress response and particular weaknesses that may hinder performance. However, it must be remembered that some somatic responses prior to competition are natural and may aid performance. However, high levels of cognitive state anxiety may adversely affect the performer and should be dealt with utilising stress management techniques.

Stress management techniques

HOT TIPS

Understand and be able to explain the methods which can be used to control the different forms of anxiety.

Following evaluation of the stress response and the identification of particular types of anxiety, the performer must be taught how to recognise the symptoms of an increased state anxiety. These may be either physiological, psychological or behavioural. Various techniques can be employed, all of which need practice. This aspect of a performer's preparation is vital if he or she is to achieve his or her potential, and as such it should form an integral part of the performer's training regime.

Remember, stress is caused by an imbalance between the perceived demands of the task and the individual's ability. The aim of all the techniques is to lower the arousal levels, allowing the athlete to feel in control of his or her emotions and actions, so that he or she feels able to complete the task successfully.

There are numerous stress management methods which can be used and they fall into two broad categories:

- cognitive strategies
- somatic strategies.

Some techniques, however, do combine elements of both.

Cognitive methods

Thought-stopping involves the individual recognising when he or she is starting to worry or develop negative thoughts about his or her performance. When this occurs a cue, action or word is used to redirect the attention to positive thoughts. For example, a netball player who has missed several shots and is beginning to have doubts about the next shot, might click her fingers or say 'focus' to herself. As a result the netball player concentrates on the action, technique or tactic for the next attempt, rather than thinks about the previous attempts.

Fig 17.06 Concentration in action

HOT TIPS

You need to be able to list and explain the specific techniques used to control somatic and cognitive anxiety.

Self-talk involves the individual developing positive thoughts about his or her actions and performances. The aim is to eradicate any negative thoughts and replace them with positive statements. For example, a sprinter at the start of a race may change thoughts such as 'Am I ready for this?' to 'My training has gone well and I'm prepared!' Similarly, a rugby team who are losing by two points towards the end of a match may have been conditioned to think 'We have plenty of time left' rather than 'We've only got two minutes left to win the game'.

Imagery involves the formation of mental pictures of successful performances. It can be used in a variety of ways to either create the expected experience of a new situation or recall the feelings of a past situation. The performer can use the technique to develop a variety of sensations. The performer may:

- create a vision of a place where he or she can retreat which has a calming atmosphere, away from the pressure of competition
- recreate the kinaesthetic feeling of a successful movement
- create images of what may happen and how to deal with them, for example, a situation within a game when confronted with two defenders
- create emotional feelings that may be experienced when placed in a stressful situation, such as success, victory and control
- create the sounds experienced in the situation, for example, either the ball on the bat or external sources that may be distracting, such as the crowd during the execution of a penalty kick.

Imagery can be either internal or external. Internal imagery involves a sportsperson seeing him or herself from within, completing the action or in the situation, experiencing the kinaesthetic feelings. External imagery involves the sportsperson seeing him or herself as if he or she were a spectator or on film.

The development of self-confidence is a key element in a performer's approach to an event. Throughout your studies in this section there are numerous examples of how a performer's personal belief in his or her own abilities can be developed. The factors contributing to an individual's self-efficacy, via past experiences, vicarious experiences and verbal persuasion, all contribute significantly. So too do the correct use of both intrinsic and extrinsic motivational factors, the appropriate use of attributions and the encouragement of approach behaviour. If all the theoretical aspects discussed are implemented correctly there is an increased chance the performer will perceive the competitive situation as challenging rather than as a threat.

TASK 2

Select a sports skill that you have previously completed well in a pressurised situation. Using internal imagery, attempt to recreate the feelings you experienced during the performance. Attempt to remember any visual and auditory cues as well as the kinaesthetic feeling involved. Repeat the action in your mind several times. Before your next event, repeat this process if you feel yourself becoming anxious and practise its use as a stress management control method.

Somatic methods

Centering/breathing control involves the performer relaxing the chest and shoulder muscles, then focusing on the movement of the abdominal muscles whilst taking slow, deep breaths. The technique is beneficial as it can redirect attention, can be performed anywhere and if practised can be completed quickly and privately.

Biofeedback

Monitoring the physiological responses of the performer. Data is collected on changes in heart rate, muscle response, respiration rate, sweat production and levels of hormone secretion.

Biofeedback involves the measurement of the body's physiological responses to stress using objective techniques. The performer is made aware of the physiological responses that are occurring and then focuses his or her thoughts to calm him or herself. The effectiveness is viewed immediately and accurately due to the machines' biological feedback. Eventually the performer can recognise the physiological changes taking place without the aid of machinery and implement other stress management techniques during competition. Commonly used methods are:

- Galvanic skin response, which measures the skin's electrical conductivity when sweating. If tense, more sweat is produced to remove the heat generated by the muscles.
- Electromyography (EMG) measures muscle tension via a series of electrodes taped to the skin, emitting a louder sound when tension is high.
- Skin temperature is measured via thermometers attached to the skin; reading are lower during times of stress.

Fig 17.07 Performers often control their breathing to help control their anxiety levels

Relaxation involves actively causing the muscles to become less tense or rigid. This can be achieved using either cognitive methods, which utilise thoughts to induce a calmer state, or somatic methods involving the control of muscle tension. Either can be used in training or competition, but care should be taken with some techniques – if employed too close to an event this may lead to under-arousal.

Progressive muscle relaxation technique involves the performer being aware of the alternating sensations of tension and relaxation of the muscles. Specific muscle groups are identified in succession, gradually reducing the tension throughout the body. Initially this may take time, but with practice athletes can focus and relax the whole body almost immediately. This is particularly useful prior to competition, to help facilitate sleep.

Goal setting

Another effective method used to control anxiety levels is goal setting. Often this method allows the performer to direct his or her attention away from the source of stress and focus on an achieveable target. If goals are set correctly they can have several effects, including:

- development of self-confidence and self-efficacy
- increased motivation levels
- improved selective attention
- approach behaviour
- persistence
- a reduction in anxiety.

The coach must take care when setting goals to ensure the performer's motivation is maintained whilst simultaneously not pushing the performer too far. The type of goal set will depend on the nature of the task, the level of ability of the performer and his or her anxiety levels. There are two types of goal which should be considered:

- outcome goal
- performance goal.

Outcome goal

Outcome goal
A goal that is set to judge the performance of the individual against others and the end result.

Performance goal
This is used to judge the performance of the individual against his or her own standards, rather than in comparison with competitors.

An **outcome goal** judges the performance of the individual against others and the end result. The performer is being compared to others and a social comparison is being made. For example, a swimmer may be set the goal of either winning the race or finishing in the top three places to qualify for the next round. The efficiency and manner of his performance is not relevant – only the final result. If the goal setting is realistic and within the performer's capability, and if he achieves the aim, his motivation is increased. Performers of this nature are said to be 'outcome goal orientated.' However, it can be demotivating if the performer is unsuccessful, especially after repeated attempts, and this can lead to an increase in anxiety levels. Therefore, with novice performers or those who tend to have avoidance behaviour, **performance goals** are more appropriate.

Performance goal

This type of goal judges the performance of the athlete against his or her own standards, rather than making a social comparison with his or her competitors. For example, the swimmer may be set a number of goals for a race, including a good reaction to the starter's gun and, effective breathing action, and his performance may be evaluated with reference to his personal best time rather than his finishing position. If the set goals are realistic the performer can evaluate his own actions and not worry about comparison with others. This helps to reduce anxiety, allowing the swimmer to remain motivated irrespective of his finishing position.

The coach may also set specific process-orientated goals which relate to the development of the tactics or technique of the performer and contribute to the overall performance goal. For example, the swimmer may set the goal of a tighter tumble turn with greater leg drive off the wall in order to improve his overall performance.

Another factor which needs to be considered is the time span of the goal. It is generally accepted that both long-term goals and short-term goals should be set to maximise their use. Many performers will use major competitions as their focus for long-term goals and sub-divide their preparation into short-term goals. For example, an international performer may base her preparation on the timing of the Olympic Games or World Championships and set her outcome goals in relation to these events. Throughout the season intermediate goals are set (which may be performance goals) allowing the performer to monitor and evaluate her progress. This not only maintains the performer's motivation levels but ensures the performer does not become anxious unnecessarily if her ultimate target appears to be beyond her reach. If the performer achieves her short-term goal, positive feelings are generated, contributing to an increased level of self-efficacy. Goals should even be set for individual training sessions and evaluated afterwards. Think back to your Personal Exercise Programme and consider if you did this and what effect it had on future sessions.

TASK 3

You are the coach of a team. During the pre-season you decide to set both outcome and performance goals. For a sport of your choice, give examples of each type of goal which may be set for the team and individual performers.

Method and principles of goal setting

In order for goal setting to be effective, in addition to the points outlined previously, many performers ensure their goals fulfil the following criteria, as proposed by Sportscoach UK, and referred to as the 'SMARTER' principle:

- **Specific** – the goal must be related to the individual performer and include precise aims, rather than simple statements such as 'you must put more effort into the race'. Ideally the goals should be clear and unambiguous, with a clear relevancc to the ultimate outcome goal.
- **Measurable** – the goal must be able to be assessed and recorded to allow the performer to see his or her progress. Ideally this should be a relatively

quick process. It may not always be possible to use objective evidence such as times or passes completed, but any subjective feedback must be as precise as possible.
- **Accepted** – the goal must be agreed between the performer and the coach. Ideally the athlete should be part of the discussion process to establish the goal, which will increase motivation levels and he or she will be more likely to commit him or herself to achieving the end result.
- **Realistic** – any goal must be within the performer's capabilities otherwise his or her anxiety will actually increase because of worry about not meeting expectations.
- **Time phased** – each goal must have a fixed deadline for evaluation, otherwise the performer may lose motivation. The length of time allowed to achieve the goal will depend on the difficulty of the task.
- **Exciting** – the goal must be viewed as a challenge to the athlete and he or she must be motivated to achieve success and to gain intrinsic satisfaction. This aspect of goal setting must be considered carefully because a target that may seem exciting initially may then lose its impact if success is not achieved; it may then appear unobtainable thus causing anxiety.
- **Recorded** – all goals should be recorded for evaluation. If a goal has been set several months before and there is no fixed record of the agreed target, disputes may arise and again there will be a negative effect on the performer's anxiety level.

If these guidelines are followed, goal setting can be highly effective in the development of a sport performer's career. It allows the performer to remain focused but be constantly challenged, always believing that he or she can improve his or her performance.

TASK 4

Before your next competitive event set yourself either an outcome goal or a performance goal. The goal must be SMARTER. For the next event set the other type of goal. Discuss your results with a partner and evaluate which type of goal was the most effective for you.

Revise as you go!

1. What is the difference between anxiety and eustress?
2. Explain the term stressor.
3. Give three examples of possible stressors that may affect a performer during competition.
4. Name the three stages of the General Adaptation Syndrome.
5. What is the difference between cognitive anxiety and somatic anxiety?
6. Explain the difference between state anxiety and trait anxiety.
7. Outline the Competitive State Anxiety Inventory (CSAI-2).
8. Comment on the validity of the Sport Competition Anxiety Test.

9. Name two physiological tests commonly used to measure levels of stress.
10. Give three examples of how a performer may display signs of somatic anxiety.
11. Explain the term competitive trait anxiety.
12. Explain the difference between somatic and cognitive methods of stress management.
13. What is the difference between internal imagery and external imagery?
14. What does the technique of centering involve?
15. Explain the term self-talk.
16. What is thought-stopping?
17. How is biofeedback used to control levels of stress?
18. What do the letters SMARTER represent?
19. Explain the difference between an outcome and a performance goal.
20. Why is it important to set short- and long-term goals?

Unit 4 Questions

Total for this question: 15 marks

Question 1

Performers in many activities require muscles to exert various levels of strength to perform actions.

a) *Spatial summation* and *wave summation* are both ways of varying the strength of contraction of a muscle. Explain what is meant by **each** of these terms. **(5 marks)**

b) Explain how the involvement of the *muscle spindles* increases the strength of a muscle contraction. **(3 marks)**

Performance in any activity will be affected by the level of arousal. **Figure 1** shows a relationship between the degree of *arousal* and the quality of performance, using the *drive* and *inverted-U* theories.

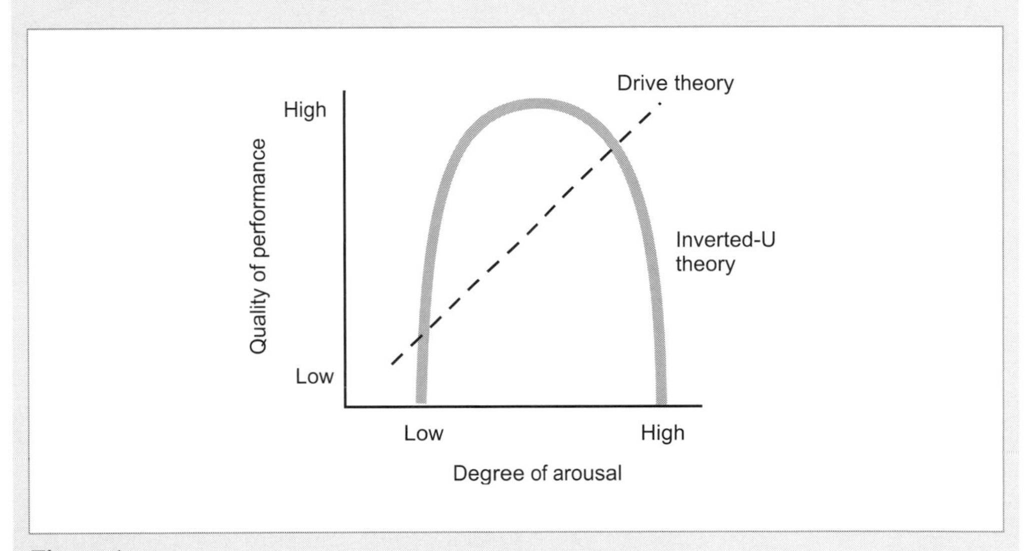

Figure 1

c) Briefly explain the **two** theories shown in **Figure 1** and compare their effectiveness in describing the relationship between the arousal and sporting performance in **differing tasks**. **(7 marks)**

Total for this question: 15 marks

Question 2

Elite performers need to control their psychological and physiological performance.

a) i) What are the similarities and differences between *aggressive* behaviour and *assertive* behaviour in sport? **(3 marks)**

ii) Discuss the *social learning* theory of aggression. **(5 marks)**

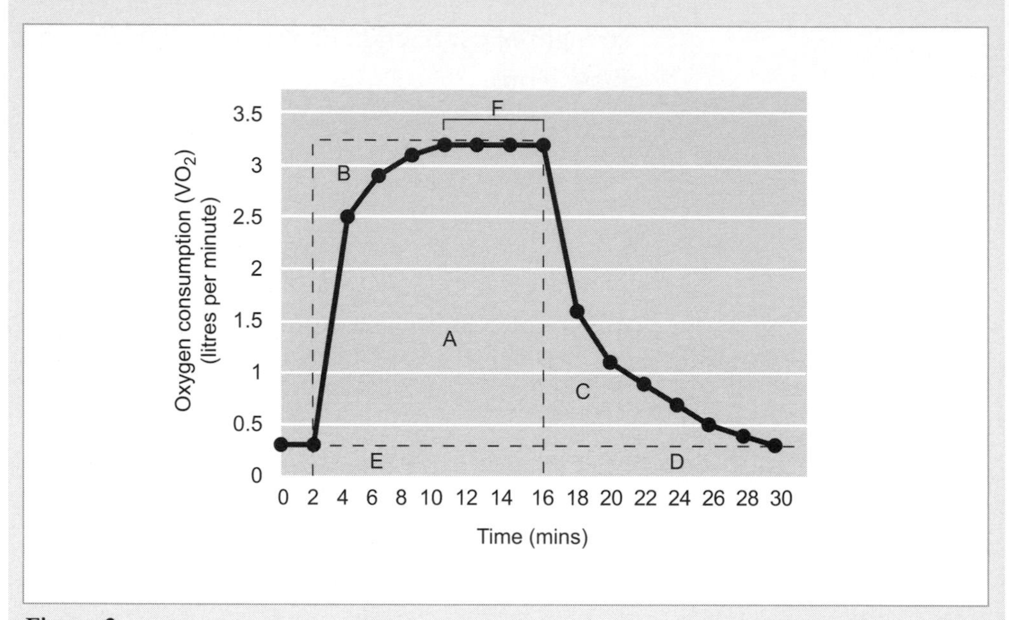

Figure 2

b) **Figure 2** shows the *oxygen consumption* ($V0_2$) of a subject during a period of rest, sub-maximal exercise and recovery.

i) State which letter (**A–F**) represents *oxygen deficit* **and** which letter (**A–F**) represents *EPOC*. **(2 marks)**

ii) How long did the exercise last **and** what does letter F represent? **(2 marks)**

c) *EPOC* consists of fast and slow components. What are the functions of the *slow component* **and** how are these functions achieved? **(3 marks)**

Total for this question: 15 marks

Question 3

Team game players tend to play and train as a group in order to improve their performances.

a) i) What do you understand by the term *group cohesion*? **(3 marks)**

ii) Explain how the size **and** structure of a group may affect its cohesiveness. **(3 marks)**

iii) Discuss whether cohesive groups are always more successful. **(3 marks)**

b) Training programmes will often include exercises to improve flexibility.

i) Describe the **method** involved in *Proprioceptive Neuromuscular Facilitation (PNF)* stretching. **(4 marks)**

ii) Using your knowledge of *muscle spindle apparatus*, explain why *PNF* stretching tends to produce better results in terms of increased flexibility than other forms of stretching. **(2 marks)**

Total for this question: 15 marks

Question 4

Marathon runners carefully plan their training to deal with the demands which they may encounter during a race.

a) Some runners may use *glycogen loading* as part of their preparation. What do you understand by this term and why would they need to do this? **(4 marks)**

b) Effective temperature regulation is vital to the marathon runner. How is body temperature regulated, and under what conditions does this process become more difficult? **(3 marks)**

c) i) Marathon runners often prefer to train in small groups. Explain what is meant by the term *group cohesion*. **(2 marks)**

ii) Explain **three** factors that are associated with group cohesion. **(3 marks)**

iii) Discuss whether cohesive groups are always more successful. **(3 marks)**

Total for this question: 15 marks

Question 5

All sports performers have attitudes. Attitudes are "ideas charged with emotion (positive or negative) which pre-disposes a class of actions to a particular social situation" (Triandis 1971).

a) Suggest **two** methods for measuring attitudes. **(2 marks)**

b) Identify and briefly explain the **three** components of attitudes. **(4 marks)**

c) Describe how **each** of the components you have identified in (b) might be used to change attitudes. **(3 marks)**

d) Use Newton's Laws of Motion to explain how a sprinter leaves the starting blocks. **(6 marks)**

Total for this question: 15 marks

Question 6

Personality profiling and biomechanical analysis can be used to prepare performers who compete at the highest level.

Morgan's Profile of Mood State (POMS) is a questionnaire given to performers to establish their relative measures on the six mental health states of fatigue, vigour, tension, depression, anger and confusion.

a) Research has shown that the profile for POMS differs between elite **and** non-elite performers. Describe these differences. **(3 marks)**

b) What are the advantages **and** disadvantages of using questionnaires to provide psychological information? **(4 marks)**

c) i) When accelerating along the track at the beginning of a 100-metre race, a sprinter generates a large impulse. What do you understand by the term "impulse"? **(2 marks)**

ii) Sketch **and** label a graph to show the typical impulse generated by the sprinter at this stage of the race. **(6 marks)**

Total for this question: 15 marks

Question 7

Research on athletes has found differing effects of *somatic state anxiety* and *cognitive state anxiety* on performance.

a) Comment on the levels of somatic state anxiety and cognitive state anxiety that an athlete might experience leading up to and during a major competition. **(3 marks)**

b) Explain, with appropriate examples, how an athlete can control cognitive anxiety. **(4 marks)**

In field athletics, the events are affected by a variety of forces.

c) To maximise the horizontal distance of a shot during flight, identify **three** mechanical factors that should be taken into account. **(2 marks)**

d) i) If air **resistance** is negligible, sketch a diagram to show the flight path of a shot from the moment of release to the moment immediately prior to landing. **(2 marks)**

ii) Add vectors to your diagram to represent the vertical and horizontal components of the velocity at:

- the point of release;
- the highest point of the flight path;
- a point in the downward flight path, level with the height of release;
- a point before landing. **(4 marks)**

Total for this question: 15 marks

Question 8

When competing on their own, elite performers such as ice skaters are affected by many factors.

a) An elite performer's motivations may be affected by his or her level of arousal. **Figure 4** shows two graphs (**A** and **B**) that may be used to explain how arousal varies during performance.

i) Identify the theories represented by graphs **A** and **B** in **Figure 4**. **(2 marks)**

ii) Describe how **each** theory may be used to explain the effects of arousal on performance. **(7 marks)**

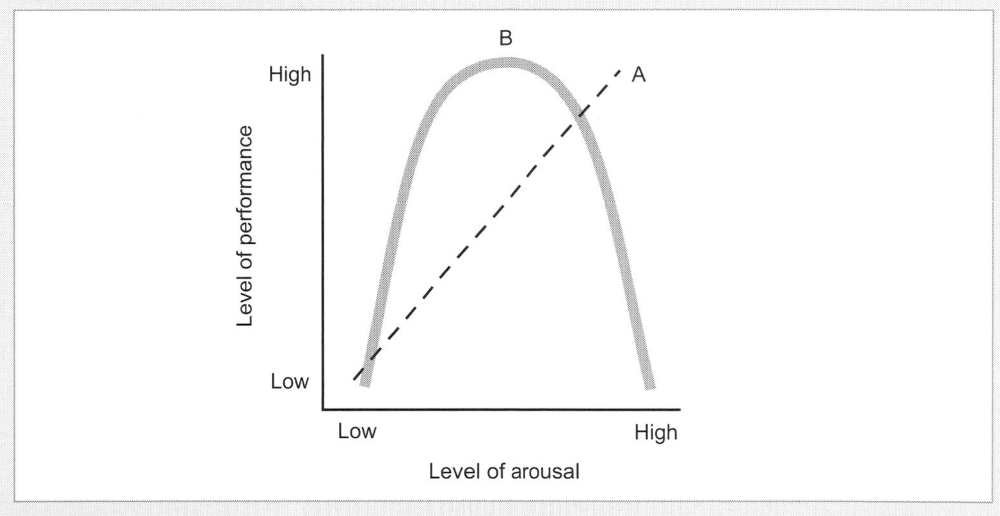

Figure 4

b) Explain how a spinning ice-skater is able to alter the speed of rotation by changing his or her body shape. **(6 marks)**

Unit 5: Factors affecting the nature and development of elite performance

Chapter 18: Talent identification and talent development

Learning outcomes

By the end of this chapter you should understand:

- what is meant by the term elite sport
- the general qualities required for the individual to progress towards elite performance
- the characteristics of talent identification and talent development programmes
- the function and policies of national organisations in terms of provision and funding
- the effectiveness of national policies in the UK.

What is meant by elite sport?

Elite sport

The most talented sportspeople. Only a few can reach this standard of performance yet require a substantial level of funding and resources.

Participation pyramid

A model to show the development of an athlete from beginner to elite level.

Elite sport refers to performers who have reached a level of excellence according to national and international standards. For our purposes excellence will mean the superior, elite athletes at both amateur and professional level, able bodied as well as disabled, who reach the pinnacle of performance in their sport.

The wider the base of sport participation the more likely it is that more athletes will reach the apex. Thus, if we encourage more people to compete at the foundation and participation levels, then more elite athletes are likely to emerge.

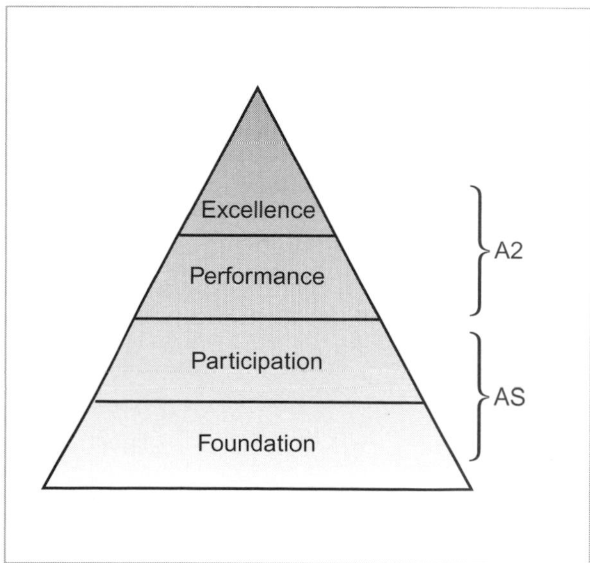

Fig 18.01 Participation pyramid

However, a country should not rely on individuals to succeed purely as a result of individual initiative and circumstances, but as a result of a national policy to spot and develop talent. A truly effective national sport policy will produce champions in selected sports on a regular basis.

Elite athletes in the modern day sport world require substantial funding and support. It is therefore vital that organisations with a remit to achieve excellence in sport do their job. There is a need for all the relevant organisations to liaise and co-ordinate their efforts.

TASK 1

Outline your progress in a particular sport. Consider the factors that influenced your initial participation and those that were significant in how far you have progressed in that sport.

Grass roots sports
Sports that take place in the community at a local level.

Why achieve excellence?

Before we go any further let us first discuss the purpose of trying to achieve excellence in the field of sport, both for the individual and society. Table 18.01 identifies some of the benefits sport can provide for both individuals and their society.

Table 18.01 Some of the benefits of sport

Individual	Society
• Sport represents a challenge • As a society we encourage excellence academically, for example, in the arts • Sport can provide an alternative employment pathway • It provides individuals with self-esteem and the ability to act as a role model for others	• Sporting success can boost national pride and morale • Helps to reduce anti-social behaviour • Sport is big business • Sport is considered a healthy pursuit which if pursued by the mass of the population will in turn reduce spending by the NHS • Elite sport can help boost **grass roots sport** • People are still curious to discover the limits of human potential.

However, not all aspects of pursuing excellence in sport are positive. Consider some of the less attractive effects:

- It is only an exclusive minority who can ever reach this level of performance and yet they require substantial funding and resources which could otherwise be directed towards the foundation and participation levels.
- The moral values of sport, such as sportsmanship, have to some extent been lost as the rewards for winning have increased and the stakes become higher. Acts of deviancy, such as doping and violence, have increased.
- Over-specialisation and excessive training leads to physical and psychological damage

However, the UK is committed to developing sporting excellence as it prepares to host the Olympic Games in 2012. Never have so many questions been asked of the organisations involved in developing sporting talent.

What qualities are required for elite performance?

The first step is to discover the talent. What qualities would be needed in a performer to attract the attention of a talent scout? A performer can be considered according to his or her physical and psychological attributes.

Physical qualities:
- natural ability
- high level of fitness and health
- high pain threshold
- possibly preferred body type for a particular sport.

Psychological qualities:
- high level of competitiveness
- willingness to train
- commitment and sacrifice
- mental toughness.

Testing for talent

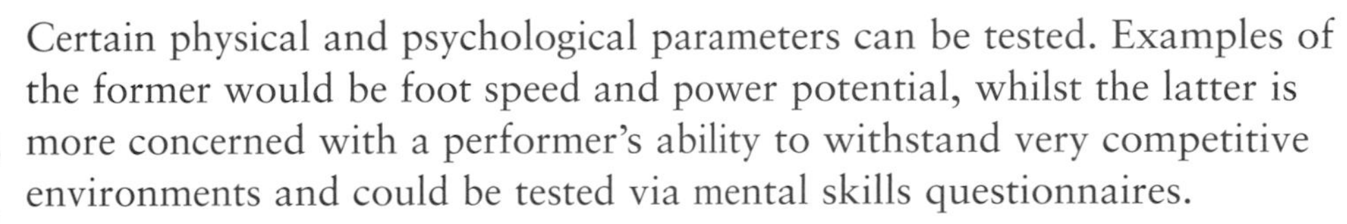

Certain physical and psychological parameters can be tested. Examples of the former would be foot speed and power potential, whilst the latter is more concerned with a performer's ability to withstand very competitive environments and could be tested via mental skills questionnaires.

HOT TIPS

You need to develop an understanding of the factors that determine whether an athlete will reach an elite level in his or her sport.

Sport specific organisations have to identify the essential characteristics of and events within their sport. They need to establish norm values, which are often adapted from accepted models based on measurements of elite performances at Olympics and World Games. The precise timing and **identification screening** is difficult to determine but there will usually be two to three phases starting in early childhood at approximately 3–8 years, then a secondary phase between 9–17 years where the athlete has already undergone some sport specific training, and finally a more complex and sophisticated phase with the high calibre athletes. These phases will vary depending on the sport and the system. The information gathered is then compared to the sport specific profiles created by the sport.

KEY WORDS

Identification screening
A system for the initial selection of people based on their potential to develop into an elite athlete.

Socio-economic status
The status of a person involving both economic and social factors.

The problems with this approach are:
- It does not take into account an individual's desire to win, ambition and drive – these factors may in fact be more important than the VO_2max of an individual.
- Whilst some hereditary factors can't be changed, such as height and length of limbs, others can, for example, weight and strength through education and training.
- The **socio-economic status** and facilities available to the individual can affect the type of sport that he or she can viably participate in. For example, a child might be identified as being physically suitable for a particular sport but her family may not be able to afford for her to take the sport up.

Social factors

The most effective talent identification programmes will be tied to the school programme as it allows wide participation, regardless of socio-economic status and the use of specialist teachers helps to alleviate the costs.

However, social factors can be just as influential in determining which sport an individual will initially begin to participate in with progression to elite levels.

Social influences that can affect a child's participation in a particular sport include:

- tradition
- ideals
- popularity of sport
- parental influence/pressure
- teacher's speciality
- accessible facilities.

TASK 2

Research the talent development plans of a National Governing body of your choice.

Talent identification and development programmes

Talent identification

A process by which children are encouraged to participate in the sports at which they are most likely to succeed, based on testing certain parameters. These parameters are designed to predict performance capacity, taking into account the child's current level of fitness and maturity (Peltola 1992).

Anthropometry

The scientific measurement of the human body.

Talent identification and development programmes need to consider:

- physiology
- **anthropometry**, e.g. height in basketball
- psychology
- hereditary factors
- sociological factors.

We have already mentioned the connection that exists between the participation level and the excellence level on the participation pyramid. That is, the larger the base of participation the more likely it is that a greater number of athletes will filter towards the apex. Therefore it is important that the base of talent identification is widened. One of the best methods is to centre the search in schools as this is the best way of reaching a maximum number of children. Also, the sports themselves need to become more democratic by reducing the incidents of discrimination, be it racial, sexual or class-based. One sign of how skewed British sport is can be demonstrated by the fact that 60 per cent of Olympic medals at the Sydney Olympics were won by athletes who had been educated at private schools, despite only 7 per cent of the population being educated privately.

National Governing Bodies (NGOs)

National governing bodies are beginning to take a lead in opening up their sport to a more diverse population. An excellent example is the Lawn Tennis Association with its development of tennis in inner cities.

- Structural aspects need to be considered, for example, facilities and the allocation of personnel, from city development officers to scouts, coaches and so on.

- The need for substantial funding is recognised as being essential, requiring a joint funding initiative from local business, the national governing body and local authorities.
- Discrimination is being tackled, structurally and through challenging attitudes.
- Sporting ambassadors such as Ian Wright are used to promote the sport.

Systematic talent identification programmes

Systematic policy
A policy that has been developed methodically in an organised, coherent manner.

Eastern bloc
The Soviet Union (USSR) and the countries it controlled in central and eastern Europe. This included East Germany (GDR).

Traditionally most countries have waited for athletes to identify themselves as a result of success in competition, but this may not be good enough for modern sport. Some countries have developed scientific methods to identify talented individuals and to help individuals choose the sport most suited to their abilities. This then becomes a **systematic policy** of talent identification and it is not new. It has operated in countries from the **Eastern bloc** and China since the 1960s and 1970s.

Table 18.02 The advantages and disadvantages of a systematic programme

Advantages	Disadvantages
• It helps to accelerate an individual's progress to an elite level. • It helps an individual to select a sport to which he or she is most suited. • It helps a coach to concentrate training methods on the most suitable athletes. • It allows a country to get the best from its resources (it can select the sport it is best suited to developing, e.g. Switzerland and skiing, and Kenya with running).	• Large numbers of young people need to be tested to produce valid results. • An expert coach's 'eye' can still be the best guide. • It requires substantial funding. • It can be difficult to reliably predict future development from a young age. • Talented children generally exhibit all-round ability so it is difficult to direct them at a specific sport early on. • Specialism before the age of 13 years can be considered dangerous both physically and psychologically.

During the 1972 Olympics quite a few medallists were scientifically selected by the GDR system. The system's features included:
- a high level of organisation and structure
- a compulsory programme of PE in schools
- the early identification of sport talent
- a club system for talented individuals in separate sports
- the ruthless elimination of those who did not 'measure up'
- a scientific approach to elite performance training
- long-range objectives

- selected schools which had to support talent scouting competition separated into age groups
- substantial financial and material support
- 2000 training centres, 70,000 young people and 10,000 full-time coaches.

Beijing is currently preparing for the Olympic Games and has some of the features of the GDR system.

Characteristics of elite sport development systems

Oakley and Green (2003) suggest that talent identification and development programmes should have the following characteristics to be effective:

- clear delineation (clearly defined roles) and understanding of the agencies involved, and effective communication between them to maintain the system
- simplicity of administration through sporting and political boundaries
- talent identification monitoring systems
- provision of sports services to create a culture of excellence in which all members of the team (athletes, coaches, scientists and managers) can interact
- well structured competitive programmes with ongoing international exposure
- well developed facilities with priority for elite athletes
- targeting of resources on focus sports
- comprehensive planning for each sport's needs
- recognition that excellence costs in terms of capital and revenue expenditure
- lifestyle support during and post elite performance phase of an athlete's career.

How does this compare to the system in the UK?

What is the track record of the UK in developing sporting excellence?

HOT TIPS

When you have understood the UK system of sport you will then be required to compare this to the sport systems of the USA and France (see Chapter 20).

Traditionally, the UK has lacked a co-ordinated, strategic plan to develop talent. This process began to take shape in the 1980s with a national organisation responsible for coaching being established, now known as Sports Coach UK. The key to achieving a nationally co-ordinated plan is for all the agencies involved to work together, integrating the support services of sport science, sport medicine, coaching, lifestyle coaching and technology.

Traditionally in the UK, school sport has been the base of the competitive organised structure. Does it still provide this base since the decline in school sport in the 1980s? If not, how can an elite sport policy at junior level be implemented?

KEY WORDS

Centralised

To draw under central control. State legislation co-ordinates and supports policies.

This is not such a problem in Germany and the Netherlands, where clubs have always provided this base. Other European countries have adopted a **centralised** strategic approach to elite sport at an earlier stage than the UK, one example being France.

Turning to gender, the gap between male and female performances has narrowed in Italy, France and the Netherlands,. Therefore they show more overall improvements as an overall team. In the UK the performance gap between men and women has widened (except in sailing and equestrianism).

Countries with successful systems produce winners in the same events year on year. In medal terms we need a strategy of converting bronze and silver medals to GOLD!

TASK 3

Read through Oakley and Green's characteristics of elite sport development systems and extract key points to answer the following questions:

1. What should an effective talent identification and development programme contain?
2. If you were in charge of your sport, what measures would you take to ensure the effective development of elite athletes?

The government is estimated to spend £2.2 billion a year on sport and physical activity in England alone. Over the last decade there have been numerous reports questioning the effectiveness of the UK system of sport. Words used to describe the system in the twenty-first century are 'amateurish' and in need of 'modernisation'. The plethora of organisations involved in sport is only one of the problems. There are currently over 500 different organisations involved in running sport in this country. However, there have also been improvements. The Carter Report (2005) cites in particular:

- the hosting of the Manchester 2002 Commonwealth Games
- performance standards in the Rugby World Cup 2003, Athens Olympic Games 2004, cricket and sailing have inspired the nation
- the building of twenty-three 50m swimming pools since 1997; nine state-of-the-art English Institute of Sport facilities; Loughborough and Bath universities have developed high quality facilities; Wembley and the new Olympic aquatic centre
- the successful bid for the 2012 Olympic Games.

The government has developed a three-pronged approach to sport which is overseen by the Department of Culture, Media and Sport (DCMS). It has become more streamlined but is still unwieldy.

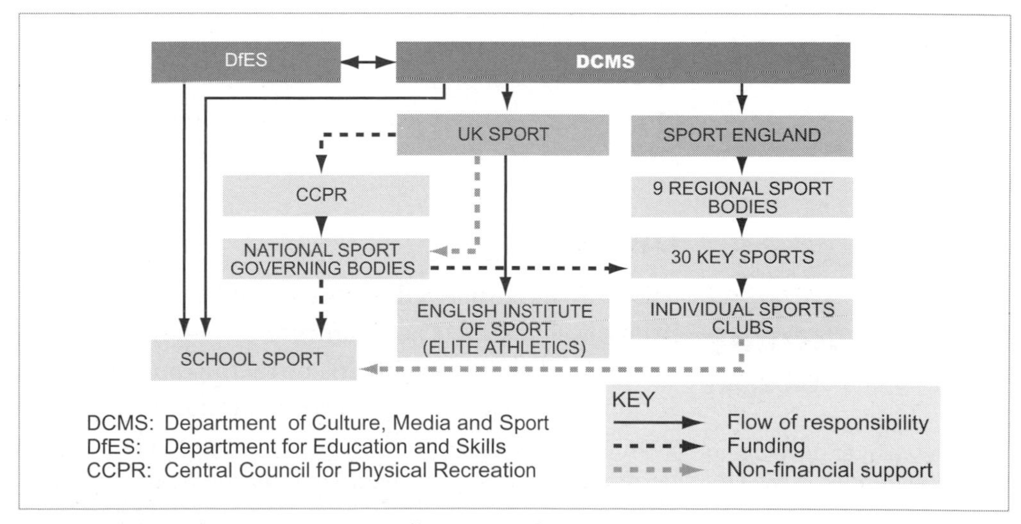

Fig 18.02 British sport – structurally unsound?

Organisations with a remit for elite sport

HOT TIPS

You will need to understand the aims and policies of the major organisations rather than their structure or funding. You only need to know about the organisations' policies for elite sport.

The organisations mentioned specifically in the syllabus specification include:
- Department for Culture, Media and Sport (www.culture.gov.uk)
- UK Sport (www.uksport.gov.uk)
- Sport England (www.sportengland.org)
- English Institute of Sport
- Sports Coach UK
- National governing bodies (can be accessed via Sport England or UK Sport)
- British Olympic Association (www.olympic.org.uk)
- National Lottery
- Sports Aid.

You can only be asked direct questions on the organisations mentioned in the specification.

Department for Culture, Media and Sport (DCMS)

HOT TIPS

It is useful to keep up to date with organisations by visiting their websites. Those recorded here are correct at time of print.

The Department for Culture, Media and Sport (DCMS) is the government department that has responsibility for sport. It promotes sport from the grass roots to elite level. The government remit for elite sport is:
- achieving excellence in national and international competition
- attracting major international events, such as the success of the Olympic bid to stage the 2012 Olympics in London.

KEY WORDS

Department of Culture, Media and Sport (DCMS)
The UK government department with responsibility for sport.

In the present day the government policies and drive for excellence have become crucial to all other sport organisations; they increasingly have a remit to fulfil government policy. Some of its recent policies are 'A Sporting Future for All' (2001) and 'Game Plan' (2002). The former highlights the importance of coordinating between schools, local clubs and organisations. The latter, in relation to elite sport, covers the broad issue of the success of the UK in international competition, the problems of funding, the complexity of the structures responsible for delivering sport policy and the hosting of massive events.

TASK 4

Outline the reasons a national government would have for devising policies for elite sport.

UK Sport

KEY WORDS

UK Sport
The organisation with the primary aim of developing elite sport in the UK.

The primary aim of **UK Sport** (founded in 1997) is the development of Britain's elite athletes a countrywide policy for the prevention and testing of doping and is responsible for attracting and running major sporting events. It is funded jointly via the government and lottery cash worth £30 million a year. The money is used to either support elite athletes directly or fund the back-up services they need such as medical care.

For the purposes of Module 5, UK Sport is more relevant than Sport England for the development of elite sport.

UK Sport has a remit to:

- encourage and develop higher standards of sporting excellence in the UK
- identify sporting policies that should have a UK-wide application
- identify areas of unnecessary bureaucracy (overly rigid or complex procedures)
- develop and deliver appropriate grant programmes in conjunction with the governing bodies and home county sport councils
- oversee policy on sport science, sports medicine, drug control, coaching and other areas where there is a need for a consistent UK-wide policy
- co-ordinate policy for attracting major international events to the UK
- represent the UK internationally and increase the influence of the UK at an international level.

UK Sport has four key directorates through which it carries out these tasks:

1 Performance development (advises governing bodies and allocates funding)
2 UK Sports Institute (central services based in London with regional network centres)
3 International relations and major events (the UK needs to be in a strong position given the benefits that accrue from major sporting events)
4 Ethics and anti-doping (co-ordination of an effective testing programme and coach education).

Significant changes to the sporting system took effect from 1 April 2006. UK Sport assumed full responsibility for all Olympic and Paralympic performance-related support in England and the UK, from the identification of talent all the way through to performing at the top level.

The transfer of the World Class Potential programme in England, together with responsibility for the direction of the Talented Athlete Scholarship Scheme (TASS), TASS 2012 Scholarships and the English Institute of Sport, integrates the funding and management of high performance sport and provides for the first time, a one-stop-shop for governing bodies and athletes. UK Sport can now have a meaningful impact on decisions across the pathway and ensure that resources are targeted where they are most required.

World Class Performance Pathway
From 1 April 2006, UK Sport assumed full responsibility for all Olympic and Paralympic performance-related support in England, from the identification of talent all the way through to performing at the top level.

In taking on this new responsibility, and remaining focused on a 'no compromise' approach, UK Sport has redefined the terms under which funding and support will be provided. It will operate on three key levels under the umbrella of the **World Class Performance Pathway** (see below).

Combined with the announcement in the April 2006 budget that much higher amounts of funding would be made available for high performance sport through to 2012, UK Sport now has the best possible environment to effect change, deliver its ambitions and make a real difference to athlete support in this country.

The World Class Performance Pathway

This will operate at three key levels:

- World Class Podium – this programme will support sports with realistic

medal capabilities at the next Olympic/Paralympic Games (i.e. a maximum of four years away from the podium).
- World Class Development – this programme is designed to support the stage of the pathway immediately beneath the podium. It will comprise of sports that have demonstrated they have realistic medal winning capabilities for 2012.
- World Class Talent – this programme is designed to support the identification and confirmation of athletes who have the potential to progress through the World Class Pathway with the help of targeted investment. Olympic athletes will be a maximum of eight years away from the podium, but again it could be much less for paralympic athletes.

Sport England

Sport England

The sports council for England. It has a remit to develop sport from the grass roots to elite level.

Since its inception in 1994, Sport England has had a dual role of developing grass roots and elite sport. Over the next decade its remit will be more concerned with grass roots, community-based and health-related programmes. However, its objectives to date remain as:
- Start
- Stay
- Succeed.

In terms of the higher levels of sport, Sport England is involved in the World Class programme, academies and sport college status.

English Institute of Sport (EIS)

English Institute of Sport (EIS)

A nationwide network of world class support services, designed to foster the talents of elite athletes in the UK.

The **English Institute of Sport** (EIS) – is a nationwide network of world class support services, designed to foster the talents of elite athletes in the UK. Services are offered from nine regional multi-sport hub sites and an evolving network of satellite centres.

High performance training venues are the platform for success. Led by Steve Cram, the former World mile record holder and Olympic medallist, it is a dynamic, pro-active organisation dedicated to realising the potential of the modern competitor.

The strategy and ethos of the EIS is set by its national team. The services are delivered by a co-ordinated network of regional teams which feature complementary skills and experience.

Podiatry

Branch of medicine which deals with conditions affecting the feet and ankles.

The range of services supplied by the EIS includes:
- the primary services of sports science and sports medicine
- support including applied physiology, biomechanics, medical consultation, medical screening, nutritional advice, performance analysis, psychology, **podiatry**, strength and conditioning coaching, sports massage and sports vision
- the Performance Lifestyle programme which provides supplementary career and education advice.

The quality of the delivery is assured by the close relationship the EIS is developing with national governing bodies, performance directors, coaches and the athletes themselves. Almost 2000 competitors are currently in the EIS system.

Funded by the Sport England Lottery fund, the EIS operates under the directorship of Wilma Shakespear, a pivotal figure in the development of the Australian Institute System embodied in the EIS ethos – 'making the best better'.

TASK 5

The EIS is based on a regional rather than a 'one centre' approach. Discuss the advantages and disadvantages of this approach.

Sports Coach UK

Sports Coach UK

This organisation provides a range of educational and advisory services for all coaches and works alongside the award schemes of the individual governing bodies.

Sports Coach UK provides a range of educational and advisory services for all coaches, and works alongside the award schemes of the individual governing bodies. It runs the 16 national coaching centres which are primarily based in institutions of higher education. The aims of the organisation are to:

- lead and develop the national standards of coaching
- work with organisations such as local authorities, national governing bodies, the British Olympic Association and higher education to improve the standards and professional development of coaches
- provide high quality education programmes, products and services such as coaching literature, videos, seminars and worksheets, factsheets and databases.

It also runs Coachwise Ltd, Sports Coach UK's wholly-owned trading company.

What should a high quality coach education programme contain? This includes:

- sport-specific knowledge (techniques/strategies)
- performance-related knowledge (fitness/nutrition/mental preparation)
- ethics and philosophy (codes of practice)
- management/vocational skills (planning/time/money)
- teaching/coaching methodology (communication skills)
- practical coaching experience.

National governing bodies

There are approximately 300 governing bodies in the UK. Many are run by unpaid volunteers, though depending on the size of the organisation this has in many cases become the responsibility of paid administrators. They are largely autonomous from government and are represented by the Central Council for Physical Recreation (CCPR) to Sport England.

National governing bodies

They are responsible for overseeing their own sport in the UK.

National governing bodies are responsible for overseeing their own sport in the country. There is no set proforma for governing bodies: some are large, some are wealthy whilst others are not. However, there are some common aims, including:

- establish rules and regulations in accordance with the International Sport Federation (ISF)
- organise competitions

- develop coaching awards and leadership schemes
- select teams for country or UK at international events
- liaise with relevant organisations such as the CCPR, Sport England, local clubs, British Olympic Association and International Sport Federations.

Fig 18.03 Performance athlete development model

Challenges for governing bodies

Performance Athlete Development Model

A ten-year development programme based on the achievement of standards rather than an age-related framework.

- New sports are attracting participants and providing competition for the older, more established sports.
- The decline in school sport has led to governing bodies having to consider how best to develop talent.
- There has been a blurring in definition of amateur and professional sport.
- The need to compete internationally with countries who have developed systematic forms of training has made the governing bodies develop the coaching and structuring of competitions and devote more money to the training of their elite sportspeople.
- Funding has become a key issue. National governing bodies receive money from their member clubs but elite sport requires huge sums of money. For this the governing bodies have had to market themselves in the modern world, especially in trying to attract television coverage which in turn brings in sponsorship deals.
- Lottery funding often brings with it certain requirements such as meeting government targets of participation and developing talent.
- NGBs must produce whole sport plans (WSPs).

Whole sport plan (WSP)

A WSP is a plan for the whole of a sport from grass roots right through to the elite level, that identifies how it will achieve its vision and how it will contribute to Sport England's 'start, stay and succeed' objectives.

PESSCLS

A major government policy to improve the links between schools and local sports clubs.

What are whole sport plans (WSPs)?

- A **whole sport plan** (**WSP**) is a plan for the whole of a sport from grass roots right through to the elite level, that identifies how it will achieve its vision and how it will contribute to Sport England's 'start, stay and succeed' objectives.
- WSPs are Sport England's new way of directing funding and resources to NGBs.
- WSPs will identify the help and resources NGBs need to deliver their whole sport plans, for example, via partners such as county sports partnerships and programmes (e.g. the Physical Education and School Sport and Club Links Strategy (**PESSCLS**). They will give us the opportunity to measure how the NGBs are delivering their sports.

What will WSPs achieve?

- In short, 'start, stay and succeed' (Sport England's objectives).
- The WSPs will allow Sport England to give focused investments to NGBs against the resources they need to achieve their objectives.
- Measurable results will give us an indication of how well NGBs are performing and whether Sport England is getting value for money from our investment.
- Whole sport plans will help create more links with regions and partners in all aspects of sport, benefiting us all through shared best practice.

International Sport Federations (ISFs)

The International Sport Federation (ISF) is the World governing body for each sport. National governing bodies are affiliated to the ISF for that sport. An example would be the Football Association being affiliated to FIFA (the Federation Internationale de Football Associations). An ISF's main responsibilities are to:

- organise events
- arrange sponsorship and television contracts
- formulate the playing and eligibility rules which will be adhered to by the national governing bodies
- take responsibility for the officials and technical aspects of their sport at the Olympics.

British Olympic Association

British Olympic Association (BOA)
A National Olympic Committee (NOC) whose aim is to:
• encourage interest in the Olympic Games
• foster the ideals of the Olympic movement
• organise and co-ordinate British participation in terms of travel and equipment of competitors and officials.

The **British Olympic Association** (BOA) is a National Olympic Committee (NOC). The International Olympic Committee requires each country to have its own Olympic committee. The British Olympic Association is free from government control and traditionally receives no money from the government. Its aims are to:

- encourage interest in the Olympic Games
- foster the ideals of the Olympic movement
- organise and co-ordinate British participation in terms of travel and equipment of competitors and officials
- assist the governing bodies of sport in preparation of their competitions
- advise on public relations with the press
- provide a forum for consultation among governing bodies
- organise an Olympic day in the UK
- raise funds through the British Olympic appeal, mainly from private sources, business sponsors and the general public
- advise on training, nutrition and sports psychology for Olympic coaches
- provide medical and careers advice for athletes
- sponsor medical research into fitness and athletic injuries.

The British Olympic Association belongs to the International Olympic Committee (IOC) (www.olympic.org/ioc). It is the umbrella organisation of the Olympic movement whose primary responsibility is the regular staging of the summer and winter games. The role of the executive board is to:

- observe the Olympic charter
- administer the IOC
- attend to all internal affairs of the organisation
- manage the finances
- inform the session of any rule changes or bye-laws.

National Lottery

National Lottery

Set up in 1994, funding from the lottery is now the primary source of sports funding in the UK.

The **National Lottery** Sports fund has earmarked £20.5 million a year for UK Sport to administer to our top UK medal hopes through the World Class Performance programme and to help attract and stage major sporting events in the UK.

TASK 6

Discuss the suggestion that National Lottery money would be better spent on other social issues such as education.

You need to be able to discuss whether or not an athlete in receipt of lottery funding should be accountable for his or her results.

Sports Aid

Sports Aid (www.sportsaid.org.uk) was established to enable top amateur athletes (at both junior and senior level) to train with similar privileges enjoyed by state sponsored athletes abroad. It is a self-financing organisation, similar to the British Olympic Association, which draws funds from commercial, industrial and private sponsors and fund raising projects. Outstanding competitors usually receive the money. They receive grants according to their personal needs, the costs of their preparation, training and competition, and are usually recommended by their governing body. Since 1976 over £5 million has been given to more than 5000 competitors. Grants are awarded through Sport Aid's charitable trust to talented athletes who are in education, on a low income or have disabilities.

Sports Aid

Sports Aid is a self-financing organisation established to help top amateur athletes with training and competition expenses.

Sports Aid has three main objectives:

1. To further the education of young people through the medium of sport.
2. To encourage those with a social or physical disadvantage to improve their lives through sport.
3. To enable those living in poverty to take advantage of the opportunities offered by sport.

A typical grant is £500 a year. To qualify, athletes would be between 12–18 years old, in genuine financial need and a member of a national squad.

In December 1999, Sports Aid was asked to play a vital role in the development of British sport talent by partnering Sport England in the World Class Start programme (see page 188).

Sporting policies for excellence

Each of the sport organisations mentioned has a remit to develop the elite level within their sport. In order to achieve this they need to develop their own policies as well as recognising that they are part of a national sport system that requires some co-ordination.

School sport

We have already mentioned that the traditional route for UK athletes has been through the school system. However,the decline in school sport, particularly since the 1970s, has become a structural problem for the development of elite sport. In the state sector about two-thirds of schools are failing to meet the government target of two hours of physical activity a week. This has now been raised to four hours!

The government policy of PESSCLS (Physical Education and School Sport and Club Links Strategy) is now firmly embedded within schools, clubs and governing bodies. The overall aim is to increase the proportion of children guided into clubs from School Sport Coordinators partnerships. Primarily, seven major sports will be focussed on (tennis, cricket, rugby union, football, athletics, gymnastics and swimming).

The policy of specialist **Sports Colleges** is part of the specialist schools programme run by the **DfES**. As of September 2003, there were 228 designated sports colleges with a government target of at least 400 by the end of 2005.

Academies are a new type of school. They are ability schools established by sponsors from business, faith or voluntary groups working in innovative partnerships with government and education. Running costs are met by the DfES. They offer a broad and balanced education whilst specialising in sport.

Sport schools are a small selection of specialist, usually residential, sports schools in the UK. Examples are Millfield, Kelly College and Reeds schools. The advantages of such schools include the combination of:

- top quality coaching
- education
- accommodation
- medical science
- a pool of similar talent
- an organised competition structure
- links with professional clubs.

However, there are disadvantages also:

- They form a private network of schools resulting in an exclusive system, drawing inevitably from a limited pool of talent.
- Young people have to experience residential, institutionalised life away from home.
- The physical and psychological demands are high.

Sports Colleges
Sports Colleges are part of the specialist schools programme. They are the regional focus for excellence in physical education and community sport.

Academies
Ability schools established by sponsors from business, faith or voluntary groups working in partnership with government and education. They offer a broad and balanced education but specialise in sport.

DfES
Government Department for Education and Skills, created in 2001.

Gifted and talented

This policy is the government's wider strategy to improve gifted and talented education. It aims to improve the range and quality of teaching, coaching and learning for talented sports people in order to raise their aspirations and improve their performance motivation and self-esteem. Up to 10 per cent of pupils in primary and secondary schools will be supported. It will include the introduction of talent development camps for pupils in Years 6 and 7 (aged 10–12 years).

TASK 7

Conduct a survey of your local area highlighting different types of educational establishments in relation to sporting excellence. Consider sport colleges, academies and so on.
Research a sport of your choice in relation to its policies for developing talent.

World Class Programme

World Class Programme
Established to help governing bodies develop a comprehensive system through which talented individuals can be identified.

Exchequer
Government department responsible for the collection and management of national revenue.

The **World Class Programme** was established to help governing bodies develop a comprehensive system through which talented individuals can be identified. This is in order to achieve success consistently in important international competitions such as the Olympics and Paralympics.

- The World Class Programme provides funding for training, coaching and so on.
- Performers are selected and recommended by their national governing body.
- The governing body is required to draw up development plans and must meet the targets they set if they are to maintain the same level of funding.
- Performers are also required to meet these targets if they are to receive a personal award.
- The money is granted by the Lottery and the **Exchequer**.
- There are four components of the programme: Start, Potential, Performance and Events:
  - **World Class Start** – local authorities and other providers will be helped to put in place coaching schemes and support programmes to give children the best possible sporting start.
  - **World Class Potential** – this part of the programme will assist the development of talented performers to win medals in future (10 years) international competitions.
  - **World Class Performance** – this programme supports the training programme of elite performers who can win medals in the next 6 years.
  - **World Class Events** – this programme aims to attract and stage major sporting events in the UK.

The **World Class Coaching Programme** aims to deliver five key services:

1. *Profiling* – the coach agrees to become involved in one of the following areas: scholarships, mentoring and expert solutions.

2 *Scholarships* – the opportunity for coaches to become involved with international and national experts and to develop experience in a world-class environment.
3 *Mentoring* – provides the coach with a one-to-one platform to exchange experiences and knowledge.
4 *Expert solutions* – provides the solutions to sport-specific issues which will benefit the athlete within the current Olympic cycle.
5 *World Class coaching conference* – a cross-sports programme for coaches in the UK which attracts national and international speakers discuss relevant issues.

In conclusion:
- Sport policy in the UK is characterised by a high degree of inconsistency and includes many organisations which are involved in creating and carrying out policies.
- Sport organisations need to continue to evolve to meet the needs of the modern athlete in the modern sport world.
- The political and economic investment in elite sport needs to be coherent and have staying power.

Revise as you go!

1 What reasons can the government have for investing in elite sport?
2 What factors can determine the level to which an athlete may succeed in a sport?
3 Define the term talent identification.
4 What characteristics should an effective talent identification and development programme contain?
5 What particular challenges does the UK face in developing effective talent identification programmes?
6 What are the main aims of the following organisations in relation to elite sport:
a) UK Sport
b) Sport England
c) Sports Coach UK
d) national governing bodies?
7 What might the advantages and disadvantages be of the British Olympic Association receiving no government funding?

Chapter 19: Sport ethics, deviancy and the law

Learning outcomes

By the end of this chapter you should understand:
- the concepts of contract to compete, mutual agreement, sportsmanship (fair play) and gamesmanship
- the traditional British sports values of amateurism, athleticism and olympism, and their place in the modern day sports world
- the changing nature of amateurism and professionalism from the nineteenth century to the present day
- the effect performing at an elite level has on an individual's sport ethics
- the effects of commercialisation and the media on sport
- the various forms of deviancy including violence (exhibited both by performers and spectators), hooliganism, doping and a 'win at all cost' attitude
- link between the law and sport.

Contract to compete

Mutual agreement

Where opponents agree to abide by the written rules of a sport.

Contract to compete

An unwritten mutual agreement to abide by the written and unwritten rules of the sport.

Etiquette

The conventional rules of behaviour embodied within a sporting situation.

Sportsmanship

Qualities encouraged in sport such as fairness and especially the observance of the unwritten rules or 'spirit of the game.'

Fair play

Equitable conduct; just or equal conditions operate for all involved in the sporting contest.

Whenever we walk onto a football pitch, a netball court, participate in a swimming competition or any other type of competitive sport, we have entered into an unwritten **mutual agreement** with our opponents.

What is the nature of such a **contract to compete**? It is an unwritten agreement whereby opponents have mutually agreed to:
- abide by the written and unwritten rules of the sport
- always give 100 per cent effort
- allow opponents to demonstrate their skill
- accept and understand the need for codes of behaviour such as sportsmanship (see below) and **etiquette**, for example, shaking hands before the start of a football match.

Sometimes such a contract may be broken; for example, when:
- these rules are not followed
- others are denied the equal opportunity to participate. (For example when other players are using drugs to enhance their performance.)

We need to define two words:
- Sportsmanship
- Gamesmanship

Sportsmanship is synonymous with **fair play**. It is a quality displayed by a person or team such as fairness, generosity, observance of the written and unwritten rules, and knowing how to lose gracefully and honourably. These qualities have been highly regarded by British society. An example might be

HOT TIPS

Do not confuse 'contract to compete' with the professional sportsman's contract.

kicking the ball out of play if someone is injured. However, there is evidence that sportsmanship is in decline (see Table 19.01).

Table 19.01 The decline in sportsmanship and possible solutions

Evidence that sportsmanship has declined	How can we encourage sportsmanship?
• Increasing numbers of sport-related prosecutions (e.g. aggression, doping) • More emphasis on winning • Monetary rewards (wages, sponsorship deals, endorsements) make the risk worth it • Spectator behaviour encourages performers to show aggression • The media hype up events and rivalries	• Fair play schemes and campaigns • Positive role models • Better quality officials and use of technology • Development of positive values early on in childhood • Punishment for negative behaviour • Encouraging codes of conduct for players, spectators and clubs

KEY WORDS

Gamesmanship
Bending the rules of the game to gain an advantage.

Gamesmanship is not the breaking of the rules but bending the rules in order to gain an advantage. An example would be tying your shoelaces before your opponent is about to serve. Technically the written rules have not been broken but it is an unethical, tactical ploy to put the opponent off.

HOT TIPS

Do not confuse the two terms sportsmanship and gamesmanship.

Amateurism, athleticism and olympism

Four sport ethics have dominated the British sporting scene. These are:

1 amateurism
2 athleticism
3 olympism
4 professionalism (see pages 194–8).

HOT TIPS

Examination questions will often require you to provide a discussion about the terms gamesmanship and sportsmanship and whether they are relevant today.

Amateurism

Amateurism is a concept which evolved in nineteenth-century England amongst the upper classes, who became known as gentleman amateurs. It was an ideal based upon participating in sport for the love of it rather than for monetary gain, and the participation was deemed more important than the winning. It encompassed the belief in fair play or sportsmanship and abiding by the spirit as well as the rules of the game. The 'all rounder' was highly regarded by the amateurs who believed that he celebrated god-given abilities. Amateurism originally had a social class distinction as it excluded the lower classes, not least because the gentleman amateurs did not wish to be beaten by their social inferiors. The 'manual labour clause' in rowing was a good example of this. The clause stated that no one could compete if 'they were a mechanic, artisan or labourer'.

KEY WORDS

Amateurism
Based on the ideal that participation in sport should be for the love of it rather than for monetary gain.

Fig 19.01 Gentlemen amateurs playing cricket

Shamateur
A term describing amateur performers who receive payments secretly.

Many amateur performers struggled in the twentieth century with commercial pressures and offers of monetary rewards. This led to a situation where some athletes were receiving 'under the table' payments leading to the term **shamateur**. Trust funds were established to try and counter this situation. A trust fund was set up by the governing body of the sport that would hold money received from advertising and so on until the athlete retired from the sport.

Over the last 100 years many changes have occurred. One of the significant changes that occurred at the end of the twentieth century was the Rugby Football Union, the bastion of amateurism, turning professional in 1996. Today the pure ideal of amateurism is difficult to adhere to, and amateurs can now officially receive financial aid from sponsorship, trust funds and organisations such as Sports Aid and the National Lottery. Even the Olympic Games now accept professional performers from sports such as tennis and basketball. Over 150 years, amateur sport has been squeezed by professional sport and become less influential.

Athleticism
Physical endeavour with moral integrity.

Athleticism

Athleticism can be defined as physical endeavour with moral integrity. It became a cult in the latter part of the nineteenth century, with its foundations in the English public schools. These schools took seriously their role of producing gentlemen with qualities of honour, integrity, courage and leadership. Athleticism could only be developed by instilling a strong moral code and was considered to nurture:

- physical qualities, such as the value and enjoyment of a healthy lifestyle, the correction of the temptation to over-study and the ability to learn to cope with winning and losing in a competitive society
- moral qualities such as working as part of a team and conforming with authority
- spiritual links of godliness and manliness (which has been called Muscular Christianity.)

Olympism

Athleticism and amateurism were to impress the travelling Baron Pierre de Coubertin in the nineteenth century. He was so impressed with the moral values the English public schools attached to sport that he established the modern Olympic Games, in 1896, along similar principles.

Olympism
A concept balancing the mind and body which encourages effort, educational values and ethical behaviour.

Olympism is a concept balancing the mind and body. It seeks to encourage effort, educational value and respect for ethical principles. The six goals are:

1 personal excellence
2 sport as education
3 cultural exchange
4 mass participation
5 fair play
6 international understanding.

Fig 19.02 Olympic Games opening ceremony

TASK 1

1 Give specific examples from a sport of your choice to explain how the contract to compete can be broken.

2 Write down some of the common characteristics encompassed in the terms amateurism, athleticism and olympism. To what extent may these characteristics hinder the progression of a performer in the modern day sports world?

TASK 2

To what extent are the values of amateurism, athleticism and olympism still relevant in modern day sport? Consider the discussion points in Table 19.02 (on page 194) and whether they best serve the modern day approach towards sport.

Table 19.02

The values of amateurism, athleticism and olympism that are:	
Still relevant in modern sport	**Less relevant in modern sport**
• We still culturally encourage respect for rules and others. • Physical Education in schools stresses the moral values as much as the physical benefits. • The Olympics are still the biggest competition in the world and they are based on amateurism and ethics (athletes take the Olympic oath). • Fair Play Awards have been given more significance in recent years at the highest level. • Athletes are considered role models for children. • Sport and society would be dysfunctional without any values. • Doping is illegal therefore we must still retain some ethical values. • Traditional values allow everyone to take part at their own level as it is about doing your best.	• Traditional values can hinder hunger for success because the end product/winning is not seen as serious. • Sport in other countries (such as the USA) is based on different principles, i.e. the **Lombardian ethic** that winning isn't the most important thing, it's the only thing (win at all costs). • These values belong to a past culture of 'gentlemanly sport' – the social values of the upper classes. Nowadays all classes compete. • Commercialisation (there are now huge monetary rewards for success) stresses the need to be good at sport. • Professional sport is more dominant than amateur sport at the highest levels. • Professional sports are creeping into the Olympics. • Increasing legislation and prosecutions in sport-related incidents suggests that these values are losing their stronghold.

Lombardian ethic

Winning isn't the most important thing, it's the only thing.

The concepts of amateurism, athleticism and olympism have formed the traditional British approach towards sport. However, it is possible that these values may not be the best preparation for developing elite athletes with the hunger to win in the modern day sports world. The dominant sport ethic in the USA, the Lombardian ethic, commonly accepted as the 'win at all costs' ethic, sharply contrasts with the more gentlemanly British mentality. The

American ethic emphasises the competitive, achievement-orientated, reward-based type of sport behaviour, i.e. the end justifies the means, encompassed in the phrase 'nice guys finish last.' This ethic is more closely connected to professional sport.

The relationship between amateurism and professionalism

Professional sport
A sporting activity that is engaged in for financial gain or as a means of livelihood.

Social mobility
Movement of an individual from a subordinate position in society to a higher or more powerful one.

Professional sport is a concept that can be traced back as far as ancient Rome and is therefore a much earlier concept than amateurism, which emerged in the nineteenth century in England. Earning money from sport has been an avenue of upward **social mobility** for centuries, starting with the Roman gladiators and continuing to the present day sport stars such as David Beckham.

Ancient Rome and industrial England in the nineteenth century shared similar social characteristics, such as the mass of a population living closely together with leisure time to fill and a disposable income to spend on entertainment. However, by the nineteenth century the dominant sport ethic in England was amateurism rather than professionalism.

Fig 19.03 David Beckham earning money from sport via advertising

Professional sport was very much in evidence in England prior to the nineteenth century in a variety of sports. Examples were pedestrianism (an early form of race walking), prize fighting (including early forms of boxing and self defence) and athletics. By the nineteenth century the middle and upper classes favoured the amateur code whilst the professional performers or athletes were always from the lower classes, as they did not have the luxury to participate in sport for the love of it. If they wished to pursue a sporting activity seriously they needed to earn money from it. Because of this they found themselves excluded from many events by the gentleman amateurs who treated professional sport with disdain, believing it lacked the moral codes they held so dear. Hence, amateurism and professionalism became part of a strict social class divide in the nineteenth century and early twentieth century, particularly in England. In the structure of professional sport, the following generalisation of roles could be made:

- lower class: performer
- middle class: agents, promoters and managers
- upper class: **patrons**.

Patron
A person who sponsors any kind of athlete or artist from their private funds.

In professional sport the performer was (and still is) paid by results, hence training and specialising in their 'trade' was important.

Sports have undergone major changes in their amateur/professional status. Rugby football is a useful case study.

Rugby football
Rugby football developed in the nineteenth-century English public schools system based on the codes of amateurism and athleticism. The popularity of the game was such that the working classes in the northern industrial towns adopted the game but needed to be paid to play or at least receive compensation for loss of earnings whilst playing. This led some clubs to pay their players when losing money from not working. This was called **broken-time payments**. The authorities of the game did not agree with this and it eventually led to the north/south split in 1896. This split had a geographical divide as the amateurs tended to be grouped in the south and the working classes in the industrial north. The two forms of rugby that evolved were:

- Rugby Union (amateur)
- Rugby League (professional).

This status quo was to last almost 100 years, with the Union game being regarded as one of the strictest adherents to the amateur code. However, sports in the modern day need to be able to survive commercially and money enables a national governing body to promote the game, finance coaching, competitions and so on. Players who realised they could be paid an income from Rugby League were being tempted to play the professional game. Therefore, in 1996 the Union game turned professional, bending to the commercial pressures of the modern day sport world.

Broken-time payments
Payments made to compensate working class players for loss of earnings whilst playing sports such as soccer and rugby football.

TASK 3
Consider some of the quotes on page 197 and answer the following question. *What are the advantages and disadvantages, suggested by the players, of Rugby Union turning professional?*
(Sources: *Professionalism: The Players' view* (BBC Sport, 2005/04/01) and *Rugby in danger of player burnout* (BBC Sport, 2005/03/01))

Professionalism at a price

In the twentieth and twenty-first centuries, many sports have become professional and amateurism has become constrained and squeezed. Note: you can be an amateur and compete for your country, such as in judo.

HOT TIPS

Do not assume professional sport means a high level of skill and amateur sport means a low level of skill. However, where the two codes exist in the sport, for example, football, the professional performers are likely to compete at a higher standard.

HOT TIPS

Remember – professional or amateur is not about the level the performer competes at but the administration of that sport – that is, does it pay its performers?

'We're better players now, without a shadow of a doubt. I played in the amateur era and you just couldn't dedicate as much time to it.'

'The game has moved on so far now you need to dedicate every day of the week to rugby.'

'I don't think there's quite the risk of player burnout that some people fear. With professionalism it means that when you're not playing or training, you're relaxing and your recovery time is good.'

'We've got great fitness coaches and great advisers who know if you're burning out; in fact many people just say "burnout" because they're tired.'

'The game has developed immensely. The physical nature is now so unrelenting and unsympathetic almost to the point that it's ridiculous.'

'England has so far avoided doping controversies suffered by other countries but players could be tempted in the future if pressures are not eased.'

'In the amateur ethos the pitches were poor, the standard of rugby was consequently poor. It was slow and not a good spectacle.'

'There are issues with regard to the politics of the game and how it is run, specifically in England where you have the club versus country debate. The issue is for guys playing international rugby who then come back to club rugby without any break.'

'From a personal point of view there are more games being put on the list and I think that's a money-making scheme.'

Fig 19.04 The advantages and disadvantages of turning professional

However, where a sport has both amateur and professional performers, the professional performers tend to be regarded as being of a higher standard.

Media

Forms of mass communication to the general public, comprising newspapers, radio, television, Internet and all forms of advertising.

Sponsorship

The provision of funds or other forms of support to an individual or event for a commercial return.

Endorsements

Where athletes display companies' names on their equipment, clothing and vehicles. The athletes are contracted to publicly declare their approval of a product or service.

Many professional performers have a high status in their sport and if the sport receives a high level of **media** coverage they become household names. As professional performers they are paid by results and therefore success in their sport is crucial. This places heavy expectations on them, from themselves, coaches, spectators, the media and so on. The pressure to perform consistently and at a high level can cause the 'win at all costs' ethic to be adhered to, overriding the more traditional British values associated with sport.

Therefore, deviant behaviour in the form of aggression, cheating and even doping can be considered necessary in order to win. (Deviant behaviour will be covered in detail later in this chapter.)

Sponsorship and **endorsements** are very good earners for sport performers and a charismatic, high profile performer is more likely to attract lucrative sponsorship deals.

Fig 19.05 Professional players are not necessarily better than amateur performers, but they are paid for their sport.

However, sponsors bring with them their own pressures, particularly expecting the performer to make regular appearances. Sponsors might even encourage a player to play when injured.

TASK 4

Research sports that have retained their amateur status. Some examples might be judo or swimming. Consider the advantages and disadvantages of this situation for these sports.

Possible examination questions, linking the topics of amateurism and professionalism from the nineteenth century to the present day, are shown below.

Role model
An individual admired for their skill, values or attitudes. They can influence young people's behaviour.

Q: *Why is the professional sport performer highly regarded in modern day society?*

- Professional sports tend to get more media coverage, giving the sport a high profile.
- The athletes become well-known, household names. They are seen as **role models**, often achieving celebrity status.
- Modern societies respect winners and high earners as most are based on a meritocratic system.
- Professional sport tends to follow the Lombardian ethic – winning isn't the most important thing, it's the only thing.
- Professional sport is often considered to be more entertaining and exciting with high standards of performance.
- Professional sport allows upward social mobility with some performers achieving the dream of 'rags to riches'.

Q: *Why did the amateur performer have a higher status than the professional performer in the nineteenth century?*

- Amateurs were from the middle and upper classes – the most powerful groups in society.
- Professionals were from the working classes who often worked for the patron (upper class).
- Amateurs applied moral values to sport which distinguished them from the lower class professionals.
- The amateurs had the power to exclude the working classes, e.g. manual labour clause in rowing and the existence of closed competitions, where amateurs and professionals were not allowed to compete together.

Q: *How can a professional performer be considered a commercial object?*

- He or she signs a contract just as a person signs a business contract.
- He or she can be 'hired and fired' by the owner or manager.
- The performer is used to advertise and endorse a company's product, bringing a financial return to a company.
- His or her image is exploited to achieve company goals. Therefore the performer needs to market and sell him or herself.
- By achieving successful results consistently the performer is financially rewarded, which is important as this is his or her income.

Q: *What are the pressures of being a role model?*

- There is an invasion of privacy by the media. The media are as interested in the private lives of athletes as much as their sporting prowess.
- Their behaviour is considered to influence the behaviour of young people and therefore they need to maintain a good, clean image.
- As they need to perform consistently and regularly this often leads to over-training and even performing when injured.
- Physical and psychological stress can be the result of a highly competitive environment.

Commercialisation and the media

Commercialisation has brought about profound changes in the structure of many sports, with media companies often able to call the shots.

The emergence of commercialism

Initial commercial developments occurred in the nineteenth century as spectator sports emerged. It is no coincidence that commercial sports first appeared in England – the first country to develop industrialisation and communication networks. Allied with this was the emergence of a mass of the population with increasing free time and disposable income in need of excitement and entertainment. People's entertainment value was exploited by individuals who saw the opportunity to organise regular sporting events. Promoters and agents emerged and **commercialism** became an integral part of sport. Since then:

Commercialism

An emphasis on the principles of commerce with a focus on profit.

- Sport has become a global product advertised and marketed across the world.
- The vast profit potential of sport in the television age was first recognised in the 1980s, attracting entrepreneurs.
- The important issues were media rights, sponsorship deals and merchandising.
- The huge sums paid for TV and other media rights have turned sport into a global business.
- Sports clothing and equipment industries form another important part of the global sport complex, such as Nike and Adidas.
- The Olympics have come to rely heavily on the money from exclusive rights deals negotiated with top sponsors.
- Building brand awareness through sport has become an important part of modern marketing.
- Top-level soccer has changed out of all recognition over the last 20 years, as huge amounts of money have flowed into those clubs able to capitalise on global media interest.
- The richest clubs buy the best players they can afford – a system that has opened a wide gap between the top ranking clubs and those without financial backing.
- The old **turnstile** system of **cash receipts** – attractive to money launderers but a nightmare for club auditors as the system could be abused by the people manning the turnstile – has given way to sophisticated electronic systems, which enable supporters to buy merchandise as well as tickets.
- Organising bodies such as the National Basketball Association, National Football League and National Hockey League behave like multinational companies, spreading their influence and products around the globe through aggressive marketing and well-directed media campaigns.
- The success of US-style business practices has jolted even traditional sports such as rugby and cricket.
- The betting industry has long been bound up with sports such as horse racing, boxing and football. In the UK horse racing accounts for 70 per cent of revenue for the top three bookmakers, yet less then a tenth of the

Turnstile

A mechanical gate or barrier with metal arms that are turned to admit one person at a time.

Cash receipts

A written acknowledgement by a receiver of money.

UK population are regular race followers.
- New technology could transform the gambling industry in the future, broadening the range of sports betting (e.g. online betting) and making it a more regular part of daily life.
- The increasing concentration of money and power in a limited number of giant sporting **conglomerates**, especially those which combine media clout with club ownership or merchandising interests, has caused increased unease. In 1998 BSkyB tried to buy control over Manchester United but the bid was blocked by the **UK Monopolies and Mergers Commission** (MMC). The MMC ruled that the takeover could damage the quality of British football by reinforcing 'the trend towards greater inequality of wealth between clubs, weakening the smaller ones'.
- Millionaires have rescued many sports clubs, but patronage by rich individuals has largely been replaced by corporate sponsorship.
- Many athletes do not have much control over their own careers.

Conglomerate
A corporation made up of several companies in different businesses.

UK Monopolies and Mergers Commission (MMC)
Independent public body that regulates the growth of major industries in the UK. Since 1999 the MMC has been replaced by the Competition Commission.

Golf and tennis are amongst the few major sports which have a relatively democratic form of government; the players decide very much how things should be run and make their own decisions about when and where they will play and which sponsorship deals to take.

The characteristics of commercial sport

Commercial sport has close links with:
- professional sport
- sponsorship/business
- entertainment (sport becomes a spectacle or display for spectators)
- gate receipts/an affluent population
- contracts (athletes/clubs/businesses/stock market/merchandise/TV rights)
- athletes as commodities/endorsements/an asset to the company
- the media
- winning and success.

Table 19.03 Advantages and disadvantages of commercialism in sport

Advantages of commercialism in sport:	Disadvantages of commercialism in sport:
• Provides capital for sport leading to improved resources/facilities/coaching • Leads to more events • Provides role models (which can encourage increased participation in sport) • Allows athletes to earn an income/train full-time • Raises the profile of sport itself	• Encourages deviant behaviour as success becomes crucial • Encourages more people to spectate rather than participate • Tends to support already popular sports and so the gap widens between other sports • Favours male over female elite over grass roots/able bodied over disabled • Leads to a squeeze on amateur sport, e.g. Rugby Union turning professional • Can reward certain types of play/behaviour to suit marketing objectives – for example, rewarding a cricketer if he hits the ball towards an advertising boarding

Professional performers

Professional performers:
- receive their income from participating in sport
- are paid by achieving successful results
- must specialise in a sport, which requires serious training
- can be owned, contracted, transferred and sold
- need to deliver high standards of performance on a regular basis
- are entertainers who become household names
- are public commodities and as such suffer from a lack of privacy.

Michelle Wie

Golfing phenomenon Michelle Wie has been adopted by publicists and marketing experts. Though an undoubted talent she has not yet won any major tournaments, however, the media hype, lucrative endorsements and the press conferences have ensured she already has a significant public profile. She has finished in the top ten in a few major women's tournaments and performed respectably in some men's events. When she played in the John Deere Classic (July 2005), takings for the tournament rose by 40 per cent and television ratings increased by more than 50 per cent. In response some television networks changed their schedules in order to guarantee Wie's tee times. Perhaps the fact that Wie has not played in so many tournaments is a clever marketing ploy; it removes the chances of too many defeats which might spoil the attraction of 'unknown potential'.

So why is so much attention paid to her by the media and commercial companies?

She looks good – tall, slim, elegant and dresses in eye-catching outfits. She captures the perfect image for the future of golf, both in terms of attracting females and young people to the game as well as promoting the game for people other than middle-aged, white members of exclusive clubs. Michelle Wie is also hugely competitive with no fears about breaking into the men's game. She has not made any secret of the fact that she is ambitious especially in 'taking on the men'. The sporting battle between the sexes is still an attractive prospect to many people. The men's tours are realising, and cashing in on, the publicity opportunities of such challenges. When Wie turned professional, it coincided with The Royal and Ancient announcement that women would be eligible to qualify for the 2006 Open. Nike and Sony have already signed her to contracts adding up to $10 million. She has become a major corporate enterprise.

How might this affect a young golfer?

Firstly, she will face the ever higher expectations, attention and subsequent pressure. She already has an entourage who follow her round on tour including image consultants, marketers, psychologists, coaches and so on. How much control will she be able to maintain in her life? Will the hype and exploitation ultimately ruin her? What is good for selling merchandise may not be the best recipe for a young developing player.

TASK 5

Discuss whether an athlete should consider the nature of a sponsor's product. For example, an athlete may be offered a contract from a tobacco company.

Who actually controls sport?

When sport became more organised and structured in the nineteenth century, sports were controlled by their own governing bodies which were established for this purpose. In the UK this was very much in the hands of the middle and upper classes who favoured the amateur code. This code did not welcome the commercial side of sport.

In the late twentieth century a shift in power occurred and the traditional governing bodies have had to change their approach towards the relationship between sport and money. In order to compete in the modern day sport world many of these traditional governing bodies have had to embrace the commercial world for what it can offer their sport.

Though sport enjoys mass participation, the power over rule-making, merchandising and media rights still lies with a small number of individuals and companies. Sports such as football, cricket and rugby are controlled by either a monopolistic ruling body or a small group of individuals or companies. Although unions have developed considerable power over the years, they act more as a blocking mechanism than an active participant in running the sport.

Ruling bodies are now losing ground to large efficient companies like News International, owned by Rupert Murdoch. He is seen as one of the most powerful men in world sport and is in control of the Fox, Sky and Star TV networks, giving him great power in broadcasting. Murdoch's companies have been expanding through the Internet, which is seen as the future of sports coverage for fans.

FIFA decides where the world cup is to be staged – the biggest commercial decision in world football. The shortcomings of the system came to an angry public attention when Germany were named as host for the 2006 competition, beating the widely anticipated winner South Africa by a single vote.

The development of the Olympics as a major global event came during the presidency of Juan Antonio Samaranch (1980–2001). His autocratic style led to much criticism, but he was a shrewd leader and guided the event into the new world of media domination.

How does the media and commercialisation affect sport?

Some sports have changed as a result of commercial and media interest. For example:

- Rules have been introduced to speed up the action to prevent spectator boredom.
- Changes have been made in scoring to create more excitement.
- Breaks are provided in play so sponsors can advertise their products.
- The format of competitions has changed such as 20/20 in cricket.
- The competitive season has been extended.
- Athletes can be put under pressure to perform even when injured.
- Business administrators now have more control of sport.
- The fourth official has been introduced to help with decisions.
- More media coverage can increase participation in a sport. Therefore less coverage of female sport can affect participation, figures and funding.
- The readers, listeners and viewers of sport are heavily influenced by the values and beliefs of those who commentate on the events, influencing their interpretation of different situations.
- The media can hype up events which can be detrimental in some circumstances.
- Interactive technology enables individual viewers to make individual choices, such as following their favourite player.
- The increase in technology has led to a more personal experience for the viewer – cameras can be fitted in a racing car, under water and in a goal.
- Action replays and freeze frames allow more detailed analysis to take place.
- Certain prestigious sport events are ring-fenced, particularly international events. Sometimes these are only available to the more exclusive satellite or cable subscription channels and not to the ordinary viewer on terrestrial TV.

Deviancy and sport

Deviancy
Behaviour which goes against societies general norms and values.

Dysfunctional behaviour
This occurs when a part of the social structure does not contribute positively to the maintenance of society, resulting in disharmony and conflict.

So far we have focussed on the traditional values of amateurism, athleticism and olympism. These values have underpinned the British sport system and as a nation we have viewed them positively. However, as we know, the sports world is also full of behaviour that goes against these principles and ethics. This type of behaviour can be referred to as **deviant** or **dysfunctional behaviour**.

Deviant behaviour is behaviour which goes against society's general norms and values. This can be criminally deviant, that is, against the law, or morally deviant, whereby no law has been broken but society would generally not consider the behaviour in a positive light. Consider looking after a four-year-old for a day. Much of what you would say would confirm society's values, such as, respect for other people, respect for property and so on. For example, you might find yourself saying 'Don't hit your little brother, be nice to him' or 'Don't stand on that, you'll break it.'

TASK 6

List examples of deviant behaviour in a variety of sports and say why you consider it to be deviant behaviour.

If we consider the phrase 'against society's norms and values' it is clear that someone or some group in society has imposed their set of ideas on others. This group would be considered the dominant group in society and in the UK could be deemed to be white, male and middle class. This is the group that has the most control and power in terms of distribution of resources and decision making at the highest levels. Therefore groups of people who fall outside these boundaries may well hold opposing views and opinions and have different behaviour patterns, but this would not necessarily mean they were 'wrong'. Thus deviancy is relative and deviants may be victims of a power system that makes the rules.

For this specification you will only be directly examined on negative deviancy – aggression and violence; doping and hooliganism.

Athletes become part of a community bonded by a sense of commitment and are often encouraged to behave in ways that would not be accepted in other areas of life. 'On the field' deviant behaviour includes 'violations of norms that occur while preparing or participating in sports events' (Coakley 1993). It can be caused by the pressure of the media, coaches, sponsorship deals and so on. If the athlete's behaviour breaks the rules of the sport it can be dealt with appropriately, but a culture has developed that accepts this type of behaviour and even deems it necessary for the sake of the win.

Negative deviancy
In sporting situations this can include violations such as deliberately fouling another player or taking performance enhancing drugs. The main motivation is to win at all costs.

Positive deviancy
Athletes are encouraged to behave in ways that would be unacceptable in other spheres of life. This can be classed as over-conformity to the sport ethic. An example of positive deviancy may be where an athlete is encouraged to over-train or perform when injured.

There are two types of deviancy:

1 **Negative deviancy** – in sporting situations this can include violations such as deliberately fouling another player or taking performance enhancing drugs. The main motivation is to win at all costs.
2 **Positive deviancy** – athletes are encouraged to behave in ways that would be unacceptable in other spheres of life. This can be classed as over-conformity to the sport ethic. An example of positive deviancy may be where an athlete is encouraged to over-train or perform when injured; in other aspects of life we would not encourage someone to cause further damage to his or her health.

Positive deviancy is a slightly more difficult aspect of deviant behaviour and might relate to the motivation for that behaviour. For example, it may be about not letting people down rather than simply wanting to be the best.

We will now focus on the specific issues of:

- aggression and violence
- hooliganism
- doping.

Aggression and violence

TASK 7

'Serious sport has nothing to do with fair play. It is a mixture of hatred, jealousy, boastfulness and disregard of all rules and sadistic pleasure in witnessing violence. In other words it is war minus the shooting'. (George Orwell, *Shooting an Elephant,* 1936)

In groups, prepare a discussion that both supports and refutes the statement made by George Orwell.

Conflict
Change and/or progress are made by one group at the expense of another.

Aggression
The intention to harm another human being either verbally or mentally.

Balanced tension
A degree of stress can be productive if it is controlled and channelled.

All sport involves some sort of **conflict**, which can be positive or negative – it is the essence of competition. If it is controlled it is functional, but if not it can soon become dysfunctional, that is, negative to the players, officials, spectators and the very sport itself.

We attempt to control any conflict situations by channelling that **aggression** in a positive way which can act as a catharsis or stress relief. Channelled aggression or **balanced tension** is the ability to utilise all your resources to achieve optimum performance without using unlawful or unethical strategies. Spectators are not able to release their tension in the same way as the performers who are actively exerting themselves. This can cause frustration which may lead to violence.

You will cover the theories of aggression (instinct theory, frustration–aggression hypotheses and the social learning theory) in the psychology aspect of the A-level, but you will not be expected to use these theories in any detail for this section.

Conflict appears in many forms:

- within yourself, for example, striving for a personal best
- against another team or within a team, for example, between top goal scorers
- against the environment/nature, for example, the conquest of a mountain
- against a crowd, for example, players becoming aggressive or abusive towards spectators
- against officials.

Conflict can also be determined by the nature of the activity, for example contact or non-contact sports.

TASK 8

Draw up a list of the causes of aggression in a sport performer.

Spectator violence – football hooliganism

Hooligan
A disorderly, violent young person usually associated with the game of football.

Professional football is by far the most popular spectator sport in Britain. Today it is estimated that between 4 to 5 million people attend a football match in England and Wales every year. However, this number is smaller than it used to be and there are many complex reasons for this, such as changing leisure patterns. However, many people blame football's relative decline up until the mid-1980s on football hooliganism.

Although football hooliganism only became recognised by the government and the media as a serious problem in the 1960s, **hooligan** behaviour at football, particularly in England, has a long history. 'Roughs' were regularly reported as causing trouble at matches in the professional game's early years at the end of the nineteenth century, on occasions attacking and stoning referees as well as the visiting players. It was not until the early 1960s, however, that the media coverage of football began once more regularly to report hooliganism at matches. Around this time, too, there was a general 'moral panic' (Cohen, 1973) about the behaviour of young people, sparked by:

- rising juvenile crime rates
- uncertainty about the future
- the emergence of a number of 'threatening' national youth styles, like that of the 'teddy boy'
- racial tensions symbolised by the Notting Hill disturbances of 1958.

It was around this time that football hooliganism in England began to take on a more cohesive and organised appearance.

Possible causes of hooliganism

The mid-1960s saw alliances being formed between groups of young men drawn largely from working-class housing estates and suburbs. Some sociologists believe this acted as an outlet for defending local masculine reputations and territories, such as streets and terraces.

An English disease?

Football hooliganism is often cited as an 'English' problem, possibly because, as mentioned earlier, England has a long history of football spectator disorders, going back to the early days of the professional sport in England in the nineteenth century. But evidence does not support this. In the early 1960s, the English wanted to pull out of European club competition because of their fears about foreign supporters and players becoming aggressive towards them. However, football hooliganism does appear to be an issue for the national side, although other countries also have serious hooligan incidents.

HOT TIPS

For the purpose of this specification you will need to understand that there are a variety of causes of hooliganism and be able to discuss the validity of these theories.

Theories of hooliganism

Most of the evidence on hooligan offenders suggests that they are:

- in their late teens or their 20s (though some 'leaders' are older)
- mainly in manual or lower clerical occupations or, to a lesser extent, are unemployed or working in the **'grey' economy**, and that they come mainly from working-class backgrounds
- ritualistic and non-violent, i.e. they do not always engage in acts of violence in their behaviour (Marsh et al, 1978)
- not always from working-class backgrounds. Unsurprisingly, London hooligans tend to be more affluent than their northern counterparts, and it is certainly 'stylish' and 'macho' in these football circles to have a distinctive style in terms of dress, etc for example
- sometimes spontaneous and 'random' in their acts of violence but can also be involved in political conspiracies and the more formal

KEY WORDS

Grey economy

Grey goods are not illegal; they are sold outside of normal distribution channels by companies that have no relationship with the producer of the goods.

organisation of hooligan assaults. Though reports of the extent to which hooliganism is 'organised' with political influences may be over-dramatised, the English national side does seem to have been something of a focus for the expression of racist sentiments among some young fans, especially in the 1980s.

However, sociologists at Leicester University (Dunning et al 1988) criticised Marsh et al (1978), not for arguing that terrace behaviour was ritualistic or rule-governed, but rather for understating the amount of 'real' violence which occurred at matches. They suggest that hooliganism is a particular form of aggressive **masculinity**, especially in lower class communities. In these 'rough' neighbourhoods young males are socialised (at home, at work, in peer group gangs, etc.) into standards that value and reward publicly assertive and openly aggressive and violent expressions of masculinity. Young men are expected to be able to 'look after themselves'.

Masculinity
Possessing qualities or characteristics considered typical or appropriate to a man. Examples might be dominant, strong, forceful.

Some fights are even pre-arranged, by telephone, away from matches, especially as police surveillance techniques have limited opportunities for fighting in and around stadia. As well as being rewarded with a manly status, the camaraderie, loyalty and 'entertainment' value of hooligan involvement is also prized by young men whose opportunities for status and excitement via other channels is relatively limited.

Heavy drinking, for example, is often a key element in a 'good day out', and drinking offences figure strongly in national football arrest statistics in England. However, drinking occurs in many other sports, for example, rugby, but does not seem to result in hooliganism.

The sociologist Ian Taylor (1987) argues that the class fraction identified by the Leicester research (1988) as the main production ground for hooliganism cannot account for the rise of the high-spending and fashionable soccer 'casual' who was at the heart of English hooliganism in Europe in the 1990s. 'Casuals' use their conspicuous consumption of expensive and stylish clothing as another means of competing with their hooligan rivals. Taylor favours the 'masculinity' theory rather than class as being the key to the current hooligan problem.

More recently, Robson's important and detailed work on Millwall fans, 'No-One Likes Us, We Don't Care' (2000) suggests that the practices of hooliganism – and racism – among some of the club's fans should also be interpreted as a form of resistance; fans are objecting to the intrusion of more middle-class sensibilities into the sport and local culture. Many working-class fans have been isolated by high ticket prices and corporate hospitality.

Armstrong (1994, 1997) asserts that gang members of 'The Blades' firm at Sheffield United come from a range of locations and backgrounds. Armstrong claims they are involved in hooliganism primarily because it provides 'social drama' and the opportunity to 'belong', achieve 'honour' and inflict shame on opponents. For him, hooligan groups are, in fact, very diverse in their make up – they can include fans drawn from across classes and anti-racists. They show few signs of organisation and they mainly enjoy confrontation rather than violence.

Finn (1994) sees hooliganism as an example of the search for a 'flow' or 'peak' experience; an intense, emotional experience not usually encountered in everyday life. Flow experiences allow for an open expression of shared, collective emotionality. Hooligans, like other fans, seek peak or flow experiences through their involvement in football; unlike other fans, however, they reject the vicarious role of a football supporter in favour of a more active and rewarding role as a direct participant in spectator confrontations. Kerr (1994) also believes that hooliganism, like other sorts of affective crimes (crimes which are motivated by emotional arousal, such as joy-riding), reflects the search for high levels of emotional arousal through risk-taking against a general background of long periods of boredom.

A summary of hooligan theories

It is clear that:

- risk and excitement are central to the hooligan phenomenon
- it is largely young men who are involved
- heavy drinking and violence seem to be linked and at least some of those young men regularly involved in hooliganism seem to be aggressive in certain circumstances with or without drink
- hooligans can be drawn from a wide variety of backgrounds with differing motivations
- racism is an issue in certain situations, particularly at a national event
- incidents of violence or poor refereeing on the field can trigger hooligan disturbances but, once again, it is difficult to argue that such incidents are a deep cause of hooliganism. After all, some hooligan incidents occur hours before a match has even kicked off! Also, there are many more violent sports than football which have not had the same problems of hooliganism
- when newspapers report on football, they use the sort of language which seems more appropriate to the world of war than that of sport (Hall, 1978). This probably helps to heighten rivalries between opposing fan groups, as do the 'predictions' newspapers sometimes make that 'trouble' is likely to occur between rival fans or that the police and local residents are preparing for an 'invasion' of visiting fans or are being placed on 'red alert'. This sort of reporting has been identified by fans themselves as being dangerous, both in terms of its identification of miscreants and also in its alleged distortions and prejudices.

Controlling hooliganism

Most Premier League matches these days require between 25 to 100 police officers to control crowds and limit hooligan outbreaks, but 'high risk' matches demand more.

The police have now established a complex intelligence network for exchanging information about 'troublesome' fans, under the auspices of the National Criminal Intelligence Services (NCIS) Football Intelligence Unit. The use of Football Trust-funded closed circuit TV (CCTV) equipment by the police in and around grounds has also contributed to limiting problems in these areas and to the successful prosecution of offenders. In fact, it is now an offence to trespass onto the pitch or its surrounds, following the Football Offences Act of 1991, and anyone who does so is likely to be traced from CCTV coverage of their activities.

Recent legislation has helped the police deal with hooliganism, though some of it is also controversial:

- The Public Disorder Act of 1986 allowed courts to make exclusion orders banning fans from grounds.
- The Football Spectators Act of 1989 allowed courts to impose restriction orders on convicted fans to prevent them attending matches abroad involving England or Wales.
- The Football Offences Act 1991 created three new offences of disorderly behaviour:
  1. Throwing missiles towards the pitch or spectators.
  2. Taking part in indecent or racialist chanting.
  3. Going on the pitch or its surrounds without lawful authority.

Over the past 20 years or so, clubs have been forced by circumstances, by legislation or both, to spend a considerable amount of money on trying to make their grounds more hooligan proof. Linked with these anti-hooligan and modernising measures is the issue of spectator safety. The post-war years have seen a number of spectator disasters, one example being the FA Cup semi-final at Hillsborough in Sheffield, where 96 Liverpool supporters were crushed to death in a section of terracing surrounded by high perimeter fencing. Since major football grounds in Britain became modernised, unfenced and all-seated in the early 1990s following Hillsborough, they do seem to have become safer and less violent venues than those of even five years ago. As football crowds have continued to rise in England, and as perimeter fences have given way to surveillance cameras and new catch-all offences for hooliganism, so match arrests and the size of police commitments at English football have steadily declined.

In addition to these changes, many clubs have also introduced family enclosures as a means of encouraging parents to attend matches with their children in safety. Clubs have traditionally provided rather poor facilities for female fans and for youngsters. A national Community Programme in Professional Football run jointly by the PFA, the FA, the Premier League and the Football League, is now in operation at almost all of the 92 professional clubs. This scheme aims to increase local community involvement in clubs and promote better behaviour among young spectators.

Recent government legislation also provides for:
- restrictions on the carriage and consumption of alcohol at football
- the banning from matches of previous football offenders
- the making of racist abuse and missile throwing offences
- the making of trespass onto the playing area illegal.

Part Two of the Football Spectators Act (1989) was designed to be used to prevent hooligan offenders from travelling abroad to watch international matches.

Despite these problems the game is currently enjoying a boom in its:
- attendance
- finances (at least at the top)
- ability to attract major foreign players
- image.

Its new commercialised and highly-marketed format may be leaving behind sections of the game's 'traditional' audience, including, perhaps, some hooligan fans. The following are all helping to regulate and control attendance at matches:
- high ticket prices
- the loss of terracing has made grounds safer and less violent
- the sometimes oppressive management and stewarding of the football audience
- the extensive merchandising of top English clubs
- the changing (more 'feminised') atmosphere at football clubs in England
- the increasing number of season ticket holders at English clubs.

HOT TIPS

Be prepared to outline strategies that the clubs, communities and security forces can use to prevent or reduce the incidents of hooliganism.

'Traditional' young male fans – 'lads' – may well be bored by, or excluded from, the 'new' football in England. One view is that some of them are now rather more interested in new dance/drugs cultures than in the 'passionless' and more 'middle-class' sport the English game is allegedly becoming (Gilman, 1994). Some people might put this change in the game down to the Americanisation of sport which is happening globally. English football clubs have imported intrusive ideas about promoting the sport from the USA:

- blaring music
- cheerleaders
- animal mascots
- licensed products from key rings to children's clothes.

Aggression, violence and hooliganism – a summary

Table 19.04 Violence in sport

Possible causes	Consequences	Solutions or remedies
• Nature of the sport, e.g. football is linked with aggression whilst gymnastics is not • History of an event, e.g. a derby involves intense local rivalry • Observed violence (if players or spectators see a violent act it can often incite a violent response) • Nature of stadium, e.g. all seater • Referee's decisions • Monetary rewards • Peer pressure • Excitement/adrenaline rush • Political groups • Loyalty/patriotism • Importance of event • Media hype • Alcohol • Frustration	• Loss of sponsors • Poor image for attracting new talent • Loss of spectators • Banning of supporters • Loss of points/elimination from competitions • Negative role models • Incites trouble within a wider population	• Crowd segregation with family zones • Limit attendance • Fair-play charters • Punishment more severe, e.g. fines/prosecutions • Develop positive role models – shame negative role models • Develop club/community links/education programmes • Tighter security/CCTV, etc. • Control alcohol availability • Responsible media reporting • Improve facilities

TASK 9

Outline the theories of football hooliganism and discuss their validity. Use a table format similar to the example shown below:

Theories of hooliganism	Discussion of validity
Hooligans come from the working-class section of the population.	Evidence shows that many offenders are from middle-class occupations.

Doping

The issue of doping in sport goes back to Ancient Greece and Rome where athletes resorted to taking drugs to either mask pain or to enhance performance. For the purposes of this specification you only need to focus on the present day. Any method used to enhance performance is called an **ergogenic aid** and includes the use of technology for improving the effectiveness of equipment. In this case we are only concerned with performance enhancing drugs.

Table 19.05 opposite outlines the types of **doping agents** that are banned by the **World Anti-Doping Agency** (WADA).

Table 19.05 Drugs banned by WADA

Drugs which are banned during competition	Substances banned during and outside the competitive season	Prohibited methods	Classes banned in specific sports
• **Stimulants** • Narcotics • Cannabinoids • Glucocorticoids	• Anabolic agents, e.g. steroids • Hormones and related substances, e.g. peptide hormones • Beta-2 agonists • Anti-oestrogenic agents • **Diuretics** and other masking agents	• Enhancement of oxygen transfer, e.g. EPO (**erythopoietin**). The synthetic version has become the cheat's way of using the drug. • Pharmacological, chemical and physical manipulation, e.g. **anabolic steroids** • Gene doping	• Alcohol • **Beta blockers**

Ergogenic aids
Refers to any substance that improves performance.

Doping agents
A term used to denote any illegal drug such as cannabis or narcotics which will help improve the performance of an athlete.

World Anti-Doping Agency (WADA)
Partnership of governments and sport in the attempt to standardise anti-doping programmes.

Stimulants
Substances such as amphetamines used to stimulate physiological activity; they improve endurance and mental alertness.

Diuretics
Drugs used to reduce the weight of athletes in sports such as gymnastics.

Erythopoietin (EPO)
A naturally occurring hormone produced by the kidneys that stimulates red cell production.

Anabolic steroid
Artificially produced male hormones which help to repair the body after periods of stress.

Beta blockers
Drugs used by athletes to steady nerves in sports such as archery.

Blood doping
The removal and reinfusion of a person's blood to improve the aerobic capacity by increasing the number of red blood cells.

Table 19.06 below highlights various types of drugs, their side effects and their use in specific sports.

Table 19.06 Different drugs, their uses and side-effects in sport

Types of drugs	Reasons for use	Side-effects	Sport
Anabolic steroids – artificially produced male hormones	• Promote muscle growth • Ability to train harder with less fatigue • Repair body after stress • Increased aggression	• Females develop male features • Liver/heart damage	• Athletics • Swimming • Power/ explosive events
Narcotic analgesics – 'pain killers'	• Reduce pain • Mask injury	• Highly addictive • Respiratory problems • Nausea	• All sports
Stimulants – stimulate body both mentally and physically	• Reduce tiredness • Increase alertness • Increase endurance	• Rise in blood pressure/ temperature • Addiction • Death	• Cycling • Boxing
Beta blockers	• Steady nerves • Stop trembling	• Lowers blood pressure • Slows heart rate • Tiredness	• Shooting • Archery • Snooker
Diuretics – remove fluid from body	• Lose weight quickly	• Dehydration • Dizziness • Faintness	• Jockeys • Boxers
Peptide hormones – naturally occurring, e.g. EPO	• Build and mend muscle • Increase oxygen transport	• Muscle wasting • EPO increases red cells in blood	• Similar to steroids
Blood doping – injection of blood to increase number of blood cells	• Body has more energy to work	• Allergic reactions • AIDS/hepatitis • Blood clots	• Running • Cycling • Marathons • Skiing

HOT TIPS

Be prepared to provide arguments and counter-arguments about the role drugs play in the modern day world of sport.

Table 19.07 highlights some discussion points including:

- why performers take anabolic steroids
- the harmful side-effects
- why the ban on drugs is not lifted
- strategies to prevent performers taking drugs.

Table 19.07 Discussion points on drug-taking in sport

Why performers take anabolic steroids	Why performers shouldn't take drugs – the harmful side-effects	Why not lift the ban on drugs?	Strategies to prevent doping
• To train harder • Build muscle for explosive events • Fear of 'not making it' • Rewards are worth the risk • To be entertaining • Pressure from coaches, media and self • Drugs easily accessible • Increased aggression	• Health risks and death • Consequences if caught, e.g. shame/ban • Not fair/ immoral (The International Olympic Committee's stance against drugs is based on their code of fair play and competition whilst protecting the health of the athlete) • Negative role model for children • Loss of earnings and sponsorship • It encourages more athletes to take drugs who would not otherwise do so	• Technologically advanced countries have an advantage in terms of coaching, scientifically-based equipment, etc • If properly monitored it is not a health risk. Many drugs are naturally occurring • Drugs may be used for normal medical care • People should be free to choose • Athletes don't ask to be role models • The money on testing could be invested elsewhere • Many of the banned substances on the WADA list are not illegal – they are available over the counter • In many cases testing has proved unsound, jeopardising athletes' careers	• Random and out-of-season testing • Better co-ordination between organisations • Education programmes for coaches and athletes • Stricter punishments and life bans • More money into testing programme • Unified governing body policies • Better technology for testing • Use of both positive and negative role models

HOT TIPS

You will not be required to know the in-depth physiological effects of drugs.

HOT TIPS

You need to be prepared to give reasons why performers take drugs. Consider the physical, psychological and sociological reasons unless the question specifies otherwise.

HOT TIPS

Be prepared to discuss the issue of doping in sport including arguments against drugs and counter-arguments to suggest drugs could be allowed.

Drugs and the International Olympic Committee (IOC)

The IOC was forced to take action in the 1960s following the death of a cyclist who overdosed on amphetamines in the Rome Olympics and after scandals at the Tokyo Games in 1964. Consequently the IOC formed the Medical Commission in 1966. In 1981 it clarified its aim to:

Sanctions

The penalty laid down in a law for contravention of its provision. The IOC has a list of prohibited substances which athletes must not violate.

- accredit laboratories around the world
- introduce the standardisation of **sanctions**
- lead an education drive against doping in sport
- encourage and sponsor research into sport science to show other viable alternatives to doping.

WADA was given this responsibility in 2002. If a substance has the following criteria it is placed on the prohibited list:

- it has the potential to be performance enhancing
- it represents a risk to the athlete's health
- it violates the spirit of sport.

Sport and the law

Sport law

The application of legal principles to all levels of competition of amateur and professional sport and to physical activity.

The deviant acts of violence, hooliganism and doping are against society's norms and values and are therefore likely to attract the attention of the law.

Sport law is:

'The application of legal principles to all levels of competition of amateur and professional sport and to physical activity.'
(Lewison/Christenson, *Encyclopedia of World Sport,* 1996)

Sport was traditionally considered to be a separate part of life to the law and they were rarely interlinked. However, the number of deviant acts within sport appears to have increased, or it may be that incidents have been more widely reported by the media. Thus, the authorities have been forced to make sport as accountable as other social institutions. Should incidents such as assaults be viewed separately to a similar instance outside the sport setting?

The needs of various groups should be considered:

Performers:

- Performers have accepted and understood the activities they participate in by abiding by the rules of the activity. However, should an opponent act outside the rules of the activity, for example, violently, the performer could legitimately claim assault. The number of prosecutions has risen. Duncan Ferguson (1995) was the first professional soccer player to be imprisoned for an on-the-field assault.
- Performers are employees like anyone else and as such can be said to have the same employment rights as any other workers. Jean Marc Bosman, a Belgian footballer, forced the authorities to address the issue of players' rights to play the game in any European country. The European Court of Justice recognised in this case that there was

no reason why professional sports players should not enjoy the benefits of the single market and in particular the free movement of workers, resulting in the abolishment of transfer fees and opening national competitions to players throughout Europe.
- Performers seek success, sometimes unethically by the use of banned substances. Should they be banned? For how long?

Referees have been prosecuted for allowing situations to occur which have caused permanent damage to a performer. The implications for referees, many of whom are voluntary and amateur, are considerable.

Supporters' behaviour has also caused a considerable amount of concern in legal circles. Hooliganism in the 1970s and 1980s brought into question the ability of football clubs to regulate the behaviour of their supporters. Various pieces of legislation have emerged such as:
- Football Offences Act of 1991
- The Public Disorder Act of 1986
- Football Spectators Act.

Participants have a right to expect that facilities and equipment are properly maintained in order that their health and safety is ensured. This applies to recreational performers as well as elite performers.

Cases where sport meets the law

Such cases can include:
- negligence and sport (for example, if a sport centre was deemed negligent in its maintenance of sport equipment for the public)
- criminal assault/manslaughter on the sports field
- the issue of whether a performer has consented to some extent to a certain level of violence (when does an opponent step over the line from what would be considered reasonable behaviour?)
- risk management and risk assessment in the sport workplace
- event management, risk and insurance
- statutory regulation, health and safety in sport
- employment relations and rights in sport
- European law (the case of Jean Marc Bosman and its implications for sport transfers)
- intellectual property and advertising
- marketing and sponsorship rights
- law of contract
- environmental law and sporting activities
- adventure tourism, risk, lawful sports and insurance issues
- doping in sport – principles, rules, cases
- disability rights – principles and cases
- gender and sexual discrimination, harassment in sport
- child protection in sport
- race relations and race discrimination in sport
- sport and leisure disasters and the law.

TASK 10

In groups, research some of the examples above involving sport and the law. Consider the following questions:

- How can the law positively support professional athletes?
- Should the law become involved in sporting incidents?

Summary

- Many of the sporting ethics established in the nineteenth century remain relevant in the present day sports world.
- Professional sport has squeezed amateur sport in the twentieth century resulting in more sports turning professional.
- Amateur sports are becoming pressurised by the need to generate money.
- The monetary rewards available today have negatively affected performer's ethics leading to an increase in deviant behaviour.
- Society has begun to demand that sports performers be more accountable for their behaviour, both inside and outside the sporting arena.
- Commercial sports have developed under certain social conditions – urbanisation, industrialisation, effective communications, increased disposable income, and a large population with high living standards and leisure time.
- The media and large commercial companies have begun to exert significant control over the national governing bodies.
- The basic structure of sports have remained the same but commercialisation and the media have been influential.
- The serious nature of high level sport and the extensive material rewards available have increased the number of deviant acts – that is, performers seem to be more prepared to commit violent and unethical acts in order to gain the rewards.
- The law has become increasingly involved with sport and the number of prosecutions has risen.

Revise as you go!

1. What is meant by the term contract to compete?
2. What would have to happen for the contract to compete to be broken?
3. What is meant by the term amateur?
4. What is meant by the term sportsmanship?
5. How does the Lombardian ethic differ to the code of amateurism?
6. Explain what is meant by gamesmanship and give a sporting example.
7. Why has sportsmanship declined over the last few decades?
8. What are some of the disadvantages of commercialisation to sport?
   What is meant by the two terms endorsement and sponsorship?
9. Suggest two ways in which the media has changed the nature of sport events.

10 Give two reasons why major international sporting events should be shown on terrestrial television rather than on satellite stations.
11 Suggest two pressures the performer may experience due to extensive media coverage.
12 Give four factors at the football match that can cause hooligan behaviour.
13 Name three prevention and control measures that have been implemented to try and combat hooliganism.
14 Early theories of hooliganism concentrated on social class. What other theories have been developed to try and explain hooliganism?
15 Hooliganism is said to be a form of deviant behaviour. What is meant by deviant behaviour?
16 What are anabolic steroids and why do athletes take them?
17 What is meant by blood doping?
18 What are stimulants and why would sport performers use them?
19 Why should athletes not take drugs?
20 What strategies can organisations implement in order to reduce/stop doping in sport?
21 Why has the number of sport prosecutions increased in the last decade?
22 State three ways in which sport and the law have become entwined.

Chapter 20: The international perspective – World Games and the sport systems of the UK, the USA and France

Learning outcomes

By the end of this chapter you should have an understanding of:
- the nature of sport within France and the USA in contrast to the UK
- the general considerations of cultural, political and economic environments and their effect upon elite sport
- the links between education systems and elite sport development
- national government policies and national sport institutes
- a comparative perspective on the issues of class, gender and ethnicity as barriers to an individual's optimal development
- the nature and characteristics of World Games
- the relationship of World Games to the individual and the state
- the differences between amateur and professional World Games
- who controls World Games – the performer, national governments or elected representatives
- modern Olympic Games and the pressures between the traditional ideals and the modern day sports world.

For the purposes of this specification you need to be able to compare the systems of sport in the UK, France and the USA. In order to do this you need to understand the basis of comparative study.

HOT TIPS

You only need to consider social and cultural factors that affect elite sport in the USA, France and the UK.

A comparative approach is widely used in many academic disciplines to:
- describe
- analyse
- explain

a variety of factors occurring within society.

A reformative approach occurs when different cultures borrow and adapt ideas from each other which may prove of benefit to their own system. For example, when deciding how to establish the United Kingdom Sport Institute, the Australian system was of great interest. However, it has been recognised that what works within one culture may not work in another, as differing political, economic or value systems may be operating.

HOT TIPS

Though you will not be examined directly on the historical factors of each country it is crucial for your understanding of the present day system of sport.

Traditional relationships between the UK, France and the USA

It is useful to have a general understanding about the history of the countries under study in order to more fully appreciate the present day system of sport they each operates.

TASK 1

Research the sports of Association football, American football and the Tour de France. Prepare a short project-style piece of work incorporating the following elements:
- origins
- social class influences
- amateur professional developments
- facilities
- gender
- visual images
- administration/organisations
- major competitions
- financial details such as sponsorship/grants
- a brief history of a particular club
- talent development.

Although you will not be directly examined on the detailed history of a specific sport you will learn a lot about the cultures they have evolved within.

It will be useful to quickly review the traditional relationships that have existed between the countries of the UK, France and the USA, their characteristics and traditions.

The UK

Modern sport began in England thus leaving a significant legacy for the rest of the world.

The UK:
- is the smallest geographically of the three countries
- has colonised many countries including the USA
- has imposed its culture on its colonies
- traditionally had a very strong social class divide which was to provide opportunities for only the more powerful classes (the middle and upper classes)
- established sporting values such as amateurism and athleticism – these values have formed the bedrock of British sport and later the modern Olympic Games
- developed sport within public schools, universities and later the sport club system
- traditionally has a **decentralised** political administration
- prefers to keep sport and politics separate.

KEY WORDS

Decentralised

The dispersal of power away from the centre. Examples would be the independent states in the USA and the local authorities in the UK.

The USA

The USA:
- is the largest of the three countries geographically (each state is the size of a European country) with the most varied terrain and climatic zones
- was colonised by the UK but gained its independence in 1776 and established a new identity

Federal government
To follow – please supply

American Dream
In theory people have the opportunity to experience upward social mobility regardless of social class.

Pluralist society
Existence in society of different ethnic groups having distinctive ethnic origins, cultural forms, religions and so on

- has a 'frontier spirit' which is reflected in the desire of Americans to push the limits of human potential – sport is called 'the last frontier'
- is geographically isolated, which allows its identity to be fairly free from external influences
- established individual states with political autonomy following independence – states' rights were hard fought for
- evolved a decentralised administration
- established a federal government to oversee matters of national importance. An example in sport is that only Olympic athletes and the national team receive federal funding
- became the land of opportunity, the **American Dream** – 'from rags to riches'
- attracted millions of immigrants from all over the world creating a multi-cultural society based upon **pluralist** values
- holds pluralist values which suggest that no one particular group should be dominant (unlike that of the British system of aristocrats). Success and power can be achieved by anyone regardless of race or, gender, etc
- adopted professional sport as it emphasised values central to the American Dream – individual hard work and ability would ensure success
- cherishes individualism and this is reflected in the American approach towards sport, e.g. taking the opportunities presented and achieving material rewards and social status for oneself. This contrasts sharply with the more collective approach in France – that is, the state comes before the individual
- encourages elite athletes to emerge through the education system rather than the club system (as in the UK and France).

Lombardian ethic
Winning isn't the most important thing, it's the only thing.

Collegiate
The university system in the USA. It provides the route through to professional sport.

Counter-culture
The process of participation is important – not the outcome of winning or losing.

Radical ethic
The outcome of a sport event is important but so too is the process.

Intra-mural programmes
Organised sports programmes within the school or college.

Three key concepts of American sport are:

1. The **Lombardian ethic** – 'winning isn't the most important thing, it's the only thing'. This contrasts sharply with the traditional British values of amateurism, where the taking part is more important than the winning. This is the dominant sport ethic and is reflected in professional sport and the **collegiate** sport system.
2. **Counter-culture**, which is the anti-competitive view, believing more stress should be placed on the intrinsic benefits from sport rather than the outcome of winning or losing.
3. **Radical ethic**, which is more similar to the British view that participation and the process is important but so is the outcome. This ethic operates in the **intra-mural programmes**.

France

France:

- shares close geographical links with the UK – both are European countries
- has a more varied climate and terrain than the UK allowing the development of winter sports
- has developed sport along similar lines to the UK with the sport club being the base of the sporting pyramid

- used to have a monarchy
- experienced the Revolution in 1789 resulting in an almost overnight change in political direction (similar to the USA but unlike the UK, which has evolved much more gradually maintaining more continuity with the past)
- founded the Republic based on socialist principles (the importance of the State, not the individual, was emphasised)
- embraced **centralised** political policies which were to become the norm
- was home to Baron Pierre de Coubertin who, during his travels in England in the nineteenth century, was impressed with the values of amateurism and athleticism in the English public schools. He founded the modern Olympic Games in 1896, based on the principles of Olympism (similar to those of nineteenth-century amateurism)
- adopted the club system similar to the UK and this is the traditional route for elite athletes
- needed to boost national pride following many military defeats and occupations in the twentieth century and poor showing in the 1960 Rome Olympics
- General de Gaulle introduced the idea of state funding for elite athletes – 'if we want medals we must pay for them'.

Centralised

To draw under central control. Government policies are carried out across a country. France has a traditional centralised administration system.

Therefore, in the three countries studied, elite athletes emerge through different pathways. The term used to signify the route taken by Olympic athletes is the **Olympic Reserve**. In summary:

- USA – education system
- France – club/governing body
- UK – club/governing body.

Olympic reserve

The most usual route through which elite athletes emerge.

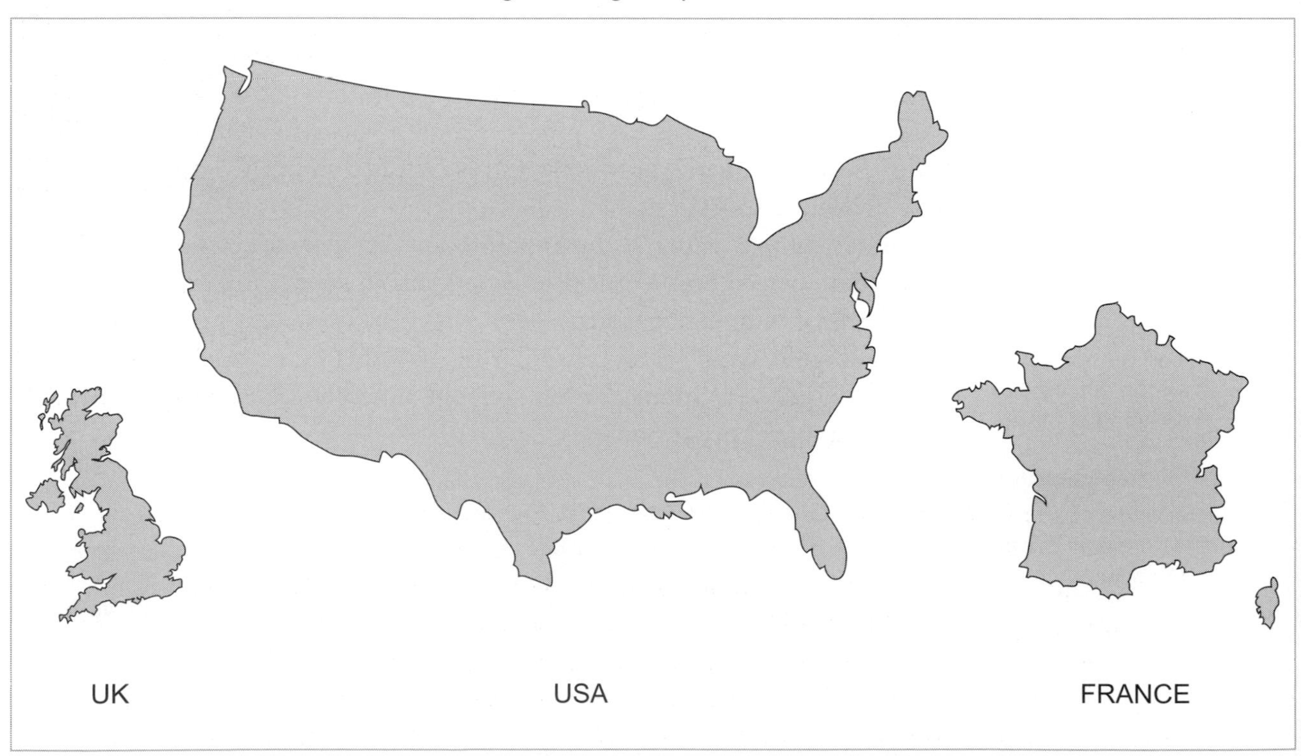

Fig 20.01 The UK, USA and France

Politics, economics and sport

We now need to consider some basic political and economic concepts and key words that will help you understand the relationships between the different cultures and their systems of sport.

Politics
Means belonging to or pertaining to the state, its local and national government and policy. Politics is about power and who wields it.

Politics and sport

Are sport and **politics** interlinked? Does sport carry with it a sense of national pride? Does international sport promote peaceful relationships between states or is it, as George Orwell said, 'war minus the shooting'?

Politics is about power and how it is wielded; it is about an individual or country exerting its will over other individuals or countries. Sport is about winners and losers and has been used by national governments to express the superiority of their political system. Sport can be used to transmit political messages.

Nationalism
National sentiment which binds a population together. Sport can develop feelings of nationalism and loyalty to one's country.

Sport can be categorised into four political themes:

1 **Sport as a means of promoting nationalism.** The Olympics is one of the best examples of sport promoting **nationalism.**The athletes represent their country; the anthems, flags and colours are all symbols of nationalism; the success and failure of the athletes are attributed as much to the countries themselves, their political system, as to the individual efforts of the athletes.

Fig 20.02 Sport – a reflection of nationalism

Propaganda
The organised distribution of information to a population, for example, using sport to sugget the political superiority of a state.

2 **Sport as a tool of political propaganda.** Governments have used sport to impose a political belief through **propaganda.** The 1936 Olympics were used by Hitler to demonstrate Germany's belief in Aryan racial superiority. In 1980 the United States led a boycott of the Olympics to protest at the Soviet invasion of Afghanistan. The UK has traditionally tried to keep sport and politics separate but in recent years there has been an increase in political involvement with more sport legislation and specific government policies for sport.

3 **Sport as a means of fostering or sustaining existing social conflict.** Sport has been used by the Western and Eastern governments to escalate political conflict. Accusations about unethical training practices, such as doping, are made regularly. Conflict in terms of discrimination within a country can be more subtle, e.g. the continuing poorer opportunities experienced by women and ethnic minority groups.

4 **Sport and the political decisions made about it** – examples include the boycott of sports events, the bidding of countries/cities for major sport events, sport legislation, etc.

Fig 20.03 Sport – can be used as a vehicle for a political message

Economic systems

KEY WORDS

Ideology
The ideas, beliefs and attitudes of a political system.

Capitalism/market economy
An economic system based on free trade and private ownership of the means of production, property and capital as the individual chooses.

Socialism
A system that involves collective ownership of the means of production and a major role for the state in the provision of services.

Mixed economy
An economy that combines a market economy with some centrally planned or state-run enterprises.

Politics and economic systems are never far apart. The values and philosophies of the former often determine the nature of the latter. The economic system often tells us a lot about the values and **ideology** of a society. We will now focus our attention on the main economic systems operating in the USA, UK and France.

1 **Capitalism or a market economy** – an economic system based on free trade and private ownership of the means of production, property and capital as the individual chooses. Some would argue that the focus on maximising profits has led to the development of the 'good life'. Others would claim that the single scale of success, namely monetary values, can alienate many people within a population. The USA is a typical example of a capitalist society. Professional sport in particular shares some of the characteristics of capitalism with its heavy emphasis on competition, winning as the only important outcome and the offer of rewards that are mostly materialistic.

2 **Socialism** – a system that involves collective ownership of the means of production and a major role for the state in the provision of services. In its extreme form of communism, socialism dominated the centrally planned economies of Eastern Europe until 1989. China, North Korea and Cuba are still mainly governed in this way. France has traditionally been based upon socialist principles and experiences. Sport here attracts heavy state funding and involvement.

3 **Mixed economy** – one that combines a market economy with some centrally planned or state-run enterprises. It is a way for governments to regulate the workings of the market through legislation. For example, the UK operates businesses within a market economy but also has a welfare system such as the National Health Service. The system of sport in the UK is a mixture of fundraising and some government funding.

Funding of elite athletes

How can the economic and political system influence the funding of elite athletes?

The funding of elite sportsmen and women varies, as does the range of political systems that support them. Funding of elite athletes is intended to support the efforts of performers who are aiming to reach international standards in their sport and not to fund those who are already wealthy as a result of their sporting success. The pursuit of excellence may be a common goal but the manner in which it is funded and run in the UK, France and the USA will depend on factors such as:

- the wealth of the country
- the type and distribution of the population
- the political philosophy
- centralised or decentralised administration
- geographical, historical and cultural factors.

HOT TIPS

The countries under study are all relatively wealthy but the manner in which they fund elite sport varies.

Types of funding

- Direct government funding – this is mostly prevalent in centralised political systems such as France. Funding is usually given for attendance at state institutes of sport, e.g. INSEP in France. This is due to the recognition in the 1960s by the French government that, if they wanted medals, they would have to pay for them. Federal funding in the USA is for Olympic athletes only. Federal influence is usually felt in matters of national importance. The Olympic team is a national team not a State team.
- Indirect government funding – an example might be the National Lottery funding in the UK. This can raise questions such as 'should athletes be accountable for the money they receive from the National Lottery'?
- **Scholarships** – these involve attendance at a university and are funded on the basis of athletic ability. In return the athletes are expected to commit themselves to the institution's athletic programme. They are very popular in the USA and funded by private, free market entrepreneurs. Limited use is made of this type of support in the UK; there are some scholarships in the sport school sector such as Millfield and there is some increase in the number of university scholarships offered. However, in comparison to the USA, this is a tiny amount. This is mostly due to the traditions of both countries, i.e. where the elite athletes originate from. In the USA, elite athletes are formally brought through the education system whilst in the UK they traditionally emerge through the club system.
- **Gate receipts** – in the USA education systems, particularly the collegiate system, huge amounts of funding are raised by gate receipts. These fund the athletic programme and many other institutional activities. The UK and France have no such comparable system.

KEY WORDS

Scholarship
Financial aid provided for a scholar because of academic or sporting excellence.

Gate receipts
Total money taken for admission to a sporting event.

- Private sources – these include businesses and corporate sponsorship. Sports in the modern day world could not cope without this contribution and it is influential in all three countries.

TASK 2

1 What characteristics does professional sport share with the ideology of capitalism?
2 The financial reward and support given to top level performers differs greatly in capitalist and socialist states. Explain how and why these differences exist.
3 How are amateur athletes funded in the UK?

Funded institutions

National Sport Institutes
A national organisation founded to promote elite sport. They possess common features such as excellent facilities, coaching, sports science and so on.

INSEP
The French National Sport Institute.

Sport study sections
Schools of excellence in France where students age 11+ years have access to excellent facilities, coaching and physiotherapy whilst undergoing normal eduction.

All three countries have developed different types of institutions with the aim of developing performance to the highest level, with either promising or already established athletes. Institutions include:

- **National Sport Institutes** – examples are the English Institute of Sport and **INSEP** in France. Any national institute of sport is going to have certain common features including high-class sporting facilities which are intended for developing elite performers but which can be used by other groups as well. They tend to specialise in targeted sports and athletes come to them for specialised training and coaching, supported by the most up-to-date sports science and medicine facilities.
- Clubs – these are sometimes attached to the National Institutes. Selected governing bodies will often operate regional and national centres of excellence at appropriate venues for junior and senior development squads.
- Sports schools – these tend to be associated with children and may be residential or local. They can be fee paying, have scholarships or be state funded.
- Schools – some schools have sport sections attached to them. In the UK there is the fairly recent development of Specialist Sports Colleges (see Chapter 18) and in France there are the well-established **sport study sections**. In the USA sport became firmly established within schools and this is the recognised route through which elite athletes emerge.

TASK 3

Research a sport of your choice. Discover where and how that sport trains its elite athletes.

National Sport Institutes

The following section is a comparison between INSEP (Institut National du Sport et de l'Education) and the EIS (English Institute of Sport).

INSEP and the EIS are both examples of Centres of Excellence for Sport and are part of the High Performance Systems operating in France and the UK. As such we can expect similarities in what they offer and provide for athletes, including high quality provision of:

- coaching
- sport science and medical support
- structured competitions at national and international level
- holistic approaches to athlete development – education, career development and social skills
- training venues and equipment
- talent identification and development systems
- administration that supports the sport system.

INSEP

HOT TIPS

Be prepared to make a comparison between the French (INSEP) and English Institutes of Sport.

HOT TIPS

As National Sport Institutes, INSEP and the EIS will share certain similarities such as high quality sporting facilities, coaching and support services such as sport science.

INSEP was established in the 1970s. Its characteristics include:

- centralised programmes – 'one centre model'
- the government is integral to INSEP (senior staff, technical directors of the sport federations and national coaches are employed by the Ministry for Youth and Sport)
- 140 coaches are employed at INSEP
- 400 athletes live on site and 140 of these are under 18 years. These youngsters follow the same regular French education as their peers
- the government issue annual directives outlining national priorities (a strategic decision has been taken to concentrate only on Olympic sports)
- five per cent tax on all TV rights; athletes receive 30 per cent of their salary tax free as payment for their image rights
- a three year 115 million euro refurbishment programme
- a total annual budget of 36 million euros
- a holistic approach is taken with a strong emphasis on career development, social skills and education – known as 'Project Life' – which all happen on site.

A high percentage of medals won for France by INSEP athletes is testament to the effectiveness of the system (France is currently sixth in the world in the Olympic medal table). INSEP athletes won 22 of France's 33 medals in Athens; 21 medallists in Sydney; 20 in Atlanta and 20 in Barcelona.

KEY WORDS

Multi-sport

Clubs catering for a range of sporting activities rather than the tradition of single sport clubs in the UK.

EIS

The EIS ethos is 'making the best better'. EIS staff visited INSEP in 2005 thus recognising that we can learn from other systems whilst realising that we have a different cultural and political approach. A few facts about EIS and comparisons with INSEP are included in Table 20.01.

Table 20.01 Facts about EIS and some comparisons with INSEP

Facts about EIS	Comparisons with INSEP
EIS was established in 2002.	France was almost 40 years ahead of the UK in its national mission to develop elite athletes.
EIS is a nationwide network of world-class support services, designed to foster the talents of Britain's elite athletes.	INSEP is an example of a 'one centre' model.
Services are offered from nine regional **multi-sport** hub sites and an evolving network of satellite centres. The services are delivered by a co-ordinated network of regional teams which feature complementary skills and experience.	Services are provided by a one centre approach but INSEP incorporates some of the most highly developed elite athlete support systems in the world.
The range of services supplied by the EIS spans sports science and sports medicine. Support includes applied physiology, biomechanics, medical consultation, medical screening, nutritional advice, performance analysis, psychology, podiatry, strength and conditioning coaching, sports massage and sports vision.	Some of the facilities at INSEP are functional but quite old. However, the quality of the knowledgeable staff and the discipline of the athletes is second to none.
The Performance Lifestyle programme provides supplementary career and education advice.	The Performance Lifestyle programme is similar to the 'Project Life' programme at INSEP. They both recognise that the 'whole' athlete needs to be developed – his or her education, social skills and career development. There is more flexibility in the French system (they have been established for a longer period of time and have had the luxury of being able to fine tune their system). In the UK there needs to be more understanding that athletes can compete at the highest level without abandoning their education. At INSEP the majority of the education is offered on site so it is offered at times specifically tailored to training, to enable the athlete to maximize both training and education. Personal tutoring and e-learning resources are also readily available.
The quality of the delivery is assured by the close relationship the EIS is developing with UK Sport, national governing bodies, performance directors, coaches and the athletes themselves.	Having a targeted, highly focussed approach to Olympic success is becoming a common factor across the world. INSEP is recognising the need to challenge and monitor the work of the Federations (similar to the national governing bodies in the UK). Similarly, NGBs in the UK are having to be more accountable for their development plans, or Whole Sport Plans (WSP).
Almost 2000 competitors are currently in the EIS system.	400 athletes live on site at INSEP; 140 are under 18 years old which means the education of these young athletes is still an important issue.
It is funded by the Sport England Lottery fund.	INSEP is state funded.
The EIS with its partnership with UK Sport needs to: • develop a generation of coaches and athletes with world-class attitudes and abilities • adopt an innovative approach to the improvement of under-performing sports • value knowledge, centralise it and share it • know where the best in the world are at • develop structures with political and intellectual credibility • access the resources needed to deliver success • realise that 'medals means money'!	The French realised that 'medals mean money' in the twentieth century!

TASK 4

What are the advantages of a one centre model rather than a regional approach in the development of elite athletes?

Education

In all three countries the education system has some influence on the development of elite athletes. The extent of this involvement differs.

HOT TIPS

Emphasis is placed on the route taken by elite athletes therefore detailed knowledge of the physical education programmes is not required.

Education and the UK

Traditionally the UK has not specifically targeted schools as the base of elite sport development. This has usually been the function of the sports clubs and national governing bodies. Competitive school sport has always been an option for British children, known as extra-curricula provision. It is based on the goodwill of physical education teachers and therefore will not operate the same way in all parts of the country. Physical education teachers are usually recognised for their all-round ability rather than specialising as sport coaches.

HOT TIPS

High schools and colleges are considered to possess the characteristics of a centre of excellence.

In recent years there has been growing recognition that schools should play a greater part in developing elite performers as they have the advantage of reaching a maximum number of children with access to many excellent sport facilities in the country. However, limitations such as funding, poor school-club links, lack of specialist coaches in schools and timetable considerations will need to be given thought if our schools are to viably replace the traditional role of the clubs.

TASK 5

1 Outline the role sport plays in British schools and the government measures that are beginning to take account of the situation.
2 The traditional British education system is decentralised – true or false?
3 Revise the UK's Specialist Sports Colleges policy.

HOT TIPS

As in the UK, sport in the USA is voluntary but a much higher status and profile is given to school sport.

Education and the USA

The USA's national education administration system is decentralised, that is, the 52 states are independent in how they run their own education system. However, at a local level it is centralised, with a local school board drawing up the physical education programme that the physical education teachers are required to implement.

Inter-scholastic sport
Competitive athletic fixtures between schools.

The physical education teacher is continuing to lose ground as PE loses its compulsory status in many school programmes. **Inter-scholastic sport,** however, remains strong.

TASK 6

Revise the terms centralised and decentralised and consider the advantages and disadvantages of each.

The development of elite athletes traditionally occurs through the high schools and colleges. The lack of an effective club structure in the USA has made this an inevitable route for athletes wishing to pursue a career in sport.

Inter-scholastic competition has its greatest impact in grades 10 to 12 (ages 14 to 17). Rivalry in local leagues is intense and competitions take place at local, district and regional levels, culminating in the state championships. State tournaments exist but the sheer size of the country inhibits national school tournaments.

Hire and fire
Lack of success of school/college teams can mean the dismissal of the coach.

The sports coach is a member of the high school faculty and money comes from donations from local booster clubs and local taxes. The sports coach tends to have a higher profile than the physical education teacher but also has a more vulnerable position due to the **hire and fire** nature of the post.

Traditionally in the UK, coaches are attached to clubs and the links between schools and clubs have been limited, due to the belief that physical education has a very different role to that of sport. The UK does not have a comparable role of the sport coach to that of the American school system.

TASK 7

Revise the concepts of physical education and school sport. See *AS PE for AQA*, Chapter 14.

Inter-scholastic sport

Inter-scholastic sport
Competitive athletic fixtures between schools.

Table 20.02 The advantages and disadvantages of inter-scholastic sport

Advantages	Disadvantages
• Encourages pride and loyalty to school • Improves fitness • Develops social skills for later life such as teamwork • Strengthens the links between schools and communities • Encourages students to become actively involved in school activities	• Too much emphasis on competition and winning • Many students spectate rather than participate • Takes resources away from many other educational programmes • Academic studies can suffer from the stress placed on sporting success

Inter-collegiate sport

By the beginning of the twentieth century, every college had an athletic committee. This was testament to the popularity that sport had already achieved in American society. With further development and expansion, inter-college regulation was required. **The National Collegiate Athletic Association** (NCAA) was established in 1906 to control and create order in **collegiate athletics**. Inter-collegiate athletics is based on two foundations:

- Division 111 – for small institutions where sport and physical education are an integral part of the students' lives.
- Division 1 – where sport is run as an entertainment business and a training ground for professional and high-level amateur sport, namely the Olympic Games. Division 11 is a transition ground between the two.

KEY WORDS

National Collegiate Athletic Association (NCAA)
A voluntary association of about 1200 colleges and universities, athletic conferences and sports organisations which administers inter-collegiate athletics in the USA.

Collegiate athletics
High level competitive sport.

Big time programmes
Athletic programmes in Division I colleges with a heavy emphasis on winning and entertainment.

Alumni
Former students of an educational institution.

Pro-draft system
Inter-collegiate sport programmes ensure a steady influx of talented players into the professional sport scene.The draft is ranked and basically the lowest placed professional club has first choice.

Scholarship (USA)
A grant of free education given by an institution of higher education to promising performers. Athletes are contracted to represent the college team.

Big time programmes

Big time programmes tend to occur in the Division 1 colleges. They are characterised by:

- materialistic incentives for athletes
- commercialism
- lip service paid to academic studies
- extreme emphasis on winning
- entertainment focus.

The extensive facilities, entertainment value, community involvement and money involved make the college programmes similar to the UK's approach to professional sport. The programmes are hugely expensive and can be a drain on other college commitments. Finance is generated through gate receipts, sponsorship, media payments and donations from the **alumni** (former students – the term used in the UK might be 'old boys').

College sport provides the route into professional and international levels of sport. The sometimes poor academic quality of potential recruits is often overlooked under the 'special admit' programmes. The reasoning behind this is simply that the colleges are under intense pressure to remain at the highest levels to sustain their revenue. The colleges' and sports' staff can earn huge amounts through their basic salaries being topped up by sponsorship and TV contracts.

The **pro-draft system** exists in the sports of basketball and American football. Talented performers are chosen by professional clubs on leaving college. However, to retain some balance the lowest ranked clubs are allowed first choice. This is the real payment for a college athlete who is not supposed to receive financial benefits whilst participating in college sport. Whilst at college the athlete will receive a **scholarship** and devote up to 50 hours a week to training and competing. Performers are prepared to accept this situation because they:

- are able to play to thousands of spectators
- become household names before they leave college
- accept the American ethic of hard work, discipline and winning.

Education and France

Don't confuse the American term for athletics with that used in the UK. Athletics in the UK is known as track and field in the USA. Athletics in the USA is a term used for sporting activities or programmes.

The traditional education system in France is similar to that of the UK with the existence of a private and state sector. France has traditionally had a strong centralised approach towards education. This means central government has promoted policies across the country with little variation allowed. In reality this was always difficult to monitor and there is now increasing decentralisation happening. This means individual schools are beginning to have some independence in how they run their schools and appoint staff.

Similarly to the USA, and in contrast to the UK, France prioritises sport rather than physical education. An organisation called the **Union Nationale de Sport de Scolaire** (UNSS) is a government organisation which runs school sport. All state schools have to be affiliated and this organisation arranges sport fixtures across France. There is no comparable system in the UK.

Union Nationale de Sport de Scolaire (UNSS)
The policy of sport afternoons is centrally controlled by the National Union for School Sport (UNSS) which is compulsory for all schools to join. The UNSS is a multi-sport federation which co-ordinates afternoon sport fixtures.

Licence system
A membership card for French students allowing them membership to a multi-sport club before they leave school.

Sport study section
The sport study sections or 'section sport etudes' provide special classes for talented children, and certain schools specialise in certain sports.

Strong links exist between schools and community sport clubs via the **licence system**. This allows membership to sports clubs for all French students before they leave school.

The **sport study sections** or 'section sport etudes' provide special classes for talented children, and certain schools specialise in certain sports. These have the usual advantages of sports schools – specialist facilities, coaching, medical and physiological testing, structured competitions – while normal schooling continues. In 1980 there were 145 sport study sections catering for 3400 children. Regional sport study sections involve 11–29-year-olds culminating at INSEP. Features of sport study sections include:

- they are part of the normal school system
- specialised groups work in certain sports.
- high quality teaching and coaching are drafted in.
- movement on to specific centres is possible for specific sports excellence.

TASK 8

1 What would be the advantages of the UK developing a similar organisation to that of the UNSS?
2 Compare France's sport study section system with the UK's Specialist Sports Colleges.

Summary of education in the UK, USA and France

UK	USA	France
• Decentralised • Physical education is the main focus in schools • Competitive sport is optional • Limited school club links • Recent policies to include schools in development of talent • Clubs are the traditional base for the nurturing of talent • EIS – National Sport Institute	• Decentralised • Competitive sport is the main school/college focus • Competitive sport is optional but carries high status • Limited club system – the education system is the base of sport participation • Colleges feed professional sport • Colleges are the main route for elite athlete development	• Centralised • Physical education and school sport are compulsory • Competitive sport has a high status • Well established school/club links • Sport study sections operate in normal schools • Clubs and schools operate closely together • INSEP – National Sport Institute

Professional sport and commercialisation

Very often the terms commercialisation and Americanisation are synonymous. The terms are associated with the manner in which the sports are played and perceived as well as how they are marketed.

The USA did not get tied down with the constricting UK amateur ethos of the late nineteenth and twentieth centuries. It also did not become involved with the state-funded Eastern bloc approach to sport.

The scholarships and spectator appeal which began in American universities are said to have been the beginnings of modern professional sport. The development of the media, especially television, was the ideal environment for professional sport to flourish. Combined with the Lombardian ethic of winning and the potential material rewards for success, this became the dominating influence of American sport.

The four main popular sports in the USA are:

- American football
- ice hockey
- baseball
- basketball.

These sports are run as businesses and the athletes are marketed as assets.

Fig 20.04

Table 20.03 Commercialisation of American sport

Sports as businesses:	Athletes as assets:
• Aim to make a substantial profit • Pay salaries/ sign contracts/ have overheads • Advertise products • Sell merchandise • Have owners and employees • Make investments (stock market)	• Are expendable (hire and fire) • Are ambassadors of the company and act as role models • Are salaried • Can be transferred/sold • Must endorse products • Must generate funds

As the dominant sports, American football, baseball, ice hockey and basketball share certain characteristics:

- the win ethic
- they are all team sports
- high scoring/excitement/no draws
- high media/spectator interest
- professional sport
- family entertainment
- heavily marketed as businesses
- excellent social and sporting facilities
- racial identities (e.g. basketball = African American, ice hockey = white)
- social class identities (e.g. American football = middle class, baseball = working class)
- well-developed children's leagues
- professional players coming through the collegiate system
- they reflect capitalism/the American Dream.

The nature of these games is often violent, technological and territorial. Why the violence?

TASK 9

Consider the following bullet points and suggest the reasons for violence in the dominant American sports.

- American sporting culture
- Media
- Political culture eg. capitalism
- Nature of the four dominant sports
- T\he American Dream.

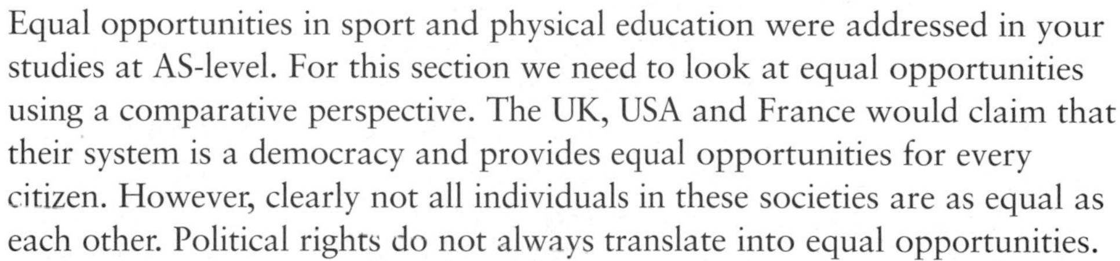

A comparative perspective on the issues of class, gender and ethnicity as a barrier to an individual's optimal development

It is very important that you observe ethical principles when discussing equal opportunity issues. The response required is a balanced judgement of the issue.

Equal opportunities in sport and physical education were addressed in your studies at AS-level. For this section we need to look at equal opportunities using a comparative perspective. The UK, USA and France would claim that their system is a democracy and provides equal opportunities for every citizen. However, clearly not all individuals in these societies are as equal as each other. Political rights do not always translate into equal opportunities.

What is involved when we discuss issues such as equality? How can unequal opportunities affect individuals reaching a level of excellence in a sport?

Society can be divided into layers. The divisions are based on biological, economic and social criteria, for example:

- age
- gender
- social class
- ethnic origin.

Dominant group
The group in society that controls the major social institutions.

Hegemonic group
One group that has leadership over other groups.

Discrimination
To make a distinction; to give unfair treatment especially because of prejudice.

Stereotypes
A standardised image or concept shared by all members of a social group.

The **dominant group** in society is the one that controls the major social institutions such as education, the Church, government, sport and so on. This group need not necessarily be the majority – merely the group who wields the most power – the **hegemonic group**. In the three countries under study the dominant group in all cases is white, male, middle-class and able-bodied. Subordinate groups therefore would be classed as women, ethnic minority groups, low socio-economic groups and people with disabilities.

Discrimination can occur when opportunities available to the dominant group are not available to all. When subordinate groups in society are discriminated against their opportunities are limited.

Sport is often described by sociologists as a microcosm of society – that is, it reflects in miniature all facets of society. This includes the institutionalised divisions and inequalities which characterise our society. Sporting institutions such as national governing bodies and sport federations are also controlled by the dominant group. Stratification in sport is inevitable when winning is highly valued. It is highlighted even more when monetary rewards are available.

Race is the physical characteristic of an individual, whilst ethnicity is the belonging to a particular group, e.g. religion, lifestyle, etc.

Discrimination can be overt or covert. The former can take the form of less tournament earnings, membership clauses to sports clubs (consider the early playing experiences of Tiger Woods who was unwelcome in some golf clubs in the USA). The latter can include attitudes and prejudices, usually based on negative **stereotypes**.

Let us look at the opportunities available in each of the three countries to:

- ethnic minorities
- women
- low socio-economic groups.

Ethnic groups as a barrier to excellence

Racism is a set of beliefs or ideas based on the assumption that the world's population can be divided into different human biological groups designated 'races'. Following on from this is the proposition that the races are ordered hierarchically, so that some stand in a position of superordinacy or superiority to others. This is a classic type of racism; ideas of superiority are often veiled in arguments concerning culture, nationalism and the ethnic identity. Quite often these contain hints of racism that are not specific but only implied. When ideas or beliefs about racial superiority are translated into action, we speak in terms of racial discrimination, or simply racialism. Racism is the idea; racialism is the idea in practice.

The first groups to become established in the UK, USA and France were white groups. They have retained this domination and in all three countries form the dominant or hegemonic group.

Examples of racism in sport

Stacking

The disproportionate amount of ethnic minorities in certain positions in a sports team usually based on the stereotypical view that they are best suited to roles requiring physical rather than mental qualities.

Stacking refers to the disproportionate concentration of ethnic minorities in certain positions in a sports team. In American football, black players have been allocated to running back and wide receiver positions; in baseball, they have been stacked in outfield positions. This tends to exclude them from, for instance, quarterback starting pitching positions – which are the most prestigious – and compels them to compete against other blacks for their team position. It could be argued that stacking is based on stereotypes and that such stereotypes are in the process of being dismantled by quarterbacks such as Doug Williams, who shows intelligence and judgement as much as power and speed in his play. Equally, recent evidence from baseball (Jiobu 1998) suggests that the stereotypes still operate.

Fig 20.05 Black athletes can experience various barriers to success in American sport

Centrality

Positions that require decision-making and interaction in a sports team. They tend to be occupied by white players.

You need to understand how centrality and stacking are different.

According to Grusky's theory of **centrality** (1963) this stereotype and subsequent forms of discrimination restricts black people from more central positions which are based on co-ordinative tasks and require a greater deal of interaction and decision-making. Significantly, coaches who make these decisions are white. Sociologocal studies have revealed the self-perpetuating coaching sub-culture which exists in American sport (J. Coakley 1994). When existing coaches need to sponsor a new coach, they are likely to select a person with similar ideas.

In the UK, national governing bodies were established by white middle-class males and this tendency still exists today. However, a recent study by Malcolm and Last (1998–99 season) at the University of Leicester suggested that in Premiership football in the UK there were initially few barriers to be overcome by black players at the elite level. Over a ten year period, 50 per cent of black players played in forward positions. This can mean occupying glamorous positions, high goal-scoring and higher transfer fees. However, the main difference occurs in the different career paths taken by black footballers. Few break their way into management positions, for example, as directors, FA committee members and so on.

Do certain ethnic minority groups have a genetic advantage?

This ongoing debate is a very sensitive issue but it should be discussed. It is imperative, however, that the discussion remains constructive and well considered.

The premise is based on the fact that athletes of West African origin feature significantly in particular sports at the highest level:

- Of the 32 finalists in the 100m in the last four Olympic Games, all were of West African origin.
- The fastest 200 times recorded for the 100m are shared by athletes with West African origin.
- In America, athletes of West African origin also lead the way in the three big sports of American football, basketball and baseball.

However, what about the sports that black people do not appear to do well in? Examples may be swimming, cycling and tennis. All sorts of crude theories have been developed over the years such as higher testosterone levels, more fast twitch fibres and so on, as well as higher density bones to limit swimming potential. Many such scientific theories have been dismissed and research methods have been called into question. No one has yet isolated a gene for advanced athletic performance.

What other reasons could there be for black success in sports such as athletics? Possibilities include:

- Judges' opinions (possibly racist opinions) do not come into play given the more objective nature of the outcome. Winning is determined by being the fastest, highest or furthest rather than by the judges' opinions, as happens in some sports such as gymnastics.
- As black people have been encouraged into sports such as athletics and team games, they have provided a sense of social acceptance and consequently provided role models for children from similar backgrounds.

Channelling

People from certain groups in society can be channelled into particular sports for which they are considered to have the appropriate physical and psychological qualities.

- **Channelling** may have been a significant factor – perhaps by *not* being channelled into tennis clubs, black people were unlikely to succeed in great numbers. Tiger Woods may have destroyed a myth that black people couldn't play golf. Surely it is more about social opportunities than genetic factors?
- Some countries target certain sports which they perceive they will be able to dominate. Examples may be poorer countries concentrating on running due to the less sophisticated facilities that are needed in comparison with other sports.

What are the problems of accepting the theory of genetic advantage?

- Genetic physical advantages have tended to be synonymous with people trying to prove this must mean a lack of intellect.
- It can undermine the 'work ethic' that is also likely to have been a significant factor. Black people in the UK, USA and France have had to fight an uphill battle to secure a better lifestyle. This can lead to a hunger for success that leads to a greater desire to win and the motivation to work as hard as possible.
- Many of the sports that cite black superiority have traditionally been considered working-class sports and therefore there have been greater opportunities for access into these sports.
- If society starts to accept these theories then white people may be put off trying to succeed in certain sports or events (**white flight**), merely perpetuating the problem. It would become a self-fulfilling prophecy.

White flight

This refers to white players being disinclined to participate in a sport believing they have no hope of succeeding. Can be seen in basketball and sprinting.

Gender

The biological aspect of a person, either male or female.

Masculinity

Possessing qualities or characteristics considered typical or appropriate to a man. Examples might be dominant, strong, forceful.

Gender as a barrier to excellence

In the UK, USA and France, women have historically experienced similar **gender** inequality. Sport evolved along the male and **masculinity** concepts of competition, achievement, aggression and dominance, which led to poorer opportunities for women and resulted in lower participation rates. Positive female sporting images have tended to be similar to other Western cultures – activities which require grace, have little physical contact and so a lower level of aggression.

Gender roles refer to what different societies and cultures attribute as appropriate behaviour for that sex. These can vary from culture to culture and also change historically within a culture. This can be further considered by reflecting on the changing and increasing opportunities experienced by women since the beginning of the twentieth century in the UK, France and the USA.

Socialisation

The learning of cultural norms and values.

The changing nature of women's roles in society and in sport

- Women and men learn their expected role through **socialisation**, which simply means the learning of cultural values. We learn these firstly through the family and then later through social institutions such as schools. Males and females are socialised into being masculine or feminine respectively.

- Sport was always seen as a male preserve. Males developed and controlled most of the modern day sports. Men as the dominant group in society denied or limited opportunities for women in the types of sports they could participate in.
- The role of women was stereotypically seen as the domestic role. The types of sporting activities women were encouraged to do tended to promote the more feminine aspects of women such as non-contact sports and improving the appearance, i.e. toning muscles (aerobics) rather than building them (weight lifting).

In the present day, opportunities for women have increased in terms of:
- more females participating in sport
- a greater variety of sporting activities available
- more clubs, facilities and competitions
- more media coverage leading to more role models
- more women in positions of responsibility in sports organisations, such as national governing bodies.

Sexism

Sexism

The belief that one sex is inferior to the other, a belief that is most often directed at women. Traditionally women have been denied the same legal, political, economic and social rights enjoyed by men.

Barr Sex Test

Sex testing was introduced in the mid-1960s and was used as recently as the 1996 Olympic Games in Atlanta.

Chromatin

The part of the nucleus that contains DNA, RNA and proteins, and forms the chromosomes and stains with basic dyes.

In spite of increased sporting opportunities for women, the fact remains that women still have less opportunities than men. Why? **Sexism**, like racism, is a set of beliefs or ideas about the purported inferiority of some members of the population, in this case women. The inferiority is thought to be based on biological differences between the sexes: women are naturally equipped for specific types of activities and roles and these don't usually include ones which carry prestige and influence.

An example of sexism directed at women is the **Barr Sex Test**. This test requires that a sample of cells be scraped from the inside of a woman's cheek and subjected to a laboratory test to determine whether a minimum number of cells contain what are called 'Barr bodies' (collections of **chromatins**). Although the exact number of these chromatins varies from woman to woman and may change over time for any given woman, usually about 20 out of every 100 cells contain this characteristic. If you count drops below a minimum percentage, the competitor is disqualified. The Barr sex test was first used in the 1968 Winter (Grenoble) and Summer (Mexico) Olympic Games. Princess Anne was the only female athlete who was not required to take this test.

The body as a social construct

The notion that the body might be of sociological interest has become popular since the 1980s. This can relate to societies' 'ideal' shape for men and women. This belief holds the view that people see themselves and others by the way their society views them. In the Western world a thin body shape for women is likely to offer high status and may be achieved using methods such as dieting and surgery. The media are heavily responsible for the extent to which ideas like these become social norms.

Femininity

Possessing qualities or characteristics considered typical or appropriate to a woman. Examples might be graceful, dainty, gentle.

The media also gives much less coverage to women's sports whilst favouring sports and athletes who match the concept of **femininity**. Women's team games are not given much coverage even though team games form the basis of many physical education programmes in schools. Individual activities such as tennis, and recently golf, are beginning to attract more media coverage. With media coverage comes more sponsorship deals – so less media coverage has significant consequences for women's sport.

Female soccer in the USA

Remember – women, ethnic minority groups and low socio-economic groups will participate in less sport for similar reasons and the strategies to improve opportunities will also be similar.

The success of the American female soccer team (who won the 1999 World Cup which was virtually ignored by the UK) highlights some interesting issues. Since their victory, members of the team have become household names and it was believed they had won a victory in the battle for sexual equality. The final was played before a crowd of 90,000, the largest audience for a women's sporting event anywhere. Big league sponsors contributed and Nike, Adidas and Budweiser beer (traditionally male products) ran adverts featuring the team.

Why was there so much social acceptance for a sport that women have had to fight to play in the UK? Reasons might include:

- America likes winners and glamour (stars like Mia Hamm and Brianna Scurry fit the feminine attractive image).
- There was no men's game to compete with (as in the UK).
- There was no governing body resistance as in the UK.
- Females do not traditionally play American football.
- Soccer is less violent and aggressive than its American counterpart.
- **Title IX** has allowed the game to be nurtured financially as well as through educational programmes.

KEY WORDS

Title IX

A piece of legislation that made compulsory the equal treatment of men and women in education programmes in receipt of federal funding.

Female participation in sport in the USA rose significantly in the 1970s due to a variety of factors:

- the women's movement
- federal legislation
- the fitness movement
- an increased public awareness of women athletes helped by increased media coverage of female sport
- federal legislation called Title IX, the education amendment of 1972, was one of the most influential factors.

Fig 20.06 The American female soccer team has enjoyed much recognition in the USA

Title IX in the USA

This piece of legislation made compulsory the equal treatment of men and women in education programmes in receipt of federal funding. Women can take a case as far as the Supreme Court – the highest court in the land. Since the 1990s hundreds of cases have been heard and many judgements made. Most of these have been resolved in favour of women, resulting in:

- women's teams being reinstated when they were due to be cut
- women's club sports being upgraded to university status
- women coaches receiving equal pay.

Part of the USA's 1972 educational amendments, Title IX reads:
'No person in the United States shall, on the basis of sex, be excluded from participation in, be denied the benefits of, or be subjected to discrimination under any education program or activity receiving federal financial assistance.'

Educational institutions were forced to accommodate females within their sport budgets. This was at first unpopular among the male dominated sports officials of schools, colleges and universities. In 1979 three women athletes from the University of Alaska sued their state for failing to comply with Title IX in providing better funding, equipment and publicity compared to the male basketball team This set in train more actions, so that by the end of 1979, 62 colleges and universities were under investigation by the Office for Civil Rights.

What are the arguments for and against the UK adopting a similar policy to Title IX? Table 20.04 below outlines a few points for consideration.

Table 20.04 Arguments for and against the UK adopting a 'Title IX' policy

Reasons for the UK to adopt a similar policy to Title IX	Reasons against the UK adopting such a policy
• Sport would be seen to reflect equality. • It would promote a higher profile of women's sport. • It would raise the profile of discrimination issues. • It might encourage sponsors to support female sport. • It might reduce the gap between male and female participation rates. • It would make administrators consider the female issue when considering resources.	• The UK and USA are two different cultures – transplanting one aspect may not work. • Sport in the UK at educational institutions is not as professionally or commercially developed. • There is not the same disparity of funding between male and female departments as in the USA. • There is little media attention at this level in the UK. • In the UK we have a tradition to keep sport and politics separate. • Scholarships are minimal compared to the USA. • The female sport role in the USA has traditionally been that of a cheerleader – more male participation.

TASK 10

Research some legal cases involving Title IX using the Internet.

Summary

Table 20.05 Unequal sporting opportunities for women and attempts to counter them

Evidence	Reasons	Action required
• Inequalities in sport • Unequal provision of facilities • Less sport for women • Fewer female coaches/administrators • Restricted club access • Participation rates less than men at all levels	• Domestic role • Social stereotyping • Concept of femininity • Physical vulnerability to perform some sports – the 'medical case'. • Sport matches the concept of masculinity • Males traditionally control sport – **male hegemony** • Less media coverage • Less role models • Less funding/ tournament earnings • Discrimination	• Equal provision at all levels from physical education to high level competitive sport • More facilities • Social acceptance of all sports • Better links between schools/clubs • Widen women's horizons • Increase media coverage of female sport • Increase training of coaches/administrators • Legislation at government level, e.g. **Sex Discrimination Act** / Title IX

Male hegemony
The dominance of males over females.

Sex Discrimination Act
A piece of legislation with the aim of working towards the elimination of discrimination on the basis of gender.

Social class as a barrier to excellence

Society can be divided into social classes defined on the basis of wealth, income, occupation and hereditary factors. The upper and middle classes or dominant group tended to occupy the highest positions of wealth, status and power. It is increasingly difficult to differentiate between the middle and working classes but generally the distinction is still based on the type of work done (manual or non-manual work).

We have already mentioned that all three countries are similar in their make-up of who has control over the major social institutions. Therefore the experiences of people from lower socio-economic groups are going to be similar in all three countries.

- Historically in the UK, France and the USA, the middle and upper classes have always had more leisure time and disposable income – opportunities necessary to participate in sport regularly.
- The middle and upper classes have controlled sports, particularly the administration of what were considered working-class sports, such as football and boxing. They have ruled the governing bodies, and been the agents and promoters.
- In the UK and France, in the late nineteenth and early twentieth centuries, professional players tended to come from the lower classes (as they needed to earn money from sport) whilst the middle and upper classes tended to be the amateurs (participating in sport for the love of it rather than for monetary gain).
- In the USA this social class divide was not quite so acute and society was happy to adopt professional sport which was more reflective of their capitalist system.
- The working classes had to wait for the provision of facilities and a right to recreation.
- This has led to a difference, even today, in the participation rates of people from lower socio-economic groups and to some extent in the achievement in gold medals in particular sports. This can be attributed to a number of factors:
  a) the cost of facilities and training
  b) the dominant middle-class culture which operates in many sports institutions, such as sports clubs, having different value systems such as rules of behaviour, dress codes and so on
  c) the lack of leadership roles in coaching and administerial positions in sports institutions
  d) lower self-esteem
  e) fewer children from lower socio-economic groups attend public schools (especially in the UK) and most of the medal winners from the UK were educated at private rather than state schools.

TASK 11

1 Sports have developed, sometimes with very clear social class identities. Suggest which social classes would be more likely to participate in the following sports:
   - football
   - athletics
   - polo
   - tennis
   - golf
   - sailing.

2 What measures could be taken in all three countries to improve the opportunities for people from the lower socio-economic groups?

HOT TIPS

World Games can be used as a base when setting questions to cover issues such as inequality, amateurism and professionalism, commercial sponsorship and so on.

World Games

Once an athlete reaches the highest standards of performance in his or her sport, he or she may have the opportunity to represent his or her country in the most prestigious sports competitions in the world. This is the pinnacle of the athlete's career. Numerous championships could classify as a World Game.

For the purposes of this specification we are going to:
- make a detailed study of the Olympic Games and Paralympics
- consider the nature of amateur and professional World Championships
- consider who controls these games.

Characteristics of World Games

Consider the Olympic Games and the World Cup. What characteristics do they have in common and what makes them different?

Table 20.06 Characteristics of World Games

International competition/elite level
Multi-sport, e.g. Olympics or single sport, e.g. football
Global/spectator events
Media/satellite
Commercialisation – TV rights/sponsorship/corporate/endorsements
Selection/trials – only the best/athlete preparation
Nationalism/patriotism
Political issues/boycotts/terrorism/propaganda
Officials/volunteers
Rewards/trophies
Benefits to host city/reasons to bid?
Amateur or professional
Deviancy – cheating/drugs/gamesmanship
Positive values – striving/effort/sportsmanship/bring countries together
Administration/bureaucracy, e.g. IOC
Symbols, e.g. five interconnecting rings for the Olympic Games
Meeting of cultures/multi-cultural sport events
Able-bodied/disabled – Paralympic
Top facilities
Individual/team events

TASK 12

Using Table 20.06 list the differences between an amateur World Game such as netball and a professional competition such as the football World Cup.

HOT TIPS

You will not need to know about the ancient Olympic Games.

Modern Olympic Games

Baron Pierre de Coubertin established the modern Olympic Games in 1896 following a visit to England in the nineteenth century when he was impressed with the amateur code in the public schools' team games and code of athleticism. He had increasingly become concerned about the poor health and lack of patriotism within his own country. He believed the English approach towards sport would help to combat these problems as well as furthering international understanding. The Olympic Games have gone from strength to strength and today are the largest and most prestigious of the World Games.

Facts about the Olympic Games include:

- The symbol of the Games are five interconnecting rings representing the five continents: Europe, Asia, Oceania, Africa and the Americas.
- The motto is – *Citius, Altius, Fortius* – meaning 'swifter, higher, stronger'.
- The following message appears on every scoreboard – 'the most important thing in the Olympic Games is not to win but to take part, just as the most important thing in life is not the triumph but the struggle. The essential thing is not to have conquered but to have fought well'.
- The six goals of the Olympic movement are incorporated in the term Olympism:
  1. personal excellence
  2. sport as education
  3. cultural exchange
  4. mass participation
  5. fair play
  6. international understanding.

The Olympic oath – taken by an athlete on behalf of all competitors, states: *'In the name of all the competitors I promise that we shall take part in these Olympic Games respecting and abiding by the rules which govern them in the true spirit of sportsmanship.'*

Let us consider these original ideals and discuss whether they are still relevant today.

Personal excellence – this competition is the largest in the world and allows athletes from the Olympic sports to show their individual level of excellence. Conversely, athletes from sports *not* accepted as part of the Olympic programme fight hard to be able to display their levels of excellence. Each year more and more sports become integrated into the Olympic programme. The Games used only to include amateur sports but today the blurring of amateurism has made this more difficult. Consequently sports such as tennis and basketball are also now included. It could be argued that for these sports the Olympics is not their real showcase and their level of performance may be best displayed at tournaments such as Wimbledon or the American championships.

The controversy of doping also brings into question whether all Olympic records have been won by natural ability or whether it is the excellence of the laboratories that have proven more significant.

Sport as education – people learn many things from participating in sport, from motor skills to appreciation of movement, to values such as working with other people. The National Olympic Committees (NOC) run Olympic Days involving schools in an effort to boost participation in sport and the popularity of the Games. Through the extensive media coverage we learn about many sports.

Cultural exchange – as an international competition many different countries and cultures are involved. Athletes travel to many different countries and again through the media the rest of the world often learns about the host cities and the cultures of the competing countries. However, it could also be suggested that the globalisation of sport and particularly the Americanisation of sports are beginning to make traditional sports 'shrink'. Also, sports such as basketball are beginning to have more coverage and influence outside the USA.

Mass participation – 'Sport for All' is a movement promoting the Olympic ideal that sport is a human right for everyone regardless of race, social class and sex. The Olympic Games is the largest competition in the world and as such is viewed by millions of people. It is widely recognised that extensive media coverage can boost participation figures at grass roots level. National Olympic Committees are supposed to make it a policy to increase participation overall. One method is the Olympic Day Run – open to men, women and children of all ages. National governing bodies and the IOC (International Olympic Committee) are implementing policies to reduce discrimination in their sports and events, and increase participation in groups that have traditionally not been overly associated with the sport.

HOT TIPS

For a discussion of how much sportsmanship is still relevant today study Table 19.01 in Chapter 19.

Fair play – this value has been very important in the sports world since the nineteenth century when the middle and upper classes in England made it an integral part of participating in sport. Also known as sportsmanship it is the observance not only of the rules but also the spirit of the game. It is the essence of the contract to compete. You need to consider positive factors such as the Fair Play Awards and negative factors such as the increase in prosecutions for sport-related offences, such as aggression and drug-taking. The IOC has taken a stance on drugs in sport by:

- co-ordinating their efforts in the prevention of drug-taking
- sponsoring conferences
- accrediting laboratories
- establishing a list of banned substances.

International understanding – with so many countries coming together and learning about one another's cultures it should be possible for us all to adopt a more understanding and tolerant approach towards our differences. The Olympic Games have rarely been cancelled but they were for World War II. Unfortunately the Games have been affected by wider political situations and are often remembered as much for the political events surrounding them as for the athletic achievements. One of the key reasons for this is that the Games have provided a focus for the country hosting the event. Their political systems are given prominent media coverage and instances have occurred when governments have used this to promote their political message.

Selected Olympics and political situations

Year	Venue	Political situation
1936	Berlin	Germany used the Games for Nazi propaganda. Hitler's Aryan race theory was discredited when Jesse Owen, a black athlete, won four gold medals.
1972	Munich	Israeli athletes and officials were assassinated by Palestinian terrorists.
1980	Moscow	52 nations boycotted as a protest against the Soviet invasion of Afghanistan.

TASK 13

Research some other political instances affecting the Olympic Games. Suggestions might be the 1968 Games in Mexico City and Sydney Olympics in 2000.

Any discussion about women and the Olympic movement must also include information from the equal opportunities section of this chapter.

Women and Olympism

Women have fought hard over two centuries to increase their acceptance and participation in the Olympic movement. The number of events and female athletes has increased, representing an increasing number of countries. This should continue with increased media coverage and more female representation in the decision-making corridors of the major sport organisations.

The IOC has made women's participation in sporting activities and the Olympic Games – and by implication in administrative and sports authorities – one of its major concerns. It recognises that while the percentage of women in physical activities and the Olympic Games has steadily increased, the percentage of women in governing bodies and sports authorities in the Olympic movement is still low.

City bids

The selection of the host city is important as the success of the Games can often be dependent on the site chosen. Each candidate city must demonstrate to the IOC that its bid to stage the world's greatest multi-disciplinary event has the support of its people and its political authorities.

Why should countries and cities bid for an event that will cost their citizens huge amounts of money? Reasons include:

- international recognition
- economic investment in infrastructure, tourism and attractive conference venues
- other cities in the successful country can gain through training camps
- the 'feel good' factor for a country
- the boost to participation figures that in turn will improve the health of the population
- social integration and inclusion
- employment benefits
- a legacy of facilities that can be used by the community once the Games are over.

Olympic marketing

Marketing
The business of selling goods, including advertising, packaging and so on.

Juan Antonio Samaranch:
*'**Marketing** has become an increasingly important issue for all of us within the Olympic movement. The revenues derived from television, sponsorship and general fundraising help to provide the movement with its financial independence. However, in developing these programmes we must always remember that it is sport that must control its destiny not commercial interests. Every act of support for the Olympic movement promotes peace, friendship and solidarity throughout the world.'* (2004)

Funds today are raised from the sale of TV rights, sponsorship, licensing, ticket sales, coins and stamps. The IOC retains 7–10 per cent of the revenues with the remainder going to the Organising Committees, the International Sport Federations (ISF) and National Olympic Committees. Included in these are the International Paralympic Committee and Paralympic Organising Committee.

Successful marketing ensures:

- the financial stability of the Games
- continuity of marketing across each Olympic Games
- equitable revenue distribution between all the committees and support for emerging nations
- free air transmission across the whole world
- the safeguarding of Olympic ideals against unnecessary commercialisation
- the support of marketing partners to promote Olympism and Olympic ideals
- a reduction in dependence on US television rights which could make the games vulnerable
- TV rights continue to account for just less than 45 per cent of Olympic revenue.

Sponsors enjoy exclusive rights in their respective business areas. Though they pay heavily for this they also recognise the potential of the global marketplace and the impact of the Olympic Games. All 200 National Olympic Committees now receive funding via the sponsorship programme – known as TOP (The Olympic Programme).

The Olympics, together with Wimbledon Tennis Championships, remain the only major sporting events that do not have stadium advertising.

Philanthropy
The effort to promote human welfare.

The future of the Olympic Games

- Commerce (business) needs to be balanced by **philanthropy**.
- The traditions of the Games must be upheld, continuing its theatrical impact as a pageant.
- Every effort must be made to reduce discrimination and enable the potential best athletes to participate.
- The size of the Games needs to be controlled.
- Cultural differences must be recognised.
- The belief in the philosophy of Olympism must be emphasised – that there is joy, and educational and ethical value in sporting effort.

The Paralympic Games

The Paralympics are for athletes with physical and sensorial disabilities. Paralympic means 'parallel' to the Olympic Games. The Paralympic Games are about ability, athletic endeavour and elite performance. Many countries have national research and training centres to provide the optimal environment, facilities and equipment for athletes with disabilities to train for their specific sports.

TASK 14

What would be the advantages and disadvantages of integrating the Paralympic and Olympic Games? Consider the viewpoints of the athletes and the organisers.

Summary

- Different cultures have different approaches towards the development of elite athletes, especially in the philosophy behind the role of sport and the type and level of funding for the athletes.
- Although the UK, USA and France are different they have some historical links with each other.
- Politics affects sport on four main levels:
  1 as a source of nationalism
  2 as a vehicle for propaganda
  3 as a reflection of social conflict or social inequalities
  4 as political philosophies affect decisions and funding for sport.
- The type of economic systems (capitalism, socialism and mixed economy) affect the nature of funding of elite sport.
- The National Sport Institutes (EIS and INSEP), though different, share similar characteristics as Centres of Excellence such as high levels of facilities, coaching and support services.
- The education systems in France and the USA have a greater role in the development of elite athletes than is the case in the UK.
- People from ethnic minorities, low socio-economic groups and women

face more barriers in their struggle to reach elite levels in sport than those from the dominant groups.

- World Games are the pinnacles of sporting achievement and as such are the focal point for commercial marketing and sponsorship, vehicles for political propaganda and individual ambition.

Revise as you go!

1. The UK has a decentralised system of sport. What does this mean?
2. How are elite athletes funded in the UK?
3. Give two differences between INSEP (the French National Sport Institute) and the EIS (English Institute of Sport).
4. What is meant by capitalism and how does it match the concept of professional sport?
5. Name the three concepts of American sport.
6. What are the advantages of using the education system as the main route for the emergence of elite athletes in the USA?
7. What is Title IX and why was it needed in the American education system?
8. Give two advantages and two disadvantages of inter-collegiate sport.
9. How is sport given more status than physical education in the USA?
10. France has a centralised system of sport. What does this mean?
11. What is the licence system and how does it benefit French sport?
12. What are the sport study sections in France and how do they operate?
13. Name four functions of INSEP as an example of a National Sport Institute.
14. How do elite athletes emerge in the UK, France and the USA?
15. What is meant by stacking, channelling and centrality theory?
16. How can an individual's social class affect his or her opportunities in achieving elite athlete status?
17. Give four characteristics of the Olympic Games as an example of a World Game.
18. How have the opportunities for women at the Olympic Games improved?
19. Give three reasons why a city would bid to host the Olympic Games.
20. Why would a company choose to be an Olympic sponsor?
21. What does the term paralympic mean?

Section B of PED5 – What can you expect?

Each question will focus on two discrete theoretical areas of the specification. They could be a combination of AS and A2 work but will be a combination of physiological, psychological and socio-cultural topics. Occasionally the question may be very broad and combine two areas into one section. For example '*outline the physiological and psychological factors required to be an elite marathon runner?*'. If you are faced with questions such as this ensure you include both aspects in your answer.

The questions are usually sub-divided into two sections each focusing on a different aspect of the course, but they will be linked in some way. The stem or introduction of the question will outline the context or scenario and the following questions will link directly to it. An example of a question is provided later in the article to illustrate this point.

Often there are questions based on training methods and the long term adaptations that may result. Many students fail to revise these fully as they are taught as part of their PEP and may be overlooked during revision. To answer these questions successfully you must develop an understanding of each type of training method, its benefits and how to apply the principles of training effectively in order to calculate the correct levels of workload intensity.

Common mistakes and preparation advice

There are numerous mistakes which can easily be eliminated with preparation, a structured revision programme and correct examination technique.

To complete the examination successfully you have to work quickly. You will have approximately 20 minutes for each question in Section A and 15 minutes in Section B, including reading time. Often students worry about the apparent lack of time and rush their answers – be methodical. Read each question carefully, allocating how many marks you feel able to achieve. Then select the questions and start writing. Be careful not to be drawn into spending too long on Section A – watch the clock.

Many students will be sitting the PED4 examination (Physiology and Psychology) immediately prior to this paper but it appears that some of the knowledge needed seems to be lost when a new paper is placed in front of them. Many students appear to switch into 'socio-cultural' mode for Section A and fail to recall information they have already displayed in the previous paper. Remember Section B is a test of the *whole* specification, so be prepared for that mentally.

In order to successfully answer these questions they need to be approached in a structured manner. Initially attempt to identify the broad topic area from which the question is drawn, possibly attempting to isolate your preferred area of strength. It will be unlikely however that you will be able to avoid one particular area entirely, therefore your revision programme should reflect this fact.

Secondly highlight the key terms being questioned and look at the mark allocation. Quickly decide how many you realistically feel able to achieve. It is at this stage many students lose marks because they confuse the key term with another or fail to identify the specific requirements of the question. On a basic level do not confuse the terms 'physiological' and 'psycholological' if mentioned in the question. On a more detailed level, for example, a recent question focused on 'type of practice'. Many students misunderstood this term and their answers focused on 'presentation of practice'.

An increasingly common mistake is to write an answer based on a question from a previous paper. The topic area is identified correctly but the answer is not specific to the question; it is based on one completed as part of the preparation for the exam. Past questions are extremely useful for your preparation but they must be used with care.

Another common mistake involves the inclusion of irrelevant information. Students who do not fully understand the requirements of the question attempt to illustrate all the knowledge they have gained when a topic area is questioned, hoping that some will be credited with marks. Whilst this 'scattergun' approach may provide the odd mark it may also mean no marks will be awarded for the correct answers, as the examiner may have been instructed to accept the first answers only. It can also waste a considerable amount of writing time.

However a useful point of examination technique is the inclusion of additional points linked to the question. If the mark allocation is given as four marks, attempt to provide either five or six points as often some of the first answers may actually be repeat answers and not be given additional credit.

When possible write in full prose rather than bullet points as the examiner may be able to credit marks if they feel you appear to have a reasonable understanding of the question requirements. An answer which contains all bullet points tends to be either right or wrong. Obviously if the time factor becomes an issue it is better to then use bullet points in order to complete the examination.

Another advantage of writing in full prose is the marks gained for your 'quality of written communication'. As mentioned previously there are up to 4 marks available and a script composed mainly of bullet point answers may only receive 1 mark. These lost marks can prove crucial in the overall grade achieved for the paper.

Frequently information is provided in the form of a table which requires interpretation. This is usually an easy way to gain marks but students fail to be specific in their responses and are often vague. Ensure you explain the data fully and make specific reference to whom or what the data refers. For example, state which event had the higher number of spectators and the figures involved rather than simply saying 'one had more than the other'.

It may seem obvious but the key to success is revision. Whilst many students will work hard to learn the topics covered in the A2 course they fail to revisit the work covered during the AS year until too late. Although the questions in the synoptic section will cover both AS and A2 work it is dangerous to gamble on not much AS content being questioned. Often many of the questions will involve a combination of each within a particular question, for example identifying energy systems used in an invasion game and a suitable training method for the game. This question requires knowledge from both the AS and A2 aspects of the physiological side of the course. Therefore you should attempt to look over your first year notes regularly throughout the second year and attempt to view your study of sport from a holistic approach rather than discrete topic areas. Use the knowledge gained from completing your 'synoptic assignment' and 'observation and analysis coursework' as part of your preparation for this examination.

In addition to a structured revision programme prepare yourself by attempting to complete past questions in a set time, helping you to adjust to the time restriction. Past questions and mark-schemes can be found on the AQA website. This is an invaluable resource to help in your preparation.

Unit 5 Questions

Total for this question: 15 marks

Question 1

The development of an elite performance requires commitment from the performer and support from a wide range of other agencies.

a) UK performers in the 2000 Sydney Olympics achieved more success than ever before.
   (i) How has the development of elite performers been supported by the National Lottery and Sport England? **(4 marks)**
   (ii) What criteria must performers meet to receive funding from Sports Aid? **(2 marks)**
   (iii) The National Lottery has given over £100 million to support elite performers. Why should we spend such large sums of money on elite sport? **(3 marks)**

b) The desire to win a gold medal may be taken too far and have detrimental effects to both the performer and society in general. What might these detrimental effects be and how may they go against the Olympic ideal? **(6 marks)**

Total for this question: 15 marks

Question 2

The development of elite performers may vary from one country to another. In the UK and the USA there is extensive support from commercial organisations.

a) How is this support given, and how do **companies** benefit? **(4 marks)**

b) Should a performer consider the nature of a company's product before accepting financial support from them? Give reasons for your answer. **(3 marks)**

c) (i) How might the development of a 16–22-year-old elite performer differ between the UK and the USA? **(4 marks)**
   (ii) Explain why these differences exist. **(4 marks)**

Total for this question: 15 marks

Question 3

Violence may sometimes occur in elite sport, both on and off the pitch.

a) Why might an elite performer commit an act of violence on the pitch? **(2 marks)**

b) Discuss whether an act of violence would be acceptable within the concept of the 'contract to compete'. **(4 marks)**

c) Hooliganism at football matches, both inside and outside stadia, is a recurring problem.
   (i) Describe **three** steps that have been taken to prevent such acts. **(3 marks)**

(ii) Discuss **three** reasons that have been put forward as to why football should suffer from hooliganism. Comment on the validity of these reasons. **(6 marks)**

Total for this question: 15 marks

Question 4

The Sydney Olympics were judged to have been a great success for the participants, Sydney and the world-wide television audience.

a) What are the characteristics of world games such as the Olympics? **(2 marks)**

b) What opportunities do the Olympic Games provide for:

(i) the individual performer? **(3 marks)**

(ii) the host city or country? **(3 marks)**

c) In the United Kingdom a number of international sporting events are "ring fenced" meaning that they must be available for viewing on terrestrial television rather than on satellite or cable subscription channels.

(i) Why should this restriction exist? **(3 marks)**

(ii) "Modern television and broadcasting technologies can give the same spectating experience as actually attending the sport event." Discuss this statement using appropriate examples. **(4 marks)**

Total for this question: 15 marks

Question 5

Elite sport is always highly competitive and increasingly commercial. Elite performers often attempt to make a living from sport and may be driven to use both legal and illegal methods to become successful.

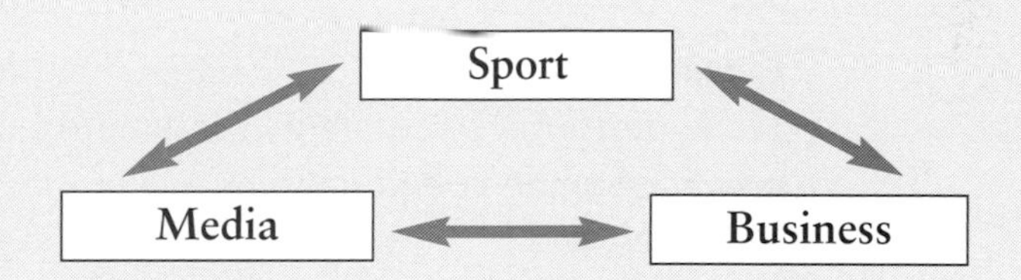

Figure 1

a) Discuss the relationships shown in Figure 1. Comment on the benefits and disadvantages of these relationships to elite sport. **(6 marks)**

b) Discuss to what extent the Lombardian ethic may have a detrimental effect upon the "contract to compete". **(4 marks)**

c) "Elite sport performers should be allowed to use performance enhancing drugs just like any other training aid.'
Discuss this statement. **(5 marks)**

Total for this question: 15 marks

Question 6

Sports attract individuals from a variety of social backgrounds and may offer an individual the opportunity to become an elite performer, either as an amateur or as a professional.

a) What social and cultural factors may account for a talented individual's choice of sport? **(3 marks)**

b) How does the modern day amateur differ from the amateur of the early twentieth century (1900–1920)? **(5 marks)**

c) What factors were responsible for the change in the status of professional performers from the early twentieth century to modern day? **(3 marks)**

d) Even though an individual may possess the right personal qualities, he or she may still fail to reach an elite standard.
A high proportion of the England football and athletic squads come from an ethnic minority group, yet in rugby and cricket the proportions are much lower.
Discuss the factors that may account for this difference. **(4 marks)**

Total for this question: 12 marks

Question 7

A mixed class of 13-year-old school children have been asked to perform a gymnastics routine during an Open Day. Some of them have negative feelings towards performing in this display.

a) Why might these children be unwilling to participate, and how can the teacher change this negative attitude? **(8 marks)**

b) How might a teacher most effectively prepare the children to perform this routine? **(4 marks)**

Total for this question: 12 marks

Question 8

Some performers require a combination of rapid application of maximum power in a controlled manner.

a) How would a performer develop power? Your answer should give general details of any training system or process used. **(8 marks)**

b) Mentally, how does a power performer attempt to ensure that he or she uses all available power, yet apply it in a controlled manner within a performance situation? **(4 marks)**

Total for this question: 12 marks

Question 9

Current physical education and physical recreation programmes play an important role in the development of skill and fitness in children.

a) Discuss whether development of skill and fitness could have been achieved through the PE syllabuses of the early twentieth century, such as the 1909 Model Course. Your answer should consider syllabus content and the conditions under which it was delivered. **(8 marks)**

b) What factors would a modern day teacher of Physical Education have to consider when devising an effective skill development session for a group of children? **(4 marks)**

Total for this question: 12 marks

Question 10

Whether or not an individual may become an elite performer is dependent upon a combination of personal strengths and external factors.

a) Explain the social and cultural factors that determine if an individual may become an elite performer. **(5 marks)**

An important individual factor is the ability to make decisions within a performance situation.

b) In terms of information processing, what factors are important in allowing a performer to make effective decisions? How can a coach help the performer develop this process? **(7 marks)**

Total for this question: 12 marks

Question 11

Teams are successful because they combine highly skilled individuals into an effective group.

a) Successful teams are often said to be cohesive. What do we mean by *cohesion* **and** how may a coach help a team to become cohesive? **(4 marks)**

b) Hockey is an example of an invasion team game. During a match, a midfield player will be running at differing speeds over a variety of distances.
Using examples, discuss the energy systems that would be dominant at specific times during a match **and** suggest the most appropriate form of training for this player. Give reasons to justify your selection of training method. **(8 marks)**

Total for this question: 12 marks

Question 12

Outdoor and adventurous activities are becoming increasingly popular.

a) What values and characteristics are associated with outdoor and adventurous activities? **(4 marks)**

b) To enable young people to take part in outdoor and adventurous activities they have to acquire a range of knowledge and skills.
Name the appropriate *teaching styles* and *type of practice* an instructor would use when teaching an outdoor and adventurous activity such as rock climbing to a group of novices. Justify your answer by discussing the factors the instructor would need to consider before making his or her selection. **(8 marks)**

Unit 6: Coursework

Chapter 21: Practical coursework

Learning outcomes

By the end of this chapter you should be able to:
- understand the requirements of the practical performance
- know how to prepare for assessment
- complete an analysis of your personal performance and compare it to that of an elite performer
- explain the causes of indentified weaknesses and demonstrate how to use theoretical knowledge to improve your practical performance.

Introduction

The aim of the practical coursework component is to build on the core skills developed in the first year of the course and to apply them in a competitive situation. The focus of the second year is to assess not only the physical skills and application of strategies and tactics, but to bring together all the various theoretical components allowing the optimisation of performance. The task you face is to use your knowledge and understanding of the theoretical aspects of the course to identify weaknesses in your performance and possible causes; you then need to use this knowledge to eradicate the faults.

The first key piece of advice is to obtain a copy of the relevant specification criteria as soon as possible. You can get this either from your teacher or download it from the AQA website at www.aqa.org.uk.

Practical performance and preparation for assessment

Table 21.01 The assessment requirements for A2 level of study

Exam board	A2 level
AQA	• One practical activity, which may be the same as that offered at AS level or different • Written/verbal observation and analysis of performance compared to an elite performer • Synoptic assignment

Much of the advice offered in this section is similar to that given for AS level. However, it is worth refreshing your memory to remind yourself how to access the marks. The table opposite outlines the examination board requirements for the A2 course. The skills developed in the first year will now be assessed in a competitive situation.

HOT TIPS

Obtain the current AQA specification criteria for your chosen activity as soon as possible. The criteria do change and include slight modifications on a regular basis.

This unit is worth a total of 17.5 per cent of the overall A2 course. The marks are allocated as shown in Table 21.02.

Table 21.02 Allocation of marks for the practical coursework component

Section A – Practical performance

- **Maximum 120 marks = 5%**
- 40 marks for each area of skill application
- For example, game activities are often split into the following sections:
  1. effectiveness of attacking skills
  2. effectiveness of defensive skills
  3. effective implementation of strategies and tactics
  4. effective implementation of physiological and psychological factors which affect performance.

Section B – Observation, analysis and critical evaluation of performance

- **Maximum 40 marks = 2.5%**
- 10 marks for identification of weaknesses when compared to an *elite performer* for each of the four assessment areas listed above

Section C – Application of knowledge and understanding to optimise performance

- **Maximum 80 marks = 2.5% (synoptic element)**
- 10 marks for identification of *possible causes of weaknesses* of each assessment area highlighted in Section B
- 10 marks for identification of *corrective practices* to allow improvement of performance

Synoptic assignment

- **Maximum 7.5%**
- Although this piece of coursework is part of this unit it will not be assessed by a visiting moderator. It will be sent to an examiner and externally marked. More detailed information concerning completion of the assignment can be found on pages 000.

Many students may often neglect the practical element of the course and tend to focus on the theoretical aspects. However, a large percentage of the final marks are allocated to this section – up to 30 per cent of the final mark allocation for the A-level course. Therefore time should be devoted to developing the skills required from the onset and not left until later when you are close to the final assessment or moderation.

To fully understand the nature of performance and how to facilitate improvement, links should be made with the theoretical components as frequently as possible. Individual strengths and weaknesses should be identified and as the course progresses, possible causes and corrective measures can be implemented.

The selection of activities must be carefully considered as there may be restrictions. In addition to your own experience, other factors may include:

- the time available to complete extra training
- the opportunity for extra-curricular activities
- the accessibility of facilities and resources
- the expertise of teachers and coaches.

HOT TIPS

Take time to analyse your performance. Highlight your weaknesses and try to work on them regularly.

The nature of assessment requires the demonstration of relevant named core skills related to a specific activity in a competitive situation. It may be difficult for some students to fulfill the requirements depending on their choice of activity. For example, many students may offer skiing during the AS course, as they are competent skiers, but they would be unable to offer it at A2 level unless they competed in actual race events. Consequently your activity must be selected carefully to avoid a panic in the later part of the course.

The marking of the practical activities is conducted by continual assessment. This allows for ongoing development of performance and caters for students who may have an 'off day' during a moderator's visit. The assessment will focus on your performance in a *competitive situation* which includes your demonstration of core skills; strategies and tactics; the application of the psychological and physiological qualities needed within a fully competitive environment or appropriate alternative.

In order to develop your skills in the competitive situation, training sessions are easier with others, not just because it is more sociable but because they can actually help to improve your performance by observing and coaching. If the practice takes place with another student who has limited knowledge of the activity, outline the identified weaknesses of the skills and prepare a sheet of the correct techniques and coaching points required.

However, if time can be spent with a teacher or another student who is experienced and is able to identify your weaknesses this may be of greater benefit. Allocated time for development may be available either during lessons or extra-curricular activities.

Further time for development may take place at a local club and the expertise of the coaches there may be utilised. If this is the case it may be advisable to inform them of the specification criteria, so that they are aware of your aims and the specific skills that need to be developed.

When possible video record any practice sessions and analyse your development. Evaluate any progress and restructure your training schedule as required.

To develop the effective application of your skills in a competitive situation, set targets for each game or event and ask someone to evaluate your performance. Do not set too many each time, possibly two or three, but try to concentrate on these and don't get over-concerned with other areas of weakness – they can be targets next time.

When developing skills don't try to change everything at once or expect a huge improvement in performance overnight. The process may take months or years to complete. Many elite performers strive to make minor modifications to their technique in order to achieve the optimum performance. The aim of the A2 course is not to make you compete at this level but to be competent performers. Try to remember this when developing your practical performance.

Assessment procedures

The school/college will be assigned an external moderator to ensure the marking criteria are applied correctly by the teachers, when compared to recommended national standards. The moderation may involve either:

- one school/college
- a group of schools/colleges
- video evidence.

The moderator may not see all the activities being offered by the school/college due to time restrictions, availability of facilities or numbers involved. However, the assumption must be made that he or she will observe any possible combination of activities and as a consequence you should be fully prepared. This may involve not only the actual practical performance but any analysis of performance requirements. The best way to prepare for the moderation is to start practising the core skills as early in the course as possible and give yourself the opportunity to experience as many conditioned situations as you can to develop your skills.

The moderation usually involves both AS and A2 students. Consequently it may be easy to lose focus and concentration. Many students assume the moderator is not watching them because they are at the other end of the sports hall or far side of the playing field. Don't be complacent – he or she may be assessing you at any time!

It also helps to make the effort to dress appropriately and 'look the part'. This will at least give the moderator the impression that some preparation and thought has been given to the assessment rather than simply turning up on the day.

The nature of physical activity inevitably involves mistakes being made during performance; it is almost unavoidable. Even the performers at the highest level make errors of judgement or are influenced by the environment, occasion and opponents. If mistakes are made do not worry about them, redirect your attention and concentrate on the task ahead. The moderator will look at the overall performance not just one small part.

If the selected activity is a team game or one that involves other performers don't try to be the centre of attention all the time. The assessment is based on your ability to fulfil a role within a specific position. Marks may be lost because of the inability to implement certain tactics, strategies and systems of play.

Analysis of personal performance

Before any personal development of skill and technique can occur, your own performance must be analysed and evaluated. This can be achieved in a number of ways:

- teacher/coach observing performance and providing feedback
- another student observing performance and providing feedback
- video recording of own performance and personal analysis.

If possible the latter is in many ways the most useful, as you can see the faults (via visual guidance) and develop a better understanding of the exact modifications needed. Video footage is also useful as a means of stopping the action and making specific comparisons to the technical model, which may be more difficult during live or full speed actions.

HOT TIPS

The analysis of your performance should include technical aspects of the skill execution and the application in a competitive situation.

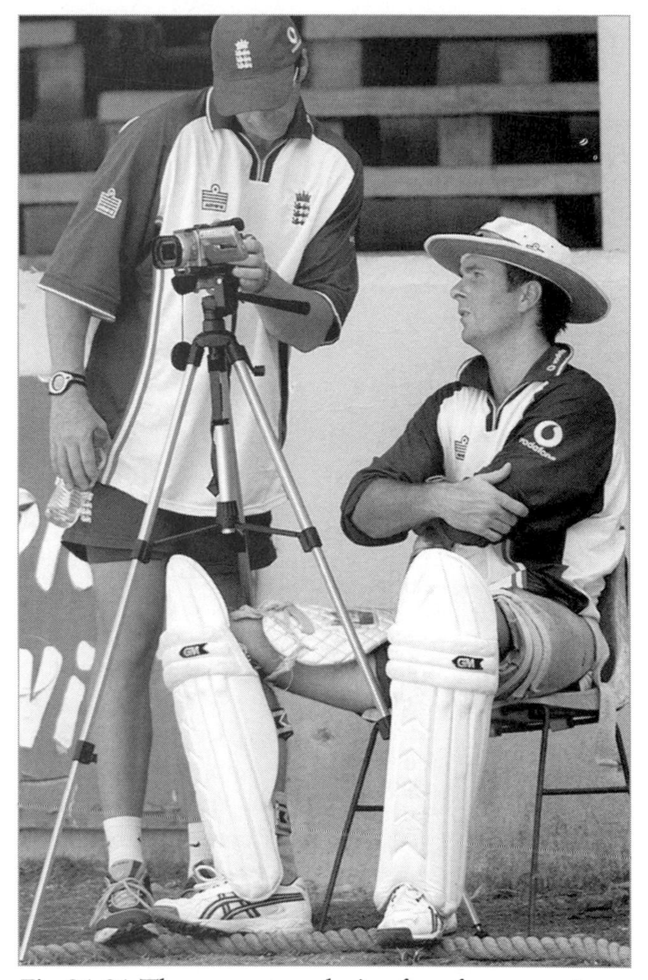

Fig 21.01 The correct analysis of performance is important if improvements are to be made

Once the actual skill has been analysed the next stage in the process involves the evaluation of the effectiveness of its application, either during conditioned practices or competitive situations.

As mentioned previously, for game activities these are split into the following sections:

- effectiveness of attacking skills
- effectiveness of defensive skills
- effective implementation of strategies and tactics
- effective implementation of physiological and psychological factors which affect performance.

Other activities have alternative categories which are more appropriate, for example, swimming and athletics may require the comments to be based on two events, and gymnastic events may be based on agilities and twists. Detailed requirements need to be obtained from the specification criteria.

TASK 1

Observe and analyse your personal performance for each of the assessment areas in a competitive situation. Identify a minimum of three weaknesses for each assessment area.

Once this process has been completed a structured training programme should be followed to develop the identified weaknesses in the skills. Frequently assess your development either via a teacher/coach or by video recording. Don't just assume because practice is taking place an improvement will occur – you may be practising the wrong technique!

Synthesis of theory and practical

The aim of this section is to assess your knowledge of the theoretical components and your ability to apply that knowledge, allowing you to improve your performance. The factors which may be potential causes of weakness can be drawn from any aspect of the specification. If possible this should be the case as it illustrates your appreciation and understanding of the whole specification, not just components within it. Many students tend to limit their answers to the psychological and physiological components and make limited reference to the socio-cultural factors.

HOT TIPS

Don't repeat courses of weakness or corrective practices – you will lose marks. You need to identify 12 different theoretical reasons from all areas of the specification.

The term 'corrective measures' or 'corrective practices' expects a student to make reference to a variety of theoretical information and not simply outline physical drills or practices.

The question could be posed for any skill or aspect of performance:
'In theoretical terms, what factors may have caused my weaknesses, what can I do to improve and how will this help?

The reasons identified may not actually have contributed to any weaknesses in performance but the process of identifying them must still take place. Try not to use the same possible cause for each skill; identify different factors. A common fault is to repeat the same cause for several skills, for example, 'lack of practice', or 'not enough flexibility', etc. If you repeat yourself you may not be credited with the marks.

Based on the analysis of performance, each weakness identified should have a possible theoretical cause explained in detail with an appropriate corrective measure. This demonstrates an understanding of the application of the theoretical components and should allow you to appreciate how many factors can actually affect the performance of an individual.

Outlined overleaf are topics which may have affected the development and performance of your chosen activities. The lists are not complete and other factors may be included. If there are other areas which may have influenced your development, explain the reasons why and outline how this knowledge can be used to rectify the situation.

Physiological factors

These might include:
- inefficient use of levers and bones
- lack of specific fitness components
- physiological composition of the individual
- dietary considerations
- inappropriate training methods
- poor application of training principles
- lack of structured training programme
- poor development of appropriate energy system.

Psychological factors

These might include:
- personality type
- plateaus and associated causes
- theories of learning experienced
- types of practice
- methods of teaching
- forms of guidance
- types of motivation
- transfer of learning
- effectiveness of information processing system
- aggression
- attitude
- group dynamics and leadership
- arousal levels
- achievement motivation
- stress, anxiety and poor stress management techniques
- self-efficacy and learned helplessness.

Socio-cultural factors

These might include:
- physical education experiences
- National Curriculum
- experiences of play, sport and physical recreation
- historical factors and traditions
- equal opportunities – gender, race, social class, disability, socio-economic group
- provision of facilities – public, private and voluntary
- National Lottery
- government initiatives
- funding
- role models
- effectiveness of national and local organisations.

As you can see from the list on page 263 there are many theoretical aspects that may be linked to your development; you just have to think about which might have had the greatest impact on you personally.

When completing this section think logically and arrange your notes in an organised manner. This makes revision and discussion more effective and thorough.

An example of this structured procedure is outlined below in Table 21.03, with a possible cause for each of the identified weaknesses taken from a different theoretical area.

Table 21.03 Exemplar of Section B and C for Assessment Area 1 – Application of Defending Skills

Course = A2 Activity = cricket (batting)	**Area of assessment = defending**
Weakness 1	Batting – play too hard at the ball against spin bowlers. I sometimes push forward too hard in defence against slow bowling. I want to get a large stride forward to counteract the spin on the ball, but I sometimes over-emphasise this and lunge forward too quickly at the ball. This often results in the ball popping up close to fielders, giving them a catching opportunity.
Possible cause (psychological factor)	I have low self-efficacy regarding this type of shot. This has been caused by the four elements outlined by Bandura: • past performance accomplishments – lost my wicket playing this shot several times before • vicarious experiences – seen others in my team playing this shot unsuccessfully • verbal persuasion – my coach has told me not to attempt the shot unless I need to • emotional arousal – I become anxious when playing against spin bowlers who bowl on the correct line and length.
Corrective practice	To develop my self-efficacy I could: • past performance accomplishments – practise the shot in training and develop my technique; I could also attempt the shot more regularly in less important games • vicarious experiences – watch how other players approach the shot and learn from their actions • verbal persuasion – my coach can encourage me to boost my confidence and we can discuss how to approach the shot in a positive manner • emotional arousal – develop effective stress management techniques, such as controlled breathing and imagery to employ when batting.

Weakness 2	Bowling – length of delivery is very erratic. I regularly bowl balls too full in length or much too short, allowing the batsman to score easy runs. I am only an occasional bowler and I am unaware of the action which I need to produce a consistent length of delivery.
Possible cause (psychological factor)	A lack of effective practice means I am not aware of the weaknesses in my bowling action. I am still in the associative stage of learning and am unable to detect if the speed of run-up, the angle of release or height of release is the major problem causing the inconsistent length of delivery. Video analysis has illustrated I often release the ball behind my head, creating a large angle of release and consequently a full delivery (too close to the batsman). The height of my release also varies and I need to release the ball further through my action.
Corrective practice	Massed practice, concentrating on my point of release, will aid familiarity with speed, angle and height of release. This should be linked with visual and verbal guidance, illustrating the good and bad points, to allow reinforcement to take place. Visual guidance could be completed through the use of video analysis and the placement of cones to highlight the target area. Verbal guidance from my coach could be used to identify when to release the ball or give me specific feedback about my technique.
Weakness 3	Running to stop a ball caused by a lack of speed over a short distance. If the ball is coming close to me I can move quite quickly a few metres either way, but if the ball has passed me I struggle to turn and chase it to the boundary. This causes me to not stop the ball crossing the boundary rope and runs are added to the other team's score.
Possible cause (physiological)	Lack of agility and speed over a short distance. Much of my training is focused on the development of skills required to play cricket rather than the fitness needed to play at a good level. Time with my coach is limited and the skill development is the focus of attention.
Corrective practice	Development of agility and speed by incorporating specific exercises into a structured training programme. Circuit training could involve shuttle runs aimed at turning quickly and sprinting in the other direction, as well as exercises to develop speed and power. These could include bench jumps, step-ups, lunges and alternate leg changes. I could also use plyometrics and speed sessions. The speed training could involve different distances up to 40m as this replicates the game situation.

Comments on the examples above:

- For each assessment area, i.e. attack, defence, strategies and tactics, and physical and psychological preparation, there must be three weaknesses, causes and corrections. In other words, you need to discuss twelve factors in total.
- For each weakness there must be a comparison made to a named elite performer. This has not been shown on this example, but once you have highlighted your weakness, explain in terms of the application of those skills why the elite performer is more effective.
- The technical terminology used is specific to the activity of cricket.
- Although all three theoretical areas are used as possible causes in this example, it is possible to use one area several times. For example, the possible causes for two weaknesses may both be psychologically-based.
- No repetitive answers – search the specification and use different reasons, to show the moderator you have an understanding of many areas from both AS and A2 modules.

Completing the analysis in this way should allow for the development of a logical and structured understanding of each area.

It may be useful to structure your analysis as shown in Table 21.04 below.

Table 21.04 Exemplar sheet of how Section B and C may be completed

	Personal performance	Elite performer
Weakness 1	*Selected skill and weakness of application in a competitive situation*	*Explanation of application of same skill and effective outcome*
Cause of weakness	*Theoretical explanation for weakness*	
Corrective practice	*Theoretical explanation of how to implement corrective strategy (not just an outline of drill/practice)*	
Weakness 2		
Cause of weakness		
Corrective practice		
Weakness 3		
Cause of weakness		

TASK 2

Using the table outlined above, complete the following tasks for the identified weaknesses highlighted in Task 1:

- Suggest a possible theoretical cause of each weakness.
- Outline a practical method which could be implemented based on this knowledge.

Repeat the procedure for two other identified weaknesses. Repeat for all aspects of performance which need to be analysed.

Key points to remember when preparing for the practical coursework

The following points can be applied to any of the different specifications:

- Check the requirements and choose the activities carefully. Don't just assume any combination of activity can be taken.
- Start preparation for the final assessment at the beginning of the course – don't leave it until the last few weeks!
- Learn the correct techniques for the chosen activities.
- Take time to analyse your strengths and weaknesses.
- Set realistic targets for performance development.
- Evaluate your progress regularly and revise your targets.
- Look for the links between the theoretical aspects of the course and personal practical performance.
- Update your notes regularly and use them as a revision resource.
- Enjoy it – the practical aspect of the course is supposed to be fun!

Index

16PF questionnaire 94, 96
400m running 18, 45

A
a-VO2diff (arterio-venous oxygen difference) 63
academies 187
acceleration 70, 72–3, 73, 74, 77
acetylcholine 39, 40
Achievement Goal theory 116–17
achievement motivation 114–16, 117
acidosis 35, 40
active recovery 45, 46–7, 48, 59
activity *see* exercise
adaptive responses to training 36, 41, 60, 64–5
adenosine diphosphate (ADP) 13
adenosine triphosphate *see* ATP
ADP (adenosine diphosphate) 13
advertising 234
aerobic capacity 3, 4
aerobic 'fitness' 20
aerobic metabolism 14
aerobic system/pathway 19–23, 24, 26–7, 28, 30, 42, 43
aggression 107–9, 191, 198, 206, 212, 214, 238
  theories of 110–12
  see also aggressive behaviour
Aggression Cue hypothesis 111–12
aggressive behaviour 89, 90, 95, 121
  reducing and controlling 112–13
  see also aggression; hooliganism
air resistance 76, 78
alactacid debt 43, 44
alactic (ATP-PCr) system 15–17, 18, 24, 27, 28, 65
alcohol 208, 209, 211
all or none law 6–7
allocation of marks 260
Allport (1935) 100
altitude training 53, 55–6
amateurism 191–2, 194–5, 201, 203, 204, 220
  Olympic Games 193, 194, 220, 244–9
  relationship with professionalism 195–6, 198, 199, 217, 243, 245
  Rugby Union 192, 196–7, 201
  UK 191–2, 195, 220, 233, 243
American Dream 221, 234
Americanisation 211, 233, 246
AMI (Athletic Motivation Inventory) 96
anaerobic capacity 3
anaerobic glycolysis 37
anaerobic metabolism 14
anaerobic pathways 15, 16, 18–19, 22, 31
  see also ATP-PCr system; lactic acid system
anaerobic threshold 34
anaerobic training 65
analysis of personal performance 263–4
angle of release 79
angular momentum 82, 83–4
angular motion 80–4
angular velocity 81, 82, 83
ANS (Autonomic Nervous System) 90, 155
anti-social behaviour 174
anxiety 120, 121, 135, 154, 155, 156–7, 163
  cognitive 121, 123, 137, 156, 157, 159
  somatic 121, 123, 156, 157, 159
approach behaviour 116, 117–18, 161, 163
Armstrong (1994, 1997) 208–9
Armstrong, Lance 29, 34, 35
Aronson et al (1994) 100
arousal 111, 119–20, 135, 136
  controlling 112, 113, 157, 160
  emotional 137
  and experience 122, 127
  over-arousal *see* over-arousal
  and performance 120–1, 121–3
  theories of 120–4
  see also social facilitation
arterio-venous oxygen difference (a-VO2diff) 63
assertive behaviour 108–9, 113
assessment procedures 262
athletes
  as assets 234
  of West African origin 237
Athletic Motivation Inventory *see* AMI
athleticism 192, 193, 194–5, 196, 204, 220
Atkinson, McCelland and (1964) 114–15
ATP (adenosine triphosphate) 13, 65
  resynthesis 13–23, 24, 26–8, 43, 44, 45, 63
  resynthesis rates 16, 19, 39, 40
  see also aerobic system; ATP-PCr system; lactic acid system
ATP-PCr (alactic) system 15–17, 18, 24, 27, 28, 65
ATPase 13, 65
attentional narrowing 124–5, 154

attentional wastage 124–5
attitude objects 100, 101
attitude scales 102–4
attitudes 99–102, 141
  changing of 104–6
  measuring 102–4
attribution process 131
attribution re-training 134, 139
attributions 117, 130, 131, 133–4, 137, 138, 161
audience 88, 126, 127, 128, 129, 154
  see also spectators
Australia, Institute System 183, 219
Autonomic Nervous System *see* ANS
autonomous phase of learning 121
avoidance behaviour 116
axes of the body 80–1
axes of rotation 80–1, 82

B
Bandura, Albert (1977) 95, 112, 135, 136–7
banned substances *see* doping; drugs
Baron (1977, 1986) 108, 128
Barr Sex Test 239
Barrow (1977) 147
basketball 79, 108, 124
Beckham, David 149, 195
'being in the zone' 123
beliefs 105–6
Berkowitz (1969) 111–12
beta-oxidation 21
betting industry 200–1
big time programmes (USA) 231
biofeedback 158, 162
black people, and sports 236–7
BOA (British Olympic Association) 183, 184, 185–6, 186
body
  axes of 80–1
  shape 83
  as social construct 239
body fat 37
body temperature 41, 44, 46, 63
Bosman, Jean Marc 215–16, 216
Bowers (1973) 95
bradycardia 64, 65
breathing control 162
breathing rates 31, 42, 45–6, 63
  at altitude 55
Britain *see* UK
British Olympic Association *see* BOA
buffering 27, 35, 65
Bull (1991) 108

C
calcium levels 40
capitalism 224, 234, 243
carbohydrate loading 26–7
carbohydrate window 46, 48
carbohydrates 26–7, 41, 46, 48
carbon dioxide (CO2) 21, 30, 63
cardiovascular system 62
Carlyle, Thomas (1795–1881) 148
Carron (1982) 140, 142
Carter Report (2005) 179
catastrophe theory 123–4
Cattell, Raymond (1965) 94, 96
CCPR (Central Council for Physical Recreation) 183
centering 162
Central Council for Physical Recreation *see* CCPR
central nervous system *see* CNS
centrality 236–7
channelled aggression 108, 206
channelling 238
cheating 198, 244
Chelladurai's Multi-dimensional model of leadership (1980) 151–2
China 177, 178, 224
Christensen, Levinson and (1996) 215
clubs 221, 222, 225, 226, 229, 230, 232
CNS (central nervous system) 9, 10, 54
CO2 (carbon dioxide) 21, 30, 63
coaches 112, 133
  goal setting by 163, 164
  role 58, 99, 117–18, 122, 129–30, 135, 143
  Sports Coach UK 183
  USA 230
  World Class Coaching Programme 188–9
Coakley, J (1994) 237
codes of conduct 191
cognitive anxiety 121, 123, 137, 156, 157, 159
cognitive arousal 119
cognitive dissonance 105–6
cognitive methods of stress management 160–1
cognitive responses to stress 154
cohesion 142–4
collegiate system (USA) 221, 225, 231, 234
commercialisation 194, 200–4, 204, 211, 217, 233–4, 244
Commonwealth Games, Manchester 2002 179
comparative approach 219
competition period 57–8
competition specific training 57
Competitive State Anxiety Inventory (CSAI-2) 96, 159
competitive trait anxiety 157, 159
competitiveness 88, 90, 114
concentration 160

concentric contractions 9
conflict 206, 224, 249
conglomerates 201, 203
connective tissue 2
contact sports 109
continuous training 28, 33, 53
contract to compete 190–1
contraction of muscles 2, 3, 4, 6–10, 40
  eccentric 9, 47, 48
  isometric 54
contracts 199, 201
control 132–3
control of sport 203
cool down 45, 46–7, 48
cori cycle 46
Cottrell (1968) 128
Coubertin, Baron Pierre de (1863–1937) 193, 222, 245
coupled reactions 16
coursework 259–69
Cram, Steve 182
creatine kinase 15, 65
creatine supplementation 16, 27
cricket 78, 106, 192
crowds 88, 126, 128, 129, 154
  see also spectators
CSAI-2 (Competitive State Anxiety Inventory) 96, 159
Cue Arousal Theory 111–12
cue-utilisation theory 124–5
cues 111–12, 124–5, 160
cultural exchange 245, 246
culture 110, 117

D
DCMS (Department for Culture, Media and Sport) 179, 180
deceleration 70, 74, 77
dehydration 27, 40, 41
delayed onset of muscle soreness (DOMS) 47–8
democracy in sport 201
Department for Culture, Media and Sport (DCMS) 179, 180
detraining effects 55, 56
deviancy 204–15, 215, 244
  increase in 174, 194, 217
  and 'win at all costs' ethic 198, 201, 217
diet 26
direct gas analysis 31
direction 74
disability rights 216
disabled athletes 201, 244, 249
discrimination 101, 176, 177, 224, 235, 248
  gender 216, 239–42
  racial 216, 236
displacement 69, 110
distance 69
Distraction-Conflict theory 128, 129
distribution of mass 82
diving 83
Dodson, Yerkes and (1908) 121–3
Dollard (1939) 110–11
dominant groups 204, 235
dominant habit 120–1, 126, 130
DOMS (delayed onset of muscle soreness) 47–8
doping 190, 194, 197, 198, 212–15, 216
  at Olympic Games 244, 246
  increase in 174, 191
  see also drugs
double periodisation 61
drinking
  alcohol 208, 209, 211
  fluids 27, 41
Drive theory 120–1, 126
Droppleman, McNair and Lorr (1971) 97
drugs 181, 190, 212–15, 216, 244
  IOC and 215, 246
  see also doping
Duda (1993) 116
Dunning et al (1988) 208
duration of exercise 15, 21, 28, 46
Dweck (1975) 138
dysfunctional behaviour *see* deviancy

E
East Germany (GDR) 177–8
Eastern bloc 177–8, 224, 233
eccentric contractions 9, 47, 48
eccentric forces 80
economic systems 224, 249
education
  France 232–3, 233, 249
  sport as 246, 246–7
  UK 229, 233, 249
  USA 229–32, 233, 249
  see also school sport; schools
EIS (English Institute of Sport) 181, 182–3, 226, 226–7, 227–8
elastic energy 9
electron transport system 20, 21, 22, 23
elite performers 86, 88, 99
  funding 174, 178, 180, 225–6, 249
  qualities 175–6
  elite sport 173–4
  development systems 178–9
  organisations with remits for 180–6
emotional arousal 137
employment rights 215–16
endorsements 198, 199, 201, 202, 234
endurance 21, 22–3, 29–30, 34–5
  training for 33, 41
energy 12
  elastic energy 9
  production 2, 63, 64, 65
  sources in the body 13–15, 23, 24

see also aerobic system; ATP-PCr system; lactic acid system
energy continuum 24
energy profiling 24–5
energy systems 15, 41
see also aerobic system; ATP-PCr system; lactic acid system
England
amateurism 191–2, 195
professional sport 195–6
public schools 192, 193, 196, 222, 245
social class 195–6
see also UK
England cricket team 106
English Institute of Sport *see* EIS
entertainment 199, 200, 201, 234
EPI (Eysenck's Personality Inventory) 92–3, 94, 96
EPOC (excess post-exercise oxygen consumption) 42, 43–7, 48
EPQ (Eysenck Personality Questionnaire) 94
equal opportunities 190, 235, 239–2
ethics 190, 191–5, 217, 221
ethnic groups 236–8, 249
eustress 154
evaluation apprehension 128
examination questions 86–7
examinations 251–3
excellence 174, 245
excess post-exercise oxygen consumption *see* EPOC
exercise
duration 15, 21, 28, 46
intensity 15, 21, 24, 36, 41, 46, 47, 48
short-term responses to 62–3
experience 122, 127, 128, 133
experiences
past 137, 161
vicarious 112, 136, 137, 148, 161
Eysenck, Hans (1995) 89, 90–4
Eysenck Personality Questionnaire *see* EPQ
Eysenck's Personality Inventory *see* EPI

F
failure 88, 133, 134, 138, 154
fair play 190–1, 191, 193, 194, 214, 246
fartlek 28, 33, 53
fast replenishment 43, 44, 45
fast twitch motor units 6, 7
fast twitch (type 2) muscle fibres 3, 4, 10, 20, 36, 65
fat 2, 64
body fat 37
fat metabolism 41
fatigue 3, 8, 10, 22, 26, 65
causes 17, 39–41
lactic acid and 20, 35, 39, 65
reducing likelihood 41
fatigue index 4
fats 2, 20, 21, 64
fatty acids 14, 22–3, 36, 63
faulty processes 144, 147
Fazey, Hardy and (1987) 123–4
female soccer (USA) 240
Ferguson, Duncan 215
Festigner (1957) 105
FFAs (free fatty acids) 21
Fiedler's Contingency model of leadership (1967) 150–1
Finn (1994) 209
fitness 20, 145
flight paths 78, 80
food *see* carbohydrate loading; carbohydrate window; carbohydrates
football 200, 206, 236
Bosman ruling 215–16, 216
community programmes 211
energy sources for 24
female soccer (USA) 240
hooliganism 206–12
World Cup 203
forces 68, 72, 72–3, 74, 75–6, 80
torques 81, 82
France 178, 221–2, 222, 224, 243, 249
education 226, 232–3, 233, 249
funding 225
INSEP 225, 226, 226–8, 232
racism 236
free body diagrams 75, 76–7
free fatty acids (FFAs) 21
Freud, Sigmund (1856–1939) 110
friction 75–6
Frustration-Aggression hypothesis 110–11
funded institutions 226
funding 177, 181, 184, 185, 186, 201
elite sport 174, 178, 225–6, 249
and gender 241, 241–2
government/state funding 179, 222, 224, 225, 228
lottery funding 180, 183, 184, 186, 188, 192, 225
Olympic Games 248
school sport 229
UK 179, 224
USA 225, 231

G
gambling industry 200–1
gamesmanship 191, 245
GAS (General Adaptation Syndrome) 155
gate receipts 200, 201, 225
GDR (German Democratic Republic/East Germany) 177–8
gender 128, 216, 238–42
commercialisation and 201, 202, 204

differences due to 33, 37
and performance 37, 178–9
General Adaptation Syndrome *see* GAS
general conditioning 57
genetic advantage, debate 238
genetics 5, 33, 35, 110, 175, 176
German Democratic Republic (GDR/East Germany) 177–8
Germany 178
gifted and talented 188
Gill (1986) 108
glycogen 14, 18, 20, 21, 35, 63
depletion 22–3, 39, 40, 41, 46
endurance events 22–3, 41
liver glycogen 14, 18, 19
muscle glycogen 2, 14, 18, 22, 36, 46, 48, 64
storage 3, 14
glycogen loading 26–7, 41
glycogen sparing 22, 64
glycolitic enzymes 65
glycolysis 18, 19, 37, 63, 65
goals 116–17, 137, 139, 163–5
golf 7, 202
golf ball, forces acting upon 72, 73
Golgi tendon organs (GTOs) 10, 54
Gould and Krane (1992) 119
governing bodies *see* NGBs
government funding 179, 222, 224, 225, 228
grass roots sport 174, 182, 184, 201
gravity 68, 72, 78
Great Man theory 148
Green, Oakley and (2003) 178–9
Greene, Maurice 70
Griffin, Moorhead and (1998) 147
Gross (1992) 89
group dynamics 141
group productivity 144–5
groups 135–6, 140–2
cohesion 142–4
developing 136, 144
Grusky (1963) 236
GTOs (Golgi tendon organs) 10, 54
gymnastics 16, 78, 80

H
haemoglobin 55, 56, 64
hammer throwing 67
Hanin (1980) 123
Hardy and Fazey (1987) 123–4
health 174, 182, 185
heart rates 31, 62, 64, 65, 137
at altitude 55
during recovery 42, 45–6
under stress 155, 156
heart size 64, 65
hegemonic groups 235, 242
height of release 79
high jump 74
Hillsborough disaster (1989) 210
'hitting the wall' 22–3, 26, 40
Hollander (1967, 1971) 89, 95
Holmes, Kelly 51, 70
home advantage 129
homeostasis 155
hooliganism 206–9, 212, 215, 216
controlling 210–11
horizontal forces 75–6
Hull (1943) 120
Husman and Silva (1984) 108–9
hydration 41
hydrogen 21, 39, 40
hyperplasia 10, 64, 65
hypertonic drinks 41
hypertrophy 10, 64, 65
hypoxic environments 55

I
ice skating 76, 83, 83–4
Iceberg Profile 97
identification screening 175
imagery 161
impulse 77–8
inertia 69
information processing 128
innervation 6–7, 7
INSEP (Institut National du Sport et de l'Education) 225, 226, 226–8, 232
instinct theory 110
institutions, funded 226
instrumental aggression 108
intensity
of exercise 15, 21, 24, 36, 41, 46, 47, 48
of training 48, 56, 57
inter-collegiate sport (USA) 231
inter-scholastic sport (USA) 229, 230
interactionist theories 95, 115–16, 148, 157
International Olympic Committee *see* IOC
International Sport Federations *see* ISFs
international understanding 245, 247
interval training 28, 33, 53
Inverted-U theory 121–3
IOC (International Olympic Committee) 185, 186, 214, 246, 247, 248
and doping 214, 215, 246
ISFs (International Sport Federations) 183, 184
isometric muscle contraction 54

K
Kerr (1994) 209
Krane, Gould and (1992) 119
Kreb's cycle 20, 21, 22, 23

L
lactacid debt 43, 44
lactate 35, 36, 48, 55
lactate anaerobic (lactic acid) system 15, 18–19, 24, 28, 65

lactate threshold 34, 37, 65
lactic acid 18–19, 34–5, 36, 42, 63
  and fatigue 20, 35, 39, 65
  removal 44, 45, 65
lactic acid (lactate anaerobic) system 15, 18–19, 24, 28, 65
Last, Malcolm and (1998–99 season) 237
law, sport and 215–17
law of acceleration 72–3
law of action/reaction 73
law of conservation of angular momentum 83–4
law of conservation of momentum 71
law of inertia 72
laws of motion (Newton) 67, 71, 72–4, 81–2, 83
leaders 90, 149
leadership 141, 143, 147–9, 243
  styles 142, 149–52
learned helplessness 117, 134, 138–9
legislation 194, 215–16, 223
  anti-hooliganism 210, 211
  Sex Discrimination Act (1975) 242
  Title IX (USA) 241–2
Levinson and Christensen (1996) 215
Lewin (1939) 95, 149
Likert Scale 102, 103
linear motion 67–71
lipase 22
Lombardian ethic, USA 194, 195, 198, 199, 221, 233
Lomu, Jonah 71
long jump 71, 79
long-term responses to training 64–5
Lorr, McNair and Droppleman (1971) 97
lottery funding 180, 183, 184, 186, 188, 192, 225

M
McCelland and Atkinson (1964) 114–15
McGrath (1970, 1984) 140, 153
McNair, Lorr and Droppleman (1971) 97
macrocycles 56, 57–9
Malcolm and Last (1998–99 season) 237
marathon running 8, 20, 22–3, 46
  energy sources 24, 40, 41
  'hitting the wall' 22–3, 26, 40
mark allocation 251, 252, 260
marketing 199, 216, 248, 250
Marsh et al (1978) 207, 208
Martens (1977, 1990) 157, 159
mass 68, 69, 71, 72–3, 76, 82
mass participation 245, 246
maximum oxygen consumption *see* VO2max
media 201, 214, 233–4
and body shape 239–40
  and commercialisation 200–4
  dealing with attention of 88, 143, 199
  effect on sport 191, 204, 217
  and hooliganism 209
  use of role models 105, 239–40
media coverage 106, 112, 184, 198, 199, 204, 239
  and gender 204, 239–40, 241, 241–2
  Olympic Games 244, 246
media rights 185, 200, 203, 248
merchandising 200, 202, 203, 211, 234
mesocycles 56, 59
MI (moment of inertia) 82–3
microcycles 56, 60
mind 86
mitochondria 2, 20–1, 35, 36
  density 3, 33, 64
modelling 136

moderation of coursework 262
moment of inertia (MI) 82–3
moments of force 81
momentum 71, 72–3
mood states 97
Moorhead and Griffin (1998) 147
Morgan (1979) 97
motivation 88, 114, 161, 238
  attitude and 99
  attribution and 131, 133–4
  goals and 163
  social facilitation and 126
  in teams 136, 141, 145, 147
  see also achievement motivation
motivational losses 144–5
motor neurons 6, 7
motor units 6–8, 10
multiple unit summation 7
Murdoch, Rupert 203
muscle belly 2, 6, 10
muscle contractions 2, 3, 4, 6–10, 40
  eccentric 9, 47, 48
  isometric 54
muscle fibres 2, 3–5, 36, 37
  recruitment 6–8
muscle glycogen 2, 14, 18, 22, 36, 64
  replenishment 46, 48
muscle spindles 2, 9, 54
muscles
  hyperplasia 10
  hypertrophy 10
  muscle spindles 2, 9, 54
  short-term responses to exercise 63
  strength of response 7–8
  structure 2, 30
  trained status 36
  see also muscle contractions; muscle fibres; muscle glycogen
myofibrils 2, 7
myoglobin 44, 45, 64

N
n.Ach (need to achieve) 115–16
n.Af (need to avoid failure) 115–16
National Collegiate Athletic Association *see* NCAA
national governing bodies *see* NGBs
National Health Service *see* NHS
National Lottery (UK) 180, 183, 184, 186, 188, 192, 225
National Olympic Committees (NOCs) 185–6, 246, 248
National Sport Institutes 226, 226–8
nationalism 223, 244, 249
NCAA (National Collegiate Athletic Association) 231
need to achieve (n.Ach) 115–16
need to avoid failure (n.Af) 115–16
negative deviancy 205
net force 74
neuromuscular system 9–10
News International 203
Newton's laws of motion 67, 71, 72–4, 75
  angular motion 81–2, 83
NGBs (national governing bodies) 176–7, 183, 183–5, 185, 188, 192, 229
  and clubs 226
  and commercialisation 203, 217
  control of 235, 243
  and discrimination 235, 246
  whole sport plans 184–5, 228
  and women 240, 241
NHS (National Health Service) 174, 224
NOCs (National Olympic Committees) 185–6, 246, 248

O
Oakley and Green (2003) 178–9
OBLA (onset of blood lactate accumulation) 34–5, 48, 63, 65
officials 185, 191, 204, 216, 244
  dealing with aggressive behaviour 107, 109, 111, 112
Ogilvie 96
Olympic Games 188, 192, 193, 200, 203, 223, 227, 244–49
  Athens (2004) 179
  Beijing (2008) 178
  Berlin (1936) 223, 247
  Grenoble (Winter) (1968) 239
  London (2012) 174, 179, 180
  Mexico City (1968) 239
  Moscow (1980) 223, 247
  Munich (1972) 177, 247
  Rome (1960) 215, 222
  Sydney (2000) 176
  Tokyo (1964) 215
  values of 194, 220, 222
Olympic Reserve 222
Olympism 193, 194–5, 204, 222, 245, 247, 248, 249
onset of blood lactate accumulation *see* OBLA
organisations 174, 180–6
organising bodies 200
Orwell, George (1903–50) 206, 223
Osgood's Semantic Differential Scale 102, 103–4
outcome goals 116–17, 137, 163, 164
over-arousal 90, 121, 122, 123–4, 124, 127, 144
  dealing with 95, 107, 113, 123, 125
over-specialisation 174, 177
over-training 174, 199, 205
oxygen 14, 15, 17, 19, 20, 22, 42, 63
  concentration at altitude 55
  consumption 30, 44, 47, 63
  transport 29, 30, 37, 56
  see also EPOC; VO2max
oxygen debt 42
oxygen deficit 15, 43, 44

P
pain 35, 39, 40, 47–8
Paralympic athletes 181, 182
Paralympic Games 188, 244, 249
participation 173, 176, 246, 247
past experiences 137, 161
PCr (phosphocreatine) 14, 15–16, 18, 45, 63, 65
peaking 56, 57, 58, 61
performance
  and arousal 120–1, 121–3
  evaluating 131
  gender differences 37
  goals for 137, 139, 163–4
  personality and 97–8
Performance Athlete Development Model 184
performance goals 137, 139, 163–4
periodisation 56–61
personal performance, analysis of 263–4
personality 88–9, 116, 122, 128, 133, 141, 150
and competitiveness 114
dimensions 90–4
  and leadership 148
  measuring 92–3, 94, 96
  and performance 97–8
  see also traits
personality factors (Cattell) 94
persuasive communication 104–5, 137, 161
PESSCLS (Physical Education and School Sport and Club Links Strategy) 184, 187
phosphocreatine *see* PCr

Physical Education and School Sport and Club Links Strategy *see* PESSCLS
Pinsent, Matt 29
pluralist values 221
plyometrics 28, 53
PNF (proprioceptive neuromuscular facilitation) 53, 54
policies for sport 174, 241–2
  France 232
  UK 187–9, 189, 223, 241–2
political systems 225
politics, and sport 223–4, 241–2, 244, 247, 249
POMS (Profile of Mood States) 97
positive deviancy 205
positive values 191
post-exercise meals 46, 48
practical coursework 259–69
practical performance 259–62
pre-season training 57
prejudice 101
preparation period 57
pressure 88, 119, 153, 155, 202, 204, 214
principles of training 52
private education 176, 192, 193, 196, 220, 243, 245
pro-draft system (USA) 231
professional performers 192, 194, 202–3
professional sport 192, 194, 195–7, 199, 217, 233–4, 244
  commercialisation and 233–4
  in Olympic Games 192, 194
professionalism 199
  at a price 198, 199
Profile of Mood States (POMS) 97
projectile motion 78–80
propaganda 223, 249
proprioceptive neuromuscular facilitation *see* PNF
proprioceptors 9
proteins 14, 21, 23
proximity effect 129
psychological testing 88
public schools 192, 193, 196, 220, 243, 245
pyruvate (pyruvic acid) 18, 20, 22, 36, 45

Q
quantities of angular motion 81
questionnaires
  personality 90, 92–4
  self-report 158
questions
  Unit 4 167–71
  Unit 5 254–8

R
race relations 207, 216
racial identities 234
racism 208, 209, 211, 236
Radcliffe, Paula 29, 55
range of movement (ROM) 54
RAS (Reticular Activating System) 90, 120
reaction forces 72, 75
recovery 42–9, 59
recruitment of motor units 6–8, 10
red blood cells 55, 56, 64
referees *see* officials
reformative approach 219
relaxation 113, 162, 162–3
  techniques 130
resistance training 10
respiratory exchange ratio 64
respiratory rates 31, 42, 45–6, 55, 137
respiratory system, short-term responses to exercise 63
resynthesis of ATP *see* ATP
Reticular Activating System (RAS) 90, 120
revision 252–3
Ringelmann effect 145
Roberts (1993) 116
Robson (2000) 208
role models
  for athletes 109, 112, 113
  athletes as 174, 194, 199, 201, 234
  for black people 237
  negative 109, 112, 214
  positive 105, 113, 120, 191
  for women 238–40, 241, 242
ROM (range of movement) 54
rotational movements 80–2
Rugby football 108, 122, 196
Rugby Union 196
  turning professional (1996) 192, 197, 201
  World Cup Finals (2003) 136, 147, 179
rules 191, 194, 204, 245
running 6, 18, 45
  see also 400m running; marathon running; sprinting

S
Samaranch, Juan Antonio 203, 248
sarcoplasm 15, 16, 22
scalar quantities 68, 69
SCAT (Sport Competition Anxiety Test) 96, 159
scholarships 181, 225, 231, 233, 242
school sport 187–8, 194
  decline 184, 187
  UK 178, 179, 184, 187
schools 176, 226, 245
  France 232, 232–3
  GDR 177
  UK 229, 233
  UK public schools 192, 193, 196, 220, 243, 245
  USA 229–32, 233
Schwartz (1977) 129
Section B of PED5 251–3
selective attention 129, 163

self-confidence 88, 135–6, 145, 159, 161, 163
self-efficacy 117, 130, 135–6, 138, 161
  developing 136–7, 139, 163
self-esteem 134, 174, 243
self-serving bias 133–4
self-talk 160–1
Sex Discrimination Act (1975) 242
sexism 239
Seyle (1956) 153, 155
shamateurs 192
short-term responses to exercise 62–3
shot put 77, 78, 78–9, 80
side-effects of drugs 213, 214
significant others 95, 104, 105, 109, 117, 137
Silva, Husman and (1984) 108–9
skating 76, 83, 83–4
skeletal muscle *see* muscles
skiing 6, 30, 83
skills 122, 127, 128, 130
slow replenishment 43, 44, 45–7, 48
slow twitch motor units 6, 7
slow twitch (type 1) muscle fibres 3, 4, 10, 20, 33, 36, 64
SMARTER principle 164–5
soccer *see* football
social class 191, 194, 199, 234, 238–9, 249
  as barrier to excellence 242–3
  and hooliganism 207, 208
  UK 195–6, 220
social cohesion 143, 144, 145
social conflict 224, 249
social facilitation 121, 126, 137, 154
social influences on participation 176
social inhibition 126, 129–30
social learning theory 95, 112, 148
social loafing 144, 145
social mobility 195, 199, 221
socialisation 238
society 106, 194, 235
  British 190–1
socio-economic status 175, 176
soda loading 27
somatic anxiety 121, 123, 156, 157, 159
somatic arousal 119
somatic methods of stress management 162–3
somatic responses to stress 154
sources of energy *see* energy; energy systems
specialised training regimes 53–6
specialism 177
specialist Sports Colleges 187, 226
spectator violence (hooliganism) 206, 206–12
spectators 112, 126, 127, 128, 201
  behaviour 191, 206, 206–12, 216
  see also crowds
speed 69
Speilberger (1966) 156–7
Spence and Spence (1966) 120–1
sponsorship 184, 185, 199, 200, 201, 204, 216, 240
  for sports performers 112, 192, 198, 202, 214
  for World Games 248, 250
sport 174, 203
  as education 246, 246–7
  effect of media on 191, 204, 217
  and the law 215–17, 217
  and politics 223–4, 241–2, 244, 247, 249
'Sport for All' 246
Sport Competition Anxiety Test *see* SCAT
Sport England 182, 183, 184, 186
Sport England Lottery fund 183, 228
sport ethics 217, 221
  UK 190, 191–5
sport law 215–17, 217
sport policies 174, 241–2
  France 232
  UK 187–9, 189, 223, 241
sport study sections (France) 226
sports, as businesses 174, 234
Sports Aid 186, 192
sports clubs 221, 222, 225, 226, 229, 230, 232
Sports Coach UK 178, 183
sports coaches (USA) 230
Sports Colleges 187, 226
sports psychology 86
sports schools 187, 225, 226, 232
sportsmanship 174, 190–1, 191, 246
sprinting 6, 17, 19, 41, 77, 84
squash 18, 24–5
stacking 236
state anxiety 157, 159, 160
state funding 179, 222, 224, 225, 228
Steiner (1972) 144–5
stereotypes 101, 235
  gender 238–9, 242
  racial 236
stress 120, 153–4, 199
  causes 154, 155, 157
  measuring levels of 157–9
  responses to 121
stress management techniques 137, 153, 158, 159, 160–3
  for aggression 95–6, 113
  for over-arousal 95–6, 123, 125
  for social inhibition 130
stressors 154, 155
stretch reflex 9, 54

stretching 53, 54
sweating 41, 63, 119
swimming 83
periodisation 58, 59, 60, 61
synoptic section 251–3
synthesis of theory and practical 264–8

T
talent
identification and development 176–9, 226–8
testing for 175–6
Talented Athlete Scholarship Scheme *see* TASS
tapering 58, 60
task cohesion 143
task-orientated goals 117
TASS (Talented Athlete Scholarship Scheme) 181
Taylor, Ian (1987) 208
teams 135–6, 140–5
television 184, 185, 200, 204, 233–4, 248
tendons 2, 10
tetanus (tetanic contraction) 7–8
thermoregulation 41
thought-stopping 160
thoughts 105–6, 160
Thurston Scale 102, 103
Title IX (USA, 1972) 241–2, 242
torques 81, 82, 83–4
training 53
adaptive reponses to 36, 41, 60, 64–5
anaerobic 65
attitude to 99
to combat social inhibition 129
competition specific 57
for endurance events 33, 41
general conditioning 57
intensity 48, 56, 57
long-term responses to 36, 41, 60, 64–5
and OBLA 35, 48
over-training 174, 199, 205
personality and 88
principles 52
to reduce fatigue 41
specialised regimes 53–6
systematic 184
for team development 144
venues 182
see also altitude training; continuous training; fartlek; interval training; plyometrics; PNF
training programmes
designing 51–2
for energy production 26, 27–8
periodisation 56–61
specialised 53–6
training pyramid 59
training units (sessions) 57, 60
trait anxiety 128, 156, 157
trait theories 90–6
traits 88, 97, 148, 150, 155
measurement 90
see also personality
trampolining 82–3
transition period 59
Triadic Model 100–1, 105
Triandis (1971) 100, 100–1
triathlon 20, 21, 39
triglycerides 14, 21, 22, 23
trust funds 192
Tuckman (1965) 141–2
Tutko 96
type 2a muscle fibres 3, 10
type 2b muscle fibres 3, 10

U
UK Sport 180–2, 228
UK (United Kingdom) 205, 220, 222, 223, 224, 231
amateurism 191–2, 195, 220, 233, 243
club system 221, 222, 225, 229, 230
development of talent 178–9
education 229, 249
football hooliganism 206–12
government funding 179, 224
lottery funding 180, 183, 184, 186, 188, 192, 225
organisations 180–6
professional sport 195–6, 243
public schools 176, 192, 196, 220, 243, 245
racism 236, 237
school sport 178, 179, 187–8
schools 192, 225, 229, 233, 243
social class 195–6, 220, 242–3
sport ethics 190, 191–5
sport policies 187–9, 223, 241–2
values 204
and women's football 240
see also EIS; England
Union Nationale de Sport de Scholaire *see* UNSS
United Kingdom Sport Institute 219
UNSS (Union Nationale de Sport de Scholaire) 232
USA (United States of America) 220–1, 222, 223, 224, 243, 249
collegiate system 221, 225, 231, 234
dominant sports 234, 235
education 229–32, 233, 249
female soccer 240
funding 225, 231
Lombardian ethic 194, 195, 198, 199, 221, 233
pro-draft system 231
professional sport in 233–4
racism 236–7
scholarships 225, 231, 233
Title IX 241–2, 242
violence in sport 234
see also Americanisation

V
values 191, 191–5, 198, 199, 204
vector quantities 68, 69, 70
velocity 69, 70, 71, 74, 76
velocity of release 78
verbal persuasion 104–5, 137, 161
vertical forces 75
vicarious experiences 112, 136, 137, 148, 161
violence 174, 212, 215, 217
  in American sport 234
VO2max 4, 29, 29–30, 33, 37
  at altitude 55
  measuring 30–2
  OBLA 34–5

W
WADA (World Anti-Doping Agency) 212, 213, 214, 215
'wall, hitting the' 22–3, 26, 40
warming up 48
water 21, 27
wave summation 7–8
weight 68, 75
weight training 53
Weiner's Attribution theory (1974, 1986) 132–3
West African origin, athletes of 237
whole sport plans (WSPs) 184–5
Wie, Michelle 202
'win at all costs' 194, 195, 198, 199, 221, 234
Winter Olympics, Grenoble (1968) 239
women 37, 201, 204, 241–2
  female soccer (USA) 240
  and Olympism 247
  roles 238–39, 242
Woods, Tiger 238
World Anti-Doping Agency *see* WADA
World Class Performance Pathway 181, 181–2, 186
World Class Programme 188–9
World Class Start programme 186
World Cup (football) 203, 244
World Games 244–49, 250
Wright, Ian 177
WSPs (whole sport plans) 184–5

Y
Yerkes and Dodson (1908) 121–3

Z
Zajonc, Robert (1965) 126–7
'zone, being in the' 123
zone of optimal functioning 123, 157